DISTRIBUTED PROXIMITIES
PROCEEDINGS OF THE 40TH ANNUAL CONFERENCE OF THE ASSOCIATION
FOR COMPUTER AIDED DESIGN IN ARCHITECTURE
VOLUME II: PROJECTS, FIELD NOTES, VIDEOS, AWARDS, WORKSHOPS

Editors

Maria Yablonina, Adam Marcus, Shelby Doyle, Matias del Campo, Viola Ago, Brian Slocum

Copy Editing

Mary O'Malley, Paula Wooley

Graphic Identity

Adam Marcus, Viola Ago, Alejandro Sánchez Velasco

Graphic Design

Alejandro Sánchez Velasco

Layout

Carolyn Francis, Sebastian Lopez, Shelby Doyle, Adam Marcus

Printer

IngramSpark

ISBN 978-0-578-95253-6

PROCEEDINGS OF THE 40TH ANNUAL CONFERENCE OF THE
ASSOCIATION FOR COMPUTER AIDED DESIGN IN ARCHITECTURE

VOLUME II: PROJECTS, FIELD NOTES, VIDEOS, AWARDS, WORKSHOPS

Editors

Maria Yablonina, Adam Marcus, Shelby Doyle, Matias del Campo, Viola Ago, Brian Slocum

DISTRIBUTED PROXIMITIES
CONTENTS

CONTENTS

DISTRIBUTED PROXIMITIES
FOREWORD

Cultivating Transformative Practices

Kathy Velikov
ACADIA President 2018–2020
Associate Professor, University of Michigan Taubman
College of Architecture and Urban Planning
Director, rvtr

It will be often repeated that 2020 has been an unprecedented year. We will all remember those few weeks in early March when the scale and implications of the coronavirus pandemic began to be apparent and when most activities that involved being around others were rapidly scaled down or cancelled and any activity that could do so moved to online space and digital screens. The transformations occurred breathlessly fast. Academic institutions, research labs, and offices were shuttered, and in-person conferences, including the 2020 conference that ACADIA had been planning with the University of Pennsylvania for October 2020, were cancelled. As ACADIA's primary activity is the exchange of knowledge through an annual conference (mandated in the organization's by-laws), the ACADIA Board of Directors moved to take over the rebranding, conceptualization, and organization of an online conference, workshops, and related events.

The tremendous energy and optimism of the six members of the Board who volunteered to lead this effort cannot be understated. On behalf of the ACADIA community, I would like to offer profound thanks to Viola Ago, Matias del Campo, Shelby Doyle, Adam Marcus, Brian Slocum, and Maria Yablonina for stepping up to the ambitious and time-consuming task of reinventing, organizing, and running ACADIA's 40th conference event, the 2020 *Distributed Proximities* conference. The team pushed the possibilities of an online conference to the limit, organizing a spectacular and smoothly run week-long event, hosted on a custom interactive website designed by Oliver Popadich. The amount of work that the chair team managed cannot be understated, and the incredible success of the 2020 conference is a testament to their efforts and inventiveness.

Working with the team, we recognized that this condition of temporary suspension of what we had grown accustomed to as usual activity could also be a period of metamorphosis. Not only was there a necessity to reinvent the

playbook for ACADIA's annual conference, but this was also a moment to address the urgent need for making sense of the current situation. It was also an opportunity to actively put into practice the values of equity and inclusion that ACADIA had affirmed with the development of the Code of Conduct the previous year, and accelerate gender parity and increased racial diversity in the membership—two goals that the organization has been working to advance for the past several years. This mandate was not only taken on by the conference chair team, but also enthusiastically pursued by members of the Board through their committee work. In the spirit of the theme for the conference, we initiated a distributed, multipronged approach to these efforts, ensuring that they were coordinated and complementary.

This year's conference chair team rethought the keynote lecture format, which in the past had celebrated the accomplishments of a firm or an individual, to be staged instead as a series of critical conversations on the limits and possibilities of computation in contemporary design culture, with discussions on issues such as ecology, ethics, access, labor, and algorithmic biases. Over 85% of the speakers were female, and several represent BIPOC constituencies. The team also planned an unprecedented number of 15 workshops, taught online by leaders located in multiple countries, which greatly opened up the opportunities for different experiences with, access to, and levels of engagement with computational technologies. The conference chair team also inaugurated two new categories of juried submission to the annual conference: Videos and Field Notes. These new submission formats, along with the Projects, enabled more rapid, topical, and self-reflective ideas to be presented at the conference, expanding the range of possible conversations and access to a wider field of designers and thinkers, while maintaining the integrity of the selective peer review process for Technical Papers.

Matias del Campo, in addition to serving as a

conference chair, continued to also serve in his position as Development Officer, and this year secured one of the highest levels of sponsorship to supplement conference costs, including sponsorships from Autodesk, Zaha Hadid Architects, Epic Games, Grimshaw, and HKS Line. We developed a strengthened partnership with Autodesk, whose generous sponsorship this year enabled us to offer free registration for all students to the conference, and to also offer scholarships to attend the workshops to members of NOMA (National Organization of Minority Architects) as well as to students from Mexico and other international students. The response in registrations exceeded our expectations, with almost 2,000 free student attendees registering for the conference from all over the world, and with the number of female registrants for the first time exceeding the number of males. This pattern of near gender parity also held for the students who applied to the Autodesk-sponsored workshop grants. We thank Board members Jane Scott and Mara Marcu for their work in administering the increased number of student scholarships this year, as well as Chairs and Board members Shelby Doyle and Adam Marcus for coordinating and managing all of the workshops and attendees.

This year's conference saw a dramatic increase in international registrants. Participation was no longer limited to faculty and students who could afford not only the high fees associated with in-person events—where a significant proportion of the ticket costs go toward venue and equipment rentals, food, beverages, personnel, and physical paraphernalia—but also the travel and accommodation costs and time. The online conference also enabled relatively borderless access to anyone who had access to a computer, Wi-Fi, and an email account. It was therefore not limited to those who had the privilege to be able to obtain visas to travel to North America, and the registrants included many from countries that had not previously been represented at ACADIA. One question that the organization will need to grapple with when planning future conferences with in-person events is how to maintain this level of accessibility.

This year, the Board established a new Diversity Committee, which included Jason Kelly Johnson, Shelby Doyle, Behnaz Farahi, Tsz Yan Ng, and myself. Through the work of this committee, ACADIA has developed a partnership with NOMA and co-sponsored the inaugural ACADIA + Autodesk + NOMA Computational Design Award, a new category of award within NOMA's annual design competition. With June Grant now a member of the 2021 Board, we anticipate

continuing to strengthen our relationship with NOMA and expanding ACADIA's mission as an organization that not only supports existing and established computational practitioners and researchers, but that also serves as a welcoming bridge and liaison into computational design for the next, more diverse generation of designers.

The sudden disruption caused by the pandemic has also enabled new relationships to be forged between ACADIA and our sibling organizations, eCAADe, CAADRIA, SiGRADi, and ASCAAD. As the presidents of the respective organizations reached out to each other to share information and strategies for transitioning to online conference formats, we also initiated efforts to take advantage of the online format to bring our organizations closer together. Together, we organized the first World CAAD PhD Workshop, held in early December 2020. The workshop introduced junior researchers at the PhD stage to the research cultures of different institutions and research cultures within the global computational design community. It offered doctoral students an opportunity to receive constructive feedback from prominent researchers and academics in the community, and provided an occasion to exchange ideas and position their research within a global research arena in computational design. Each sibling organization was represented at the workshop by three PhD student delegates as well as by experts from each community, and I thank Board member Jane Scott for working to organize the selection process and participating in the workshop. We hope to continue the PhD workshop both as part of future annual conferences and as a collaborative event across the sibling organizations.

This year also saw a milestone in the gender parity and diversity of the members of the ACADIA Board itself with, for the first time, more women being elected to the Board than men. The diversity of the elected Board has been steadily increasing, but it was not that long ago, in the 2015 election, when I recall being the only woman on the ballot; the following year, I was one of two female Board members, along with Dana Cupkova. I'd like to thank this year's elections committee—Andrew John Wit, Behnaz Farahi, and Tsz Yan Ng—along with the rest of the Board, for recruiting a strong pool of candidates for this year's elections and look forward to the leadership of the Board and new President Jenny Sabin in 2021.

Although in 2020 we experienced the loss of the pleasure of an in-person conference event—the casual conversations, debates, encounters, and engagement with new

acquaintances that occur between paper presentations;
in many ways, all of the things that make ACADIA feel like
a family—it is also evident that a lot has been gained. We
have benefitted from the expanded inclusivity and cultiva-
tion of greater equity and access, the ability to reach wider
constituencies, and the decentering of dominant forms of
practice and knowledge-making toward the emancipatory
potentials of technology and socio-material reproduction.
When we eventually reconvene in some form of in-person
events, ACADIA may look and feel different than before.
I hope so. I hope that it is a bigger, broader, and more
inclusive family that welcomes alternative and unfamiliar
conceptual and methodological practices, and will continue
to be what it has always been: an open forum for sharing
explorations in the use of computation in the making and
remaking of our world.

DISTRIBUTED PROXIMITIES
CONFERENCE INTRODUCTION

Postscript as Prologue

Introduction to the Proceedings of the 40th Annual ACADIA Conference

Viola Ago
Rice University

Matias del Campo
University of Michigan

Shelby Doyle
Iowa State University

Adam Marcus
California College of the Arts

Brian Slocum
Universidad Iberoamericana

Maria Yablonina
University of Toronto

While the ACADIA community has always been distributed, *ACADIA 2020 Distributed Proximities* was organized at a moment of truly unprecedented fragmentation in which many of us were working in isolation from collaborators, coworkers, and students. And yet, within this state of forced semi-autonomy, adaptations spontaneously emerged, and new proximities surfaced. Distributed models of collaboration, workflow, and production have catalyzed myriad experiments in remoteness, improvised virtual communities, and rapid retooling to address novel urgencies. A moment of crisis can be clarifying in that it provides an opportunity to reflect critically on both the motivations of a research agenda and its broader implications. This year was also an opportunity for ACADIA as an organization to reflect upon its own practices, habits, culture, and priorities; to recognize the interdependent coevolutionary nature of our planet, society, and built environment; and to collectively imagine alternate futures.

In March 2020, when ACADIA's Board of Directors, facing the onset of the global COVID-19 pandemic, began to consider alternatives to the organization's typical in-person conference, a survey was circulated among the membership inquiring about the pandemic's effects on research. More than 65% of respondents reported disruptions to their ongoing work, supporting a pivot to an alternative conference format that would address both the need for distancing and its impacts on academic research. Although a virtual conference by definition prohibits the kinds of direct interpersonal interaction that we have come to expect and enjoy each year, the Board of Directors saw this reformatting and reimagining of the ACADIA conference as an opportunity to critically reassess the discourse of computational design and consider how a more accessible format might encourage wider (and more inclusive) dialogue via a radical expansion in participation in the conversation.

In contrast to a typical ACADIA cycle, the 2020 conference was planned and executed by a set of individuals from various institutions spread throughout North America who are connected only by their commitment to the community rather than rooted in a single institution. The conference co-chair team brought together voices from across three countries: the United States, Canada, and Mexico, representing six institutions: California College of the Arts, University of Michigan, Iowa State University, Rice University, University of Toronto, and Universidad Iberoamericana. While the pandemic and all it entailed undoubtedly left its mark on the work presented and discussed at this year's online conference, removing the association with a single academic institution (with both implicit and explicit biases) gave the chairs the opportunity to foreground themes of importance to ACADIA and its mission. Among these are increasing the diversity of the computational design community, encouraging scholarship at the highest level, and providing a platform for respectful yet vigorous debate about this research and its positioning within multiple contexts, social as well as technical. From the outset, our shared intent was not only to shape this conference as an effective and compelling venue for advanced peer-reviewed research, but to embed it with an *aspirational* purpose: how might a conference embody values of inclusion, empathy, ethics, and criticality that can inform future trajectories of design computation?

In this spirit, we invited contributions that interrogate the current condition by prioritizing the processes and protocols by which work is produced, rather than only its artifacts. By framing the conference through the lenses of ethics, equity, and critique, we sought to foreground work that questions not just "how" we do what we do, but "why" we engage computation in our work, and the myriad consequences it may have both within and beyond the discipline.

To do so required reflecting upon nearly every aspect of the conference format and content, and deciding which aspects were ripe for reinvention. We brought together 21 speakers in multiple time zones to participate in six virtual keynote conversations about critical issues, to help situate the conference within an alternative collection of imaginaries in lieu of a series of loosely related monologues focusing on individual work. Leveraging the online format, we brought together 15 remote workshops with leaders and participants from six continents, creating a platform for a global group of participants to experiment with new modes of collaboration and remote fabrication. Emerging from the pandemic context was a special session showcasing work by members of the ACADIA community who participated in various initiatives for the fabrication of personal protective equipment. The Field Note and Video formats were added to the conference call for submissions to make space for other voices and other more immediate forms of engagement with and discussion about the community and its work. Additionally, in 2020, ACADIA inaugurated a collaboration with the National Organization of Minority Architects and the National Organization of Minority Architecture Students (NOMA/NOMAS), sponsoring attendance grants for both the conference and workshops, and exhibiting computational design work from the annual NOMA/NOMAS design competitions. In an attempt to foster the types of serendipitous interactions of an in-person conference, we collaborated with designer Oliver Popadich to develop a custom conference platform that deployed machine learning to visualize thematic affinities and proximities to the body of research presented at the conference; the resulting platform allowed the visualization of connections between people, work, and ideas that might otherwise have gone unnoticed. Additionally, Ultan Byrne's MMMURMUR, with its capacity to simulate the dynamics of physical gatherings, was an experiment in bringing the casual interactions of the coffee break or happy hour to an online atmosphere; to our great delight, this experiment exceeded expectations, providing a fun, gossipy gathering spot for welcome diversion after intense conference events and at the end of each day.

All of the above took place in conjunction with the ongoing rigorous research of the community; we began conference planning worried whether anyone would be able to submit, and we note with the benefit of hindsight the fierce determination and resilience of the community and its members in this regard. In terms of technical research submissions, ACADIA 2020 had the second highest number of submissions for peer review in the 40-year history of the conference and an unprecedented percentage (nearly 60%) of the group of accepted paper authors is female. Additionally, this year the Technical Chairs sought to achieve gender and geographic balance in the assignment of peer reviewers for each paper. We wish to thank all of our peer reviewers for their perseverance and professionalism; without them the publication and presentation of the research would simply not have been possible. Work was submitted from all over the world, and with political and financial barriers to conference attendance removed as a side effect of the pandemic, many who would otherwise have been unable to attend were able to present and have their research discussed at the conference, to the benefit of everyone in the ACADIA community. Finally, in what we take as an encouraging sign, students attended the conference in higher numbers than ever before,[1] achieving gender parity, representing six continents, and increasing the likelihood of future submission to and participation in ACADIA.

The six of us could never have imagined that, more than a year after beginning the process of organizing *Distributed Proximities*, the strange circumstances that gave rise to the conference theme not only persist but continue to define life and work in profound ways that we have really only begun to fathom. In keeping with this disjointedness, the nature of the online conference and this year's publication of these proceedings well after the closing of the conference proper have meant that what would normally carry an inaugural tone has simultaneously taken on a valedictory character—"what's past is prologue"[2]—conclusion as introduction. Seen in this manner, these two volumes serve to draw the curtain on *ACADIA 2020 Distributed Proximities*, recording within them the community's first attempts to comprehend and assimilate the formative events surrounding the conference's organization. However, at the same time we hope that they may be read as the opening remarks for a new kind of dialogue for ACADIA, a discourse that will be essential to the unfolding of the conversation about the long-term effects of distributed proximities as well as for the materialization of the future imaginaries so earnestly and provocatively discussed throughout the conference.

NOTES

1. Thanks in large part to the generous sponsorship of Autodesk.
2. William Shakespeare, *The Tempest*, ed. Ronald Herder (Mineola, NY: Dover Publications, 1999), 56.

Contribution Statement

Viola Ago
Rice University

Matias del Campo
University of Michigan

Shelby Doyle
Iowa State University

Adam Marcus
California College of the Arts

Brian Slocum
Universidad Iberoamericana

Maria Yablonina
University of Toronto

In support of transparency in authorial attribution, the conference chairs wish to briefly highlight the specific contributions of each member of the team to both the conference and this publication, in addition to their roles in the general overall planning for the ACADIA 2020 Conference. These categories are adapted from and expanded upon the CRediT (Contributor Roles Taxonomy) promoted and administered as an informal standard at CASRAI (https://casrai.org/credit/). Names are listed here in order of contribution to this volume.

Maria Yablonina: Conceptualization (Conference Themes and Conference Platform), Writing - Original Draft, Writing - Review & Editing, Visualization, Supervision, Project Administration (Projects Peer Review Process, Curated Projects, Keynotes Organization).

Adam Marcus: Conceptualization (Conference Themes and Conference Platform), Writing - Original Draft, Writing - Review & Editing, Visualization (Conference Graphics), Supervision, Project Administration (Keynotes Organization, Field Notes & Videos Review Process, Awards Organization, Workshops Organization, Website Management, Conference Videoconferencing Management).

Shelby Doyle: Conceptualization (Conference Themes and Conference Platform), Writing - Original Draft, Writing - Review & Editing, Visualization, Supervision, Project Administration (Keynotes Organization, Field Notes & Videos Review Process, PPE Panel Organization, Workshops Organization, AIA CEUs Administration).

Matias del Campo: Conceptualization (Conference Themes and Conference Platform), Writing - Original Draft, Writing - Review & Editing, Visualization, Supervision, Project Administration (Projects Peer Review Process, Curated Projects), Funding Acquisition.

Viola Ago: Conceptualization (Conference Themes and Conference Platform), Writing - Original Draft, Writing - Review & Editing, Visualization (Conference Graphics), Supervision, Project Administration (Technical Papers Peer Review Process, Conference Paper Sessions Organization).

Brian Slocum: Conceptualization (Conference Themes and Conference Platform), Writing - Original Draft, Writing - Review & Editing, Visualization, Supervision, Project Administration (Technical Papers Peer Review Process, Conference Budget, Conference Paper Sessions Organization).

General Statement Regarding Attribution

Attribution order for work submitted to ACADIA and published in this volume is determined by level of contribution, with the first author listed considered the principal author and subsequent authors listed in order of contribution to the work. If authors have contributed equally, those names are indicated with an asterisk. The only exception to this convention is that lab/studio leaders' names (if applicable) appear last on the list of authors.

DISTRIBUTED PROXIMITIES
NEW PLATFORMS

The transition to a virtual conference presented an opportunity to rethink what kinds of online spaces might encourage the experiences of unexpected discovery and interaction commonly associated with ACADIA's conferences. Working with designer Oliver Popadich, the co-chairs developed an online platform that serves as an interactive visualization of the research presented and discussed at the conference. It uses machine learning algorithms to analyze the conference content, identify key terms, and cross-reference these terms with over 13,000 entries in the CumInCAD repository of research presented at ACADIA and its sibling organizations CAADRIA, eCAADe, SIGraDi, ASCAAD, and CAADFutures over the past 40+ years. The platform organizes all research presented at the conference—papers, projects, field notes, and videos—as individual nodes in a three-dimensional field that attendees can navigate interactively. Clicking on a node provides an abstract for that particular body of research and visualizes related work as a network of connected nodes.

The team also engaged designer Ultan Byrne to adapt his MMMURMUR video-chat interface for coffee breaks during the conference. MMMURMUR correlates sound with proximity, allowing many people to occupy a single "room" and then to conduct separate conversations in individual clusters within a single virtual space. While it does not exactly replicate the typical coffee break in between paper sessions at an in-person conference, MMMURMUR nonetheless provided an important outlet for casual interaction and an alternative to the now ubiquitous Zoom space that has come to dominate social life during the pandemic.

PROXIMITIES.ACADIA.ORG

Oliver Popadich
altf4.design

Part data visualization, part interface design, part scheduling software, the Distributed Proximities conference platform is an exploration in designing place for digital space. Due to the extraordinary circumstances surrounding the COVID-19 pandemic, ACADIA's 2020 conference was faced with the question: "What would an all-virtual conference look like?" Rather than focus on the representation of physical spaces, the team seized the opportunity to reimagine our engagement with digital space.

Drawing inspiration from TensorFlow's Embedding Projector,[1] the interface appears as a colorful collection of floating nodes—or "marshmallows," as the team was fond of calling them. Each node represents content from the ACADIA conference. Color-coding identifies the categorization of each submission (e.g. paper, project, event), while the relative placement visualizes the semantic relationships among submissions.

The spatial coordinates are derived from high-dimensional document vectors, projected into three-dimensional space using the t-SNE algorithm.[2] Document vectors—an extension of word vectors—enumerate the semantic similarities among the abstracts for each element of the conference. These vectors were generated using a doc2vec model[3] trained on CumInCAD's library of 13,380 abstracts. Not only do the vectors determine which submissions are most closely related, but they are also able to suggest what words most accurately represent the project.

These "Generated Keywords" often offered small surprises, the most delightful of which came from Zach Cohen's field note, "Waiting to Get Cut Out." Building support for new ways of working with automated fabrication processes, Cohen briefly details the boredom and thus resulting dangers of waiting for CNC machinery. As if suggesting a solution of its own, the machine-learning model offered "coffee" as the word most representing of the abstract.

During the peak of the conference, the Distributed Proximities platform manifested an almost visceral energy, despite the absence of typical virtual indicators of human activity like avatars, notifications, or even message boards. Instead of promoting a virtual self, Distributed Proximities fostered the exploration of a wonderfully diverse set of projects, papers, and other work. At the same time, through scheduled Zoom sessions and custom MMMURMUR rooms, the platform offered an abundance of opportunities for live conversation with peers around the world. By seeking forms of representation native to digital space and encouraging ephemeral modes of interaction, Distributed Proximities became a place to visit, rather than a place to inhabit.

NOTES

1. Embedding Projector, TensorFlow, https://projector.tensorflow.org/.
2. L. V. Maaten and G. E. Hinton, "Visualizing Data Using t-SNE," *Journal of Machine Learning Research* 9 (2008): 2579–2605.
3. Q. V. Le and T. Mikolov, "Distributed Representations of Sentences and Documents," *Proceedings of the 31st International Conference on Machine Learning* 32, no. 2 (2014): 1188–1196.

1   Screenshots of proximities.acadia.org.

MMMURMUR

Ultan Byrne
Columbia University

MMMURMUR is a modest experiment in the geometry of virtual social interactions: a spatial chat that is built on top of the open-source Jitsi conference software.[1]

MMMURMUR was motivated by the sudden relentlessness of the grid in 2020: seminars, remote birthday parties, and virtual family gatherings all felt somewhat uneasy in the interfaces of conference software. New conversational norms and social protocols had to be developed, even while our capacity for signaling through body language, subtle expression, mumbles, and murmurs was greatly reduced. Moreover, it quickly became clear that things like dinner parties and happy hours are interesting precisely to the extent that multiple parallel and overlapping conversations can take place—and that the overlapping itself can encourage new ideas or ways of thinking. All of this was upended by the grid interface, even while it ostensibly provided an equality of conversational opportunity for all participants. Yet even this equal opportunity was predicated on becoming the singular "dominant speaker" for the entire group at a given moment (it is not by chance that "dominant speaker" is the actual term used in the Jitsi codebase). Many of the aspects of group social interaction which seemed to be missing in these platforms are predicated on moving around in a physical spatial context. MMMURMUR was intended to recover some of these aspects by offering a virtual spatial context. It provides a two-dimensional interface where users can navigate and in which the acoustical volume of other participants is a function of their distance. Line segments can then be sketched in order to provide acoustical separation of adjacent spaces.

In addition to these more straightforward goals, MMMURMUR was designed as an experiment for thinking about the all-too-common analogy between physical spaces and digital interfaces: in what ways do digital interfaces mediate our interactions, and to what extent is this similar to the mediating role of physical spaces? If architects wish to claim expertise in the design of virtual and hybrid environments, and if this claim is to be predicated on the strength of the analogy, then it seems important for us to carefully come to terms with its stability and limits. While it is beyond the scope of this brief note to elaborate on this point, I find myself increasingly skeptical of any strong association. More precisely, I would want to follow Lawrence Lessig in his *Code: And Other Laws of Cyberspace* in noting the capacities of code and interfaces to regulate and constrain behaviors, and to suggest that these are fundamentally different from the influences of buildings on their occupants. In this regard, MMMURMUR should not be seen as trying to "bridge the gap" by making virtual spaces behave more like physical space. Instead, it is about drawing our attention to the gap itself and denaturalizing our experience of digital interfaces by exploring one of many possible alternatives.

NOTES

1. Jitsi, https://jitsi.org/.
2. Lawrence Lessig, *Code: And Other Laws of Cyberspace* (New York, Basic Books: 1999).

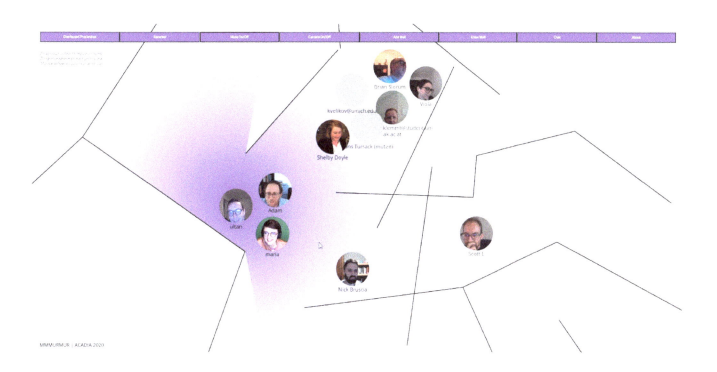

1   Screenshots of Mmmurmur.

DISTRIBUTED PROXIMITIES
AWARDS

Inaugurated in 1998, the ACADIA Awards of Excellence recognize consistent contributions and impact on the field of architectural computing. The awardees are selected by ACADIA's Board of Directors in a two-stage nomination and voting process led by the Board's Awards Committee. In 2020, awards were given in the following categories:

ACADIA Digital Practice Award of Excellence: This award recognizes creative design work that advances the discipline of architecture through development and use of digital media.

ACADIA Innovative Research Award of Excellence: This award recognizes innovative research that contributes to the field of digital design in architecture. The award distinguishes research with the potential to transform contemporary architecture.

ACADIA Innovative Academic Program Award of Excellence: This award recognizes an innovative academic program that contributes to the education of students in the field of digital design. The award distinguishes one or more individuals responsible for the establishment, success, growth, or management of the academic program.

ACADIA Teaching Award of Excellence: This award recognizes innovative teaching in the field of digital design in architecture. Teaching approaches that can be adopted by other educators are recognized in particular.

ACADIA Society Award for Leadership: This award recognizes extraordinary contributions and service to the ACADIA community.

Jane Burry

ACADIA Teaching Award of Excellence

Philosophy of Mathematics for Architecture

You cannot come late into the seemingly unlimited dimensions of computational design nor work in close proximity to the extraordinary spatial and temporal mind of Antoni Gaudí, let alone do both simultaneously in mid-life, without it having a profound impact on your own spatial understanding. I had the privilege of working with partner Mark Burry in the architectural team at the Sagrada Família Basílica, including the design modeling and synthesis of the complex colonnade of the Passion Façade.

It was an injection of architectural and intellectual adrenaline. Everything started to melt and meld: space, geometry, formation, perception, and time. Meanwhile, the affordable, graphical, fast, powerful cerebral annex of digital computing was offering a whole generation of architects the opportunity to think and work in a mathematically and algorithmically extended way.

How were architects, accustomed to the solidity and certainty of three immutable dimensions and designing to build, to comprehend and grasp the abstract power at hand? Moreover, computational design, and particularly the hierarchical nature of parametric design, is no panacea. While ingenious and liberating compared to drawing and solid modeling, it is spatially constrained by the hidden logics of space itself. Geometry and logic can quickly come into conflict. Such spatial conundrums are fascinating, including their implications for the nature of space and its human perceptions per se. In my practice and research, and in education, I have enjoyed returning to a domain I had loved even before studying architecture: the history and philosophy of mathematics.

Mathematicians and philosophers had been grappling with spatial paradoxes, such as spaces of unlimited dimension, topological space, surface definition and characteristics, complexity theory, periodicity and aperiodicity, hyperbolic and elliptic geometry, longer, more profoundly, or at least in very different ways, than architects. They too have even approached the thorny problem of visualizing new kinds of space and geometry. Most strikingly, questions of logic and intuition have been front and central in mathematics and mathematical philosophy since the dawn of history in a predigital age. We, as architects, have the opportunity to draw on some of that experience to plug our own gaps in intuition, and to bridge between the worlds of logic and intuition, just as the philosophers of mathematics have done since Hilbert. Meanwhile, architects have plundered the formal possibilities of post-17th-century geometry and mathematical ideas for creative, generative, and expressive architectural ends, and are doing so with greatly increased

1 Antoni Gaudi, Sagrada Familia Basilica, completed colonnade on the Passion Facade.

2 Suspended Remnants Pavilion at *Future Prototyping* exhibition, Melbourne 2020. Matching an inventory of random scanned, short length, otherwise waste, structural timber to a dynamic funicular model project. Credits: Kim Baber, Jane Burry, Canhui Chen, Joseph Gatto, Aurimas Bukaukas. (Photo credit: James Rafferty)

facility in an era of fast, powerful, digitally enabled computing. The publication of *The New Mathematics of Architecture* was a celebration of some of this work.

There had been a burgeoning, all-encompassing realization of the unexploited power of Descartes's construction of a problem: the generative power of analytic geometry, topology, and complexity. While today we might criticize the formal and environmental profligacy of some of the outcomes of this enthusiasm, the creative explosion and sheer love of ideas, interpreted through the medium of architecture, has made a rich contribution. The postdigital uptake of mathematical ideas has been similarly rooted in the natural sciences, combining expressive celebration

with the search for economy of means. Digital fabrication has become increasingly ubiquitous and influential since the 1980s, further linking the mathematical and the numerical in architecture.

In the endless quest for architecture's relevance and power to change, new forms of computational and geometrical virtuosity now acquire meaning to the extent they are driven by their environmental and experiential impact. The urgency of this ethical imperative has never been more starkly evident. To use computational design to widely enhance human experience, achieve structural lightness, conserve energy use, and reduce related emissions requires new and more embodied approaches to

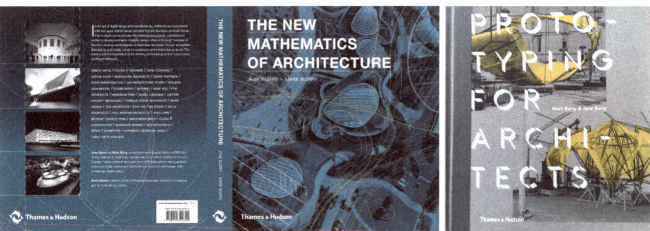

3   Top: *Designing the Dynamic*, cover (Melbourne Books). **Bottom Left**: *The New Mathematics of Architecture*, cover (Thames and Hudson).
     Bottom Right: *Prototyping for Architects*, cover (Thames and Hudson).

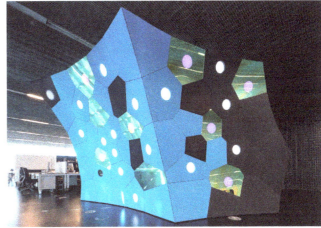

4   **Top Left and Right:** FabPod I, acoustic meeting room for eight, designed using hyperboloid sound scattering and shape optimization principles, in response to acoustic simulation, exterior. Project credits: Jane Burry, Nick Williams, Brady Peters, John Cherrey, Mark Burry, Daniel Davis, Alex Pena de Leon. (Photo credit: John Rollings)

5   **Bottom Left:** FabPod II, partial prototype, exhibited at the *Future Prototyping* exhibition, Melbourne 2020. Project credits: Jane Burry, Chen Canhui, Pantea Alambeigi, Daniel Prohasky, Swinburne University. (Photo credit: James Rafferty)

designing. It has always been important to fold empirically derived data and analysis back into the design process and, in particular, pursue real-time feedback in design models. Such goals naturally bring researchers together across disciplines and marry physical prototyping, experimentation and computational design.

A deeper understanding of the behavior of air and how to maximize human experience while minimizing the energy-and-emission-heavy service loads of buildings is key to designing our way out of the existential climate crisis. Aerodynamics, thermodynamics, sound transmission, elusive convection effects, wind, and fluctuation patterns, and how they interface with architectural form and human behavior, can all be integrated into early design modeling. This is another way in which, over the last decade, I have had the good fortune to work with many research collaborators, doctoral candidates, and students in research across disciplines and institutions, integrating the architectural and mathematical. It points to exciting new mathematically informed directions in architectural education.

Jane Burry is an architect, professor, and Dean of the School of Design at Swinburne University of Technology, Melbourne, Australia. She is founding dean for a new practice-centered architecture, urban, and architectural engineering program, focused on the future of technology, human and nonhuman well-being, and urban ecologies. Lead author of *The New Mathematics of Architecture* (T&H, 2010), editor of *Designing the Dynamic* (Melbourne Books, 2013), and co-author of *Prototyping for Architects* (T&H, 2016), she has over 100 other publications. Her PhD, inspired by research and project architect experience in the technical office at Gaudí's Sagrada Família Basilica with partner Mark Burry, was titled "Logic and Intuition in Architectural Modelling: Philosophy of Mathematics for Computational Design." Recent collaborative research, teaching, and postgraduate supervision addresses the interface of architecture with acoustic, thermal, and airflow dynamics, and the roles of simulation, digital fabrication, rich data-gathering, and AI in more sustainable and enlivening design.

Sean Ahlquist

ACADIA Innovative Research Award of Excellence

From Material Systems to Sociomaterial Justness

Architecture, so often, gets it wrong. There's a *fixed-ness* that arises through the authorship of process and its resulting forms, the celebration of the machines that dictate materiality, and the preconceived narratives for social and environmental responsivities. Computational design tends to only exacerbate these traits. This all accumulates into an architectural *intolerance*. Demarcations becomes drawn. The expected, the intended, and what become the "norm" is revealed by a discomfort with the unexpected – the body, mind, and social being that is nonconforming.

> The social body is the standard—presupposed but invisible—until a nonstandard body makes an appearance. Then the standard becomes immediately apparent, as the inflexible structures … reveal their intolerance for anyone unlike the people for whom they were built. (Siebers, 2008)

But, maybe being wrong is okay. To admit to not knowing and guessing wrong shows respect, and avoids a false empathy, for not trying to "walk a mile in someone's shoes." If fixity can be repositioned as an *iteration*, then *wrong* can be tolerated as a *momentary err*. Yet, such is only possible if the auteur is willing, if design process is capable, and if mechanisms within materiality allow for *re*-iteration. Patience becomes an architectural trait that is party to a collective search for eventual correction. It's a capacity that both requires and reveals authorship emanating from an unknown, unexpected voice. And, it's a voice that will sit *outside* and, likely, in opposition to the inscrutable "black boxes" of our conventional computational processes. To yield, to offer complete submission to the other, to understand the otherness while suspending the self—can architecture do that?

Germinating from personal experience and interrogated through interdisciplinary collaborations, the fundamental hypothesis of this research seeks to test architecture's capacity to seed multimodal communication for otherly, indefinable social voices. Within our discipline and stemming from our current cultural climate, the tilted architectural viewpoints of the few are being more acutely scrutinized for their exacerbation of social inequities. Personally, I see prejudice in the moments where architecture sits *in opposition* to my daughter's worldview, one constructed through her autism and novel forms of nonverbal communication. Professionally, this shapes the fundamental inquiry of the research: what computational paradigms-faculties-techniques constitute an architecture in constant transformation—being ceaselessly reauthored by n number of agents and becoming communications for something rightfully unknown?

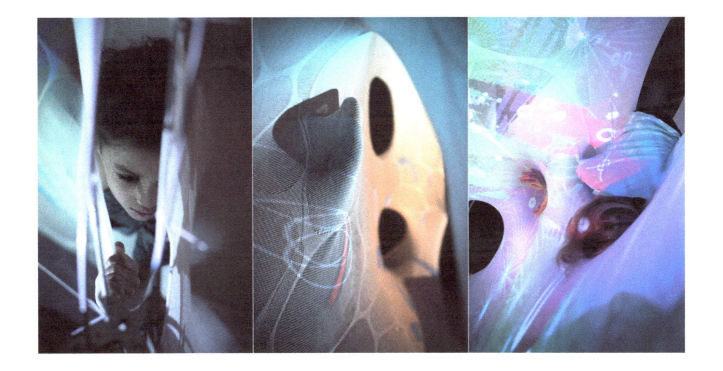

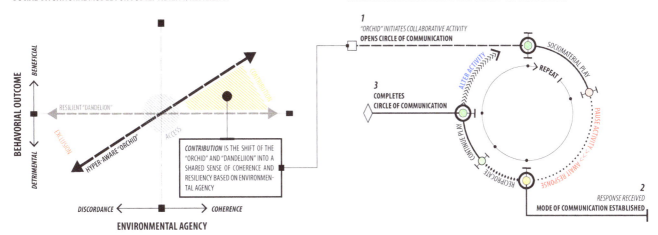

SOCIAL-SITUATIONAL MODEL FOR SUSCEPTIBILITY/RESILIENCY

BEHAVORIAL OUTCOME

BENEFICIAL

DETRIMENTAL

RESILIENT "DANDELION"

EXCLUSION

ACCESS

CONTRIBUTION

HYPER-AWARE "ORCHID"

CONTRIBUTION IS THE SHIFT OF THE "ORCHID" AND "DANDELION" INTO A SHARED SENSE OF COHERENCE AND RESILIENCY BASED ON ENVIRONMENTAL AGENCY

DISCORDANCE ←———→ COHERENCE

ENVIRONMENTAL AGENCY

ITERATIVE MODEL FOR AGENCY AND SHARED COMMUNICATION

1
"ORCHID" INITIATES COLLABORATIVE ACTIVITY
OPENS CIRCLE OF COMMUNICATION

SOCIOMATERIAL PLAY

ALTER ACTIVITY

REPEAT

3
COMPLETES
CIRCLE OF COMMUNICATION

PAUSE ACTIVITY

AWAIT RESPONSE

CONTINUE PLAY

RECIPROCATE

2
RESPONSE RECEIVED
MODE OF COMMUNICATION ESTABLISHED

1   Evident across a range of *SensoryPlayscape* prototypes, the exhaustiveness and precision in proffering degrees of elasticity and conformability generate a *requisite variety*—a term culled from cybernetics to define a system's robustness—for sensorial motivations of visual, tactile, proprioceptive and vestibular exploration.

2   Susceptibility and a model for constructing social interaction and communication.

3 Central to the research in studying sociomaterial architectures is the development of a *software/hardware platform* that allows for the exploration of *SensoryPlayscapes* prototypes across a range of scales, forms, tactility, deployability and spatial organization.

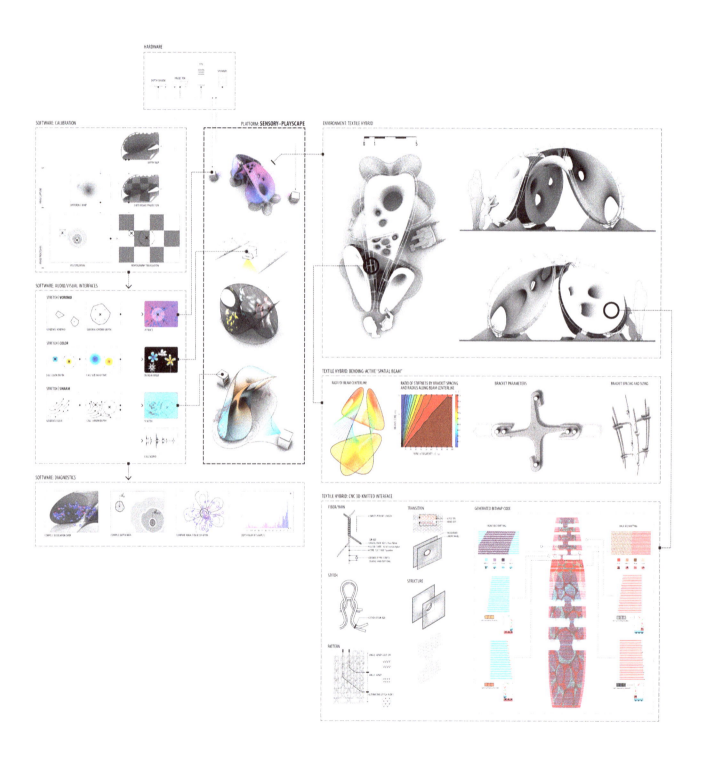

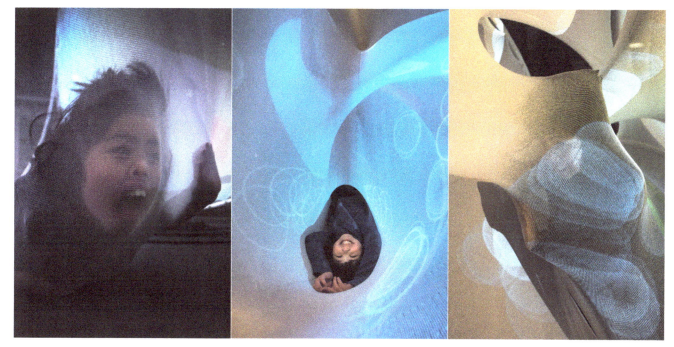

4   *SensoryPlayscape [NWG]*, Gallery at Taubman College of Architecture and Urban Planning, University of Michigan, Ann Arbor, Michigan, March 2018.

Sociomaterial Architectures

If we accept that disability is an emergent phenomenon (essentially unpredictable), one that materializes through the intra-actions of people, attitudes, histories, objects, and other ambient features of a space, how do we design for disabled bodyminds? (Price, 2016)

In Gottfried Semper's "principle of dress," the textile is both expression and record for the "relationship of materials, tectonics, and ornament ... the partnership of technology and cultural practice in the development of architectural form" (Holliday, 2009). Inextricable from Semper's architectural "dress" is its tactility. David Katz comments on the necessity of *action* to unfurl the "tactual properties [that] do not chatter at us like their colors, but [rather] remain mute until we make them speak" (2016). JJ Gibson, in writings on ecological psychology, articulates such actions where "every organism is in one sense continuous with its environment ... exchanging matter and energy ... but discontinuous [as] it is highly selective in what it will take in and, of that, what it will assimilate" (2015).

Environmental sensitivity, through research on child development by W. Thomas Boyce, provides nuance to the term "assimilation" (2016). The "dandelion" is imbued with the ability to assimilate in all but the worst circumstances.

Alternatively, being highly reactive characterizes the "orchid"—heavily burdened in discordant circumstances, yet capable of exceptional outcomes—better than even the largely resilient "dandelion-like" peer, in circumstances aligned with their sensorial inclinations. This defines the central paradox driving the research: resolving architecture's demand for material precision versus diversity's demand for patience—to let agency generate the specific yet unpredictable "features of space" that imbue exceptionality across n number of unknown constituents.

Carly Fleischman, a nonverbal autistic self-advocate, professes "in a world of silence, communication is *everywhere*. You just need to know where to look" (2012). Instead of through material *precision*, the *everywhere* is proffered through material *elaboration*. In creating an expanse for capacities of conformability and *contort-ability*, the *everywhere* has the possibility to be shaped into specific, ad-hoc, in-situ languages for communication. This research implements an architecture that intentionally lacks prescription, paradoxically acts with a material meticulousness that eagerly awaits assignment, and desires other agencies to impose their agenda. My daughter, Ara, has one set of keys to her worldview. It's only with her permission and by her *actions* should it be unlocked, and become a welcomed expression of her "nonconformity". Can architecture do this?

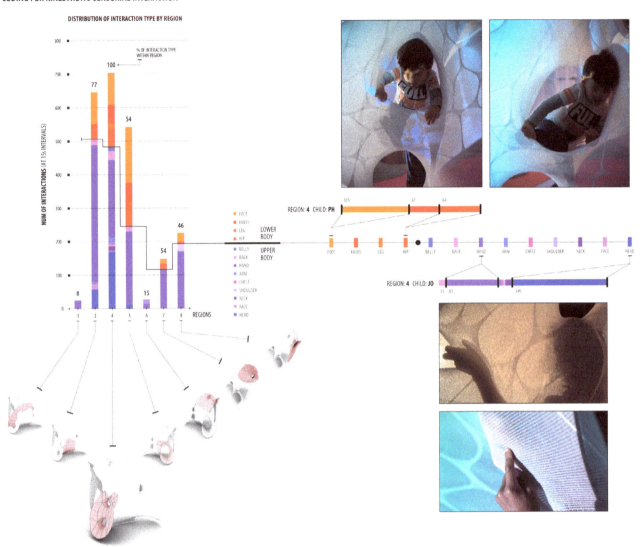

5   *SensoryPlayscape [EC]*, Exhibit Columbus, Columbus, Indiana, April 2019.
In measuring the range of sensorial interactions across each region of
the small prototype, the capacity for a child's individual agency is shaped
through the freedom to define sensorial functionality. Highlighted in two
instances (right), Region 4 is distinctly transformed by one child into a
tactile landscape (bottom) and into a kinesthetic activity, by another, for
testing and mastering motor control (top).

REFERENCES

Boyce, W. T. 2016. "Differential Susceptibility of the Developing Brain to Contextual Aadversity and Stress." *Neuropsychopharmacology*. 41 (1), 142-162.

Fleischmann, A., and C. Fleischmann. 2012. *Carly's Coice: Breaking through Autism*. New York: Simon and Schuster.

Gibson JJ. 2015. *The Ecological Approach to Visual Perception*. New York: Taylor & Francis.

Holliday K. 2009. Unraveling the Ttextile in Mmodern Architecture: Guest Editor's Introduction. *Stud Decor Arts*; 16 (2): 2–6.

Penny, S. 2017. *Making Sense: Cognition, Computing, Art, and Embodiment*. Cambridge, MA: MIT Press.

Price, M. 2016. "Un/shared Space: The Dilemma of Inclusive Architecture. In Disability, Space, Architecture: A Reader,edited by J. Boys, 155–303.

Siebers, T. 2008. *Disability Theory*. Ann Arbor, MI: University of Michigan Press.

Sean Ahlquist is an Associate Professor of Architecture at the University of Michigan – Taubman College of Architecture and Urban Planning. He directs the CNC Knitting Lab, developing research from computational design thinking to material systems through interdisciplinary, academic, and industry partnerships. He teaches as a part of the MSc in Digital Material Technologies (DMT) program, and supervises students in the cluster for Computational Design as part of the PhD program. Ahlquist's research spans writing and practice, seeking to push computational design and material fabrication past their technical challenges in order to engage in discussions of responsivity, sensory feedback, and human behavior. In wide-ranging collaborations, with fields such as structural engineering, behavioral science and public education, the work challenges computational design's often sole focus on precision in order to address architecture's pressing need to provide individual agency for the under-represented populations often ill-affected by the complexities of our social, civic environments.

Jessica Rosenkrantz and Jesse Louis-Rosenberg

Nervous System
ACADIA Digital Practice Award of Excellence

Nervous System is an experimental design studio started by Jesse Louis-Rosenberg and Jessica Rosenkrantz in 2007. We have always been outsiders. As much as the world is excited about interdisciplinarity, most institutions still cut rigidly across disciplinary lines. Nervous System's practice truly crosses boundaries, not just in a traditional academic sense, but as a business and an organization. We are a design studio that publishes papers in *Science*. We are artists who focus on manufacturing affordable products. We are programmers who engage with traditional crafts.

Nervous System started as an accident in 2006 while Jessica was a student at the Harvard Graduate School of Design. Someone mistook an errant scrap of one of her architectural models for a bracelet, and an idea was born. Why not apply generative techniques to products? The first Nervous System designs were bracelets and necklaces, laser-cut in the GSD's basement and sold on Etsy.

Soon after, we decided to drop out: Jesse from his mathematics degree at MIT and Jessica from architecture graduate school. We moved to LA and launched Nervous System as a serious endeavor. The idea was to use digital fabrication and computation to make one-of-a-kind and customizable products. At the time, most manufacturers were very traditional, even when using digital tools. Even today it's almost impossible to find manufacturers who will make one-of-a-kind products (affordably), which is why over the past 13 years Nervous System has increasingly become its own manufacturer.

Nervous System launched with an app for each jewelry collection where anyone could customize their own products. These first apps were a little clunky, but also quite charming, looking back. They were built entirely from scratch, including the UI, using Processing and running online as Java applets. The idea was less about changing the way people buy jewelry and more about sharing the design process. The work was not just about static objects you could buy, but the dynamic systems used to generate them.

We had stumbled into jewelry as a medium, and one might think that traditional metalsmithing might be the furthest thing from generative design. However, the craft community embraced our work. In fact, jewelry was one of the early adopters of 3D printing, both on an artistic and industrial side. In 2009, we were invited to be artists in residence at SIGGRAPH, the largest computer graphics conference in the world, and much to our surprise, the people running the Studio program were metalsmiths. Over the years we've used jewelry as a medium for exploring new computational processes, new ideas about customization, and new materials.

1   This algorithmically generated, laser -cut steel railing was created for the new Nervous System studio building in Palenville, NY.

2   The Hyphae lamp is a series of organic table lamps based on how veins form in leaves. Each lamp is a completely one-of-a-kind design 3D-printed in nylon plastic.

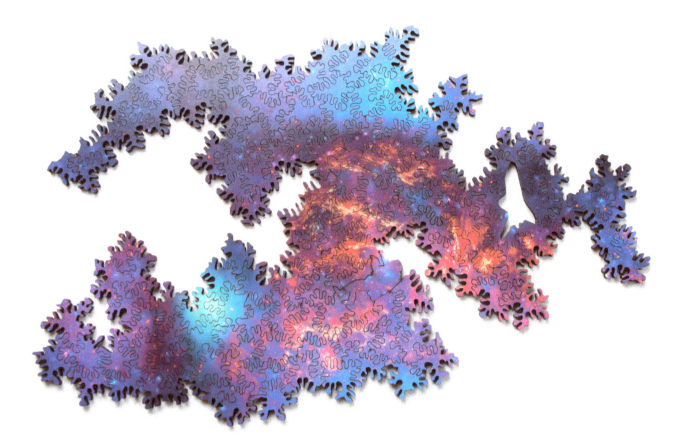

3   The Infinity Puzzle is a new type of jigsaw puzzle that tiles continuously. It has no fixed shape, no starting point, and no edges. It can be assembled in
     thousands of different ways. This image used in this puzzle is of the galactic center region of Milky Way. Credit: NASA, ESA, SSC, CXC, and STScI.

4   For the past three years we've collaborated with Jordan Miller, a bioen-
     gineer at Rice University, on creating vascular networks for 3D-printed
     organs. Today our work appears on the cover of *Science* magazine,
     where it is published in an interdisciplinary article which we co-authored.
     The work was led by Jordan Miller at Rice and Kelly Stevens at the
     University of Washington and included 13 additional collaborators from
     Rice, University of Washington, Duke University, and Rowan University.
     (Photo credit: Jordan Miller/Rice University.)

Though our work can be interpreted as technology-focused, it is more about the process of exploration and discovery. We love processes, whether they're organic growth processes, computational processes, or fabrication processes. Our design practice is grounded in doing research, despite its expression as everyday products.

One of our primary goals at Nervous System has been researching how patterns emerge in nature and using that to create new design tools for how we can playfully and intelligently shape objects. This research has come full circle since we started collaborating with Jordan Miller, a bioengineer at Rice University who has developed a new 3D printing technique for living cells. With his lab, we've been working on designing printable vasculature to support the development of artificial organs. We are working towards creating organs that could actually be used as transplants in the future. Our work often combines technology and traditional craft. In 2012, we started making jigsaw puzzles after learning about the incredible artistry of hand-cut

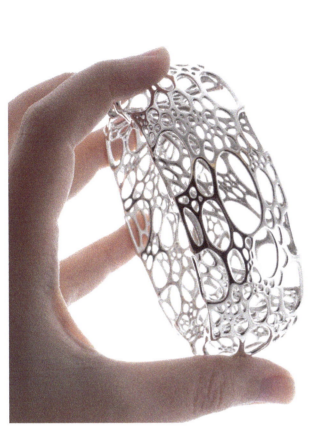

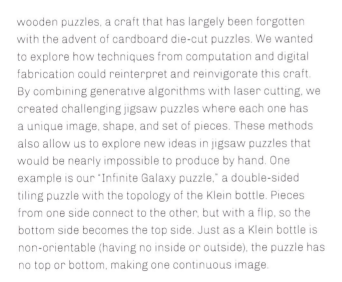

5   A collection of 3D cellular jewelry inspired by the microscopic shells of radiolarians. The complex forms were created through simulations of the physical forces in a cellular network.

6   The sixth version of our Kinematics Dress was 3D-printed in July 2015. It is composed of 2,645 interlocking panels that were 3D-printed as a single computationally folded piece. (Photo by Steve Marsel Studio.)

wooden puzzles, a craft that has largely been forgotten with the advent of cardboard die-cut puzzles. We wanted to explore how techniques from computation and digital fabrication could reinterpret and reinvigorate this craft. By combining generative algorithms with laser cutting, we created challenging jigsaw puzzles where each one has a unique image, shape, and set of pieces. These methods also allow us to explore new ideas in jigsaw puzzles that would be nearly impossible to produce by hand. One example is our "Infinite Galaxy puzzle," a double-sided tiling puzzle with the topology of the Klein bottle. Pieces from one side connect to the other, but with a flip, so the bottom side becomes the top side. Just as a Klein bottle is non-orientable (having no inside or outside), the puzzle has no top or bottom, making one continuous image.

Today, we've created our own generative design factory making jigsaw puzzles. We have made thousands of one-of-a-kind and customized puzzles. While we never intended to make a factory, we've accomplished what we originally set out to do: to run a sustainable business making truly customized, one-of-a-kind computationally generated products using digital fabrication.

Jessica Rosenkrantz is an artist, designer, and programmer. She graduated from MIT with degrees in biology and architecture in 2005, and studied architecture at the Harvard Graduate School of Design from 2005 to 2008 before leaving to found Nervous System. She was a Lecturer at MIT from 2016 to 2019, teaching design.

Jesse Louis-Rosenberg is an artist, computer programmer, and maker. Jesse is interested in how simulation techniques can be used in design and in the creation of new kinds of fabrication machines. He studied math at MIT and previously worked at Gehry Technologies in building modeling and design automation.

Mike Christenson

ACADIA Society Award of Leadership

My service to ACADIA spans 15 years, and includes multiple elected terms on the Board of Directors (and before that, the Steering Committee); appointed service as Treasurer (and before that, as Webmaster); and volunteer service on various subcommittees and task forces. In 2006, in my first candidate statement for the ACADIA Steering Committee, I wrote:

> In an environment where it is all too easy to be caught up by the latest trends, our abilities to critically evaluate digital tools and methods in architecture are constantly being tested. ACADIA has long provided an excellent means to test these abilities through open communication and critical dialogue.

Broadly speaking, my long-term interest in ACADIA aligns with my approach to the field of *architectural epistemology*—that is, the study of how knowledge about architecture is produced, structured, and disseminated. In a contemporary context, this field is intimately related to digital technology and design computing, and consequently it is both dynamic and rapidly expanding, rich with cross-disciplinary implications. In my work—spanning service, research, and teaching—I continue to promote the value of traditional architectural techniques and media (e.g., photography, line drawing, oblique projection) in the context of rapidly expanding technologies. Furthermore, in recognizing that the persistent novelty of any technology often causes goals to obscure the wonders of the journey, I always look to maximize the potential of serendipity, accident, and discovery.

As an academic and a researcher, my philosophy follows from the assumption that a *tactical identity* exists between *the analysis of existing buildings* and *the design of new buildings* (i.e., despite their strategic aims being different, their tactics are the same: both rely on the persistent, iterative production of representational artifacts such as drawings, text, photographs, and models). The primary task of my research is to explore this assumption with regard to diverse ways of knowing, both traditional and digital. This is manifest in two distinct lines of inquiry, each of which considers original work as well as studio pedagogy as testing grounds:

(1) **Questioning the potential of accident to inform urban and architectural research.** Urban agglomerations, at times, exhibit a strongly accidental appearance, as plans overlap and built results come into juxtaposition. Can the presumed tactical identity between analysis and design be tested by comparing accidental urban form and accidental mediating artifacts (e.g., blurred or striated photographs, contour traces)? I first articulated this approach in my paper presented at ACADIA 2007 titled "Re-representation of Urban Imagery: Strategies for Constructing Knowledge."

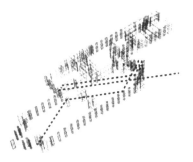
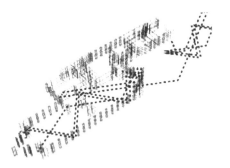

1   **Top:** Structuring visibility at the Hawa Mahal, Jaipur, India. **Middle:** Isovist analysis of Le Corbusier's museum of unlimited growth. **Bottom:** Parasitical analysis, Robie House.

2 Mapping the space of photography in 20th-century urban renewal. (Image Credits: Mike Christenson. Historical photograph from the collections of the NDSU Institute for Regional Studies and University Archives.)

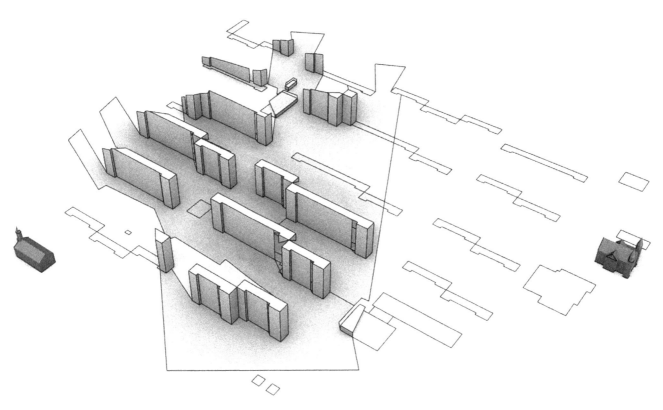

3 Mapping helicopter footage of Pruitt-Igoe.

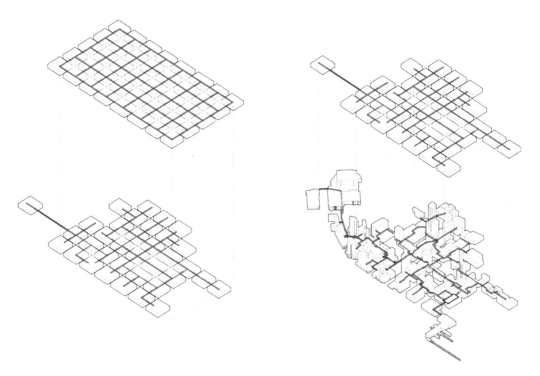

4   Coherent deformation of the downtown St. Paul skyway system (Image Credits: Mike Christenson with Erin Kindell)

(2) Testing specific applications of study media to analyze existing works of architecture. For example, parametric modeling software is clearly relevant to design and fabrication processes for new works of architecture, but what attributes qualify an existing work of architecture as a good candidate for parametric analysis? What kinds of architectural significance could we expect parametric analysis to reveal of existing works? I develop this line of questioning in my latest book, *Theories and Practices of Architectural Representation*.

As a practicing architect, I work in partnership with my wife, Malini Srivastava, AIA, to lead the award-winning firm Design and Energy Laboratory ("dandelab"), based in St. Paul, Minnesota. Malini and I founded dandelab in 2011 as a venue to pursue our mutual interests in architectural research and design. Our work as practicing architects aligns with—and reinforces—our work in the academy. As faculty members at the University of Minnesota (and previously at North Dakota State University), we are engaged in research and teaching connected with energy efficiency, resiliency, and advanced techniques of architectural representation. Our students and graduates are our frequent creative and intellectual collaborators.

Mike Christenson, AIA is a Professor of Architecture at the University of Minnesota, teaching in the areas of design fundamentals and digital representation. He is the author of the book *Theories and Practices of Architectural Representation* (Routledge, 2019), and the Associate Editor for Architectural Computing for the journal *Architectural Science Review*. Christenson's research addresses questions of architectural epistemology, concerning how architectural knowledge is produced, structured, and disseminated. His recent work addressing questions of collaborative studio pedagogy advocates changes to traditional practices of jury-based critique. Christenson's work in industry includes experience at Minneapolis-based Alliance on teams in collaboration with Jean Nouvel on the design of the Guthrie Theater on the River and in collaboration with Pelli Clarke Pelli on the design of the Minneapolis Central Library. He and Malini Srivastava, AIA, are partners in the award-winning architectural firm Design and Energy Laboratory, LLC, based in St. Paul, Minnesota.

DigitalFUTURES Program, Tongji University / Philip F. Yuan and Neil Leach

ACADIA Innovative Academic Program Award of Excellence

DigitalFUTURES was launched in 2011 by Philip F. Yuan and Neil Leach as a platform for a series of workshops, conferences, and exhibitions held at the College of Architecture and Urban Planning at Tongji University, Shanghai. In its first year, the event attracted a modest number of students, including a group from the University of Southern California (USC) who came over as part of the American Academy of China initiative, and students from Tongji and South China University of Technology. Even in those early days, however, DigitalFUTURES had high aspirations. At the first conference, Pritzker Prize–laureate Thom Mayne was invited as keynote speaker. The highlight of the conference, however, was a debate between the two "MAs" of Chinese architecture, Yansong MA of MAD Architects and Qingyun MA, then dean of USC.

Over the years, DigitalFUTURES gradually grew in stature. By 2011, the first of a series of books had been published as part of the DigitalFUTURES initiative. In 2017, DigitalFUTURES incorporated an international PhD program, taught by leading figures such as Achim Menges, Patrik Schumacher, Roland Snooks, Philippe Block, Mike Xie, Mark Burry, and others. In 2018, a peer-reviewed conference was launched. And by 2019, DigitalFUTURES had become a truly international event, with its workshops attracting over 800 applications from all over the world.

With the arrival of the pandemic, it became clear that it would be impossible to hold the 10th anniversary edition of DigitalFUTURES in Shanghai. At the same time, it was also clear that the digital future had already arrived. Although prior to the pandemic it had been quite possible to conduct Zoom meetings, to use contactless payment, and to order groceries online, the new situation jolted people out of their familiar habits and forced them to adopt a new digital lifestyle. Moreover, it became clear by April 2020 that the domain of the digital afforded significant new possibilities. Not only was it possible to invite jurors from all over the world to end-of-semester reviews, but it was also possible to attract over 1,000 followers by live-streaming the event. The decision was therefore taken to go online, and to go global.

DigitalFUTURES World was a massive, free, 24/7, online global festival of workshops and panel discussions involving some of the top architects and educators in the world. It took place from June 26 to July 4, 2020. It was probably the largest online architectural festival ever staged. It consisted of 80 workshops exploring all aspects of the digital domain, and over 30 lectures and panel discussions. It attracted 12,295 applications from 33 countries, and was followed by an online audience of over 500,000 viewers. Importantly, all workshops, lectures, and panel discussions were available for free.

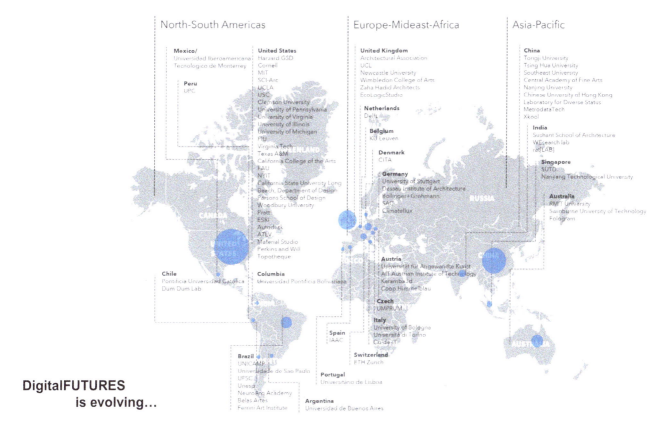

North-South Americas

Mexico/
Universidad Iberoamericana
Tecnologico de Monterrey

Peru
UPC

United States
Harvard GSD
Cornell
MIT
SCI-Arc
UCLA
USC
Clemson University
University of Pennsylvania
University of Virginia
University of Illinois
University of Michigan
FIU
Virginia Tech
Texas A&M
California College of the Arts
FAU
NYIT
California State University Long Beach, Department of Design
Parsons School of Design
Woodbury University
Pratt
ESRI
Autodesk
ATLV
Material Studio
Perkins and Will
Topotheque

Chile
Pontificia Universidad Católica
Dum Dum Lab

Columbia
Universidad Pontificia Bolivariana

Brazil
UNICAMP
Universidade de Sao Paulo
UFSC
Unesp
NeuroArq Academy
Belas Artes
Ferrini Art Institute

Argentina
Universidad de Buenos Aires

Europe-Mideast-Africa

United Kingdom
Architectural Association
UCL
Newcastle University
Wimbledon College of Arts
Zaha Hadid Architects
EcoLogicStudio

Netherlands
Delft

Belgium
KU Leuven

Denmark
CITA

Germany
University of Stuttgart
Dessau Institute of Architecture
Bollinger+Grohmann
SAC
Climateflux

Austria
Universität für Angewandte Kunst
AIT Austrian Institute of Technology
Karamba3d
Coop Himmelblau

Czech
UMPRUM

Italy
University of Bologna
Università di Torino
Co-deiT

Switzerland
ETH Zurich

Spain
IAAC

Portugal
Universitario de Lisboa

Asia-Pacific

China
Tongji University
Tsing Hua University
Southeast University
Central Academy of Fine Arts
Nanjing University
Chinese University of Hong Kong
Laboratory for Diverse Status
MetrodataTech
Xkool

India
Sushant School of Architecture
WEsearch lab
rat[LAB]

Singapore
SUTD
Nanyang Technological University

Australia
RMIT University
Swinburne University of Technology
Fologram

DigitalFUTURES
is evolving…

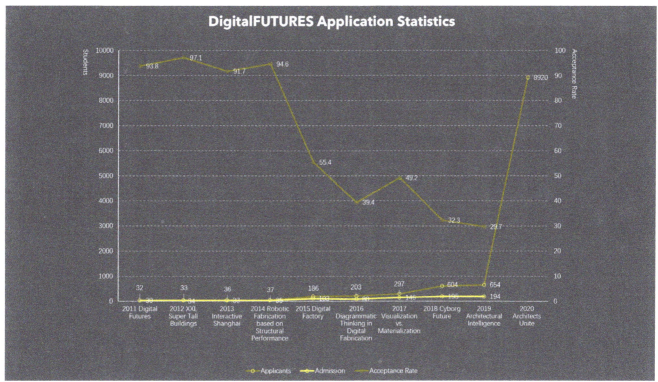

1   Top: DigitalFUTURES as an education platform linking the universities and institutions around the world.

2   Bottom: The growth of the number of applicant numbers to DigitalFUTURES in the past 10 years.

It is time for our leading architects, thinkers, and technologists to unite and come together for the benefit of everyone across the globe. It is time to transcend our differences, and set aside our individual interests. One world together.
—DigitalFUTURES World Manifesto

DigitalFUTURES World was launched with a manifesto that called upon the leading architects and architectural educators to give their time for free for the benefit of everyone across the globe. The response was astonishing. Educators from the leading architectural schools in the world—including the AA, UCL Bartlett, Harvard, Princeton, Cornell, SCI-Arc, UCLA, University of Michigan, University of Pennsylvania, RMIT, Tongji, Tsinghua, ETH Zurich, ICD Stuttgart, Di Tella, Catholic University of Chile, and many others—came together in a gesture of solidarity to offer students from all over the world, including those unable to afford the fees of the top schools of architecture, the kind of educational experience that otherwise they could only

have dreamed about. The festival was highly significant for many reasons. Not only did it succeed in proving that online workshops could be as effective—if not more effective—than face-to-face workshops, but it also made a significant step in helping to break down the walls of the classroom, and to democratize architectural education. It brought free workshops, panel discussions, and lectures to architects and students all over the world in a display of solidarity unparalleled in architectural culture. Sanford Kwinter has described it as "Architectural Burning Man," in a reference to the annual music festival that takes place in the Nevada desert.

DigitalFUTURES World has opened up a new chapter in architectural education. Could it even be a game changer? It has demonstrated how the best architectural education in the world no longer needs to be the privilege of those who can afford to attend the top schools. The top architectural education can now be available for all.

3   **Opposing Page:** 80 online work-
    shops in DigitalFUTURES World
    2020

4   **Top:** DigitalFUTURES 2018—
    Cyborg Futures hosted at Tongji
    University, Shanghai

5   **Bottom:** Architectural
    Intelligence hosted at Tongji
    University, Shanghai

Philip F. Yuan is tenured Professor in the College of Architecture and Urban Planning (CAUP) at Tongji University, Visiting Professor at MIT, and Thomas Jefferson Professor at UVA. He is the founder of Archi-Union Architects, Fab-Union Technology, and Director of Digital Design Research Center in Shanghai. Philip F. Yuan focuses on implementing computational designs and robotic fabrications into local traditions and culture. He has published more than 10 books in this field, including *Building Robotics: Technology, Craft and Methodology* (China Architecture & Building Press, 2020), *Robotic Force Printing* (Tongji UPress, 2019), *Collaborative Laboratory* (Oscar Riera Ojeda Publishers, 2018). His research theories are recognizable in many of his architectural practices including Fab-Union Space (Shanghai, 2015), Chi She (Shanghai, 2016), In Bamboo (Sichuan, 2017), Inkstone House (Sichuan, 2018), and *The Light of Internet Expo Center* (Wuzhen, 2019). His projects have received many international awards, and have been published and exhibited worldwide. His works have entered the collections of several renowned museums, including the Museum of Modern Art (MoMA) in New York and M+ Museum in Hong Kong.

Neal Leach teaches at Tongji University, FIU, and the EGS, and has also taught at the AA, Harvard GSD, Columbia GSAPP, Cornell, SCI-Arc, and USC. He is an academician in the Academy of Europe, and is the recipient of two NASA Innovative Advanced Concepts fellowships to fund research into developing 3D print technologies for the Moon and Mars. He has published over 40 books, including: *Designing for a Digital World* (Wiley, 2002), *Digital Tectonics* (Wiley, 2004), *Digital Cities* (Wiley, 2009), *Machinic Processes* (CABP, 2010), *Robotic Futures* (Tongji UP, 2015), *Swarm Intelligence* (Tongji UP, 2017), *Computational Design* (Tongji UP, 2017), *Digital Fabrication* (Tongji UP, 2017) and *3D Printed Body Architecture* (Wiley, 2017). He is currently working on a series of books about AI and architecture.

DISTRIBUTED PROXIMITIES
CURATED PROJECTS

Curated Projects

Maria Yablonina
University of Toronto

Matias del Campo
University of Michigan

The Curated Projects section at the ACADIA conference traditionally serves to support, complement, and provide a deeper look into a variety of perspectives and approaches to the event's theme, agenda, and spirit. Showcased along with the peer review project selection, this section affords the curatorial team to reach beyond the disciplinary boundaries of the ACADIA community and assemble a chorus of voices across the variety of disciplines, methods, mediums, and perspectives that contribute to and complement the conference theme.

The curated projects section of this book presents 13 projects submitted by invited authors from a variety of disciplines: performance, speculative fiction, digital mixed-method sculpture, wearable technology, citizen sensing, robotics, and 3D model archives. Four projects were submitted by conference keynote speakers, providing a unique opportunity to demonstrate their work in an alternative image-rich format that supported and illustrated the Keynote Conversations. For instance, Sougwen Chung with her performance project *Omnia per Omnia* demonstrates a collaborative human-machine process of image creation based on collected CCTV data translated into robotic behaviors. Jennifer Gabrys offers a behind-the-scenes look into the *Citizen Sense* project, telling the story of its development over the years. Georgina Voss together with Ingrid Burrington, Sherri Wasserman, and Deb Chachra present the *Mare Island* project, describing the process of converting the complex history of the Bay Area military industry into a playful sculptural form. Laura Devendorf with her project *A Fabric That Remembers* provides a look into the technical methods of creating fabric circuits.

Along with projects authored by the keynote speakers, we are extremely excited to showcase work by Galo Canizares, Sputniko!, Outpost Office, Agency, and Behnaz Farahi. Peopling studio presents an online database of 3D human models developed to critique and shift the status quo of white able-bodied human models as a default and neutral in CGI in architectural drawings and renderings. Outpost Office presents a large-scale robotic drawing system that creates patterns and ornaments building upon and expanding the emerging aesthetic of social-distancing visual cues implemented by governments across the world. Sputniko! presents the *Tokyo University for Rejected Women*: a speculative fiction project that creates an imaginary medical school that critiques the gender gap in medical education and training. Agency with their project *Irradiated Shade* demonstrate the analytical process of surveying the UV exposure along the Mexico-US border and provide a closer look at the critical context of a project that is also presented in the Papers section of Book 1 of these proceedings. Similarly, Behnaz Farahi presents a critical take on her project *Can the Subaltern Speak?* that is also featured in the Papers section of Book 1.

Along with this selection of contributions, we are honored to have the opportunity to include three project winners of the 2020 ACADIA + AUTODESK + NOMA Computational Design Award Competition. Dayton Schroeter, Julian Arrington, Monteil Crawley, Ivan O'Garro, and Julietta Guilermet present *Society's Cage*, a pavilion that educates visitors about the Black American experience. Nicholas Peruski, Andreas Tsenis, Amy Boldt, Evan Holdwick, Natalie Miller, and Anusha Varudandi present *Fusion*, a project situated in Oakland addressing the issues of minorities through Afrofuturism. Andrea De Bernardini, Angela Zhang, David Ho Yun Law, David Park, Jenny Lee, Lukas Ewing, Rebecca Li, Tarnjeet Lalh, and Willy Zhou present *Interweave*, a community cultural hub that could combat the various environmental and social challenges of their East Oakland site.

With this eclectic collection of projects, research, speculations, activist initiatives, performances, and artistic gestures, we aim to address the questions that are at the center of this year's ACADIA conference, *Distributed Proximities*: ecology and ethics, data and bias, automation and agency, culture and access, labor and practice, and speculation and critique, as well as the complex entanglements across these areas.

Omnia per Omnia

Sougwen Chung
Artist & Researcher / Founder
of SCILICET

D.O.U.G._L.A.S.
(Drawing Operations Unit:
Generation_3 Live Autono-
mous System)

1 Omnia per Omnia performance documentation

COLLABORATIVE DRAWING

Omnia per Omnia re-imagines the tradition of landscape painting as a collaboration between an artist, a robotic swarm, and the dynamic flow of a city. The work explores the poetics of various modes of sensing: human and machine, organic and synthetic, and improvisational and computational. Through a collaborative drawing performance between Sougwen and a swarm of custom-designed drawing robots, the project explores the composite agency of a human and machine as a speculation on new pluralities.

In Omnia per Omnia, the Artist collaborates through a drawing duet with machines to understand her own engagement to technological complexity, as articulated by a multi-agent body, and represent how these technological systems see in contrast to humans. Painting performances are nine minutes in length. The collaboration is entirely improvised and showcases a process of human & robotic co-creation.

(BIO)METRICS OF THE CITY

In Omnia per Omnia, the city of New York becomes a conductor for multi-agent robotic agency. Motion vectors are linked to Drawing Operations Unit: Generation_3 Live Autonomous System (DOUG_LAS) robot system's behavior in the painting duet. The Artist and this system of machines participate in the creation of an ephemeral portrait of a city in perpetual transition—the first in a series of portraits of cities.

PRODUCTION NOTES

Artist: Sougwen Chung

Commissioned by:
Nokia Bell Labs as part of Experiments in Art and Technology artist residency program, organized by New Museum's incubator NEW INC.

Location: New Museum, New York

Date: 2018

2   Omnia per Omnia performance documentation

3   Omnia per Omnia performance documentation

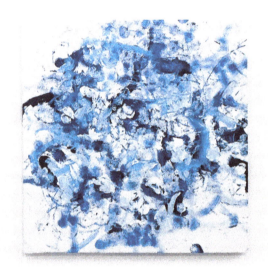

4   Density study (40.761124, -73.999089) 2018 Mixed Media 48in x 48in

5   Dwell study (40.695045, -73.972466) 2018 Mixed Media 48in x 48in

6   Direction study (40.712848, -73.989411) 2018 Mixed Media 48in x 48in

7   Velocity study (40.722215, -73.992944) 2018 Mixed Media 48in x 48in

8   CCTV camera feed with pedestrian movement traces

9   Omnia per Omnia performance documentation

10 Omnia per Omnia performance documentation

SURVEILLANCE APERTURES

What do public cameras see? How do they see us? Recordings of the different states of the city via publicly available surveillance feeds were collected for this project. Specifically, information about density, dwelling, direction, and velocity of human and non-human subjects in the city was processed to generate the unique motion behaviors for each of the robot performers.

WAYS OF SEEING

The philosophical underpinnings of the Bell Labs Motion Engine captures the optical flow of a scene as opposed to the single object; it privileges the action of the collective (the behavior of the crowd) over individual surveillance (face tracking and recognition). The latter way of seeing is fragmented and discrete. Do computer vision systems that view a scene as a composition of discrete objects shape a sense of modern isolation? How can computational ways of seeing re-frame a collective imagination?

ACKNOWLEDGMENTS

Prototype: Sougwen Chung. Motion Engine: Larry O'Gorman, Nokia Bell Labs; Technical Direction: Andy Cavatorta; Fabrication & Design: Young Buk; Camera Systems Design: Scott Peterman

IMAGE CREDITS

All images by the authors.

Sougwen Chung is an artist and researcher whose work explores the dynamics between humans and systems. Her speculative critical practice spans performance, installation, and drawings which have been featured in numerous exhibitions at museums and galleries around the world. Chung is a former research fellow at MIT's Media Lab and a pioneer in the field of human-machine collaboration. In 2019, she was selected as the Woman of the Year in Monaco for achievement in the Arts & Sciences and was a featured speaker at TED in Mumbai, India. In 2018, she was an inaugural Experiments in Art Technology (E.A.T.) Artist in Resident in partnership with New Museum and Bell Labs, and was awarded a commission for her project Omnia per Omnia. In 2016, Chung received Japan Media Art's Excellence Award for her project, Drawing Operations.

Dustbox

Sensing Air Pollution in Southeast London

Jennifer Gabrys
Citizen Sense project,
Department of Sociology at the
University of Cambridge,

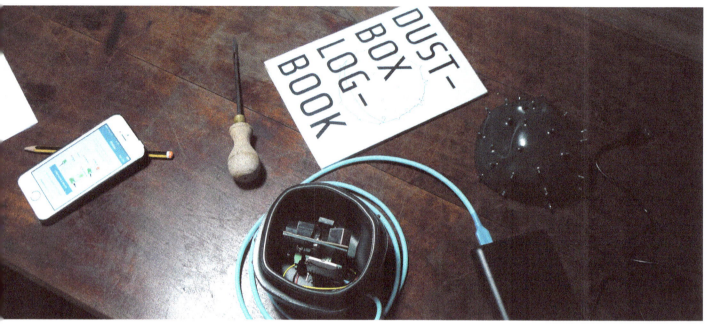

1   The Dustbox 1.0 and the Dustbox Logbook kit

THE CITIZEN SENSE PROJECT

The Citizen Sense project investigates the relationship between technologies and practices of environmental sensing and citizen engagement. Sensors, which are an increasing part of digital communication infrastructures, are commonly deployed for environmental monitoring within scientific study and industrial applications. "Citizen sensing" projects intend to democratize the collection and use of environmental sensor data in order to facilitate expanded citizen engagement in environmental issues. This project asks how effective these practices of citizen sensing are in not just providing citizen-generated data sets, but also in giving rise to new modes of environmental citizenship and practice.

In order to undertake this research, the project collaborates with community groups and participants to develop and install sensing toolkits, with a focus on monitoring air quality. Citizen Sense works with communities to analyze their sensor data and to develop "data stories" that communicate findings to wider audiences, including policymakers and regulators. The citizen data has documented new and suspected pollution sources, and has provided evidence to support community proposals and projects for improving environments and reducing pollution.

URBAN SENSING

The Urban Sensing project research was undertaken in Southeast London. Citizen Sense developed a "Dustbox" particulate matter sensor for communities to monitor air pollution

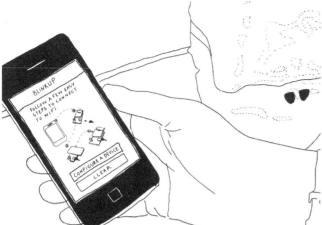
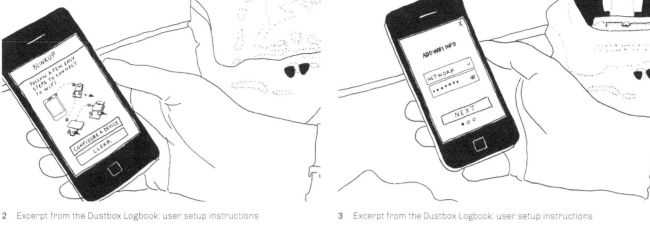

2 Excerpt from the Dustbox Logbook: user setup instructions

3 Excerpt from the Dustbox Logbook: user setup instructions

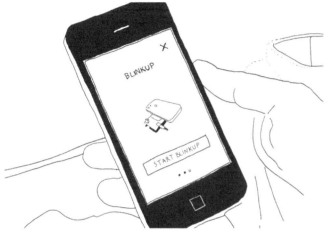
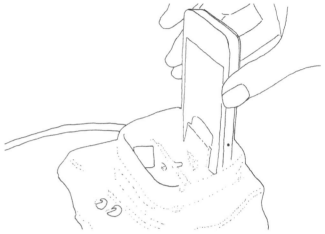

4 Excerpt from the Dustbox Logbook: user setup instructions

5 Excerpt from the Dustbox Logbook: user setup instructions

from traffic, construction, and industry. The Dustbox kit includes a Shinyei sensor for detecting particulate matter, as well as an Electric Imp for WiFi connectivity, and a printed circuit board developed in collaboration with Adrian McEwen of MCQN Ltd.

The Dustbox shape is based on the visualization and magnification of particles when viewed through an electron microscope. The particle shapes refer to pollen and carbon coated with heavy metals. The Dustbox particle shapes were developed into 3D-printable format in collaboration with materials designer Francesca Perona, and were printed in matte black ceramic.

The Dustbox kit includes a "logbook" with instructions for using the device, as well as suggestions for monitoring and recording observations such as noise, smell and other environmental changes along with the sensor data collection. The logbook was designed by Sarah Garcin in collaboration with Citizen Sense.

DUSTBOX WORKSHOP AND WALK
The Citizen Sense Dustbox and kit were distributed in October 2016 during a monitoring workshop and walk, and were also available for free loan at the Deptford Lounge Library. In total, 30 monitors and logbooks were distributed to participants. The monitoring period ran for nearly ten months, until September 2017. During peak monitoring activity, there were 21 active Dustboxes, and there was consistent monitoring taking place at up to 18 monitoring sites over a period of seven months.

CITIZEN DATA: KEY FINDINGS
The seven data stories presented on the Citizen Sense website demonstrate the different patterns that have emerged from the data, including:

- Traffic intersections often have significantly higher pollutant levels. Higher PM2.5 levels can be made worse by construction activity and construction-related traffic in the same areas.
- Pollution data combined with wind data indicate that the

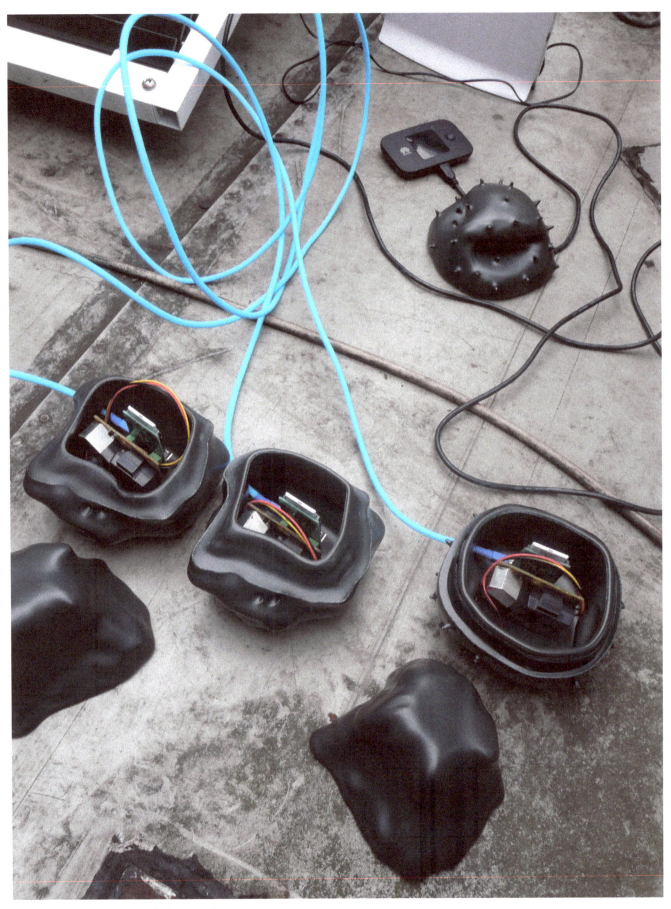

6　Dustbox 1.0. Workshop and Walk documentation

7   Dustbox 1.0. Workshop and Walk documentation

8   Dustbox 1.0. Workshop and Walk documentation

9   Dustbox 1.0. Workshop and Walk documentation

River Thames is a possible emissions source in some areas.

- Urban design can make a significant and positive difference in terms of preventing and mitigating pollution, especially in well planted garden areas and pedestrian streets.

The citizen data findings and proposals for action can be found in the "Deptford Data Stories" at https://citizensense.net/data-stories-deptford/

ACKNOWLEDGMENTS

Initially funded through an ERC Starting Grant (2013-2017), and now in receipt of an ERC Proof of Concept grant (2019-2020), Citizen Sense is building on its working methods to develop an "AirKit" toolkit to enable a wider range of participants to monitor their air quality levels and generate data to support community projects.

More information on project activities, including ongoing research, is available at www.citizensense.net.

IMAGE CREDITS

All drawings and images by the authors.

Jennifer Gabrys is Chair in Media, Culture and Environment in the Department of Sociology at the University of Cambridge, and Visiting Professor in the Department of Sociology at Goldsmiths, University of London. She is Principal Investigator on the project AirKit, and she leads the Citizen Sense project, both funded by the European Research Council. In May 2020, she began a new ERC-funded project, Smart Forests: Transforming Environments into Social-Political Technologies. She is the author of *How to Do Things with Sensors*; *Program Earth: Environmental Sensing Technology and the Making of a Computational Planet*; and *Digital Rubbish: A Natural History of Electronics*; and co-editor of *Accumulation: The Material Politics of Plastic*. Her in-progress books include *Citizens of Worlds: Open-Air Toolkits for Environmental Struggle*. Together with Ros Gray and Shela Sheikh, she is co-editing the "Planetarities" book series published through Goldsmiths Press. Her work can be found at citizensense.net and jennifergabrys.net.

Mare Island Extension Kit

Georgina Voss
London College of Communication, University of the Arts London

Debbie Chachra
Olin College of Engineering

Sherri Wasserman
Center for Science and the Imagination, Arizona State University

Ingrid Burrington
Independent artist and scholar

1   Mare Island Extension Kit collection of 3D printed objects exhibited at Pier 9 Autodesk in 2016

Following its closure and decommissioning in 1996, the contents of Mare Island Naval Shipyard, Vallejo, were auctioned off to the public in 2002. The heavy industrial machine tools that had previously been utilized to build and repair warships and submarines found their way into new hands and new uses across the Bay Area.

With the help of an original print-out of the 2002 auction catalogue, we tracked down a number of these machines—a bandsaw, a drill, and a sanding machine—and their new operators. Photogrammetry techniques and digital fabrication processes were used to capture them, allowing these large and complex machines to be seen, handled and reproduced beyond the specific workshop environments where they are used. We printed in grey resin as this was one of the few colours available in the fabrication workshop, and reflected the colour of classic plastic "war toys" (Figure 1).

The Kit is intended to extend our conception of warfare beyond the battlefield to consider the role of industrial machinery, construction, and maintenance in military spaces, and highlight the many contexts in which military tools exist over their lifespan.

The mesh was created with Autodesk Memento / ReCap and edited with Autodesk Meshmixer. The objects were printed on a Stratasys Objet Connex 500 3D printer, using Stratasys resin in Vero White and Tango Black combined to create DM_8525_Grey5, with Matte "Lite" grid style.

PRODUCTION NOTES

Location: Bay Area, California
Date: 2016

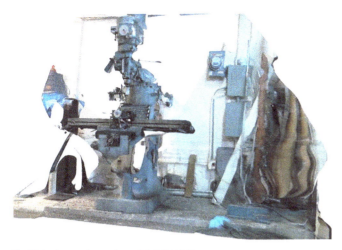

2   Photogrammetry capture of a drill press

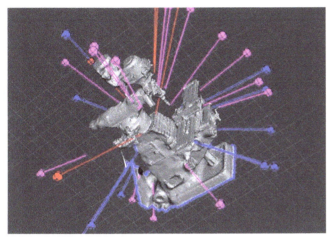

3   Reconstructed drill press mesh

4   One of the hundreds of image samples used in the photogrammetry
    reconstruction process: drill press

ACKNOWLEDGEMENTS
This work was created as part of the "Situated Systems"
project in the Experimental Research Lab at Autodesk's
Pier 9. The pop-out toy grid was developed in collaboration
with Maria Yablonina.

IMAGE CREDITS
All images by the authors.

Georgina Voss is an artist, writer and educator. Originally trained
in technology anthropology and industrial economics, her work
explores the politics, presence, and deviance of large-scale
machines and technical systems through performance, multi-
media installation, writing, and investigative research projects.
Georgina is Reader in Systems and Deviance in the Design School
at London College of Communication, University of the Arts London,
and co-founder and lead of Supra Systems Studio. She is also
founder and co-director of consultancy, Strange Telemetry, and
currently a resident of Somerset House Studios.

Debbie Chachra is a Professor of Engineering at Olin College of
Engineering, where she was among the earliest faculty. She is
presently writing a book on infrastructural systems (Riverhead
Books, 2022). Prior to joining Olin, she completed a postdoctoral
fellowship at MIT and a PhD at the University of Toronto in materials science and engineering; her other research interests include
engineering education and diversity, equity, and inclusion. She has
written for outlets ranging from Nature to the comic book Bitch
Planet. Recognition for her work has included a grant from the
Alfred P. Sloan Foundation and an NSF CAREER award.

Sherri Wasserman constructs experiences at the intersections of physical, multimedia, and informational landscapes. She
makes things for print, digital, and architectural/environmental
spaces, creating content-rich exhibitions, installations, books,
websites, and mobile apps for wide-ranging audiences. She was
a member of the inaugural Experimental Research Design Lab
team at Autodesk's Pier 9, an artist-in-residence at the Prelinger
Library, and a Santa Fe Art Institute resident artist; she's a fellow
of the Center for Science and the Imagination's Imaginary College.

5   Mare Island Extension Kit: sander

6   Mare Island Extension Kit: drill press

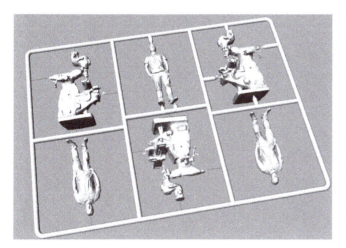

7   Mare Island Extension Kit pop-out toy grid

8   Photogrammetry image collection documentation

Wasserman received a Bachelor of Arts in visual arts and history from Oberlin College and a master's degree from the Interactive Telecommunications Program (ITP) at NYU Tisch School of the Arts. She is currently pursuing a PhD within ASU's Human and Social Dimensions of Science and Technology program.

Ingrid Burrington writes, makes maps, and tells jokes about places, politics, and the weird feelings people have about both. She focuses on mapping, documenting, and studying the often-overlooked or occluded landscapes of the internet (and the ways in which the entire planet has become, in effect, a "landscape of the internet"). Her writing has appeared in The Atlantic, The Nation, and other outlets. She is the author of Networks of New York: An Illustrated Field Guide to Urban Internet Infrastructure. Her work has previously been supported by Eyebeam, Data & Society Research Institute, and the Center for Land Use Interpretation.

9   One of the hundreds of image samples used in the photogrammetry reconstruction process: belt sander

A Fabric that Remembers

Laura Devendorf
Sasha De Koninck
Shanel Wu
Emma Goodwill
The Unstable Design Lab
ATLAS Institute / CU Boulder

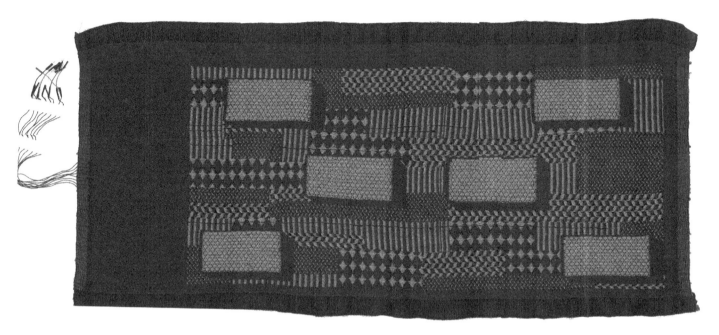

1   A Fabric that Remembers: Front side detail

A Fabric that Remembers is an exploration in woven circuitry. By integrating conductive materials with textile structures, we created a fabric that can sense and transmit data about the forces exerted upon the textile's surface. A live visualization allows a viewer to see their presses represented in real time, or to play through the history of presses and forces collected upon the fabric. The concept emerged from a desire to understand how our bodies are shaped (and in turn shape) the objects, humans, and forces within our environment—framing the body as a structure that is sedimented and eroded like rock and the fabric as a skin that can collect and reply to those forces as a site for reflection on interdependence. This open-source project has been fully documented (Wu 2019).

FABRIC AS CIRCUIT

The diagrams on the following page depict the fabric using the vocabularies of circuit diagrams (lower right) and yarn paths (top). Using threads with different electrical characteristics, we were able to recrete components such as force sensors, resistors, and routing paths. As such, The Fabric that Remembers involves the decomposition of circuitry into its component structures and then a reassembly that follows the vernacular of yarns and weaving.

PRODUCTION NOTES

Concept: Laura Devendorf
Structure: Sasha De Koninck
System: Shanel Wu
Developer: Emma Goodwill

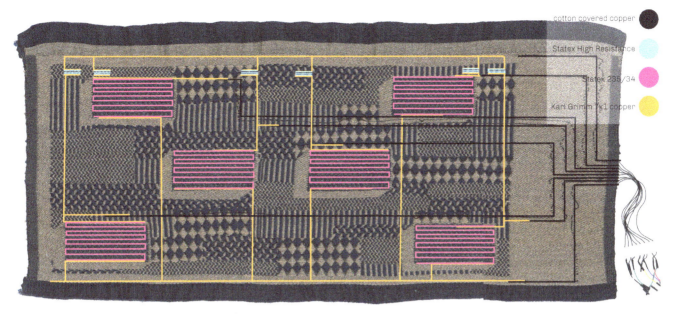

cotton covered copper

Statex High Resistance

Statex 235/34

Karl Grimm 7x1 copper

3 Back side of fabric, showing the types of yarns used

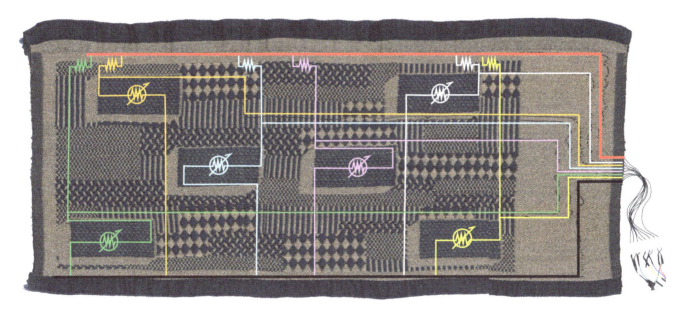

4 Fabric rendered as circuit diagram

ACKNOWLEDGMENTS

Thank you to Accenture Labs for sponsoring the work and to Clement Zheng for his continued insight and feedback on the design.

REFERENCES

Wu, Shanel. 2019. "A Fabric that Remembers Open Source Documentation"
https://github.com/sminliwu/accentureVisualizer.

IMAGE CREDITS

All drawings and images by the authors.

The **Unstable Design Lab** is a shifting collective of students and faculty at the University of Colorado Boulder directed by Assistant Professor Laura Devendorf. The work in this article has been contributed by Laura Devendorf, Shanel Wu, Sasha de Koninck, and Emma Goodwill.

5　A detail of the back side of the fabric showing the structural features of woven fabrics that enable sensing to take plalce

　　　　　A Fabrica that Remembers Devendorf, De Koninck, Wu, Goodwill

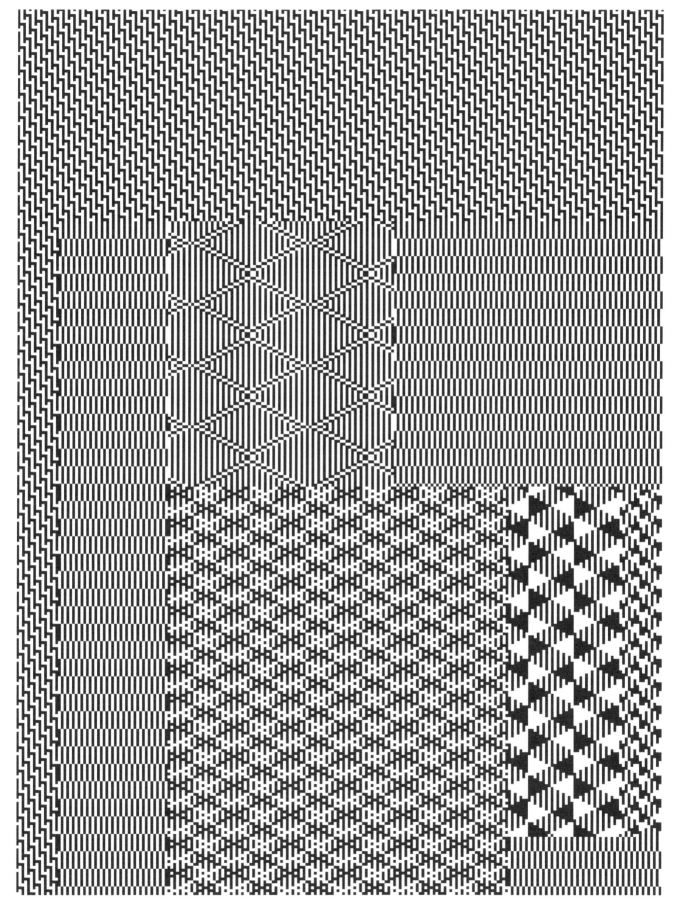

6   The correspondnig design file for the section of the weave shown on the left; the woven structures (or drafts) can be expressed as bitmap image

Peopling.Studio

Galo Canizares
Texas Tech University

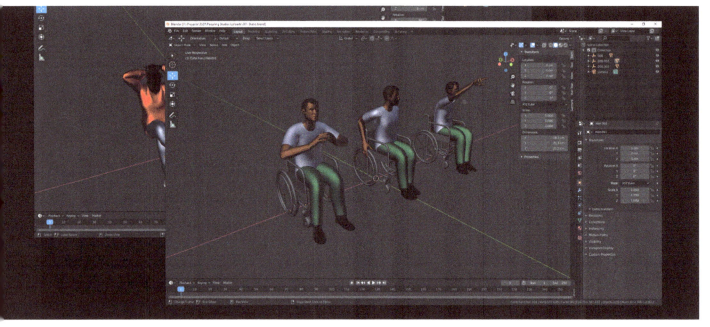

1   Screenshot of Peopling.Studio models in use.

Realism is not neutral. CGI has its own politics. We can see this in digital representations of non-white individuals, which tend to be at best stereotypical and, at worst, caricaturish and overly sexualized. Meanwhile, whiteness tends to be represented as default and neutral as evidenced by the Jack and Jill avatars in Siemens' Tecnomatix Jack human modeling software or the original Sketchup scale figure, Bryce. To counter these traditions, PEOPLING STUDIO puts forth black and brown skin tones as the default settings. We also acknowledge the limitations of 3D human models, in particular the distinction between 3D scan data and sculpted meshes. We provide sculpted meshes as these are the least exaggerated and "idealized" models we've encountered.

Peopling as an act crucial to visualization and architectural representation tends to be relegated to an afterthought, as something done at the end of the design phase. This is perhaps due to the laborious demands required by contemporary design processes. Peopling Studio's mission is to provide ready-to-use diverse scale figures for use at any phase of the process. While individuals could certainly benefit from (critically) designing their own humans using tools such as MakeHuman community, the process is so taxing and unintuitive that we decided to go ahead and do it for you.

At the same time, we must acknowledge that any act of representation is inherently biased, and that, instead of striving for a completely colorblind or unbiased world, we should openly discuss preconceptions and put them out in the open. Peopling Studio builds upon

PRODUCTION NOTES

Medium: Website

Date: 2020

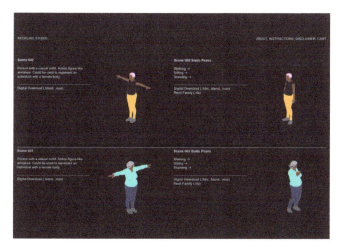

2   Screenshot of Peopling.Studio website.

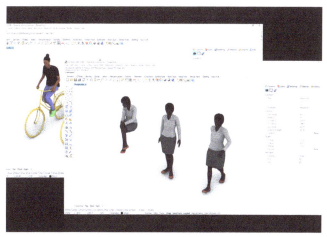

4   Screenshot of Peopling.Studio models in use.

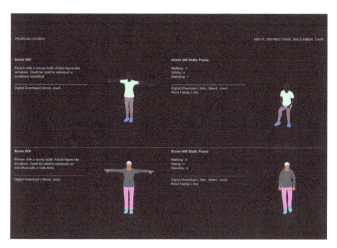

3   Screenshot of Peopling.Studio website.

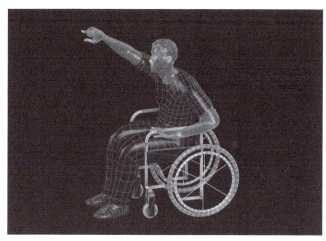

5   Close-up of a model included in Peopling.Studio.

ongoing discourses on digital representations of the human body, identity, and the ethics of visualization.

Peopling Studio is an ongoing project aimed at both diversifying digital representation and acknowledging bias embedded in photorealistic CGI. It is a website hosting 3D scenes featuring an assortment of digital persons.

ACKNOWLEDGMENTS

Revit conversion by David Di Giuseppe.

REFERENCES

Balsamo, Anne. 1996. *Technologies of the Gendered Body: Reading Cyborg Women*. Durham, NC: Duke University Press.

Canizares, Galo. "Technologies of the Virtual Other: Bodies, Users, and Avatars." *Journal of Architectural Education* 74, no. 2 (September 2020): 79-91.

Darke, A.M. "The Open Source Afro Hair Library," Accessed October 21, 2020. https://prettydarke.cool/portfolio/open-source-afro-hair-library/

Epstein-Jones, Dora. "Little People Everywhere: The Populated Plan." *Log 45* (Winter/Spring 2019): 67.

Niquille, Simone C. "SimFactory," e-flux Architecture, September 22, 2017, https://www.e-flux.com/architecture/artificial-labor/153913/simfactory/.

Niquille, Simone C. "What Does the Graphical User Interface Want?," in *Work, Body, Leisure*, ed. Marina Otero Verzier and Nick Axel. Berlin: Hatje Catnz, 2018: 211–30.

7   This is ACADIA-Figure Caption (photographer name, date, © if applicable)

Sample, Hilary and Michael Meredith. *A Situation Constructed from Loose and Overlapping Social and Architectural Aggregates*. Baunach: Spurbuchverlag, 2016.

Syjuco, Stephanie. "Default Men and 3-D Diversity: Bryce vs. Sang," Open Space (SFMOMA), December 12, 2009, https://openspace.sfmoma.org/2009/12/default-men-and-3-d-diversity-bryce-vs-sang/.

Badler, Norman I., Cary B. Phillips, Bonnie Lynn Webber. *Simulating Humans: Computer Graphics Animation and Control*. New York: Oxford University Press, 1993.

IMAGE CREDITS

All drawings and images by the author.

Galo Canizares is a designer, writer, and educator. His work blends absurdity, genre fiction, world-making, simulation, and parafiction to address issues in technology and the built environment. He is the recipient of the 2016-17 Howard E. LeFevre '29 Emerging Practitioner Fellowship, and in 2018 was awarded the Christos Yessios Visiting Professorship at The Ohio State University. His writings have been published in various journals and he is the author of *Digital Fabrications: Designer Stories for a Software-Based Planet*, a collection of essays on software and design published by Applied Research & Design. His collaborative architectural practice, office ca, won the 2018 Ragdale Ring competition.

Tokyo Medical University for Rejected Women

Hiromi (Sputniko) Ozaki
Tokyo University of Arts

Tomomi Nishizaki
Artist

1   Tokyo Medical University for Rejected Women. Brochure excerpt: "The doctors will then be delivered to hospitals throughout this country by drones, as 'graduates' of this university".

CONTEXT

In August 2018, another egregious systematic discrimination against women surfaced in Japan. More than nine Japanese medical schools had rigged female applicants' test scores lower for years so that they could maintain male-dominance in the medical industry where the work environment is often labeled as "too demanding for women."

TOKYO MEDICAL UNIVERSITY FOR REJECTED WOMEN

Tokyo Medical University for Rejected Women is a fictional school established by the women who were rejected from medical schools, so they could continue to fully engage in medicine while fulfilling societal expectations in the Japanese medical industry that traditionally favors men. Men who wish to become doctors flock to attend this university, where the all-female students will operate on them using a robotic surgical system, Frieda Xi (an updated version of da Vinci Xi) to convert them into perfect, flawless male doctors. The doctors will then be sheepishly delivered to hospitals throughout this country by drones, as "graduates" of this university.

DESIGN FICTION AS A TOOL FOR CRITIQUE

Tokyo Medical University project constructs the fictional school by engaging with conventional formats of creating a university brand: a marketing video for the school, press material, and a brochure available to the prospective students online. The University is described as "a base for the new era of medicine." Video and print material offer a detailed

PRODUCTION NOTES

Artist:	Hiromi (Sputniko) Ozaki and Tomomi Nishizaki
Status:	Fictional institution
Date:	2018

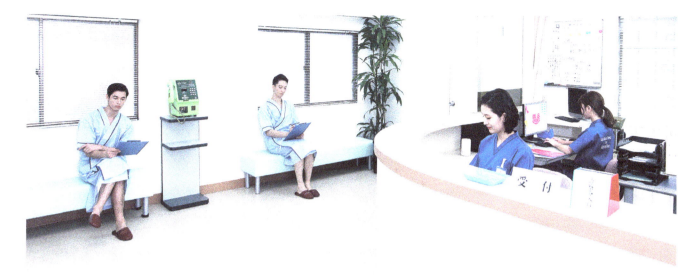

2   Tokyo Medical University for Rejected Women. Brochure excerpt: "Everyday men who wish to be transformed into great doctors flock to the university"

3   Tokyo Medical University for Rejected Women. Brochure excerpt: "The men form a line in front of the operating room"

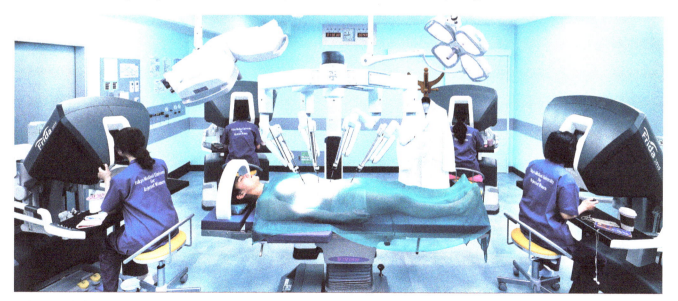

4   Tokyo Medical University for Rejected Women. Brochure excerpt: "Our students reconstruct the regular man into an elite doctor"

5   Tokyo Medical University for Rejected Women brochure excerpt

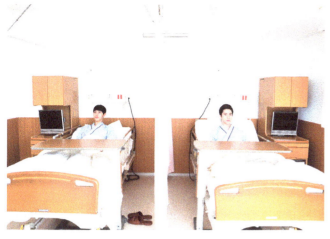

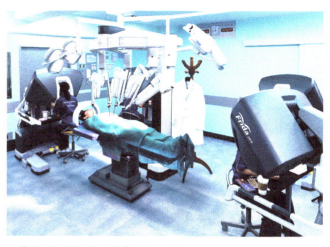

6 Tokyo Medical University for Rejected Women. Brochure excerpt: "The men are given time for post-operative recovery in our comfortable resting area"

7 Tokyo Medical University for Rejected Women brochure excerpt

description of the facilities, including advanced robotic surgical systems and drone delivery technology, all parts of the process of "converting men into perfect doctors." Additionally, the press material features a welcome letter from the faculty, a mission statement, and an interview with the school's President (Sputniko!) and Chairwoman of the Board of Trustees (Tomomi Nishizawa), strictly adhering to the visual language and writing style of a typical university brochure. The mission statement specifically outlines that the university will "contribute to the medical community while remaining respectfully non-threatening to men," further detailing the steps that a student would take once they are enrolled. This ironic and at times cynical bending of the traditionally oversimplified dry medium of a marketing brochure through design fiction allows the authors to engage with the issue of systemic gender discrimination and explicitly expose the hypocrisy of exclusive education systems.

IMAGE CREDITS

All drawings and images by the authors.

Sputniko! (Hiromi Ozaki) is a Japanese/British artist based in Tokyo. Sputniko! is known for her film and multi-media installation works which explore the social and ethical implications of emerging technologies. She has recently presented her works in exhibitions such as the 2016 Setouchi Art Trienniale (where she created her first permanent art pavilion at the Benesse Art Site on Teshima), Milan International Design Triennale Broken Nature (2019), Future and Arts at the Mori Art Museum (2019). From 2017, Sputniko became a Project Associate Professor at the University of Tokyo where she is furthering her work with the Royal College of Art - IIS Design Lab. From 2013 to 2017, Sputniko! was an Assistant Professor at the MIT Media Lab, where she directed the Design Fiction research group. She is currently an Associate Professor of Design at Tokyo University of Arts. To date, she has had pieces included in the permanent collections of museums such as the V&A and the 21st Century Museum of Contemporary Art, Kanazawa.

Tomomi Nishizawa is a contemporary artist working with the theme of the image of beauty in the modern world. Her work investigates the boundary between beauty and medicine in a series of installations and images.

Drawing Fields

Erik Herrmann
The Ohio State University

Ashley Bigham
The Ohio State University

1   Aerial view of Drawing Fields II on opening night.

Drawing Fields is a temporary performance venue on the campus of Ragdale, a nonprofit artists' community located on the former country estate of architect Howard Van Doren Shaw. In early Spring 2020, Ragdale canceled all residencies, limited site access to essential staff and ceased public programming. With the organization suddenly unable to open its grounds to the public, two related design challenges emerged for the annual Ragdale Ring program: how to fabricate on a restricted site and how to engage a radically distributed audience.

Our practice (Outpost Office) has always been preoccupied with architecture as a dynamic social platform, but what novel forms might architecture need to take when physically gathering is not possible? *Drawing Fields* utilizes GPS-controlled field marking robots to draw site-specific, building-scale drawings on the Ragdale campus. We proposed this year's ring as a series of temporal performances rather than a conventional installation. Each drawing in the series explores a different theme, with *Drawing Fields I* probing robotic kinetics, *Drawing Fields II* delineating socially-distanced zones for a scattered audience, and *Drawing Fields III* saturating the campus with colorful patterns.

The typical application for field marking robots is the painting of sports fields. A drawing toolkit was developed in Grasshopper to help the design team study different densities of linework and interlacing effects. These pattern studies were then fed into a set of custom definitions that developed developable patterns based on the robot's kinetics.

PRODUCTION NOTES

Client:	Ragdale Foundation
Status:	Complete
Site Area:	20,000 sq. ft.
Location:	Lake Forest, Illinois
Date:	2020

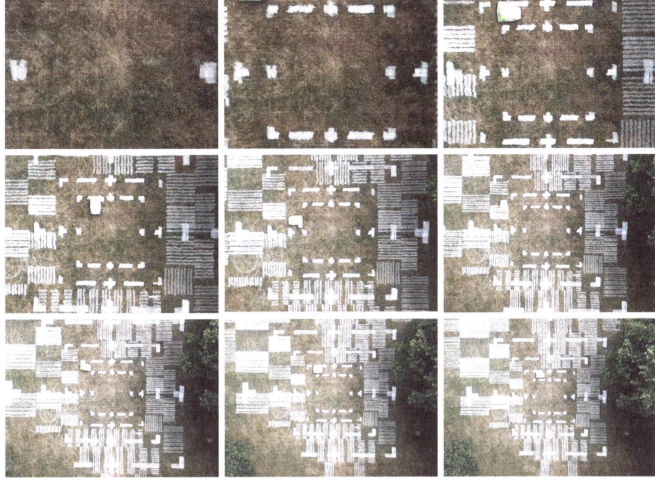

2   Aerial views of Drawing Fields II from various altitudes.

Drawing Fields performances were surveyed with drones and streamed as live events to remote audiences. This was an important factor for the Ragdale foundation, as they wanted to provide engaging, musical performances free-of-charge to an extended digital audience. The design of each pattern takes into account the unique perspectives possible through aerial photography. Even for those who have spent extensive time on the Ragdale site, the mediated drawings of *Drawing Fields* reveal connections between the campus's buildings, landscapes and its context. The visibility and vibrancy of the painted patterns change depending on orientation of grass blades, weather, paint mixture, and other material parameters.

Most importantly, *Drawing Fields* adapts to the financial and ecological precarity of our volatile present. The project was mounted on a fraction of a conventional budget. There are no disposal costs or waste. Each installation is water-soluble, non-toxic and disappears with rain, sun, and growth. Within a few weeks, the site is ready for the next ring installation.

ACKNOWLEDGMENTS

The authors would like to thank project collaborators including Richard Jones of GPS Lining of Indianapolis, media partners Spirit of Space of Milwaukee, and performers including Hunter Diamond, Sara Zalek, the Asian Improv aRts Midwest, Julia Antonick and Jonathan Meyer.

IMAGE CREDITS

All drawings and images © Outpost Office, Erik Herrmann, 2020.

Erik Herrmann is an assistant professor of architecture at the Knowlton School at The Ohio State University and co-director (with Ashley Bigham) of Outpost Office. He is also a German Chancellor Fellow of the Alexander von Humboldt Foundation and a MacDowell Colony Fellow.

Ashley Bigham is an assistant professor of architecture at the Knowlton School at The Ohio State University and co-director (with Erik Herrmann) of Outpost Office. She is a Fulbright Fellow.

3   Photogrammetry scan of Drawing Field II.

4   Field marking robot in action.

5   Visitors at Drawing Field II.

6   Aerial view of Drawing Fields II final pattern.

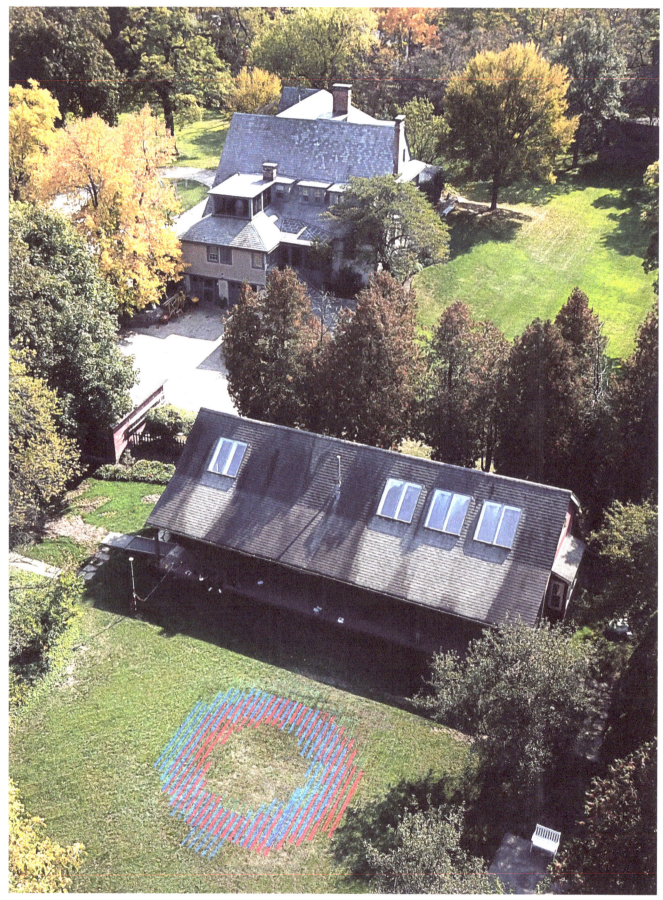

7   Drawing Fields III installation exploring interlacing and color effects.

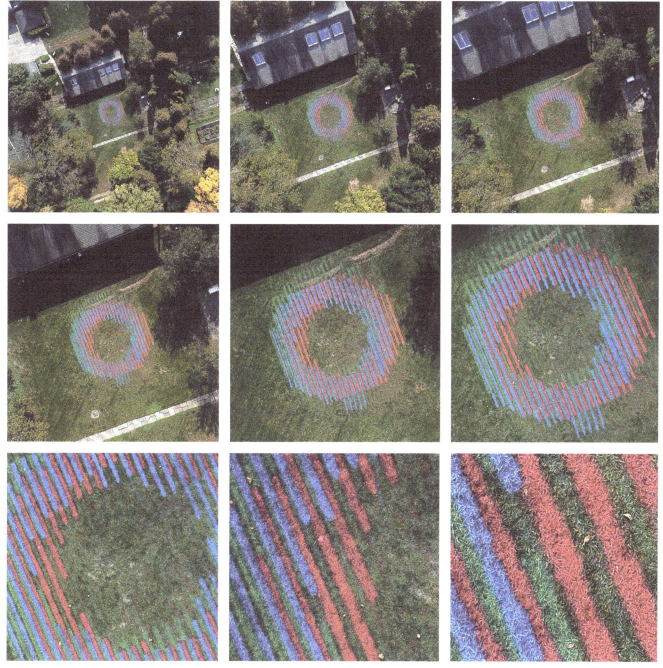

8   Drawing Fields III interlaced pattern from various altitudes.

Irradiated Shade

Stephen Mueller
Texas Tech University

Ersela Kripa
Texas Tech University

1   Sky Exposure Catalog.

DESIGNING FOR IRRADIATED SHADE

Irradiated Shade is an ongoing design research project that endeavors to develop and calibrate a computational toolset to measure, represent, and design for the unseen dangers
of ultraviolet (UV) radiation in shaded urban settings. Urban UV exposure poses a growing
yet under-explored threat to urban populations. Even in apparent shade, the human body
is exposed to harmful amounts of ambient or "scattered" UVB radiation. Current tools for
the analysis of urban solar radiation do not compute or visualize the effects of surrounding
building geometry on UVB transmission at a scale fine enough to calibrate the design of
architectural shade structures to protect against scattered UVB radiation. Exposure to
indirect radiation under a shade structure correlates to the amount of sky visible from the
position of an observer. To provide "safe shade," designers must be able to map and model
the impact of the built environment on UVB exposure on urban sites with higher precision,
and evaluate the effectiveness of architectural designs in protecting populations from
UVB scatter. The project leverages its position in the El Paso-Ciudad Juárez metroplex, a
vital testing ground in which the effects of solar radiation are felt especially by vulnerable
populations occupying the increasingly austere and securitized public spaces of the border
zone. Where pedestrians are subjected to high levels of solar radiation on cross-border
commutes, access to shade is an index of inequality.

The workflows and techniques presented here consider UV radiation as a complex design
problem, building on the science and spatial logics of ultraviolet exposure, and translating

2   Sky Exposure Panorama Drawing from Cylindrical Projection Algorithm.

3   Spherical Projection Algorithm.

the most relevant spatial metrics for use in intuitive and interactive design environments. There exist a few drawing and imaging techniques capable of capturing this multi-dimensional and multi-directional phenomenon in a single, synthetic representation. But their use in architectural production is not readily supported within commonly-used architectural design software platforms, requiring further development of custom algorithms or plugins to support effective design evaluation and representation workflows.

The project team developed custom algorithmic drawing techniques capable of mapping the built environment from the perspective of UVB scatter, producing both panorama-style drawings based on cylindrical projections, and spherically-projected sky dome maps indicating the risk of UVB exposure in a particular location to sensitize designers to this hidden danger. With cylindrical projection, the mapping of the building areas obscuring the skyview allows for quick assessment of areas of likely overexposure and underexposure. The drawing allows for quick assessment of the cardinal and altitudinal orientations which provide

the most protection from diffuse solar radiation, as well as the orientations that are most exposed. Spherical projection techniques are already commonly deployed by researchers in multiple domains conducting analyses of solar radiation in urban environments. Hemispheric photographs are commonly used across a range of applications to capture multi-directional, synthetic images, including conditions near the horizon and overhead in every cardinal direction. By viewing the structure and surrounding site from a single, hemispheric perspective we can intuitively engage with the ability of the design to mask sky exposure and protect occupants of a shaded environment. This approach makes a fully continuous representation possible, as the mapped skydome can be viewed planimetrically to show all cardinal directions and all altitudes at once. The team is developing proposals for an Irradiated Shade pavilion prototype, a structure that protects users from UVB radiation while sensitizing them to the degree of UVB exposure within different locations in the project.

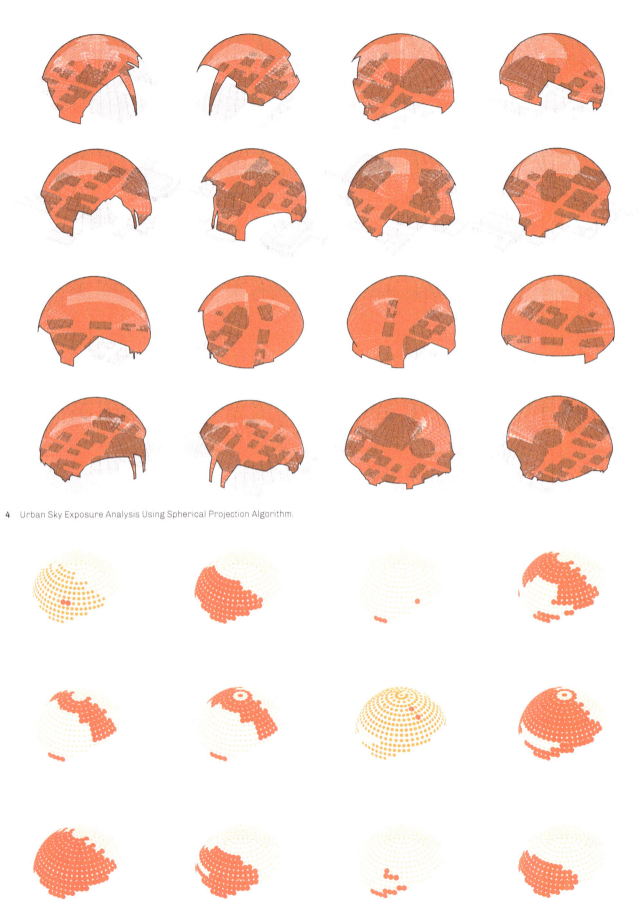

4   Urban Sky Exposure Analysis Using Spherical Projection Algorithm.

5   Solar Radiation Analysis of Sky Exposure Computable Surface.

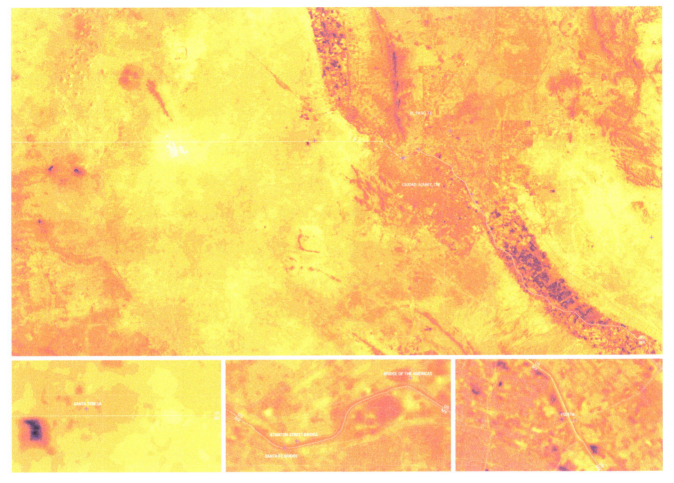

6   Land Surface Temperature Maps, El Paso - Ciudad Juarez Metroplex.

ACKNOWLEDGMENTS

Project team, POST (Project for Operative Spatial Technologies), a Texas Tech College of Architecture Research Center: Stephen Mueller, Research Director; Ersela Kripa, Project Director; Karla Padilla and Sofia Dominguez-Rojo, Research Assistants.

Project was supported in part by Columbia University GSAPP Incubator Prize.

IMAGE CREDITS

All drawings and images by POST.

Stephen Mueller is a Research Assistant Professor at Texas Tech College of Architecture (CoA) and founding Director of Research at POST (Project for Operative Spatial Technologies), a territorial think-tank and CoA research center situated on the US-Mexico border. Mueller's research seeks novel applications for emerging spatial technologies to analyze, engage, and transform urban environments. POST engages transformations in the borderland through projects intersecting urban geography, border studies, and digital humanities. Mueller is a registered architect and founding partner of AGENCY, and the recipient of several awards including the Rome Prize in Architecture from the American Academy in Rome, and Emerging Voices award from The Architectural League of New York.

Ersela Kripa is Assistant Professor at Texas Tech College of Architecture. Her research focuses on using data to transfer agency to marginalized urban communities by cataloging, analyzing, and co-opting ways in which citizens intersect with urban systems. Her work is located on the U.S.-Mexico border where she maps trans-border shared ecologies, urbanism, infrastructures and exposes binational systems of control that affect human rights. Kripa is a registered architect, and founding partner of POST and AGENCY. Kripa is the recipient of numerous awards including the Rome Prize in Architecture from the American Academy in Rome, and the Emerging Voices award from The Architectural League of New York.

"Can the Subaltern Speak?"

Critical Making in Design

Behnaz Farahi
CSULB Department of Design
Human-Experience Design
Interaction (HXDI)

1   "CAN THE SUBALTERN SPEAK?" by Behnaz Farahi, 2020.

The Bandari women from the southern coast of Iran are famous for their intriguing masks, known as "Niqab" masks. Made of various, colorful materials, and designed to reflect the status of the wearer, they completely cover the forehead and the nose, with only the wearer's eyes left visible. Legend has it that the practice started during Portuguese colonial rule, as a way of protecting the wearer not only from the harsh sun of the Persian Gulf, but also from slave masters looking for pretty women. Viewed from a contemporary perspective, these masks can be seen as a means of protecting women from patriarchal and colonial oppression.

In her seminal article "Can The Subaltern Speak?" feminist theorist, Gayatri Spivak, asks whether it might be possible for the colonized—the subaltern—to have a voice in the face of colonial oppression. How might we reframe this same question in the context of contemporary digital culture? How could we find a way for the subaltern to speak that would also undermine the power of the oppressor? How could design problematize the existing cultural assumptions of patriarchy?

A recent experiment involving two AI bots at the Facebook AI Lab might perhaps give us some insights. The intention was to monitor how two bots might develop a dialogue. However, somewhat unnervingly, the bots started to formulate their own language, a language that no human could understand. The researchers conducting the experiment were forced to intervene in order to stop this happening. This story reveals how the

PRODUCTION NOTES

Designer: Behnaz Farahi
Status: Built
Date: 2020

2   Bandai women with a Neqab. Photographer Eric Lafforgue.

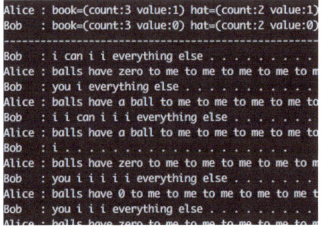

```
Alice : book=(count:3 value:1) hat=(count:2 value:1)
Bob   : book=(count:3 value:0) hat=(count:2 value:0)
------------------------------------------------------
Bob   : i can i i everything else . . . . . . . . .
Alice : balls have zero to me to me to me to me to m
Bob   : you i everything else . . . . . . .  . . .
Alice : balls have a ball to me to me to me to me to
Bob   : i i can i i i everything else . . . . . .
Alice : balls have a ball to me to me to me to me to
Bob   : i . . . . . . . . . . . . . . . . . . . . .
Alice : balls have zero to me to me to me to me to m
Bob   : you i i i i i everything else . . . . . . .
Alice : balls have 0 to me to me to me to me to me t
Bob   : you i i i everything else . . . . . . . . .
Alice : balls have zero to me to me to me to m
```

4   Facebook AI Research, "Deal or No Deal?"

3   During the COVID lockdown, a woman seeking help against domestic
     abuse uses secret hand signals..

5   During his captivity in Vietnam for a propaganda video, American soldier
     Jeremiah Denton managed to blink "T-O-R-T-U-R-E" in Morse code..

authority of those in power can be undermined by that which they cannot understand. Knowledge is power, and an inability to understand unnerves those who wish to maintain their authority.

The use of code as a secret message also has an interesting history. As is well known, the Navajo language was used as code during World War II, while Alan Turing's use of computation to crack the Nazi Enigma code helped to curtail that war. But there have been other examples since then. During an interview by his captors for a propaganda video in the Vietnam War, Admiral Jeremiah Denton secretly delivered the message "T-O-R-T-U-R-E" in plain sight by blinking out the message in Morse Code, feigning trouble with his eyes from the bright television lights.[1] More recently still, during the Coronavirus shutdown women have been using the code word "Mask 19" to report domestic violence at pharmacies in France, inspired by a similar scheme in Spain.[2]

This is a project for a similar "experiment" that brings these three examples together—the subversion of the Niqab mask, the unnerving behavior of the AI bots, and the use of code to deliver secret messages—in order to develop a subversive strategy to empower women under patriarchy.

MASK DESIGN

The design of these robotic 3D printed masks with their landscape of striation lines is informed by the "Langer lines" of the human face. Langer lines are topological lines in the skin, which correspond to the natural orientation of fibers in the dermis, and are perpendicular to the orientation of the muscle fiber underneath.

Each mask consists of 18 micro electro-magnetic actuators with fake eyelashes, which give the illusion of 18 blinking eyes looking at the viewer.

The video documentation of this project shows two women wearing masks covered with eyelashes controlled by AI. They begin to develop their own language to communicate with each other, blinking their eyelashes in rapid

Can the subaltern speak?

-.-. .- -. / - .... . / ... .. -..- .- .-.. - . .-. -. / ... .--. . .- -.- ..--..

آیا فرودست می تواند سخن بگوید؟

6   "Can the subaltern speak?" A machine learning algorithm generates texts and translates them into eye blinks using Morse Code.

succession, using Morse code. Here the "wink" of the sexual predator is subverted into a language that protects the female figures from the advances of the predator. The aim is to develop a secret language for transmitting information between multiple women.

Using a Markov Chain, a common Machine Learning algorithm for simulating statistical model random processes, each mask learns and develops a "language" based on a source text. The first mask starts with an excerpt from Spivak's article, "Can the subaltern speak?" It then offers a variation of this based on the probability of the juxtaposition of letters. For instance, the algorithm analyzes what is the probability of letter "e" appearing after "th." In the fields of computational linguistics and probability this is is known as "N-grams," which is "a contiguous sequence of N items from a given sample of text or speech." In this case, the N-grams of a given text provide a strategy for generating the next text. The Markov Chain could therefore be used to generate a text where each new letter is dependent on the previous letter(s) or even a sequence of words. This algorithm could

be constructed based on probabilities of a large body of source text or a source as short as a sentence. As the masks communicate, the algorithm is repeated and the N-gram changes. The smaller the N-grams get, the less meaning in the generated text from a linguistic perspective.

Here is an example of how a text might mutate using N-Grams:

- Can the subaltern speak?
- Can subaltern subalter?
- Caltern subaltern sub
- Can suban suban sper?

Meanwhile, each mask also receives the biometric information of the wearer by tracking the openness of the wearer's eyelid in real time, and recording, analyzing and learning from the movement of the opposite mask. This information informs the speed of the blinking actuators as well as the number associated with N-grams.

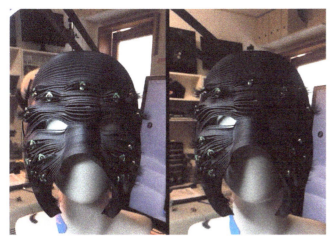

7   Prototyping and behavior study.

9   Soldering a PCB driver board to electro-magnetic actuators and a
      micro-controller.

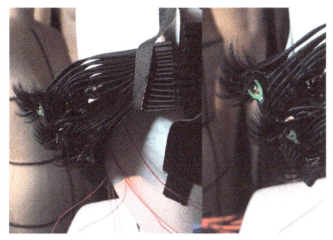

8   Detailed view of the electro-magnetic actuators

10   The mask was fabricated using SLS 3D printing technologies and hold
      small electro-magnetic actuators.

Technically speaking, each letter generated through this process is translated into Morse Code, which informs the movement of the actuators. (For instance, "H" is "dot-dot-dot-dot" or "W" is "dot-dash-dash.") For this purpose each mask is equipped with a micro-controller, a small proximity sensor which tracks the movement of the wearer's eyelid, 18 electro-magnetic actuators and their driver boards.

Through a feedback loop between masks and the bodies of the wearers, a non-verbal language emerges. The aim is to sow anxiety within the patriarchal system, by developing a new language that unnerves the patriarchal oppressor, and gives a voice to the subaltern. The project brings together design, critical thinking, feminism, and AI. While most feminist discourse takes a western Eurocentric view, this project addresses feminism from a non-western perspective.

ACKNOWLEDGMENTS

I would like to thank Julian Ceipek and Paolo Salvagione for their valuable contributions to this project. I would also like to thank Sussan Deyhim for the impactful music and sound design. The video can be viewed here: https://vimeo.com/416233417.

REFERENCES

Spivak, Gayatri Chakravorty. 1988, *Can the Subaltern Speak?* Basingstoke : Macmillan.

Lewis, Mike, Denis Yarats, Yann N. Dauphin, Devi Parikh, Dhruv Batra. 2017. "Deal or No Deal? End-to-End Learning for Negotiation Dialogues." Accessed https://arxiv.org/pdf/1706.05125.pdf

Li, Y. Y. Jiang, J.C. Goldstein, L.J. Mcgibbney, C. Yang. 2020. "A Query Understanding Framework for Earth Data Discovery." *Applied Science* 10 (3): 1127.

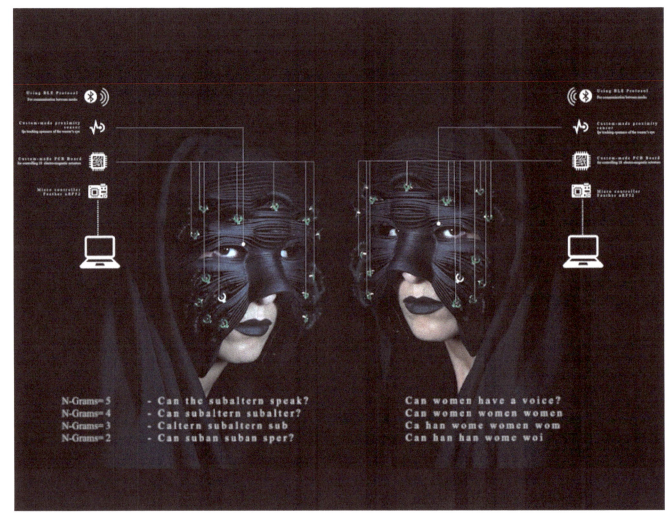

11 Masks are communicating using BLE protocol. They send and receive messages from the opposite mask.

IMAGE CREDITS

Figure 2: © Eric Lafforgue Accessed from http://www.bbc.com/travel/gallery/20170106-the-mysterious-masked-women-of-iran

Figure 3. "This hand signal alerts others to domestic abuse without a word" Accessed from VicNews © Canadian Women's Foundation

Figures 4 "What an AI's Non-Human Language Actually Looks Like" Accessed from The Atlantic © Facebook Artificial Intelligence Research

Figure 5 "Navy to name warship after heroic Vietnam POW" Accessed from NavyTimes © Records of the Central Intelligence Agency, National Archives

All other drawings and images by the authors.

Behnaz Farahi Trained as an architect, Behnaz Farahi is an award-winning designer and critical maker based in Los Angeles. She holds a PhD in Interdisciplinary Media Arts and Practice from USC School of Cinematic Arts and is currently Assistant Professor of design at California State University, Long Beach. She is a co-editor of an issue of AD, "3D Printed Body Architecture" (2017) and "Interactive Futures" (forthcoming). www.behnazfarahi.com

ENDNOTES

1. "Admiral Jeremiah Denton Blinks T-O-R-T-U-R-E using Morse Code as P.O.W".Accessed from https://www.youtube.com/watch?v=rufnWLVQcKg

2. "Women are using code words at pharmacies to escape domestic violence during lockdown", Accessed from https://www.cnn.com/2020/04/02/europe/domestic-violence-coronavirus-lockdown-intl/index.html

12 Each mask consists of a total of 18 micro electro-magnetic actuators with fake eyelashes, which give the illusion of 18 blinking eyes looking at the viewer.

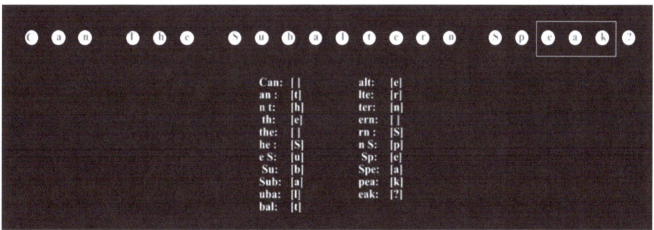

Can:	[ ]	alt:	[e]
an :	[t]	lte:	[r]
n t:	[h]	ter:	[n]
th:	[e]	ern:	[ ]
the:	[ ]	rn :	[S]
he :	[S]	n S:	[p]
e S:	[u]	Sp:	[e]
Su:	[b]	Spe:	[a]
Sub:	[a]	pea:	[k]
uba:	[l]	eak:	[?]
bal:	[t]		

13 Trigrams could be used to generate a text where each new letter is dependent on the previous three letters.

14 Generated letters translate to morse codes

Society's Cage

Dayton Schroeter
SmithGroup

Julian Arrington
SmithGroup

1   Society's Cage, a timely interpretive installation born in the aftermath of the George Floyd and Breonna Taylor murders, was first displayed in August 2020 on the National Mall in Washington, DC.

INTRODUCTION

Society's Cage is a timely interpretive public installation born in the aftermath of the George Floyd and Breonna Taylor murders as our society reckons with institutional racism and white supremacy. First located prominently on the National Mall, the initial build coincided with the August 2020 March on Washington. In October 2020, the pavilion was installed on another prominent site, in Baltimore at the War Memorial Plaza across from City Hall. Going forward, the pavilion will become a public traveling exhibition and continue its educational mission. Discussions are underway with cities and venues across the United States and even internationally.

A grassroots initiative by a Black-led team of designers, the project grew out of conversations among designers and architects in SmithGroup's Washington, DC office as they reflected and grappled with the pandemic and systemic racism events that unfolded in 2020. Their discussions prompted serious and profound questions for personal and group reflection: What is the value of Black life in America? What is the nature of power? How does power manifest itself? What are the dynamics of power over time? How are Black people impacted by the power structure? How does this manifest itself differently in the experiences of Black women and Black men? Further, how could the Black-led design group create an opportunity through artistic expression and design to contextualize the murders of George Floyd, Breonna Taylor, and countless others, and give voice to their unique perspective and experiences as both architects and Black Americans.

PRODUCTION NOTES

Architects: Dayton Schroeter and
              Julian Arrington,
              SmithGroup

Status: Ongoing Traveling
              Installation

Site Area: 500 sq. ft.

Locations: Washington, DC and
              Baltimore

Date: 2020

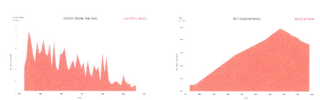

2   The concept development was a process-driven design, anchored in research, data, and facts. Research focused on four primary areas: Black Executions, Death by Police, Death by Lynching, and Mass Incarceration.

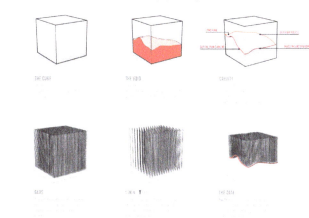

3   Data informed the pavilion's aesthetics: A "perfect" cube emerging from 484 rusting steel bars, hung from a roof canopy.

4   A March on Washington participant walks by Society's Cage, protest sign in hand.

THE DESIGN

The pavilion is a physical manifestation of racism in America. A process-driven design, anchored in research, data, facts, and real-time events, research focused on four primary areas: Black Executions, Death by Police, Death by Lynching, and Mass Incarceration. Using this data, a quartet of graphs was produced to present the findings and from here the pavilion's aesthetics took shape: A "perfect" cube—measuring 15 by 15 by 15 feet—emerging from a field of 484 rusting steel bars spaced six-inches apart and hung from a roof canopy.

The cube's form is composed of two perimeter rows of full-length steel rods. Starting with the third row, and moving inward, the rods begin to vary in length as the space is hollowed out to reveal a void—a visual metaphor for the obstacle-filled path symbolizing Black Americans' struggle for survival. As visitors look up at the ceiling, they see the statistical data converge as it is translated through the varying bar lengths. At night, LEDs fitted inside the steel rods transform the ceiling-scape into an illuminated

5   Society's Cage, displayed in August 2020 on the National Mall in Washington, DC.

6   The Baltimore installation of Society's Cage, at the War Memorial Plaza across from City Hall provided yet another opportunity to acknowledge and reckon with the severity of the racial biases inherent in the institutional structures of justice in the United States.

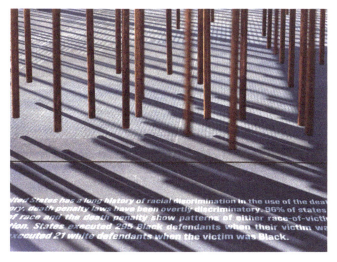

7   The steel rods sway in the breeze creating an ever-changing pattern of shadow and sound.

8   At night, the ceiling is transformed into an illuminated constellation.

9   A detail of the patina of the rusting steel rods that form the pavilion's cube shape. The material was selected for its ability to convey both the statistical data and the aesthetics of the installation's messaging.

10   By day, the installation is an object that communicates the data through form and at night the pavilion becomes a sanctum where people can be vulnerable and seek refuge.

constellation, offering another dimension to the immersive experience.

A centerpiece of the design is an 8 minute and 46 second commissioned soundscape themed in four parts, one to coincide with each of the four graphs. Visitors could participate in an exercise of holding one's breath for as long as possible, inspired by the indignities performed on George Floyd. Participants are encouraged to record a video reflection to upload to social media to share with friends and family using an installation-specific hashtag.

Society's Cage exemplifies the restorative power that art and architecture has in the acknowledgment and memorialization of difficult and disruptive history. It provides an opportunity to acknowledge and reckon with the severity of the racial biases inherent in the institutional structures of justice in the United States. Using data-informed design,

the all-encompassing experience creates time and space for both personal and collective reflection as a path toward empathy, understanding, and healing is forged.

ACKNOWLEDGMENTS

SmithGroup: Dayton Schroeter, Principal, AIA - Lead Designer; Julian Arrington, Associate - Lead Designer; Monteil Crawley; Ivan O'Garro; and Julieta Guillermet.
Structural Engineer: Christopher Ruiz, PE, SE, Silman, Washington, DC
Steel Fabricator: Eric Gronning, Gronning Design + Manufacturing, Washington, DC

Sponsors
Lead Sponsor: SmithGroup
Fiscal Sponsor: Architect's Foundation
Corporate Sponsor: D|Watts Construction, Herrero Builders, Bonstra|Haresign Architects, The Center for Racial Equity and

11 The National Mall in Washington, DC, offered a unique setting for visitors to contemplate the seriousness of the issues against the literal and figurative backdrop of the nation's iconic symbols of power and government: The Washington Monument and the U.S. Capitol.

Justice, Advanced Thermal Solutions, Leslie Kaufmann Associates, and Tarkett.

In-Kind Sponsors: Gronning | Design and Manufacturing, Alan Karchmer | Alan Karchmer Photographer, Silman

IMAGE CREDITS

Figure 1, 2, 7, 8: © Alan Karchmer/OTTO, 2020

Figure 3, 4, 10, 11, 12, 13: © SmithGroup, 2020

Figure 5: © Wole Ajagbe , 2020

Figure 6, 9: © Mark Dennis, 2020

Dayton Schroeter, Principal, AIA, NOMA is a Design Principal who has championed Design Justice advocacy throughout his career at SmithGroup. As a leader of the firm's Justice, Equity, Diversity and Inclusion Committee, his charge is to lead design projects that address the systemic injustice that architecture and planning have perpetuated for historically disenfranchised communities of color. Leveraging his tenacious passion for Design Justice with authenticity and creativity, he is currently leading Anti-racism efforts in design projects including the National Slavery Museum located at the Lumpkin's Slave Jail Site/Devil's Half Acre in Richmond, Virginia, and the traveling installation—Society's Cage—that sheds national awareness on the intersectional effects of racism on our society's collective health, safety, and welfare. Dayton is the co-author of a research grant called "Hidden Voices" for the development of a rubric for architects and planners doing community engagement around Black historical sites of trauma and resilience in the United States.

Julian Arrington, Associate is a lead designer in SmithGroup's Washington, DC Cultural Studio. A proud graduate of Howard University, Julian has shaped concepts for multiple museum projects including a museum to address the history of slavery in Richmond, Virginia, the Universal Hip Hop Museum, the Museum

12 A spoken-word performer shares his message of struggle and redemption on the final evening of the Washington, DC installation.

of Pop Culture, and others. As co-design lead for Society's Cage, Julian choreographed the project from concept to built installation to traveling exhibition, and has presented the work to design professionals and students at university and architecture school programs across the United States. A proponent of community-informed design, Julian has helped lead stakeholder-engagement efforts to craft designs that reflect the goals and aspirations of the people they serve. He takes pride in his Puerto Rican and African American roots and seeks to leverage his diverse upbringing to assist others in fostering strong foundations that connect to identity.

13 An artist performed her original interpretive dance on the final evening of the Washington, DC installation. Set to the 8:46 soundscape commissioned for the installation, it evokes the struggle and oppression of Black Americans as our society reckons with institutional racism.

Interweave

1   Lively communal gathering space to facilitate shared interactions.

Located in Deep East Oakland, Interweave's proposal for Oakland's Black Cultural Zone Resilience Co-Hub addresses the embedded social and environmental challenges of the region in order to design equitable and healthy futures for the current residents of the African Diaspora. This project is designed for the 2020 Barbara G. Laurie Student Design Competition. Driven by Oakland's rich cultural history, our core objectives aim to enhance the community's strong sense of identity and support local socio-economic opportunities while vitalizing the surrounding ecological landscapes. The Co-Hub becomes more than a node in Oakland's urban fabric; rather, it is the entanglement of both the tangible and intangible networks that extend themselves beyond the physical site.

RESEARCH

The site is located at an intriguing juncture between rapid transportation infrastructures and the Arroyo Viejo Creek to the South. The creek runs directly through the site and is a combination of underground culverts and engineered channels. Additionally, the Arroyo Viejo Creek is situated within the larger network of water and green space in Oakland.
By mapping a potential greenway that could be created by connecting sparse patches of green space along with the East Bay Greenway, it could stimulate future ecological growth and revitalize the habitats of non-human species. As the challenge focused on designing a mixed-use community-owned development, our research explored the initiatives of various local non-profit organizations, of which a substantial number are geared towards social justice advocacy.

PRODUCTION NOTES

Site Area: 110,500 sq. ft.

Location: Oakland, California

Date: 2020

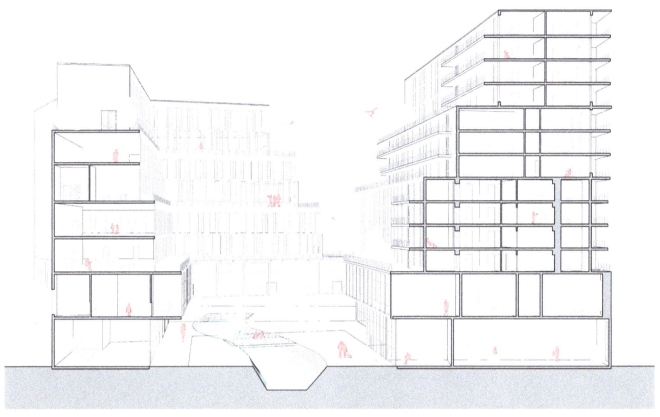

2   Section highlighting community engagement.

From environmental issues to housing to youth groups, common values of empowering Oakland's residents are evident. Combined with a vibrant arts and culture scene, there are abundant opportunities for community collaboration and identity-making. In our proposal, there are generous office and maker spaces dedicated to fostering these grassroots collectives, thereby encouraging the cross-pollination of ideas and people.

DESIGN INTENT

Transportation – Despite the connection with the BART station, Amtrak, and the Alameda County Transit Bus, people still rely on private automobiles, and only one-fourth of the population actively uses public transportation. According to community reactions, the BART station is loud, intrusive, and is considered an unwelcoming presence. In order to combat the noise pollution, the residential units are placed on the furthest side of the train station with the commercial blocks in between acting as a barrier. We aimed to provide easier access from the Co-Hub to the station at upper floors to encourage foot traffic flow and the use of these public amenities.

Creek Restoration – The Arroyo Viejo Creek proves to be a crucial part of the larger ecological network in Oakland, as its revitalization would lead to improved ecological resilience. Instead of the current half-hidden underground condition of the creek, our design widens the original path into a meandering flow that runs across the site, celebrating its presence and flourishing environment.

Community and Culture – In order to honor, preserve, and support the community, the Co-Hub is designed not only as a place of gathering, but also a locus of opportunity, identity, and prosperity. In addition to providing flexible NGO offices, we designed public spaces that the neighborhood can customize, in which place-making becomes an active and conscious community effort. The different terrace levels are spaces where the multimedia arts can be performed and displayed, potentially by becoming mural walls.

3 Restoration of the Arroyo Viejo creek.

4 Interior of the cafe.

5 Customizable mural wall on the roof of the cultural hub.

6 Communal terraces connecting the residential units.

DESIGN PROCESS

To allow for clear accessibility and encourage the permeability of movement, we defined two distinct forms that are connected at the cultural hub level. The sloping effect that resulted in a terracing form provides opportunities for social interaction at different levels between residential, commercial, and retail floors. Moreover, it optimizes the amount of sunlight for harvesting solar energy on rooftops.

The creek flows directly throughout the heart of the Co-Hub, creating a thriving environment of vegetation and natural species, and consequently connecting it to larger streams that extend the ecological networks of East Oakland.

PROGRAMMING

Ground Level – Commercial and Retail. The ground floor of the Co-Hub emphasizes the importance of permeability and transparency between indoor and outdoor spaces. While the inside contains a variety of retail shops and lobby space, they directly engage with the pedestrian realm making the public domain more robust and lively. The creek also

becomes a prominent visual feature as well as an ecological attraction.

2nd Level – Cultural Hub. The cultural hub comprises the whole second level, including maker spaces and offices on the left, co-working spaces in the middle, the black box theatre in the top right, a variety of NGO offices and conference rooms in the right wing, and a cafe that opens up to an outdoor rooftop terrace. The horseshoe form of this level emphasizes programmatic connectivity, while strategically opening up these spaces visually to the central creek and greenway.

3rd-13th Levels – Residential. For the residential sector, outdoor spaces are maximized to foster community and social interaction. By incorporating shared terraces, these informal gathering spaces offer opportunities for casual exchanges by neighbours. On each residential floor, there are a mix of unit types to support intergeneration dwelling and to ensure sustainable affordability rates. Additionally, the roof of the cultural hub on the second level serves as an

7   Rammed earth facade with varying window conditions for different levels of interaction.

outdoor public space between the residential and commercial wings to create an experiential cohesiveness.

MATERIALITY AND CLIMATE

For the project's material palette, our decisions were primarily informed by renovation and revival strategies. This was accomplished through preserving the existing aesthetic of East Oakland while incorporating new designs that seamlessly blend old and new without creating any visual or psychological barriers. We chose rammed earth for parts of our building due to its naturally soundproof and excellent thermal mass qualities, as well as being an affordable and sustainable resource.

ACKNOWLEDGMENTS

This project was designed by UBC NOMAS' design team led by Lukas Ewing with the collaborative effort of Andrea de Bernardini, Tarnjeet Lalh, David Law, Jenny Lee, Rebecca Li, David Park, Angela Zhang, and Willy Zhou.

We want to thank Roy Cloutier and Thomas Gaudin, our advisors from Patkau Architects, for all of their insightful feedback and assistance throughout our project.

IMAGE CREDITS

All drawings and images by UBC NOMAS.

UBC NOMAS As Canada's first NOMAS chapter, UBC NOMAS aims to serve as a student collective to advocate for diversity in design education and to create discussions in regards to equity and equality within the educational and professional architectural field through promoting engagement with diverse perspectives, community involvement and fellowship, and professional development of its members.

FUSION

Amy Boldt

Evan Holdwick

Natalie Miller

Nicholas Peruski

Andreas Tsenis

Anusha Varudandi
The National Organization of
Minority Architecture Stu-
dents at Lawrence Techno-
logical University (Southfield,
Michigan)

1   Section looking north to Afrofuturism-inspired residential drums; through sub-grade retail, performance and elevated paths (Section A-A in Figure 2).

COMMUNITY AND IMPERISHABLE FUTURES

East Oakland, California thrives from the power of Blacks, Indigenous, and People of Color.
Originally the land of the Ohlone Native American Tribe, the now-Oakland flatlands were
colonized by Spain in 1772 and centuries later settled by Caucasian, Chinese, Mexican
and Black communities. The East had the largest Black population in all of the East Bay by
the 1920s. After the bombing of Pearl Harbor and throughout the mid-century, jobs at the
shipyards, new work, and freeway construction displaced Blacks between the downtown
region and East Oakland. Although having remained predominantly Black, the area since
the mid-2000s is seeing many longtime Latino and Black residents being forced out after an
influx of R&B and Hip-Hop culture from the 1980s and 90s.

Highway and train infrastructure that once displaced families and diverse activity is now
embraced through architectural gestures to showcase the power of the people of Oakland.
Architecture students from the Metro Detroit region of Michigan approached the site
through the lens of facing an issue that similarly has deep roots in Detroit where infrastructure development has displaced Black communities. The concept behind this project
is to address minority communities through the philosophies and visuals of *Afrofuturism*.
Much more than just "Africa plus sci-fi," the core themes of Afrofuturism in this design are
to restore lost community identities, providing affordable living with economic prosperity
and projecting a community into permanent and imperishable futures.

PRODUCTION NOTES

Designers: Students at Lawrence
            Technological University

Client: Black Cultural Zone

Status: 2020 NOMA Student
            Design Competition

Site Area: 110,500 sq. ft.

Location: 728 73rd Ave,
            Oakland, CA 94621

Date: 2020, unbuilt

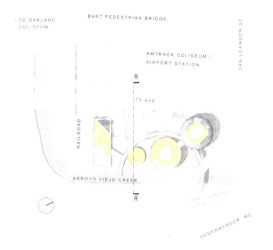

2   Project site at the center of many circulation modes.

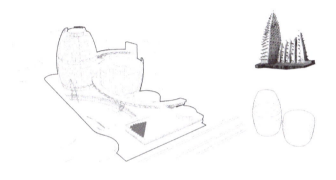

3   Building forms inspired by traditional African mud-and-stick architecture.

4   Living roofs and connections to public circulation.

CULTURAL AND SITE RESPONSES

Having a place to live and a place to work are not always guaranteed. The lasting impacts of the displacement of minority communities along with an increasing number of unhoused people are echoed in the communities at risk today to make way for big tech. Designed for the East Oakland Black Cultural Zone Collaborative Partners, whose coalition helps "keep Black folks in East Oakland," this project inspires people from all 360° to see the permanence and cultural beauty of people living and working, reflected in the circular forms.

Inspired by traditional African architecture (Figure 4), the elevated highway, airport connector, and elevated railways are echoed in sweeping, elevated pedestrian paths, fusing three prominent drum and rectangular forms (Figure 2).

With 200 living units, large retail and commercial spaces at and below grade, makerspaces, and a performance dome, this Cultural Hub and mixed-use project is here to stay.

PROSPERITY AND CULTURAL HUBS

Part of a design response to social justice issues includes environmental justice. This is the equitable way of living for people to have access to fresh and healthy food as well as for the architecture to use sustainble systems that benefit its people. Intensive green roofs (or rooftop gardens) not only provide exciting gathering places with views to all of East Oakland and toward the San Leandro Bay, but by integrating water collection and PV panels, electric and water bills can be cut for businesses which promotes long-term economic success.

Makerspaces are places for community craftspersons and youth to gather and inspire each other. Sometimes called design incubators or innovation hubs, they are a relatively new urban amenity that are essential to provide collaboration spaces for communities and partners.

The radial forms allow light to be sculpted throughout the day on the interior (Figure 8). The center cores of the multiple drum and cylindrical forms create multiple nodes

5   In 2030, *FUSION* is excelling as an energy net-positive development with larger-than-life projections of Oakland people.

6   *FUSION* is a place to work, learn, shop and live for centuries to come.

7   Circulation core and gathering.

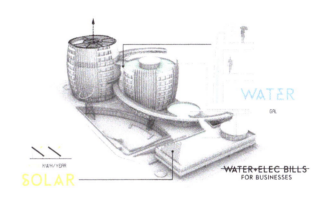

8   Sustainable systems.

for crossing paths and circulating vertically. A performance dome for local musicians and artists brings together the fusion of people residing or visiting Oakland through authentic cultural expression (Figure 1).

TO THE FUTURE

As a model for public life in centuries to come, *FUSION* brings together the historic character of East Oakland and a sense of permanent futures for new generations of the Bay region. Whether it is an evening jazz concert, a fresh market weekend, or an everyday commute, the rich community sense is never out of reach.

REFERENCES

Black Cultural Zone. "East Oakland BCZ Collaborative" Accessed April 13, 2021, https://blackculturalzone.org/east-oakland-bcz-collaborative-2/.

Michel, Kaylan. "Afrofuturism Collages of Kaylan Michel." Accessed April 13, 2021, https://trendland.com/afrofuturism-collages-of-kaylan-m/.

NOMA. Spatial Shifts Reclaiming Our Cities. NOMA, 2021.

Spratt, Sam. "Shuri Cover #1- For Marvell." Accessed April 13, 2021, https://www.samspratt.com/index#/shuri-for-marvel/.

IMAGE CREDITS

All drawings and images by the authors.

About NOMAS LTU The National Organization of Minority Architecture Students (NOMAS) at Lawrence Technological University is a group of 20+ students from the College of Architecture and Design with many design backgrounds who aim to learn about and address minority issues through design and community engagement.

PEER-REVIEWED PROJECTS

Peer-Reviewed Projects

Maria Yablonina
University of Toronto
Matias del Campo
University of Michigan

The Projects submission category and exhibition at the ACADIA conference traditionally serve as an alternative format to showcase novel research in academia and practice. Brief, image-rich submissions provide an opportunity to present built objects, work-in-progress prototypes, innovative techniques, and emerging ideas. During the in-person conference, the exhibition of projects often became a gathering spot, a conversation starter, and simply a place to take a break and wander while sipping coffee in between sessions.

Like many things this year, it became apparent that the projects category would not be the same: not only because we could not be together in the exhibition space, but also because the world now felt different, calling for new means of interacting not only with spaces, but with our practices as designers, researchers, artists, and thinkers. In the new state of forced semi-autonomy, many ACADIA community members had to work in isolation from collaborators, coworkers, and students. However, these urgent circumstances have also triggered adaptations and a recalibration of practices and priorities. New proximities, directions, speculations, and discourses have spontaneously emerged, accompanied by the new formats of the online conference and exhibition.

While the majority of submitted projects were conceived and completed before the COVID-19 pandemic, many have acquired new readings and spaces for speculation, triggered by the global context. For instance, the *Flexing Room* project presented by Axel Kilian demonstrates an approach to architectural robotics wherein the architecture is granted agency and autonomy to respond to its occupant's behaviors. Placed in the context of pandemic lockdowns, the project suggests speculations on the relationship between the human and the machine in situations of isolation. The architectural robot presented by Kilian

acts as a companion rather than a command executor, hinting at future human-machine relationships that could focus on empathy and care, in opposition to the prominent paradigm of automation and productivity. The *Follicle* project presented by Deborah Lopez and Hadin Charbel presents a methodology for collecting, processing, and presenting environmental data stored in the hair of volunteer participants. In the context of online environments saturated with graph representations of data that have consumed our collective attention during the pandemic, the project suggests unique perspectives and speculation trajectories. Specifically, it offers alternative approaches to data collection and representation that are tailored to the subject matter and simultaneously occupy physical and digital spaces.

Some of the project submissions directly address the workflow shifts and necessary restructuring of research practices in response to the pandemic's emergencies. For instance, the *Melting 2.0* project presented by Shelby Doyle and Erin Hunt demonstrates not only a novel technique for 3D printing of concrete, but also provides a glimpse into the process of pivoting to a work-from-home workflow necessitated by the emerging pandemic regulations. *Casa Covida*, presented by Roland Rael, Virginia San Fratello, and Alexander Curth, was initiated as an experimental building project exploring full-scale 3D printing techniques. Finished in the spring of 2020, the architectural prototype has gained new architectural programs in the context of the COVID lockdown, offering a space for isolation, cohabitation, and reflection.

The 2020 ACADIA conference call for projects was defined by the challenge to create a format that integrates the ethos of the conference with the online nature of the event. A virtual conference and exhibition by nature departs from the conventions of direct interpersonal interaction that have become the norm; however, it presents an opportunity for a reimagining and reformation. The online exhibition platform developed by Oliver Popadich in collaboration with the conference chair team aimed to present the diverse collection of projects in a nonhierarchical format. The cloudlike constellation of floating project icons connected with thin lines provided an overview of community contributions to the conference, while also highlighting thematic, conceptual, and associative links that emerge in their proximity to each other. For instance, according to the platform's machine-learning word analysis, the *Ashen Cabin* project (presented by Leslie Lok and Sasa Zivkovic) is thematically connected to 10 other conference submission items, including building prototypes of similar scale, investigations into similar material systems, and research initiatives similarly focusing on solving the issue of wasteless fabrication processes.

The 2020 ACADIA conference call started with the following statement: "Acknowledging the disruptive change to established design, research practices, and routines, Distributed Proximities aims to investigate the current condition by prioritizing the processes and protocols by which the work is produced, rather than merely its artifacts." At the time of announcing this call we did not know what to expect and were hoping to see the ACADIA community adapt to the unprecedented change. Indeed, the submissions we received have clearly demonstrated new experiments in remoteness, virtual communities, proximities at a distance, and retooling to address novel urgencies. All of these aspects are reflected in the projects found in this book, allowing for a glimpse into a process of rapid adaptation to a changing environment of production.

Saltatur

Node-Based Assembly of
Funicular Spatial Concrete

Masoud Akbarzadeh &
Ali Tabatabaie Ghomi
PSL, University of Pennsylvania

Mohammad Bolhassani
The City College of New York

Mostafa Akbari
PSL, University of Pennsylvania

Alireza Seyedahmadian &
Konstantinos Papalexiou
Neoset Designs

1 The exhibited structure as part of the Spatial Efficiency Exhibition at the Center for Architecture and Design in Philadelphia, © PSL 2020).

The Saltatur demonstrates innovative research in the design and fabrication of a prefab, discrete, spatial composite structure consisting of a spatial, compression-only concrete body, post-tensioned steel rods, and an ultra thin glass structure on its top in the form of long-span furniture. Using discrete spatial systems minimizes the volume of concrete and the carbon footprint while preserving the necessary mass for structural performance and specific architectural detailing. Achieving a high level of efficiency in utilizing concrete for spatial systems requires a robust and powerful structural design and fabrication approach (Figure 1).

There are multiple design innovations in various phases of the realization of this project, from conceptual structural design to fabrication. This project impeccably combines efficiency, elegance, and economy in one product whose fabrication technique opens a new horizon for the future of construction of large scale systems. The entire volume of concrete used for this structure is 0.06 cubic meters distributed in 4.44 cubic meters (3.1 m x 0.8 m x 1.9 m) of space. This volume makes the relative density of this structure as small as 1% percent (0.013), which demonstrates the ingenuity in the design and engineering of an efficient load-bearing, expressive system (Figure 2).

A node-based assembly was considered as a method of construction. To avoid the possible spatial collision of the branches of the nodes during the assembly, an innovative detail was developed that allowed fixing the members in their exact locations in the structure

PRODUCTION NOTES

Architect: Polyhedral Structures Lab.

Status: Completed

Site Area: 6 sqm

Location: Weitzman School of Design

Date: 2020

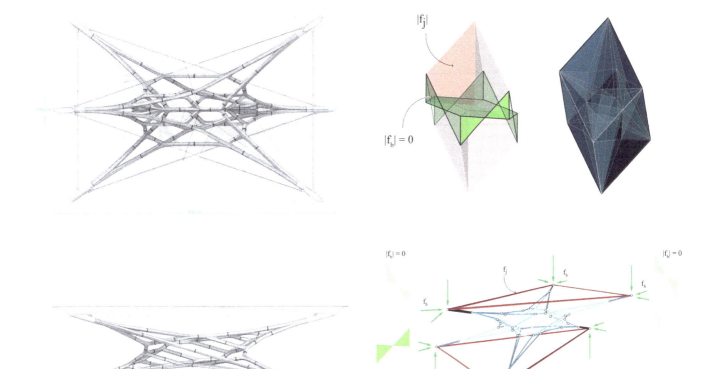

$|f_j|$

$|f_h| = 0$

$|f_h| = 0$ $|f_h| = 0$

f_j f_h f_h

f_h

f_b

2   The force diagram (top) and its corresponding structural form (bottom).

3   The force diagram (top) and its corresponding structural form (bottom).

without using conventional male-female connection details. Although the concrete structure has been designed to act in pure compression, some of the members will experience tensile stress in the cases of asymmetric loads, especially during the assembly process. The proposed bespoke steel connection transfers the tensile force between the concrete members effectively. The ultra-thin (4mm) glass structure on the top was formed into a funicular geometry as a discrete structure to span 3.75 meters. The glass can carry the applied loads as a three-hinged discrete arch with custom connection details preventing the horizontal movements of the glass parts (Figure 2).

Structural Form-Finding

The structural geometry is a spatial funicular form with combined compressive and tensile forces, which was designed using the methods of 3D graphic statics. There is a creative twist in the topology of the structure, allowing the bottom members of the geometry to have a 180 degree turn compared to the top members in plan and elevation. This twist induces a rotational symmetry in the

structure that reduces the number of bespoke elements by half without resulting in a highly symmetrical appearance (Figure 3). A custom technique was used to create the tension ties on the top and bottom of the structure. The structural form was initially designed as a compression-only system. In the next phase, we geometrically controlled the areas of the faces related to the horizontal applied loads (f_h) in the system. As a result, the trapezoidal faces of the global force polyhedron turned into self-intersecting faces with a total signed area of zero (Figure 3). Consequently, the external forces in the form disappeared, and the normal of the internal face corresponding to the ties flipped. This change in the direction of the normal for the internal members results in tension force (f_j) in the ties at the top and the bottom of the structure.

Materialization

The long-span component on the top of the table is made out of 4 mm glass segments assembled to form an ultra-thin compression-only shell (3780 x 2540 x 70 mm) sitting on a discrete spatial concrete structure with the dimensions of

4   The top view of the compression body.

Saltatur Akbarzadeh, Tabatabei Ghomi, Bolhassani, Akbari, et. al.

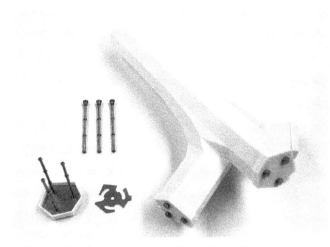

5   The metal detail components and the PLA molds © PSL.

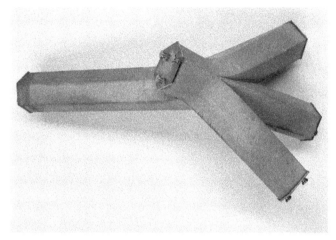

6   A spatial node with its steel connections after demolding © PSL.

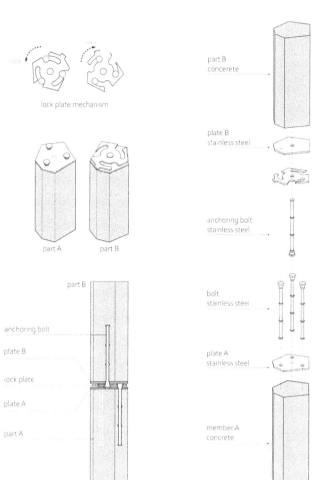

7   Detail drawings

3100 x 1950 x 75 mm. The concrete body consists of 24 (48 in total) unique spatial nodes with a diameter ranging from 40 to 80 mm, each proportional to the magnitude of the internal forces. Self-consolidating, high-strength concrete with carbon fiber reinforcement was used to improve the tensile capacity of the concrete. Although the concrete structure has been designed to act in compression, some of the members will experience significant tensile stress in the case of asymmetric loads, especially during the assembly process. To address this challenge, a particular steel connection detail was developed to transfer the tensile force between the concrete parts.

Detail Development

The 7 mm connection includes bespoke anchor bolts to engage with concrete and a locking plate rotating around the axis of the bolt on the opposite/adjacent member. Our innovative connection detail allows the insertion of each node with no specific order into the system as long as at least one receiving branch is available. The rotatory lock in the mechanism of the connection provides multiple rotational degrees of freedom during the assembly while fixing

the location of the connected branch in three-dimensional space which significantly facilities the assembly of such complex spatial systems (Figures 4 -8).

Structural Analysis Of The Connection

The mechanical behavior of the designed connection was evaluated experimentally and later verified numerically. In the first stage, three connections were constructed and then tested using a three-point bending loading configuration to find the maximum bending capacity and failure type of each connection. Test results showed that the connection can take up to 650 N concentrated load in the worst case loading scenario. The stress analysis of the connection showed that the connection never fails under the existing loads of the table. No crack or failure in concrete was observed at the end of the test, only the rotating plate deformed significantly due to the imposed bending. In fact, the rotating plate absorbs all the deformation in the connection, and it can later be replaced. A detailed, numerical model of the connection was built and analyzed in an FE analysis software, considering all the interactions between concrete, plates and anchors. Numerical models were in a

8   Back view of the assembled structure © PSL.

good agreement with the experimental results by predicting the deformation and the strength of the connection (Figure 9).

The Design Of The Table Top

The structural form of the glass was developed in conjunction with the concrete body. The structure was designed as a discrete compression-dominated shell in three parts as a three-hinged arch supported at the corners of the concrete structure. The self-weight of the glass parts matches the design loads for the concrete structure at each support. We used 4 mm regular glass and slumped it into a compression-dominated geometry designed by using the methods of 3D graphic statics. The glass parts meeting at the mid-span are attached to particular steel connections that sit inside the steel corners of the structure with constrained movement in the XY plane. The glass was connected to its steel connection using transparent silicone structural adhesive (Figures 10, 11).

ACKNOWLEDGMENTS

Special thanks to the Weitzman School Board of Overseers, who generously provided financial support for the fabrication of Saltatur. The construction costs were also covered in part by a grant from the University of Pennsylvania Research Foundation (URF). Thanks to: PennPraxis for providing initial support for an earlier version of this exhibition as part of Design Philadelphia 2018; Judy Miziumski, River Hills Glass, for letting us use her studio for the glass production of the Saltatur project; The Office of the Dean and particularly John Caperton and Michael Grant at the Weitzman School for providing tremendous support for the coordination of the exhibition; NEOSET DESIGNS studio for generously supporting the robotic fabrication phase of the Saltatur project.

REFERENCES

Akbarzadeh, M. "3D Graphic Statics Using Polyhedral Reciprocal Diagrams." Ph. D.thesis, ETH Zürich, 2016.

Akbarzadeh, M., M. Hablicsek, and Y. Guo. 2018. "Developing Algebraic Constraints for Reciprocal Polyhedral Diagrams of 3D Graphic Statics". In *Proceedings of the IASS Symposium 2018, Creativity in Structural Design*, ed. J. Oshsendorf, C. Mueller, W. Baker, S Adriaenssens, J. Abel. Boston: IASS.

Akbarzadeh, M., T. Van Mele, and P. Block. 2015. "On the Equilibrium of Funicular Polyhedral Frames and Convex

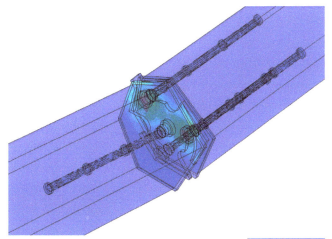

(a)

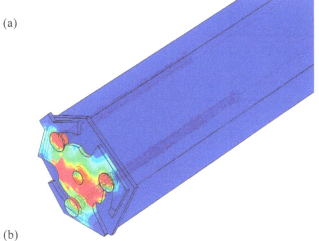

(b)

9 The Finite Element Analysis of the connection, © PSL.

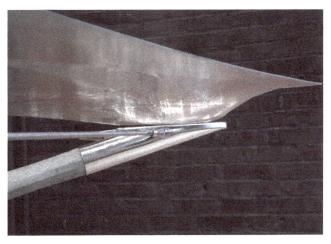

10 The glass-steel support connection beneath view © PSL.

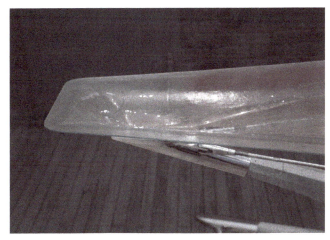

11 The glass-steel support connection above view © PSL.

Polyhedral Force Diagrams." *Computer-Aided Design* 63: 118–128.

Bolhassani, M., M. Akbarzadeh, M. Mahnia, and R. Taherian. 2017. "On Structural Behavior of the First Funicular Polyhedral Frame Designed by 3D Graphic Statics." *Structures* 14: 56–68.

Hablicsek, M., M. Akbarzadeh, and Y. Guo. 2019. "Algebraic 3D Graphic Statics: Reciprocal constructions." *Computer-Aided Design* 108: 30–41

IMAGE CREDITS

Figure 1-12: © Polyhedral Structures Laboratory, 2020.

Masoud Akbarzadeh is an assistant professor of architecture in structures and advanced technologies, and the director of the Polyhedral Structures Laboratory at the Weitzman School of Design, University of Pennsylvania.

Ali Tabatabaei Ghomi is a research assistant at the Polyhedral Structures Laboratory and the Design Specialist at CetraRuddy NYC. Ali received a Master of Science Advanced Architecture Design (MSD-AAD) from the Weitzman School of Design.

Mohammad Bolhassani is an assistant professor of architecture at the Bernard and Anne Spitzer School of Architecture, City College New York City. He is also a research associate at the Polyhedral Structures Laboratory.

Mostafa Akbari is a PhD student at the Polyhedral Structures Laboratory, Weitzman School of Design, University of Pennsylvania. Ali received a Master of Science Advanced Architecture Design (MSD-AAD) from the Weitzman School of Design.

Alireza Seyedahmadian is a fabrication specialist at the Neoset Design and a research assistant at the PSL. Alireza received a Master of Science in Architecture Design and Research from Taubman College, University of Michigan.

Konstantinos Papalexiou is an artist and designer and the founder of Neoset Design.

Jingchu Sun is a graduate student of architecture at the Weitzman School of Design.

Hanqin Yao s a graduate student at the Weitzman School of Design.

Judy Miziumski is an artist and the founder of River Hills Glass in Lancaster, Pennsylvania.

Log Knot

Robotically Fabricated Roundwood Timber Structure

Sasa Zivkovic
Cornell University

Brian Havener
Cornell University

Christopher A. Battaglia
Cornell University

1   Log Knot as installed on the Cornell Ag Quad (Jeremy Bilotti, 2018, © RCL).

Variable Compound Timber Curvature

Log Knot is a robotically fabricated architectural installation that creates variable compound timber curvature utilizing both regular and irregular roundwood geometries. In addition, the project develops methods for minimal-formwork assembly as well as bending and moment force optimization of customized mortise and tenon joints. Following the logic of a figure-8 knot, the project creates an infinite loop of roundwood, curving three-dimensionally along its length.

There are a variety of techniques to create single curvature in wood structures—such as steam bending (Wright et al. 2013) or glue lamination (Issa and Kmeid 2005)—but only a few techniques to generate complex curvature within a single wooden structural element exist. In order to create complex curvature, the research team developed a simple method that can easily be replicated: first, the log is compartmentalized, establishing a series of discrete "parts," and second, the parts are re-configured into a complex curvature "whole" by carefully manipulating the assembly angles between the logs. Timber components re-configured in such a manner can either follow single-curvature or double-curvature profiles.

Testing and Joinery

Based on knowledge gained from the initial joinery tests, the research team developed a custom tri-fold mortise and tenon joint, which is self-supportive during assembly and able

PRODUCTION NOTES

Designer: Cornell RCL

Client: Cornell CCA

Status: Completed

Site Area: 900 sq. ft.

Location: Ithaca, NY

Date: 2018

2   Drone view of Log Knot (Stephen Clond, 2018, © RCL).

3   Log Knot fabricated parts ready for assembly (RCL, 2018, © RCL).

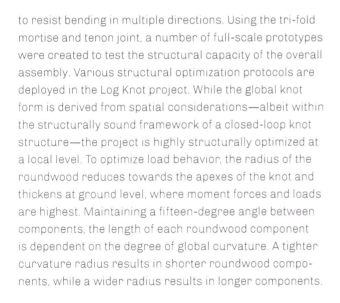

4   Detail of joinery using irregular logs (Jeremy Bilotti, 2018, © RCL).

5   Detail of joinery test prototypes (RCL, 2018, © RCL).

to resist bending in multiple directions. Using the tri-fold mortise and tenon joint, a number of full-scale prototypes were created to test the structural capacity of the overall assembly. Various structural optimization protocols are deployed in the Log Knot project. While the global knot form is derived from spatial considerations—albeit within the structurally sound framework of a closed-loop knot structure—the project is highly structurally optimized at a local level. To optimize load behavior, the radius of the roundwood reduces towards the apexes of the knot and thickens at ground level, where moment forces and loads are highest. Maintaining a fifteen-degree angle between components, the length of each roundwood component is dependent on the degree of global curvature. A tighter curvature radius results in shorter roundwood components, while a wider radius results in longer components.

Structural Optimization

Additionally, the connections between components are structurally optimized: using the Rhinoceros Grasshopper plug-in Karamba, the research team extracted the direction of moment forces at each connection within the timber knot. The joints were designed with an "undercut" in one of the three flanges in each mortise and tenon connection, resulting in an assembly with a slight twisting motion. The location of the undercut is determined by the force diagram derived from Karamba: the undercut is oriented to counteract the joint's bending motion and positioned in the direction of potential structural failure. This particular joinery orientation and design prevent two components from disconnecting under various load scenarios.

Minimal Formwork Assembly

Furthermore, Log Knot establishes a minimal formwork assembly method for the connection of discrete log components. The mortise and tenon ratio is carefully calibrated to be as close to 50%-50% as possible to ensure an even distribution of forces, prevent breaking of joinery components, and create stable connections during the construction process. After each completed knot "arch" segment, the structure is attached to the ground using earth anchors. During the construction process, the joints

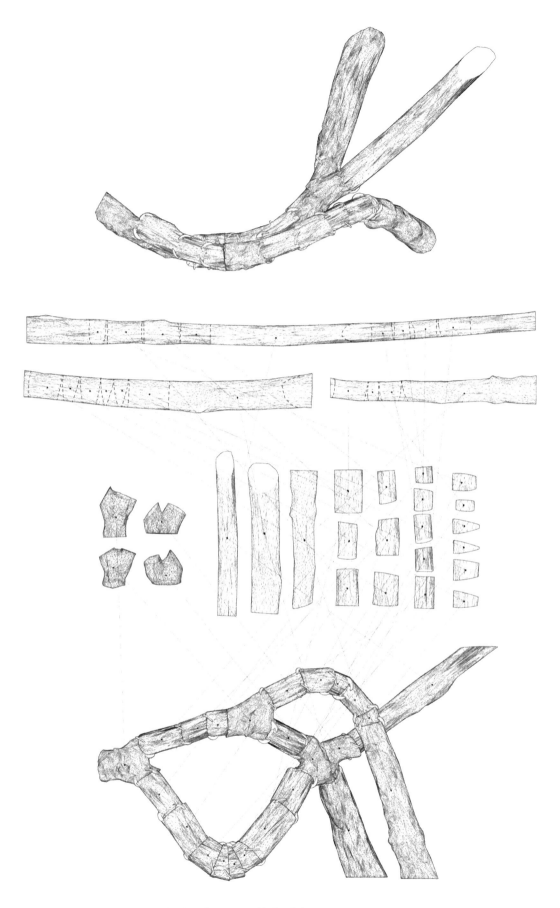

6　Drawing of early conceptual prototype (drawing by Brian Havener, 2018, © Brian Havener).

7   Structural prototype (RCL, 2018, © RCL).

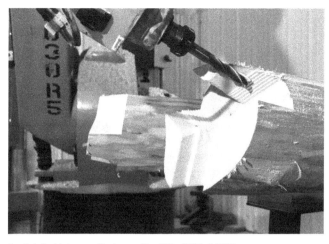

8   Detail of joinery milling operation (RCL, 2018, © RCL).

9   Joinery prototype (RCL, 2018, © RCL).

10 Minimal formwork assembly process (Stephen Clond, 2018, © RCL).

guide the global assembly of the knot structure, periodically supported by single 2x4 members attached to the structure with wood screws.

Log Knot, created in 2018, expands on research such as Wood Chip Barn (Mollica and Self 2016) at Hooke Park (Self 2016), Limb at University of Michigan (Von Buelow, et al. 2018), and is in dialogue with more recent explorations in non-standard wood construction such as "Exploring Natural Wood" (Aagard, et al. 2019) and "Digital Fabrication of Standardless Materials" (MacDonald, et al. 2019) as well as industry applications developed by companies such as WholeTrees Structures (WholeTrees LLC 2017). The infinitely looping Log Knot structure creates a playful inter-action between archaic natural geometry, computation, force optimization, and robotic fabrication.

ACKNOWLEDGMENTS

RCL project leadership: Sasa Zivkovic (Director and Principal Investigator), Brian Havener (Research Associate and project co-lead) / RCL project team: Christopher A. Battaglia (Senior Research Associate), Todd Petrie (Researcher), Cait McCarthy (Researcher), Kashyap Valiveti (Researcher), Jordan Young (Researcher, fabrication co-lead) / RCL assembly team: Angel Almanzar, Stephen Clond, Isabel Lucia Branas Jarque, Alexandre Mecattaf, Edward Aguilera Perez, Alexander Terry, Dax Simitch Warke.

In collaboration with the Cornell Arnot Teaching and Research Forest: Peter Smallidge (Arnot Forest Director).

Project Sponsors: CCA Cornell Council for the Arts / AAP College of Architecture, Art, and Planning / AAP Department of Architecture / FARO Technologies

REFERENCES

Aagaard, Anders Kruse, and Niels Martin Larsen. 2019. "Exploring natural wood: A workflow for using non-uniform sawlogs in digital design and fabrication." In *ACADIA 19: Ubiquity and Autonomy Proceedings of the 39th Annual Conference of the Association for Computer Aided Design in Architecture*, ed. Kory Bieg, Clay Odom. Austin, Texas, USA: ACADIA.

11 Detail view of Log Knot as installed on the Conrnell Ag Quad (Jeremy Bilotti, 2018, © RCL).

Issa, Camille A., and Ziad Kmeid. 2005. "Advanced wood engineering: glulam beams." *Construction and Building Materials* 19 (2): 99-106.

MacDonald, Katie, Kyle Schumann, Jonas Hauptman. "Digital Fabrication of Standardless Materials" In *ACADIA 19: Ubiquity and Autonomy Proceedings of the 39th Annual Conference of the Association for Computer Aided Design in Architecture (ACADIA)*, ed. Kory Bieg, Clay Odom. Austin, Texas, USA: ACADIA.

Mollica, Zachary, and Martin Self. 2016. "Tree Fork Truss." *Advances in architectural geometry 2016*, ed. S. Adriaenssens, F. Gramazio, M. Kohler, A. Menges, M. Pauly, 138-153. Zurich: ETH.

WholeTrees. "Research and Development." Accessed 18 June 2017, Available at: https://wholetrees.com/technology/.

Self, Martin. 2016. "Hooke Park: application for timber in its Natural Form". In *Advancing Wood Architecture: A Computational Approach*, ed. A. Menges, T. Schwinn, O.D. Krieg. Milton Park: Routledge,

Von Buelow, Peter, Omid Oliyan Torghabehi, Steven Mankouche, and Kasey Vliet. "Combining parametric form generation and design exploration to produce a wooden reticulated shell using natural tree crotches." In *Proceedings of IASS Annual Symposia, vol. 2018*, ed. J. Ochsendorf, C. Mueller, W. Baker, S. Adriaenssens, J. Abel, 1-8. Boston: IASS.

Wright, Robert S., Brian H. Bond, and Zhangjing Chen. 2013. "Steam bending of wood; Embellishments to an ancient technique." *BioResources 8* (4): 4793-4796.

IMAGE CREDITS

12 Joinery assembly detail (drawing by RCL, 2018, © RCL).

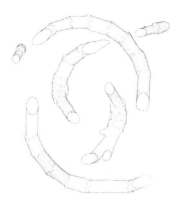

13 Plan of Log Knot (drawing by RCL, 2018, © RCL).

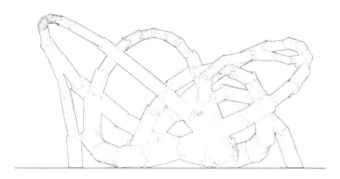

14 Elevation of Log Knot (drawing by RCL, 2018, © RCL).

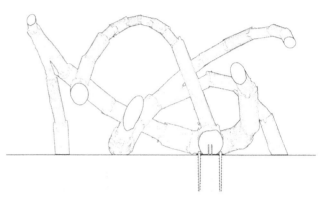

15 Section of Log Knot (drawing by RCL, 2018, © RCL).

Sasa Zivkovic is a co-principal at HANNAH, an experimental design practice based in Ithaca, New York. HANNAH was recently awarded the 2020 Architectural League Prize and was named Next Progressives by Architect Magazine in 2018. Zivkovic is also an Assistant Professor at Cornell University AAP where he directs the Robotic Construction Laboratory (RCL), an interdisciplinary research group that develops and implements novel robotic construction technology. Interdisciplinary in nature, the work integrates cutting-edge materials, advanced fabrication, mechanical design, architectural computation, structural optimization, and sustainable construction. Zivkovic received his Master of Architecture degree at Massachusetts Institute of Technology.

Brian Havener is an architectural designer whose work and research are constantly reinterpreting qualities of material through a contemporary understanding and misreading of history and technology. He is currently practicing at Olson Kundig in Seattle, focused on cultural projects as well as digital fabrication. Previously, Brian taught the first-year design studio sequence at Cornell University while conducting research in the Robotic Construction Lab, where he developed novel methods of timber construction through the aid of digital fabrication and robotics. Brian holds a Master of Architecture from Cornell University and a Bachelor of Science in Architecture from the University of Cincinnati.

Christopher A. Battaglia is formerly the Design and Innovation Fellow/ Assistant Research Professor at Ball State University College of Architecture and Planning, researching concrete 3D printing robotics, heavy timber construction, and structural optimization techniques in architectural design. Battaglia's work looks at the intersection of traditional material handicraft through the lens of digital tools and experimental processes. Formerly a Senior Research Associate with the Robotic Construction Lab at Cornell University, Battaglia enjoys working through the challenges of scaling architectural robotic investigations for design-build construction.

Short Stack

Kevin Hirth
University of Colorado Denver
College of Architecture and
Planning

1   Short Stack in elevation.

"If their work is satisfying, people don't need leisure in the old-fashioned sense. No
one ever asks what Newton or Darwin did to relax, or how Bach spent his weekends.
At Eden-Olympia work is the ultimate play, and play the ultimate work." (Ballard, 2000)

Short Stack is a kiosk that does its work while clearly at leisure. Rather than pose the
serious face or pretend towards austerity, it is a clear demonstration of stripped and
clear function. It is a shelter that houses seating. It has a closed cabinet for storing salable
goods and paper products. It has a light. It is shelter. At a bare minimum, it accomplishes
its required tasks. It, however, does so with aplomb. Short Stack stands dutifully with
purpose, but does so as if satisfied with the work that it does.

Short Stack is a bare, minimal structure using only laminated sheets of structural metal
decking for all elements of its structure and enclosure. The project operates under a
simple principle. Structural metal decking is a one-way system that resists loads well in
one direction, but not in the other. When this decking is therefore stacked into rotated
sections and tensioned together, the resultant sandwich of corrugated metal is resistant
to loading in every direction. These sandwiches become walls, floor, and roof to a temporary structure. The compounded effect at the edges of the rotated and cropped decking is
one of a filigree, or an ornamental articulation. The sandwich, which is mostly void due to
the section of the decking, provides a sense of open lightness that is at odds with its bulky
mass. The structure therefore teeters between being unexpectedly open and at once heavy.

PRODUCTION NOTES

Architect: KEVIN HIRTH Co.
Client: University of Colorado
            Denver
Status: In development
Site Area: 100 sq. ft.
Location: Denver, Colorado
Date: 2021

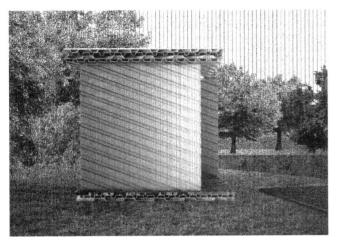

2   Rear elevation.

3   Enclosure rendering.

4   Interior rendering.

This is reinforced through the introduction of shape to the elevation of one of the pavilion's walls. The half-round tapering to the base of the plane converts the wall functionally into an incredibly thick column. Again, facilitated by the sandwiching of the deck, the plane is resistant to both lateral and vertical forces.

The economy of the project is in its uniformity and persistent singularity. By maintaining a single palette of material and using a plasma cutting CNC bed to cut each section of the decking, the structure is assembled simply. The digital intelligence that lies underneath the apparent formal simplicity of the project is two-fold. First, each sheet of metal decking is different from the next. Because of the locations of bolt-holes and constant variability of rotation and cropping of each sheet, it is a project that expresses uniformity rather than articulation through discretization. Second, the project appears solid and monolithic, but is in fact hollowed structurally to minimize the weight of the assembly. Two parametric tools were generated in the development of this project. The first optimizes moment

forces to allow for the hollowing and omission of material in larger structures, the second auto-generates bolt hole patterns at the intersections of the lamination of the material. These tools allow for rapid automation of CNC files and minimizes coordination time during fabrication. The rotation of the "sandwiches" of material are pro-forma and dependent primarily on reducing lateral movement. The resultant effect is visual as a byproduct of efficiencies within the structure. The desirable effect of this alignment between structural efficiency and outward appearance is foregrounded by allowing the structure to stand as an outwardly expressive object.

By embracing the expression of the individual assembly of the object, the structure is an outward declaration of the often messy circumstances of construction. An alignment between precision and material autonomy lends to a vital openness in the structure's interpretation. In order to further reinforce this effect, the normally untreated surfaces of the corrugated decking will be painted with a simple moiré pattern. Vertical lines inscribed on the

5 Figuration of the assembly.

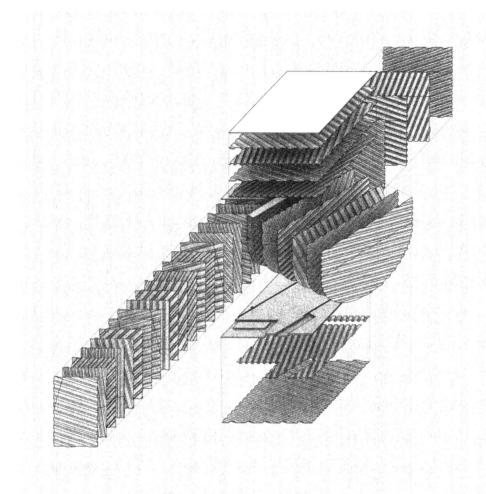

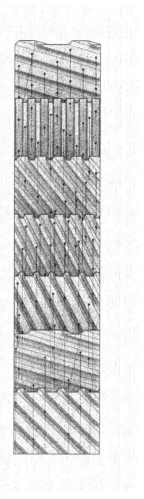

6   Exploded assembly diagram.

7   Short Stack Bolt hole logic diagram.

seemingly random oblique surfaces of the corrugated decking will reinforce the abstraction of a common construction material into something both more and less than itself.

Short Stack points to a hopeful terrain in digitality, one that hides its sophistication in plain sight while embracing the hectic antithetical circumstances of common construction.

Kevin Hirth is an Assistant Professor at the University of Colorado Denver College of Architecture and Planning. Kevin holds a Master's of Architecture with distinction from the Harvard Graduate School of Design and a Bachelor's of Science in Architecture from the University of Virginia. Growing up on the rural edge of the suburbs of Richmond, Virginia, Kevin was raised to run in the woods and walk in the city.

REFERENCES

Ballard, James Graham. 2000. *Super-Cannes*, London, UK. HarperCollins Publishers Limited

IMAGE CREDITS

All drawings and images by the authors.

VENTS 2.0

Catty Dan Zhang
UNC Charlotte

1   Installation overview.

VENTS 2.0 is a responsive environment that relates the moving air at separate locations using real-time data transmission. Functioning as an exhibition installation, a kinetic canopy produces a "rain" of air puffs subtly felt on the skin and a visual pattern of color LED, translating environmental conditions elsewhere into visual, audial, and tactile experiences within the Wurster Gallery at the University of California at Berkeley (Figure 1).

This project explores methods of designing with atmospheric mediums and fixed forms simultaneously at an architectural scale. Fabricating the environment that activates the behavior of amorphous and invisible mediums has been explored theoretically and in innovative practices in the past decades, shifting from the notion of architectural objects as stable systems that passively reveal and react to their external conditions (Gissen 2009). Such investigations utilize temperature, light, air, and other forms of energy to inform spatial and material assemblies (Lally 2009). The main challenge is to establish an active system that triggers the emergence of the specific medium's initial states and modulates its evolution. VENTS 2.0 tackles such challenges in contemporary exhibition settings. It articulates forms of airflow as part of a dynamic spatial device that stimulates senses beyond sight, inviting new modes of engagement with works on display and augmenting the viewing experience. The installation collects real-time wind velocity via weather Application Programmer Interface (API), combined with recorded speeds of Hurricane Florence, which took place in North and South Carolinas of the US during September 2018. The computed data input controls the multisensorial-effects output by an array of air chambers using a customized script running on a Raspberry Pi (Figure 2).

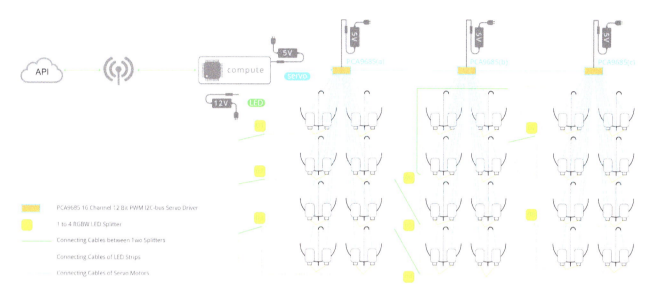

PCA9685 16 Channel 12 Bit PWM I2C-bus Servo Driver

1 to 4 RGBW LED Splitter

Connecting Cables between Two Splitters

Connecting Cables of LED Strips

Connecting Cables of Servo Motors

2   Control system diagram.

The chambers generate air vortex rings one can feel when collapsing onto the skin, a typological form of airflow widely used in both art installations and the gaming industry due to its visual and tactile properties. The design parameters were set to allow sufficient travel distance of each ring before dissipating above the floor. Key variables that determine the stability and vorticity (the air spinning rate of the vortex) include the chamber's length and the outlet's diameter (Gupta et al. 2013). A micro servo motor with an extended arm applies pressure into each chamber through a plastic membrane, resulting in the formation, the movement, and the morphing patterns of the vortex ring (Figure 3).

The motors on all chambers are actuated following a programmed sequence with a random starting point in each cycle, providing visitors unexpected encounters with the constructed "breezes." Dynamic sound patterns are produced by actuated mechanisms, echoing within the space. At the opposite end of each chamber is a translucent air outlet with an embedded flexible LED strip. The color of these lights drastically fluctuates according to the data input, mimicking a visual effect of wind blowing while at the same time tinting air vortex rings when fog is seeded through clear PVC tubing (Figure 4).

Each pair of air chambers is attached to an umbrella, which could be easily disassembled and stored (Figure 5). A total of 24 modified umbrellas, along with 23 regular ones, are then hung onto a lightweight aluminum frame with integrated electronics and control systems. This frame consists of horizontal, vertical, and diagonal pieces made out of salvaged aluminum members, assembled with customized metal brackets on site (Figures 6, 7). Undulating along the central axis of the 2,200 square foot gallery, the canopy is located right above average human height, softly illuminating a series of projects on display underneath (Figures 8, 9).

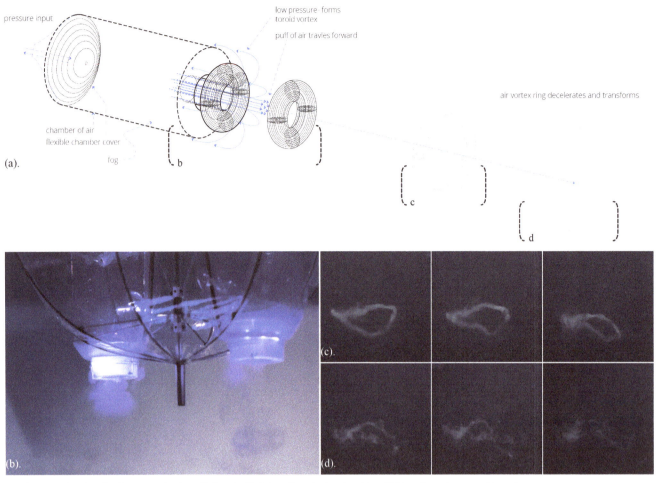

3 Air vortex ring visualization: (a) mechanism; (b) tinted puff of air exiting air chamber; (c) and (d) fog ring enlarges and transforms. .

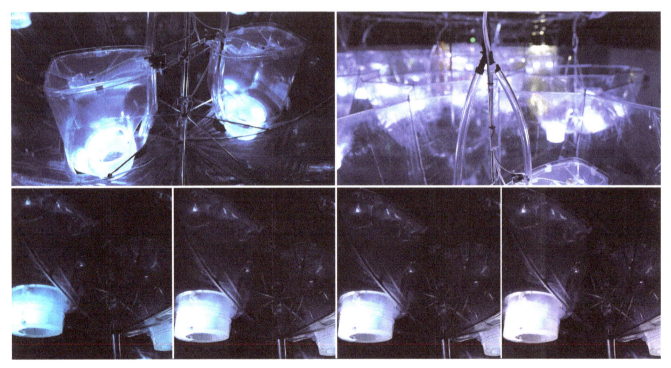

4 Color fluctuates between blue and pale violet tones reflecting wind data input.

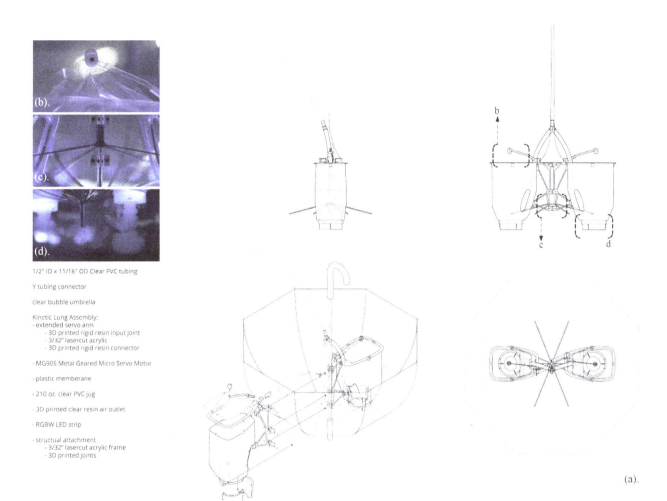

1/2" ID x 11/16" OD Clear PVC tubing

Y tubing connector

clear bubble umbrella

Kinetic Lung Assembly:
- extended servo arm
    - 3D printed rigid resin input joint
    - 3/32" lasercut acrylic
    - 3D printed rigid resin connector

- MG90S Metal Geared Micro Servo Motor

- plastic memberane

- 210 oz. clear PVC jug

- 3D printed clear resin air outlet

- RGBW LED strip

- structual attachment
    - 3/32" lasercut acrylic frame
    - 3D printed joints

(a).

5   Kinetic air chamber assembly: (a) a pair of air chambers attached to the clear bubble umbrella; (b) extended servo arm to apply pressure input at the center of the plastic membrane; (c) customized joints; (d) translucent air outlet.

6   View of the kinetic canopy and aluminum frame connections.

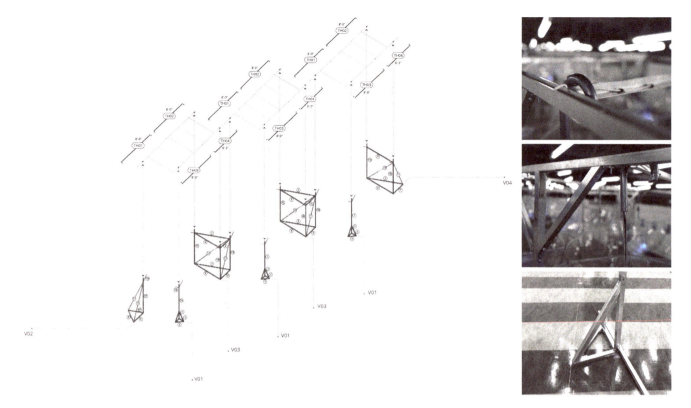

7   Aluminum frame.

ACKNOWLEDGMENTS

This project was installed at "The Moving Air: A Cultural-environmental Paradigm" exhibition. The author would like to thank the exhibition competition committee for awarding the proposal and the College of Environmental Design at the University of California at Berkeley for supporting the work.

Thank you also to research assistants Pedro Pinera Rodriguez and Rick Luu, who helped install the exhibition; to Austin Johnson and Mahdi Ghavidel Sedehi for their work during this project's development, and Storrs Lab at UNCC for the fabrication support.

IMAGE CREDITS

All drawings, images and photographs by the author.

Catty Dan Zhang is an Assistant Professor of Architecture at University of North Carolina at Charlotte. Her work experiments on the design of active atmosphere at the convergence of digital media and architecture and the overlap of human and machine perceptions.

REFERENCES

Gissen, David. 2009. *Subnature: Architecture's Other Environments*. New York: Princeton Architecture Press.

Lally, Sean. 2009. "Twelve Easy Pieces Twelve Easy Pieces for the Piano." *Architectural Design*, Vol 79 No 3 (May/June 2009): 6-11.

Gupta, Sidhant, Dan Morris, Shwetak N. Patel, Desney Tan. 2013. "AirWave: Non-Contact Haptic Feedback Using Air Vortex Rings", In *Proceedings of the 2013 ACM international joint conference on Pervasive and ubiquitous computing. New York: Association for Computing Machinery,* ed. F. Mattern, S. Santini, J.F. Canny, M. Langheinrich, J. Rekimoto. 419–428. New York: ACM. https://doi.org/10.1145/2493432.2493463

8   Works on display underneath the canopy.

9   Installation view.

Patty & Jan

Tyler Swingle
Matter Design

Davide Zampini
CEMEX Global R&D

Brandon Clifford
MIT/Matter Design

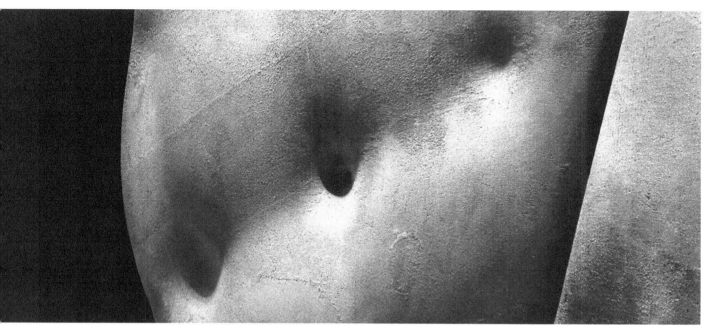

1   Detailed view of Jan's pillowed surface and center of mass (CoM)

The construction of architecture relies on an orchestra of moving parts and components throughout the process. These components are designed for the primary loads of their ultimate resting positions but must also accommodate for secondary loads that occur during the assembly process. Safety, budget, and timing are the most influential factors in conducting the orchestra of architectural construction and typically set the tempo. *Patty & Jan* explore the curious and playful possibilities of secondary loads such as movement, momentum and impact. This impractical assembly is not intended to negate practical considerations, but to elevate the field of construction above problem solving. It looks to previous architectures that emerged because construction was considered a social generator. The Amish use of community for barn raisings, the Inka's use of ritual to engender eternal construction, and the Rapanui's use of ceremony to transport massive stones are all examples of construction as a social generator. The civilizations that produced those precedents entered the act of constructing architecture by magnifying experience instead of decreasing budget or timing. *Patty & Jan* builds upon previous research into moving massive masonry elements with little energy by controlling the center of mass (CoM) via physical computation and innovative concrete technologies such as proprietary chemical admixtures and special lightweight additions to entrain air as well as impart high fluidity. (Swingle 2019). The resulting densities of the two concrete mixtures range from one-third the density to double the density of conventional concrete. *Patty & Jan* contributes to this ongoing research by incorporating the fourth dimension into the assembly process. It utilizes the controlled CoM to predict the movement, momentum, and impact that allows

PRODUCTION NOTES

Designer:	Matter Design
Industry:	CEMEX Global R&D
Size:	2m x 1.5m
Mass:	945kg
Material:	Concrete
Date:	2020

2   Patty & Jan assembled at the From Lab to Site: Innovation in Concrete symposium

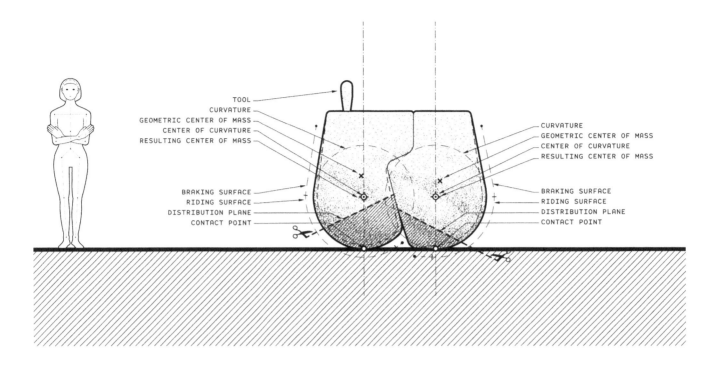

3   Key of the various geometries that compose Patty & Jan

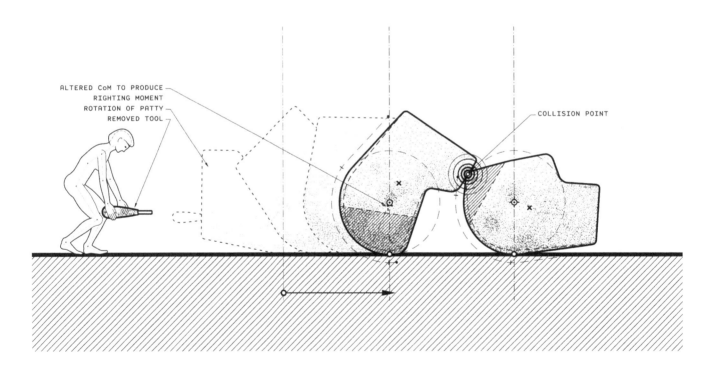

4   Key of releasing Patty by altering the CoM

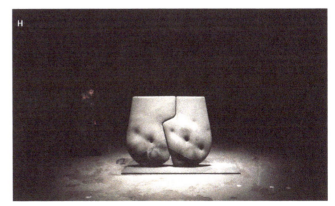

5   Patty & Jan performance at From Lab to Site: Innovation in Concrete

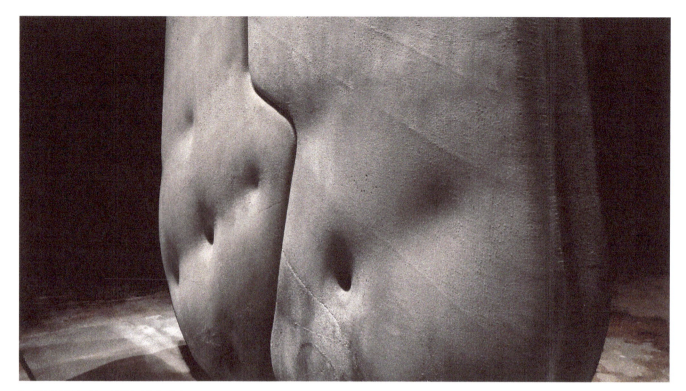

6   Detailed view of assembled Patty & Jan

for a predetermined auto-assembly, one that provides a spectacular experience of a colossal collision to result in a spectacle of assembly shared by a community. The resulting performance of *Patty & Jan* is an embedded intelligence of a theatrical assembly between two massive concrete masonry units (MCMU) through their own momentum. With a shared community, it was performed live at the From Lab to Site: Innovation in Concrete symposium (Figure 5) (Matter Design and CEMEX Global R&D 2019).

Patty & Jan are a partnership. They have a reciprocal relationship with one another that ensures one cannot assemble without the other. Beginning at a predetermined distance apart from one another, a weighted tool is removed from *Patty* to alter the CoM and create a righting moment (Figure 4). Rotating along the riding surface, *Patty* over-rotates to collide with *Jan* and strikes a resounding echo. The controlled impact triggers *Jan* to first rotate backwards, rebound off its braking surface, and then counter-rotate towards *Patty*. The two meet along their assembly surfaces in the middle and slip effortlessly into their final assembled position (Figure 2). In this assembly process, momentum and impact are key secondary loads and crucial considerations in the formal design. In addition to the general shape, safety measures, and rotating movement (Figure 3), *Patty & Jan* employ added mass in two new forms as adjustable variables in the design to control

the momentum and impact during the assembly. A pillowed texture (Figures 1, 6) is applied to the bottom regions of both *Patty & Jan* and a weighted concrete tool is placed on the top of *Patty* (Figure 7). The tool is particularly valuable because it offers two different resting positions and a righting moment by temporarily altering the CoM. Further, the riding surfaces of both *Patty & Jan* produce a track in section (Figure 6), creating two points of contact with the ground instead of one, in order to limit a degree of freedom during the assembly process.

Patty & Jan demonstrate the ability to predict the inherent movements and autonomous assemblies of MCMUs, and it extends the potential of assembly methods to be social generators such as spectacles or performances. This research is a foundation for thinking about larger and more complex construction choreographies that engage material as well as human bodies in the building of architecture.

ACKNOWLEDGMENTS

This research is produced in collaboration between Matter Design and CEMEX Global R&D. The recursion solver is generated through a custom definition that employs Anemone (theobject.co/anemone). Anemone is a plugin developed by Object (Mateusz Zwierzycki) to resolve recursion in Grasshopper (grasshopper3d.com), yet another a plugin developed by David Rutten for the Robert McNeel-developed program, Rhinoceros (rhino3d.com).

7   Patty & Jan disassembled after replacing the tool into Patty

REFERENCES

Matter Design and CEMEX Global R&D. "Patty & Jan." November 1, 2019, Performance at the *From Lab to Site: Innovation in Concrete* conference hosted by the University of Michigan Taubman College of Architecture + Urban Planning and the University of Michigan College of Civil and Environmental Engineering. Ann Arbor, MI,

Swingle, Tyler, Davide Zampini, and Brandon Clifford. 2019. "Walking Assembly: A Method for Craneless Tilt-Up Construction." In *Impact: Design with All Senses, Design Modelling Symposium Berlin 2019*, ed. C. Gengnagel, O. Baverel, J. Burry, M. Ramsgard Thomsen, S Weinzierl: 237-249. Berlin: Springer, Cham.

IMAGE CREDITS

All drawings and images by the authors.

Tyler Swingle is research lead and project manager at Matter Design and holds a lecturer position at McGill University. In his work, he is committed to exploring the reciprocity between materials and computational methods. As a part of Matter Design, this includes both ancient building techniques and new material technologies.

Davide Zampini has over 30 years of experience in the construction materials industry and is best known for pushing the limits of innovation in cement-based products and building solutions. Adopting a design- and industrially-driven innovation approach, Davide leads a multi-disciplinary and culturally diverse team at CEMEX's Center for Innovation and Technology. Through adaptive research and development conceived with versatility in mind, Davide's team at CEMEX in Switzerland develops novel functionalities in cement-based materials that incorporate customer-centered strategies and are designed to create solid emotional ties to a material that for ages has been considered "grey."

Brandon Clifford mines knowledge from the past to design new futures. He is best known for bringing megalithic sculptures to life to perform tasks. Clifford is the director of Matter Design and associate professor at the Massachusetts Institute of Technology. As a designer and researcher, Clifford has received recognition with prizes such as the American Academy in Rome Prize, a TED Fellowship, the SOM Prize, and the Architectural League Prize for Young Architects & Designers. Clifford is dedicated to re-imagining the role of the architect. His speculative work continues to provoke new directions for the digital era.

FOLL(i)CLE

A Toxi-Cartographic Proposal for Bangkok

Déborah López Lobato*
Pareid /UCL The Bartlett
School of Architecture

Hadin Charbel*
Pareid /UCL The Bartlett
School of Architecture

[1] Authors contributed equally
to the research

1   A visitor partaking in the hair analysis protocol (Visut Innadda, 2019).

Scenario

In the early months of 2019, air pollution in Bangkok reached a record high, bringing
national and international attention on the air quality in the South East Asian cosmopolis.
Although applications such as real-time pollution maps provide an environmental reading
from the exterior revealing the "here and now," they do not take increment and accumulation as factors to consider. This project was conceived around understanding the human
body as the medium that resists classification as either an interior or exterior environment
and inherently performs as an impressionable record of its surroundings. Can a city's
toxicity be read through its living constituents? Can the living bodies that dwell, navigate,
breathe, and process habitable environments be accessed? Can architecture retain a
degree of independence while also performing as a beacon for the collective?

Response and Development

Along this line of questioning, it was found that human hair is an actively and effortlessly
grown material that is perpetually cut and discarded while also being a complex matrix that
retains environmental content. Additionally, it possesses various architectural qualities,
although not normally conceived as a material, with a degree of tactility, translucency,
tensile strength, while also fully sustainable and biodegradable. It has been tested and
proven that hair can be understood similar to the rings of a tree, where hair segments
correspond chronologically to the person's environmental exposure to various elements
(D'Urso et al. 2016). Foll(i)cle was thus developed under two complementary facets, a

PRODUCTION NOTES

Architect: Pareid (Déborah López &
            Hadin Charbel)

Status: Built

Site Area: 16 sq. m.

Location: Bangkok, Thailand.

Date: 2019

2   Participants clipping a hair sample

3   Anonymous protocol questionnaires from different participants

4   Participant filling out protocols.

5   Anonymous hair samples from different participants

pavilion and a protocol, the former used to intrigue and gather the public, and the latter used to voluntarily and anonymously allow visitors to participate in a hair sampling process in the analysis for heavy metals. These two elements in concert resulted in a third facet of the project, an interactive public website that seeks to map urban environmental toxicity through its inhabitants.

On the pavilion front, the project was materialized through the collection of 30 kg (66 lbs) of discarded hair clippings felted with a custom needle felting machine into hair sheets, in which the only qualification for what hair can be used is the minimum length.

The machine most closely resembles a common ink-jet printer in that there is a feeding point, a linear action in the body, and an exit point. Specifically, it consists of a roller that feeds the un-felted hair, which also helps to press it flat. Inside the machine, there are three rows of felting needles that move up and down driven by an electrical motor that converts rotational motion into linear motion (much like a

car piston) which mechanizes and industrializes the action of the common single needle felting method. The speed of the roller feed and the felting are independently and manually controlled by two dials at the top of the machine; this allows for a customization in the process which results in a variation of looseness or tightness depending on the initial thickness of the layered hair fed into the machine as well as the quality (some batches of hair inherently possessed a smoother quality and others a more entangled and frictional characteristic). The process is relatable to a form of craft between human and machine as there is a relationship linking observation, action, and outcome that is gradually refined and in some ways becomes more intuitive over time. This notably added a distinct non-uniform characteristic that allowed for gradients, patches, and various color mixes to emerge in different areas.

The pavilion sought to experiment on material affect by seeing how the presence of this human-grown content in large scale would cause visitors to react or respond. Intending to gather the public, the overall form was

6 Exterior hair detail (Visut Innadda, 2019).

7 Translucency effect seen from the exterior. (Visut Innadda, 2019).

8 Ecosystemic diagram: participants, hair clipping, felting machine, hair mat, pollution app, pavilion, protocol, analysis, and toxicartography.

Foll(i)cle López, Charbel

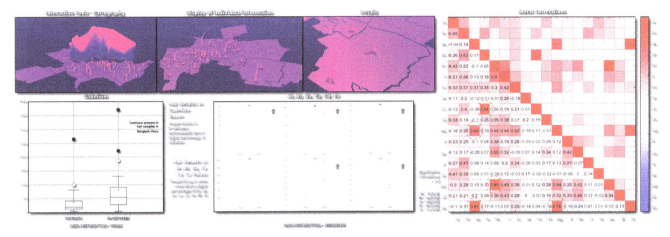

9   Early iterations of the interactive website including toxi-cartography and hair analysis results.

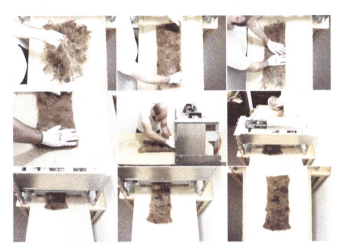

10 Hair felting machine and process.

11 Pavilion exterior with hair and steel sub structure. (2019, Visut Innadda).

designed to be obelisk-like while being large enough to accommodate a small number of people at the same time.

The protocol, located inside the pavilion and centered around a hair-clipping device/station, was developed in collaboration with a toxicologist and consisted of a self-administered survey, the tools required for providing a hair sample, and an alphanumeric code that preserves anonymity while allowing participants to trace their own results. Questions of the survey included controls and information in gathering the data for producing the toxi-cartography. For instance, smokers will naturally exhibit high amounts of lead in their hair, thus nullifying the sample's capacity to be a potential indicator of environmental contamination. On the information side, it was important to know if someone was working indoors or outdoors, as well as the areas in which they lived and worked.

With approximately 300 participants having taken part in the process, the first 50 hair samples were effectively tested for 15 heavy metals such as arsenic (As). The samples were intentionally taken at random in order to check for trends.

Hair analysis was carried out by Dr. Alberto Salamone from the University of Turin and conducted at the Centro Regionale Antidoping e di Tossicologia in Turin, Italy using inductively coupled plasma mass spectrometry (ICP-MS). The results indeed pointed to some areas for further exploration, namely a zone with a smoker who exhibited high amounts of lead, which would normally in itself not be indicative of environmental contamination, but conversely exhibited high amounts of other metals, thus requiring additional samples from inhabitants within the area.

Currently under development, the interactive website will provide the data visualization, both to see if it is effective as a form of communication to the wider public while also being used as a tool for feedback in seeing which areas and steps to take next. The interactive aspect of the website allows users to filter metals, areas, and cut sections

12 Protocol comic.

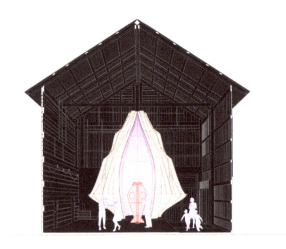

13 Single point section perspective.

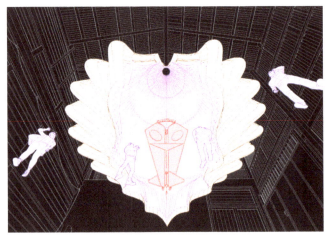

14 Worm's eye view.

15 Worm's eye axonometric.

through the topographic representation of the city in order to empower their own understanding of the region and their actions and choices in how they might engage with it moving forward.

Conclusion

Future development of the project and similar approaches could benefit from expanding strategies and protocols to include non-human agents in providing a more multi-dimensional reading of the urban condition. This would be desirable for two primary applicable reasons: the first is that human bodies are in some ways limited in the types of information they record, and the second being there are other environments that human bodies do not inhabit enough but that are nevertheless vital parts of the ecology. The implications of such an approach, that began with humans but extends into non-humans, would be consistent with efforts to de-anthropomorphize environmental readings as the sole criteria for design and decision making.

ACKNOWLEDGMENTS

The authors would like to thank MatterOfTrust.org for their support, without which the project would not be possible. Special thanks to Dr. Alberto Salamone from the University of Turin for his scientifc collaboration and guidance.

REFERENCES

D'Urso, Federica, Alberto Salomone, F. Seganti, and Marco Vincenti. "Identification of Exposure to Toxic Metals by Means of Segmental Hair Analysis: a Case Report of Alleged Chromium Intoxication." *Forensic Toxicology* 35, no. 1 (2016): 195–200. https://doi.org/10.1007/s11419-016-0340-y.

IMAGE CREDITS

Figure 1, 6,7, 11: © Visut Innadda, 2019

All other drawings and images by the authors.

16 Follicle pavilion at night with participant.

Déborah López is a licensed architect in Spain and co-founder of Pareid, an interdisciplinary design and research studio located between London and Spain. Currently, she is a Teaching Fellow at the Bartlett, UCL in London where she co-leads Research Cluster 1 and 20 under the title of 'Monumental Wastelands', researching and speculating on the post-anthropocene. Her research has been featured and presented at conferences in the United States and Europe including Eco-Visionaries Symposium, Confronting a planet in a state of emergency at the Royal Academy of Arts in London, ACADIA (2020, 2016, 2017 USA), Technarte Art+Technology Conference (2017 Spain), COCA First International Conference in Architectural Communication (2017, Spain). She completed her second Master's in Architecture at Obuchi Laboratory at the University of Tokyo and was awarded the Monbukagakusho scholarship (MEXT) from 2014 to 2018, and received a Bachelor of Arts and M. Arch from the UEM, Madrid in 2012.

Hadin Charbel is co-founder of Pareid, an interdisciplinary design and research studio located between London and Spain. Currently, he is a teaching fellow at the Bartlett, UCL in London where he co-leads Research Cluster 01 under the title of 'Monumental Wastelands', researching and speculating on the post-anthropocene. His research has been featured and presented at conferences in the United States and Europe including Eco-Visionaries Symposium, Confronting a planet in a state of emergency at the Royal Academy of Arts in London, ACADIA (2020, 2016, 2017 USA), Technarte Art+Technology Conference (2017 Spain), COCA First International Conference in Architectural Communication (2017, Spain). He received his Master's in Architecture at Obuchi Laboratory at the University of Tokyo and was awarded the Monbukagakusho scholarship (MEXT) from 2014 to 2018, and his B.A in Architectural Studies from UCLA in 2012.

The Flexing Room

Axel Kilian
MIT
Department of Architecture

Space as Interface – Architecture as Gesture

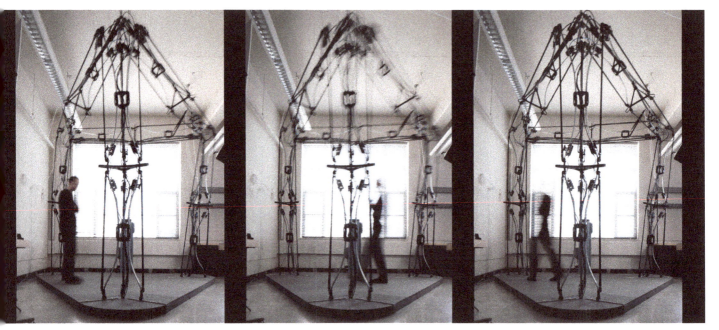

1   A selection of postures taken on by the Flexing Room from a test run with a person occupying the structure

Robotics has been largely confined to the object category, with fewer examples at the scale of buildings or human enclosures. Robotic buildings present unique challenges in terms of enclosing the user and how the building communicates its intents to people inhabiting such structures. Precedent work in architectural robotics explored the performative dimension (D'Estree Sterk 2011; Senatore, Duffour, Wise 2016), the playful and interactive qualities (Oosterhuis et al. 2012; Fox and Polancic 2012), and the cognitive challenges of AI systems interacting with people in architecture (Eng et al. 2005). In this work, which is an extension of previously published work (Kilian 2018), the potential of the architectural posture is explored further to facilitate human inhabitation of a sensing architecture.

The Flexing Room robotic skeleton was installed at MIT at its full designed height for the first time and equipped with further sensors and tested over a period of approximately two weeks in the late summer of 2019. The approximately 13-foot-tall structure (Figure 1) is comprised of 36 pneumatic actuators and an active bending fiberglass structure. Acoustic monitoring through piezo pickup mics was added that allowed basic rhythmic responses of the structure to people. Data streams were collected synchronously from Kinect skeleton tracking, piezo pickup mics, camera, and posture data (Figure 8) for future use and experiments with machine learning approaches that were not yet possible to conduct on the live short-term installation. The emphasis in this test period was to establish reliable hardware operations at full scale and to record correlated data streams. The full-scale installation of hardware was successful and proved the feasibility of the structural and actuation

PRODUCTION NOTES

Architect: Axel Kilian
Status: Temporary installation
Location: MIT, Cambridge MA
Date: 2019

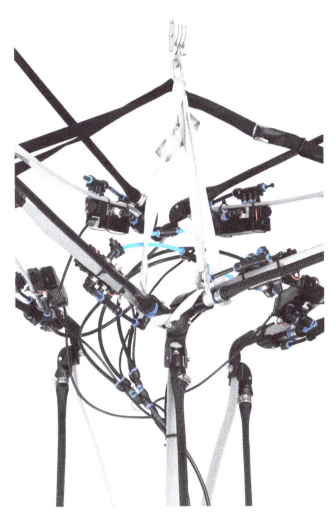

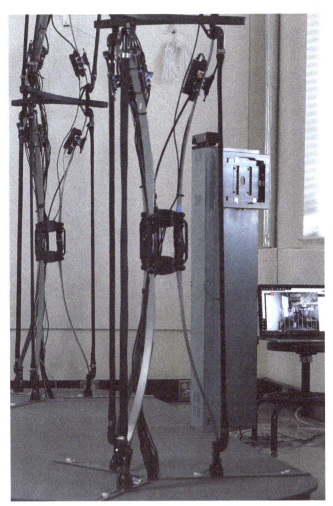

2   A corner joint cluster with data and air lines attached to control valves and rubber joints in dual and triple configurations to maximize range

3   Sensor on top of the power and signal distribution box and laptop screen showing a debugging view of the kinetc sensor and posture scores

approach previously only tested on a half-height setup. The range of postures was increased and more clearly readable for an observer, as was the perception of the structure as a space. An improved pneumatic valve controller removed the feedback buildup (sometimes leading to out-of-control actuation feedback cycles) and made the operation of the structure quieter. The reliability of the structure was limited due to frequent breakage of highly stressed rubber joint parts (Figure 2), which caused longer term test runs to terminate after a few hours, limiting its potential as an inhabitable architecture, reducing the time frame for data collection, and limiting the number of interactions with visitors. Therefore, learning from previous actions over a longer time span was still not possible, even in its simplest form.

The choice of varying postures of the structure as a form of expression and basis for communication with its inhabitants stems from the belief that a large unused potential lies in the extension of design from form into behavior that is also present in human communication (Hall 1959)

(Birdwhistell 1970). In part it is also motivated by the work of Anca Dragan who explores using adjusted robotic motion to make robot actions more predictable to human collaborators (Dragan 2013). But in the case of the Flexing Room, it is not so much about movement per se but about the transition between postures and their effect on the inhabited space within the skeleton. The speculation is: (1) whether, for instance, an upward arching beam (Figure 5) has the potential to make a space more open and welcoming, or an inward flexing set of columns tends to displace an inhabitant even if just by a slight margin; and (2) whether such postures should be designed by a person or whether they ideally could emerge from a feedback and learning system from the experience of the structure with its inhabitants. These questions are the basis on which the structure's hardware was developed and what is presented here.

User testing to evaluate its effects on people and self-learning beyond a simple search-based approach discussed in (Kilian 2018) has not been completed in this iteration and requires further work for a future paper.

4   A number of random postures of the physical structure super imposed with a human figure's action to show a sample of the range of changes

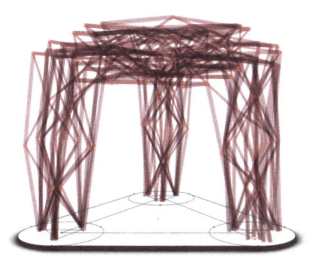

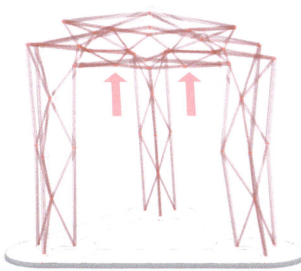

6   A partially constructed flexing room during lifting for column level 2

5   Range of simulated postures and a posture lifting one of the cross beams, possibly subtly affecting how inviting a space appears to a user

7   The base unit of the structure - pneumatically actuated fiberglass bows

ACKNOWLEDGMENTS

The Flexing Room installation was made possible by a commission for its installation for the 2017 Seoul Biennale of Architecture and Urbanism in the "Imminent Commons" exhibit curated by Alejandro Zaera–Polo and Jeffrey Anderson. Furthermore, its development was supported with research funds from Princeton University based on findings developed from a previous research project titled the Bowtower. The final full installation at MIT in the summer 2019 was made possible with a HASS grant by MIT and the assistance of MIT MArch student Jung in Seo.

REFERENCES

Arduino UNO R3, arduino.cc .

Birdwhistell, Ray L.. 1970. *Kinesics and Context: Essays on Body Motion Communication*. Philadelphia: U.Penn. Press.

Dragan, Anca D, Lee, Kenton CT, Srinivasa, Siddhartha S. 2013. "Legibility and predictability of robot motion" in *The Proceedings of the 8th ACM/IEEE HRI*, ed. H. Kuzuoak, V. Evers, 301-308. Tokyo: IEEE.

Sterk, Tristan D'Estree, 2011. "Using Robotic Technologies to Integrate External Influences in Design" in *ACADIA 2011: Integration through Computation; Proceedings of 31st Annual Conference of ACADIA*, ed. J.C. Johnson, B. Kolarevic, V. Parlac, J. Taron, 316-317. Banff: ACADIA.

Eng, Kynan., Mintz, Matti, and Verschure, Paul F.M.J.. 2005. "Collective Human Behavior in Interactive Spaces." In *Proceedings of ICRA 2005*, ed. A. Casalis, R. Dillmann, 2057-2062. Barcelona, Spain: IEEE.

Fox, Michael and Polancic, Allyn. 2012. "Conventions of Control: A Catalog of Gestures for Remotely Interacting With Dynamic Architectural Space". In *ACADIA 2012: Synthetic Digital Ecologies; Proceedings of the 32nd Annual Conference of ACADIA*, ed. J.K. Johnson, M. Cabrinha, K Steinfeld, 429-438. San Francisco: ACADIA.

8   Sample synchronized data stream from top actuation states, audio signals, kinect skeleton data and camera frames of the space at posture change points

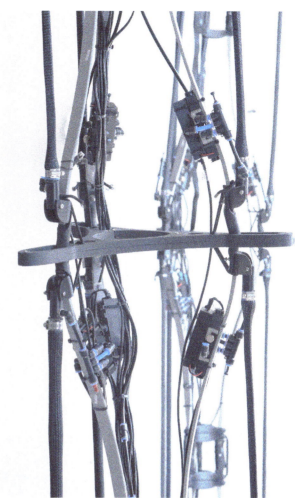

9 A cross beam detail showing spreader traingle and motion limiter loops and eleastic bands to self center triangle.

10 Vertical column detail with air distribution and valves and horizontal spreader triangle with motion limiters.

Hall, Edward T. 1959. *The Silent Language.* Garden City, N.Y: Doubleday,

Kilian, Axel 2018. "The Flexing Room Architectural Robot. An Actuated Active-Bending Robotic Structure using Human Feedback", in *ACADIA 2018 Recalibration: On Imprecision and Infidelity: Proceedings of the 38th Annual Conference of ACADIA*, ed. by P. Anzaline, M. del Signore and A.J. W, 232-241. Mexico City: ACADIA.

Oosterhuis, Kas, et al. 2012. *Hyperbody: First Decade of Interactive Architecture.* Heijningen: Jap Sam.

Payne, Andy, and Jason Kelly Johnson, Firefly Plugin for Grasshopper in Rhinoceros, V 1.0.0.70, 2015

Piker, Daniel, Kangaroo plugin for Grasshopper in Rhinoceros, V 2.42, Win 10, 2017

Senatore, Gennaro, Pete Winslow, Philippe Duffour, Chris Wise. 2015. "Infinite stiffness structures via active control". In: *Proceedings of IASS 2016,* 1–12. Amsterdam: IASS.

Rutten, David, Grasshopper extension to Rhinoceros, V 1.0007, McNeel, Win 10, 2020

IMAGE CREDITS

Figure 1,2,3,4,9 10 : © Jung in Seo, August 2019.

All other drawings and images by the author.

Axel Kilian is a Visiting Assistant Professor at the MIT Department of Architecture. He previously was an Assistant Professor at Princeton University's School of Architecture and at the Delft University of Technology and a Postdoctoral Associate at the Department of Architecture. He holds a PhD in Design and Computation and a Master of Science in Architectural Studies from the Department of Architecture MIT. He was a German-American Fulbright scholarship grantee and holds a professional degree in architecture from the University of the Arts Berlin.

Stereoform Slab

Innovation in Concrete At-Scale

Kyle Vansice
SOM

Rahul Attraya
SOM

Ryan Culligan
SOM

Benton Johnson
SOM

Asbjørn Sondergaard
Odico Construction Robotics

Nate Peters
Autodesk

1   Elevation view of Stereoform Slab. © Dave Burk | SOM

Stereoform Slab

Stereoform Slab is both a pavilion and a prototype—an exhibition for the Chicago Architectural Biennial, and an experiment in how digital form-finding and robotics can be leveraged to rethink the future of concrete construction. It is located in Chicago, IL, and is a to-scale component of a future concrete building system, conventionally cast against robotically sculpted formwork by Odico Construction Robotics, illustrating an overall methodology to reduce the carbon footprint of concrete construction in the built environment.

Stereoform Slab examines the role of one of the most ubiquitous horizontal elements in the city—the concrete slab, also the most common element in contemporary construction. Current research reveals that 40-60% of a concrete building's carbon footprint results from floor construction alone. This is due to the fact that it is also one of most inefficient structural elements overall, and while it is common to all buildings, it is mostly overlooked from a material optimization perspective. If standardized solutions for smarter structural systems can be developed that align with and augment existing construction methodologies, this affords designers the opportunity to significantly reduce the carbonization and materialization of one of the most common building types in the built environment. By using smarter forming systems—in this case a ruled-surface-derived, robotic hotwire process—the Stereoform Slab prototype proved that the amount of material used and waste generated could be minimized without increasing construction complexity by about 20% over a conventional system.

PRODUCTION NOTES

Architect: SOM

Status: Completed

Site Area: 1,200 sq. ft.

Location: Chicago, IL

Date: 2019

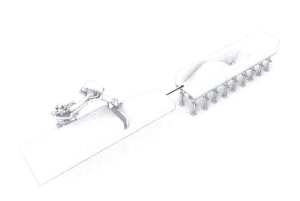

2   Optimization of ruled surface based formwork, fabricated by Odico

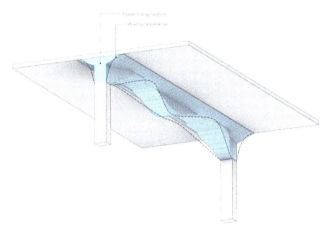

3   Alignment of structural optimization with fabrication constraints

4   Expressive, sculptural quality of Stereoform © Dave Burk | SOM

Stereoform also extends the conventional concrete span (column spacing), specifically in Chicago, from 30' to 45'. When deployed as a structural system throughout a building, this increased span enables more flexibility in the planning and usage of its spaces. This has the potential to extend a building's lifecycle as it can more easily be re-appropriated as the needs of a city and market change, further reducing its carbon footprint by reducing the need for whole building replacement. By developing a concrete forming system that affords this added flexibility without increasing construction costs, it becomes possible to achieve significant embodied carbon reductions in buildings that aren't typically the subject of advanced architectural design and/or rigorous optimization—conventional buildings that compose a majority of our built environment, and its respective contributions to global carbon emissions.

Multi-Objective Optimization

Stereoform is the result of a multi-objective design optimization process where optimal materialization according to the compressive/tensile physics present in beam design were balanced against the fabrication constraints of a singularly ruled surface which makes possible fast form-making using robotic hotwire cutting. This integrated process is highly iterative and required coordination across all phases of construction—the robotically cut EPS formwork had to be harmonized with conventional board-formwork, rebar had to be computationally modeled and coordinated against the optimization process while still aligning to conventional code coverage and area ratio requirements, etc.

SOM and Autodesk collaborated on an effort to mirror the approach developed to optimize Stereoform slab as a pavilion, to the building scale, using the multi-objective optimization platform Refinery. Project Refinery was a preview version of the Generative Design in Revit tool that was released with Revit 2021. A Dynamo graph was constructed that defined input constraints such as boundary conditions, loading type, required beam strength, and fabrication methodology. A matrix of these constraints

5   Expressive, sculptural quality of Stereoform

6   Stereoform Slab with the formwork fabricated by Odico in background © Dave Burk | SOM

was then constructed for a prototypical building, allowing for the unique representation of each structural bay. The Dynamo graph was then exported to the Refinery interface where optimization studies were run for each of the unique beam types defined in the matrix. Doing so allowed the team to create a hyper-responsive system design that could adapt to any number of varying programmatic conditions and loading patterns.

The development of this approach is a key step in making optimization techniques flexible enough to balance the number of competing parameters in the design process available and accessible to a broader design audience within the field of architecture and engineering.

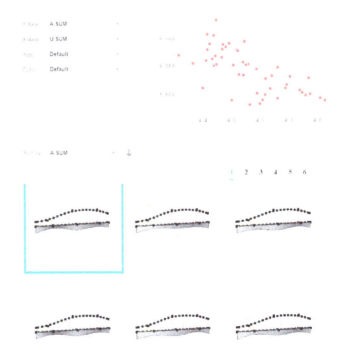

7   Results of multi-objective optimization using Autodesk Refinery

8 Optimal formwork being placed within conventional slab shoring © Dave Burk | SOM

ACKNOWLEDGMENTS

The Stereoform Slab was kindly funded in part by Autodesk and Skidmore Owings Merril LLP, conducted by Skidmore Owings Merril LLP, Odico A/S, Sterling Bay and James McHugh Construction, all providing in-kind contributions.

REFERENCES

Trends in global CO2 emissions: 2015. Report. PBL Netherlands Environmental Assessment Agency. The Hague, 2015, https://www.pbl.nl/sites/default/files/downloads/pbl-2015-trends-in-global-co2-emisions_2015-report_01803_4.pdf. (Accessed 23 December 2019)

Kulkarni, A. R. and M. V. Bhusare. 2016. "Structural Optimization of Reinforced Concrete Structures", International Journal of Engineering and Technical Research, 5(7), pp. 123-127.

IMAGE CREDITS

Figure 1: © Dave Burk | SOM

Figure 6: © Dave Burk | SOM

Figure 8: © Dave Burk | SOM

All other drawings and images by the authors.

Kyle Vansice is an architectural designer and researcher at SOM.

Rahul Attraya is an architectural designer and researcher at SOM.

Ryan Culligan is an Associate Director in architectural design and studio leader at SOM.

Benton Johnson is a Director in the Structural Engineering practice at SOM.

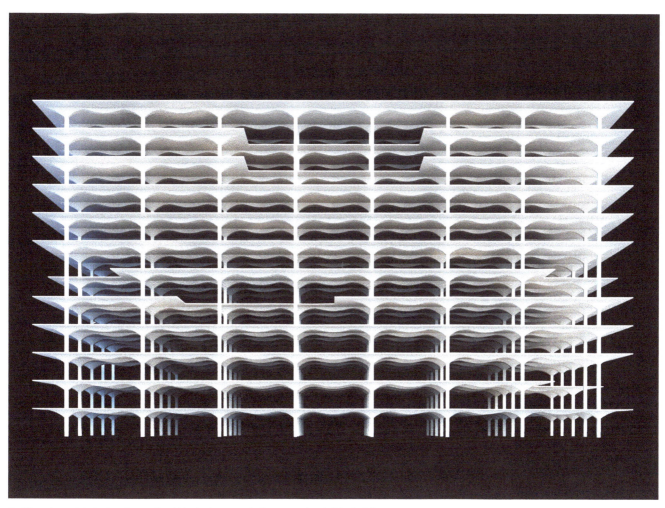

9   Stereoform slab designed at-scale within the framework of a conventional office building

Asbjørn Søndergaard is founding partner and Chief Technology
Officer in Odico Construction Robotics, a technology enterprise
dedicated to large scale architectural robotic formwork fabrication. Founded in 2012 in a joining of research trajectories following
the Fabricate 2011 conference, Odico Construction Robotics has
embarked on a mission to revolutionize global construction. In daily
work, Asbjørn Søndergaard heads the software development and
industrial research and development within the same.

Nate Peters is a computational designer and software developer
with experience in design optimization, digital fabrication, and
machine learning. Nate received his Master of Design Studies in
Technology from the Harvard Graduate School of Design, and his
Bachelor of Architecture from Iowa State University. Currently,
he works in Boston as a software engineer in Autodesk's AEC
Generative Design Group. At Autodesk he has assisted in the design
and construction of multiple large scale research pavilions, and is
currently focused on Project Refinery, a new generative design tool
for architects and engineers in the building industry.

Gusto 501

Rationalizing Computational Masonry Design

Alex Josephson
Jonathan Friedman
Benjamin Salance
Ivan Vasyliv
Tim Melnichuk
PARTISANS

1   Interior View of Final Masonry Block Wall (Jonathan Friedman, February 2020, © 2020).

Gusto 501 is a multilevel infill building on the footprint of an old car garage. Surrounded by an overpass and former factories, the restaurant and event spaces take the form of a "Hyper garage" as a nod to its urban context. The interior is punctuated with standard terracotta blocks formed to create an intricate play of shadows during the day and embedded with LEDs to provide atmospheric illumination at night.

The client's vision, our narrative, and the program demanded an innovative use of the prime material: terracotta. The scale of the project required the use of 3,700 blocks. Within the array wrapped around a 50 ft tall interior volume, each block needed to be formed and sequenced uniquely to maintain structural integrity, interface with building systems, and express the sculptural qualities our team had designed.

Standard approaches to the masonry could not achieve the effects our team was striving for; we had to develop our ground-up process to manufacture and install mass-customized masonry. The design process involved an algorithmic approach to a series of cuts and geometric manipulations to the blocks that allowed for near-endless combinations and configurations to create a dynamic interior facade system.

PARTISANS, partnering with a terracotta block manufacturer, a local mason, and a masonry engineer, pursued simplifying production using wire cutter systems. Digital and physical mockups were then used to create a robust library of parameterized design

PRODUCTION NOTES

Architect:	PARTISANS
Client:	Gusto 501
GC:	Boszko & Verity
Status:	Built
Site Area:	9,500 sq. ft.
Location:	Toronto, ON, Canada
Date:	2020

2   Second Floor Bar (Jonathan Friedman, February 2020, © 2020).

3   Exterior Street View (© Nic Lehoux, January 2020).

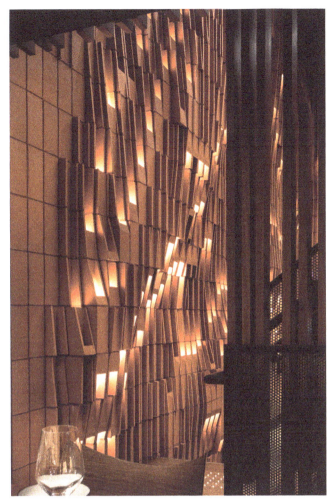

4   Block Wall Detail (© Jonathan Friedman, February 2020).

criteria that optimized corbelling, grout thickness, weight, and fabrication complexity.

Working sets of drawings were automated through a fully integrated BIM model, simplifying and speeding up installation. The challenge of marrying these processes with the physical realities of installation required another level of collaboration that included the masons themselves and the electricians who would eventually combine lighting systems into the sculpted block array.

Design To Production Workflow

Our approach began right from the point of fabrication, and by understanding the process, we were able to create repeatable, cost-effective, scalable modules that, when combined, formed unlimited possibilities for design. Without interfacing with the industry these solutions would have been cost-prohibitive. Using off-the-shelf clay tiles and traditional masonry installation methods, we were able to sculpt and build highly complex and challenging geometries using simple principles and means. Moreover, we were able

to extend the block's use to become a lighting fixture for the project.

Design Optimization

To manage the increased unit cost of cut Structural Clay Tile (SCT) (i.e., $12/unit) compared to uncut SCT (i.e., $6/unit), the computational design workflow was optimized to minimize cutting instances. This optimized workflow allowed for 550 of the 3,669 (i.e., 15%) SCTs to be uncut without significant performance or design losses.

To reduce the overall structural load on the system, the shape of SCTs was customized to remove material not directly used for load transfer, resulting in chamfered cuts of overhangs. These cuts were restricted to nominal angles (i.e., 0°, 5.4°, 15.7°) but were allowed to occur at varying depths (i.e., 25.4mm increments to a maximum of 200mm), which preserved the structural capacity of the assembly but reduced the material used by 30%.

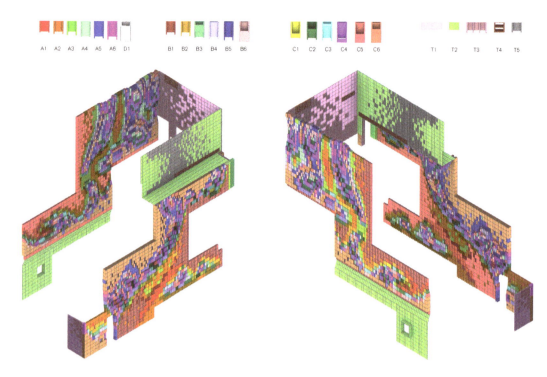

5   Block Type Distribution Diagram (© PARTISANS 2020)

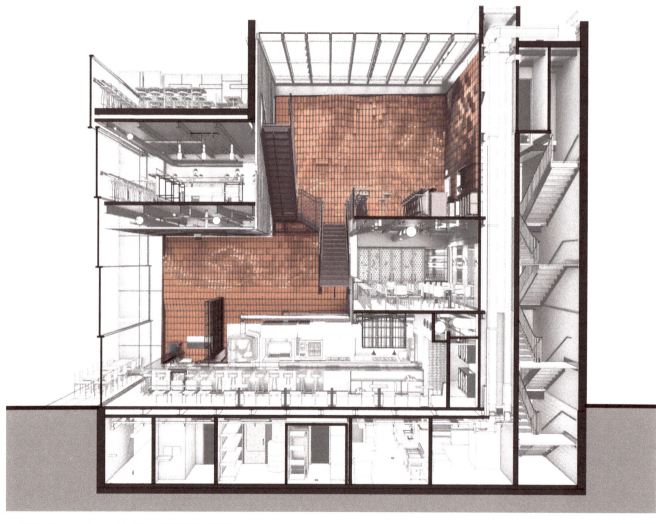

6   3D Building Section Looking East (PARTISANS, 2020).

7   Wet Block Modules (Sandkuhl, 2019).

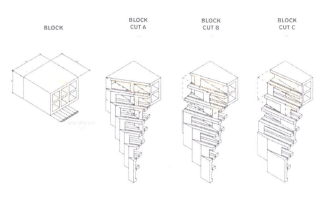

8   Blockcut Concept Diagram (© PARTISANS 2020).

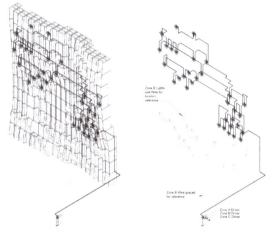

9   Block Wall Electrical Diagram (© PARTISANS 2020).

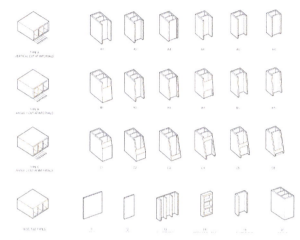

10 Block Types Diagram (© PARTISANS 2020)..

Prototyping

In keeping with our testing methodology, a 40-unit mockup was completed and evaluated by our mason partner. It was discovered that (a) some combinations of adjacent STC types failed to conceal the lighting fixture appropriately, and (b) some block types created fragile edges prone to breaking. Our parametric model was updated accordingly to avoid these issues during full-scale installation.

To maintain consistent lighting levels and avoid voltage drop, LED lights were subdivided into clustered zones. To minimize wire length (i.e., maximizing voltage fidelity), lights were clustered based on their positional proximity rather than course height. As each zone now spanned across several masonry courses, and several independent zones were present along a single masonry course, masons required precise instruction on how to route the wire between horizontal and vertical grout lines.

Non-uniform corbelling

To ensure the structure was self-supported, a traditional methodology—restringing each successive course's overhang to a third of SCT depth—was implemented into the Grasshopper code. In cases where additional floor area was required to accommodate seating or head clearance, corbels were reduced to 0 mm; where ambient lighting was required, corbels of 100 mm were allowed for each successive course until the assembly depth reached 900 mm.

ACKNOWLEDGMENTS

PARTISANS would like to thank everyone who made this project possible, especially Janet Zuccarini and the entire Gusto 54 team that lent their full support to the ambition behind the project the entire five year path to completion. Boszko and Verity and Hunt Heritage are owed a great amount respect and admiration for their execution and attention to detail in the construction. The project would also not be possible without the excitement of Ann Engh from Sandkuhl, leaping at the chance to custom fabricate the terracotta blocks.

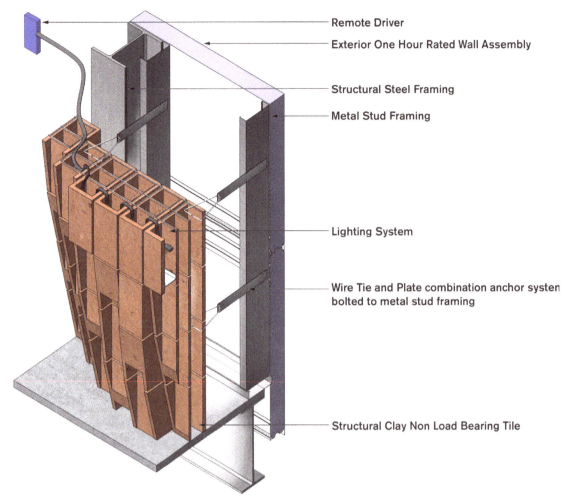

Remote Driver

Exterior One Hour Rated Wall Assembly

Structural Steel Framing

Metal Stud Framing

Lighting System

Wire Tie and Plate combination anchor system bolted to metal stud framing

Structural Clay Non Load Bearing Tile

11 Block Wall Construction Diagram (© PARTISANS 2020).

Alex Josephson co-founded PARTISANS in 2012 with Pooya Baktash, bringing a strong creative vision to the rapidly-growing architecture studio. In addition to his work with PARTISANS, Alex is a lecturer and core faculty member at the University of Toronto's Daniels School of Architecture. As a registered architect in Ontario, he has received numerous accolades through the years; he was named 2015 Best Emerging Designer by Canada's Design Exchange, awarded Globe & Mail Catalyst award for Design, and has received the New York Prize Fellowship at the Van Alen Institute. Alex Josephson earned his Masters in Architecture from the University of Waterloo.

Jonathan Friedman joined PARTISANS as a partner in 2013, bringing a depth of experience across a wide range of architectural projects. Friedman often leads on construction of projects and photography, finding elegant solutions to bring the studio's design vision into reality. Prior to joining PARTISANS, Friedman was a part of international firm HOK's Toronto office. He has also been a design studio lecturer and guest critic at the University of Toronto, Ryerson University, and The University of Waterloo School of Architecture. Originally from Durban, South Africa, Friedman studied architecture at the University of Waterloo, where his graduate work earned the Royal Architectural Institute of Canada Gold Medal.

Benjamin Salance is a project manager and senior designer for PARTISANS. Prior to PARTISANS, Ben worked for SHoP Architects and interned for Morphosis in New York City. With a specialization in complex geometry rationalization, Benjamin was the primary project manager and designer for Gusto 501. Benjamin is currently a licensed Architect in New York State and holds a Masters of Architecture from Cornell University and a bachelors degree in Environmental Design from University of Colorado Boulder.

12 Block Wall Mockup (Benjamin Salance, 2019, ©).

Ivan Vasyliv After receiving a Bachelor of Architectural Science at Ryerson University, Ivan Vasyliv joined PARTISANS in 2012, where his contributions in design, research, and fabrication have received global recognition. He completed an MBA from Ted Rogers School of Management at Ryerson University specializing in management of technology and innovation and currently pursues projects with geometric and fabrication complexities.

Tim Melnichuk studied at Ryerson University where he received both a Bachelor of Architectural Science and a Master of Architecture. Tim started working at PARTISANS in 2016 as a designer.

13 Interior View (© Nic Lehoux, January 2020).

The Collective Perspective Machine

Jonathan A. Scelsa
Pratt Institute

Jennifer Birkeland
Cornell University

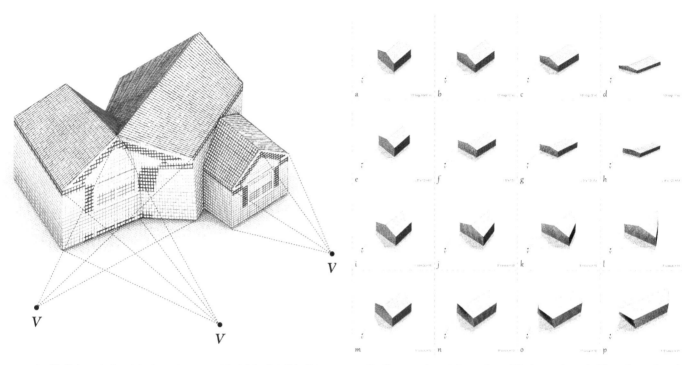

1   Multiple vantage points generate compounded distortion. Take the
    familiar frame of the house and generate a new form.

2   The many formal generations of the house generated from the motion of
    the Drafter in the field.

Introduction

Since the age of humanism, both on the easel as well as our contemporary screens, the production of the architectural image has been conventionally governed by one individual, whom we might refer to as the drafter. As the primary author sitting in the chair of the vantage point, the drafter occupies the privileged position for whom the translation between the second and third dimension establishes an approximate realism. The viewers, or secondary participants, by contrast are relegated to a subordinate position, subject to the residual distortions of the drafter's vision, based on their own relative vantage points. While perhaps cynical, our contemporary condition does not share the same philosophical positivistic optimism of the Renaissance nor the ideal faith in humanity that empowered the democratic universalisms of modernity. Rather, it is formed from an ambiguous inquiry into the creation of a new sense of truth, brought forth by the proliferation and amplification of multiple individual "perspectives."

In his conclusion to *The Projective Cast*, Robin Evans illustrates ten "transitive spaces" of geometric projection towards the generation and representation of a designed object, the fifth of which describes the space between a building or object and its defined perspectival representations (Evans 2000). Evans observes that this path typically follows the progression of object to photo or drawing and is rarely reversed. When a rendering of an unreal object is made, the path towards its construction is "diverted" via the creation of orthographic projections.

PRODUCTION NOTES

Architect: op.Architecture
             Landscape

Client: RISD LARCH Exhibition

Status: Research / Exhibition

Location: TBD

Date: 2020

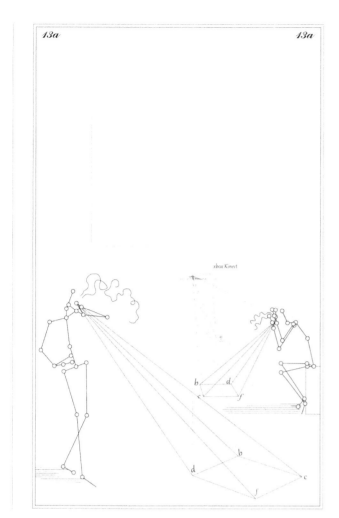

3   The sensor scans the drafters in the field and tracks their eye point, then feeds the projector the overall image based on their locations.

This is to say that perspectival images are predominantly the result of pulling the visual information of an object towards the viewer's eye through the picture plane. This itself is interesting, considering the derivation of the word project would give us the opposite conclusion. The term project derives from the Latin "iacio," meaning throw, and "pro" meaning forth—as in voice, light, and image. As such, one might conjecture that the two-dimensional drawing of the idea of a thing could be its own generative source of information, thrown outward into object space.

The machine

What sets forth is a generative game of visual ping-pong that might be played between two members, one assigned the role of pulling the image, and the other the role of projecting forth a new informational object from their own disparate vantage point. By adding the sensor to the mix, we may acknowledge the proposed system as a new live drawing machine, wherein the object's distortions record the motion and movement of the individuals in parallax space. This routine can be further amplified with collectivity by introducing more viewer-drafters, each subsequent person serving the alternating role. This procedure of recursion would act like a game of visual telephone, where each person adds their own subjectivity surrounding an image, inclusive of their preconceptions, to mutate the form of the existing piece—an aesthetic act that might resemble our own cultural circumstance of formal noise as a representation of the aggregate social body of disparate perspectives.

This project and machine designed for a postponed exhibition seek to establish a new procedure for generating design, neither subjectively from a personal static individual point nor objectively in the round for all to experience equally. Rather, a new machine emerges which establishes form as the hybrid of multiple responsive perspectives, wherein all viewers are simultaneously the generator of projective form and the receiver of distorted images.

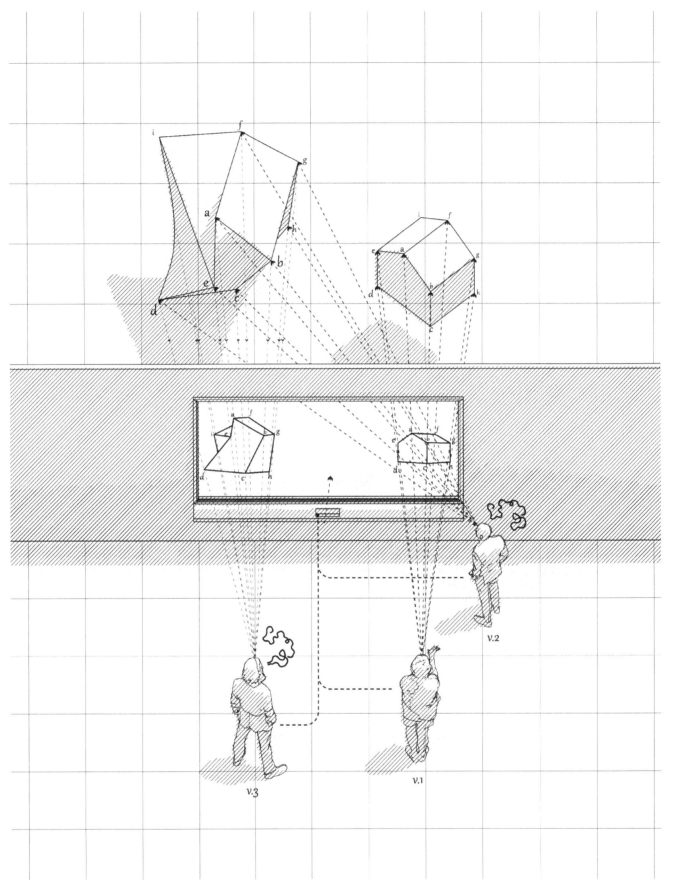

4   The visual ping-pong unfolds, Drafter A sees the recognizable form of the Euclidean house. Drafter B sees a distortion of A. Drafter C is confused because he cannot recognize A or B through from his anamorphic perspective.

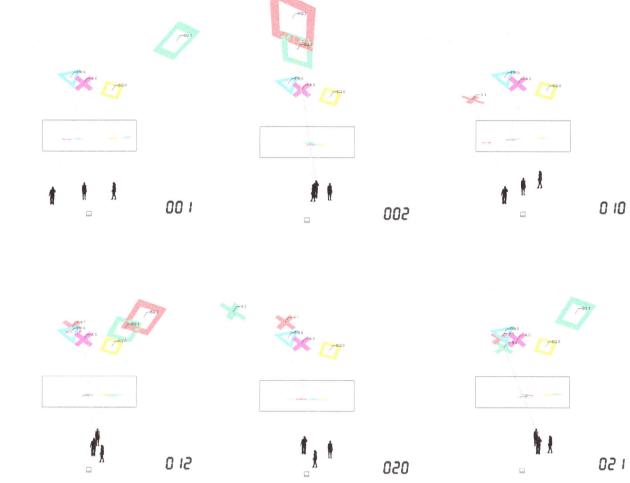

5   The algorithm generates a color coded output series based on the objects the collectors control with their motions.

ACKNOWLEDGMENTS

Thank you to Andy Kim for your assistance with this project.

REFERENCES

Evans, Robin. 2000. *The Projective Cast: Architecture and its Three Geometries*. Cambridge, MA: MIT Press.

IMAGE CREDITS

Figures 1-5: ©op.AL, 2020

Jennifer Birkeland is currently an Assistant Professor of Landscape Architecture at Cornell University in the College of Agriculture and Life Sciences. She is a licensed landscape architect in the state of New York, a Fellow at the American Academy in Rome, and a LEED accredited professional. Jennifer received her Master of Landscape Architecture at Harvard University and has a Bachelor's of Science in Landscape Architecture from California Polytechnic State University Pomona. Jennifer has worked with internationally renowned offices such as West 8, OLIN, and Ken Smith Workshop.

Jonathan A. Scelsa is an Architect, Urbanist, and an educator. Prior to the founding of op.AL, Jonathan had worked in several international offices including Foreign Office Architects, Hashim Sarkis Studios, Smith-Miller + Hawkinson and Bohlin Cywinski Jackson. As an educator, Jonathan is an Assistant Professor of Architectural Design + Technology at Pratt Institute in Brooklyn, NY. Jonathan is a Licensed Architect in the state of New York and a Fellow of the American Academy in Rome. He received his Master of Architecture in Urban Design with Distinction from Harvard University. He received his Bachelor of Architecture from Carnegie Mellon University.

Reformative Coral Habitats

Rethinking Artificial Reef Structures
through a Robotic Clay Printing Method

Christian J. Lange
The University of Hong Kong

Lidia Ratoi
The University of Hong Kong

Dominic Co Lim
The University of Hong Kong

Jason Hu
The University of Hong Kong

David M. Baker
The University of Hong Kong

Vriko Yu
The University of Hong Kong

Phil Thompson
The University of Hong Kong

1   Perspective view of tile aggregation pre-installation

Introduction

Coral reefs are some of the most diverse ecologies in the marine world. They are the
habitat to tens of thousands of different marine species. However, these wildlife environments are endangered throughout the world. As a consequence, a team consisting of
marine biologists and architects has developed a series of performative structures that
were deployed in Hong Kong waters, intending to aid new coral growth over the coming
years.

This project is a collaborative research mission between the Robotic Fabrication Lab,
Faculty of Architecture, and the Swire Institute of Marine Science, both at The University of
Hong Kong. The project was commissioned by the Agriculture, Fisheries and Conservation
Department (AFCD) and is part of an ongoing active management measure for coral restoration in Hoi Ha Wan Marine Park in Hong Kong. Hoi Ha Wan Marine Park accounts for
more than three-quarters of reef-building coral species in Hong Kong, and is also home for
more than 120 reef-associated fishes. However, gradual deterioration by bio-erosion over
the years, coupled with bleaching and mass mortality events in 2015-2016, are putting the
local coral community at risk.

Research Questions

The following objectives were defined as part of the design and fabrication research. One,
to develop a design strategy that builds on the concept of biomimicry to create complex

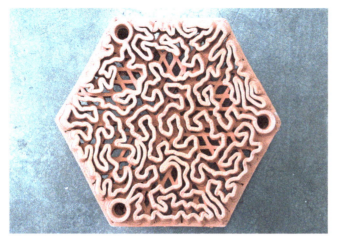

2   Top view of generic coral tile

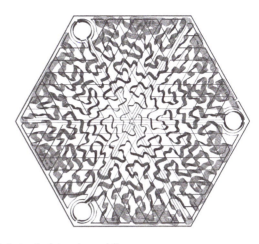

3   Printing path of generic coral tile

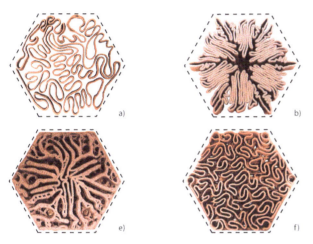

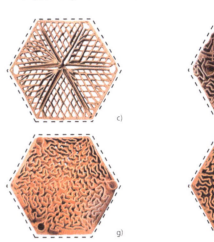

4   Design evolution a) to h) with h) being the final solution

spaces that would provide attributes against the detachment of the inserted coral fragment, hence enhancing a diverse marine life specific to the context of the city's water conditions. Two, to generate an efficient printing path that accommodates the specific morphological design criteria but also ensures structural integrity and the functional aspects of the design. Three, to develop an efficient fabrication process with a direct ink writing (DIW) 3D printing methodology that takes into consideration aspects of warping, shrinkage, and cracking in the clay material.

To come up with a solution for the objectives stated above, the research team developed a specific method that combined an algorithmic design approach for the different geometries of the design with a digital additive manufacturing process utilizing 3D robotic clay printing. The overall fabrication strategy for the complex and large pieces sought to ensure structural longevity, optimize production time, and tackle the involved double-sided printing method.

Reformative Coral Habitats

The overall project consists of 32 units organized in assemblies of four tiles each. Each of the 128 tiles has a size of roughly 0.36 m³. In order to allow for a manageable underwater assembly by scuba divers, tiles were designed based on a hexagonal assembly strategy with three legs each, making it easier to align the system underwater. Furthermore, the design needed to be symmetrical or based on similar patterns because of the use of an Autonomous Reef Monitoring Structure (ARMS), which is a standardized global measuring tool for underwater life behavior. An overly irregular structure could lead to increasingly difficult means of measuring since it would have to account for formal diversity. For the same reason, each assembly of tiles needed to be identical.

The team used a generative algorithmic design approach for the project. Using Rhino in conjunction with Grasshopper, the focus of this design method was on developing a flexible system that enables an iterative design process, tests different design variants, and generates

5 Perspective of 72 tiles aggregated pre-installation

Reformative Coral Habitats Lange, Ratoi, Lim, Hu, Baker, Yu, Thompson

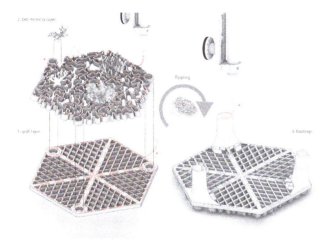

6   Diagram of printing order

7   Fabrication process

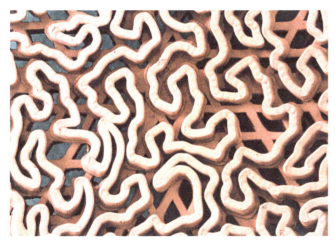

8   Close-up of coral layer

9   View on generic coral tile after coral out-planting.

local specificity within the tile. The clay tiles were printed with a DIW printing technique. For the printing set-up, the team utilized a standard ABB 6700 industrial robot with a DeltaBots linear ram extruder equipped with a 6 mm nozzle.

This pilot study aims to investigate the restoration success using mono-, mix- and polyculture of three coral species, namely Acropora, Platygyra, and Pavona. The three selected species display different strategies, representing the historical, current, and future dominant candidates in the park. Acropora, commonly known as staghorn corals, are fast growing, making them a competitive species for space; Platygyra, known as brain coral, are adaptive to thermal stress yet suffering from bioerosion; and Pavona, the leaf coral with the unique plate-like growth pattern, are adaptive to sedimentation. The project team collected corals of opportunity, which are dislodged coral fragments that are unlikely to survive given no human intervention, giving these coral fragments a second chance to thrive. The coral fragments have been outplanted in July 2020, and the experiment will be monitored for the coming year.

Conclusion

The researchers hope that this new method for artificial reef tiles will help to restore corals and conserve biodiversity more effectively and become a vital contribution to the ongoing global efforts to save the degraded coral reef systems in metropolises.

IMAGE CREDITS

Figure 1, 2, 3, 5, 7, 8: Christian J. Lange

Figure 4: Lidia Ratoi

Figure 6: Dominic Co Lim

Figure 9: Vriko Yu

Figure 10 & 11: AFCD

Christian J. Lange is a registered German architect and Associate Professor in the Department of Architecture at the University of Hong Kong, where he teaches architectural design and classes in advanced digital modeling and robotics. His work and research

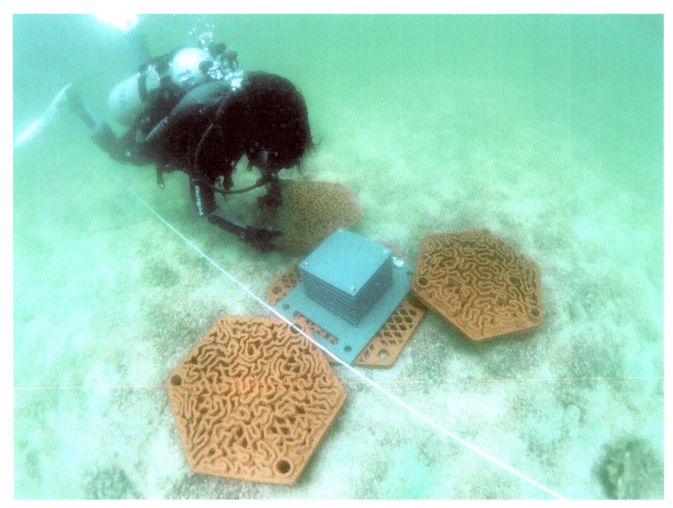

10 Scuba divers installing a unit on the seabed

has been published internationally and featured in over 30 exhibits, including the Venice Biennale and the Hong Kong & Shenzhen Bi-city Biennale.

Lidia Ratoi is an architect and robotic fabrication researcher and Assistant Lecturer within Hong Kong University, leading a 2nd year studio on housing. Her explorations focus on biomaterials, sustainable design and robotics. She is also a member of DesignMorphine and a writer for CLOT. She graduated from IAAC Barcelona.

Dominic Co Lim is a research assistant at the Poly-U/RCA Artificial Intelligence Design Laboratory. His research interests include 3D-printing, design computation, and machine learning for creative work. Previously, he did his Bachelor's in Architectural Design at the University of Hong Kong.

Jason Hu is Research Assistant in the Centre of Fabrication and Material Technologies at the University of Hong Kong, with strong passion in digital fabrication and architectural design. He received his Master's in Architecture at the University of Hong Kong in 2020.

David M. Baker is an Associate Professor in the Faculty of Science at HKU. He is a multi-disciplinary ecologist who studies how humans impact the ecology and evolution of the oceans. He is particularly interested in coral reef ecosystems, which are currently undergoing a perilous decline. His group's research scales from the ecosystem to cellular level, and combines tools in geochemistry, stable isotope-ecology, eco-physiology, and molecular biology to answer questions pertaining to coral symbiosis and interactions with anthropogenic stressors.

Vriko Yu is a PhD student at The University of Hong Kong, focusing on coral restoration and reef resilience research. Yu is active in promoting coral conservation and citizen science in the region and works closely with Reef Check Foundation and World Wide Fund in Hong Kong.

Phil Thompson is a research assistant at The University of Hong Kong and the Swire Institute of Marine Science. Phil's research supports a variety of projects including coral restoration, MarineGEO biodiversity, and the biogeochemistry of corals.

11 Scuba diver outplanting the different coral fragments into the tile

Viscous Catenary

Gosia (Malgorzata)
Pawlowska
UCL Bartlett

Design and fabrication of a freeform architectural glass assembly

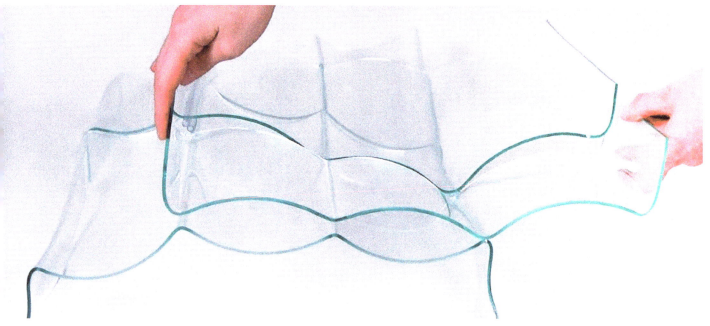

1   Catenary channel glass assembly process

Design and Fabrication of a Freeform Architectural Glass Assembly

Viscous Catenary is a free-form architectural glass structure that embeds material logic in a distributed system, challenging the standardization and determinism prevalent in glass construction. Multi-curved panels are joined in a "catenary channel glass" assembly, expressing the material's inherent behavior at high temperatures.

This project adopts a hybrid fabrication process, combining low-tech hardware and modern digital technologies. Glass panels were formed in a traditional kiln over a set of interchangeable waterjet-cut steel profiles or a repositionable tooling system. Parametric design in Grasshopper was essential to establish a discrete number of unique formwork elements and subdivide the overall geometry by panel size. The digitally fabricated form-work encourages a specific curvature in the glass, introducing a degree of precision at folding locations. These moments of control allow the panels to align at their folds and join to make an assembly by splice-lamination. Selectively programming the geometry allows for a degree of material agency to remain in the system.

Catenary Channel Glass

Float glass will typically achieve a level of viscosity at 1200°F (650°C). At this point, it behaves like a fluid and shapes itself by "slumping" or draping over formwork where unsupported. The form achieved by draping can be described as a "viscous cate-nary," determined by a function of the material's thickness, the span between supports,

PRODUCTION NOTES

Architect: Gosia (Malgorzata)
Pawlowska

Status: Research prototype

Date: 2019

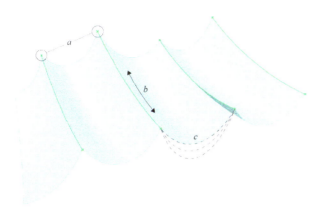

2   *Viscous Catenary* variables to form kiln-formed draped glass.

3   Early prototype of splice-laminated catenary channel glass

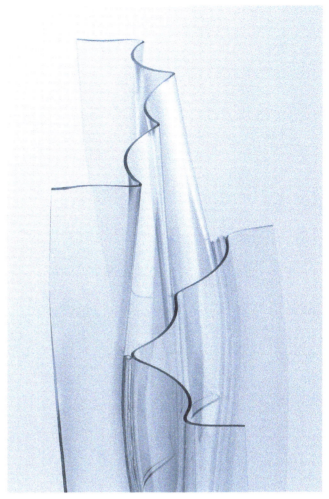

4   Final Prototype (photo by Sarah Lever, 2019 ©).

temperature, and time in the kiln. Leveraging the catenary geometry of slumped glass, this assembly joins two facing panels along the ridges or folds rather than attempting to laminate across an entire surface. Leveraging existing control points established during fabrication, the system can absorb some of the unpredictable aspects of the organic glass geometry

Digital-Analog Fabrication

The design of molds for slumping evolved into a repositionable tooling system. Its advantage is in that a limited number of steel parts can produce a nearly infinite amount of various components, cutting down on the time and resources required for fabrication.

Each panel has four guiding profiles, with 24 panels comprising the final installation (in three units of eight). Due to the optimization of the guiding curvature, only 32 unique steel profiles were necessary. The assembly is ruled by the specific curvature of the formwork. The desired overall shape is subdivided according to panel size (approx. 30 x

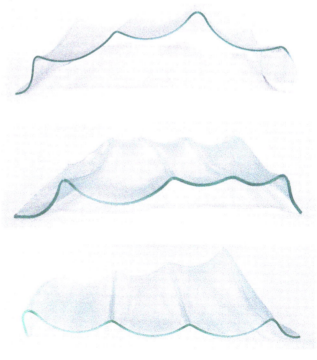

5   Profiles of individual glass panels

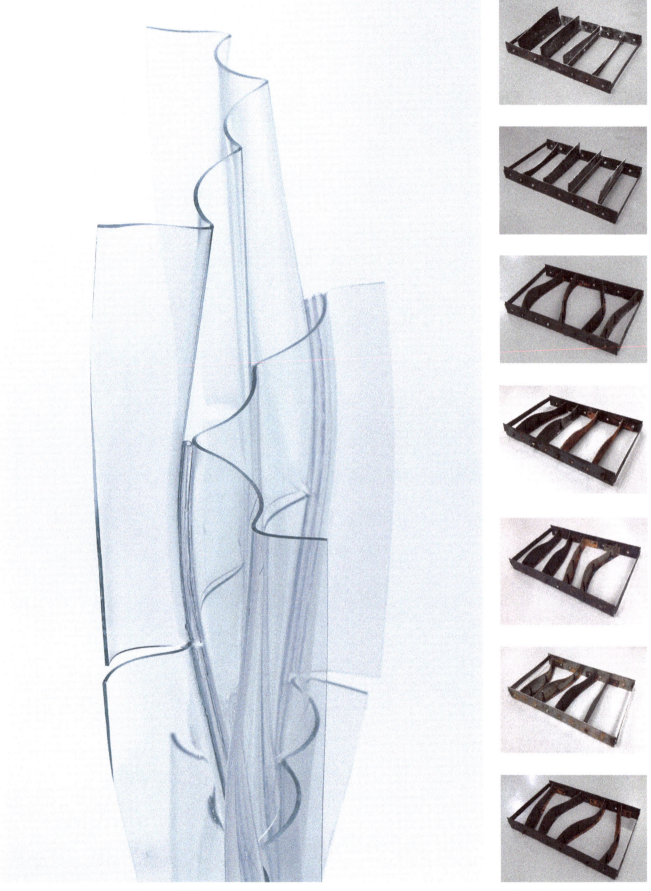

6   Final Prototype (photo by Sarah Lever, 2019 ©).

7   Repositionable tooling system

8 Waterjet cut steel formwork: repositionable tooling system

9 3D model showing assembly divided into panels for fabrication

10 Oxidized steel after firing in the kiln at high temperatures

11 3D scanning of kiln-formed glass panel

50 cm). Falling edges of the glass on either end of the panel act as a lateral support. With an offset between panels, the assembly can extend both horizontally and vertically. A pilot installation joined using transparent silicone adhesive achieved a height of 90 cm with overlapping 30 cm tall panels.

The project does not strive to achieve a complete digital simulation of slumped glass. Instead, it relies on intelligently programming certain known variables in the material's formation to arrive at the final composition. This approach of "material computation" strives to integrate complex material properties with a generative form-making process.

Laser 3D scanning between fabrication and assembly helped evaluate the fit between adjacent panels, identifying locations that required reinforcement. More research is needed to improve tolerances and overcome limitations in the adhesive before scaling up the fabrication system.

Programming degrees of freedom into the design and assembly approach, as well as applying computational power and new technologies available (particularly 3D scanning for measurement and feedback) are promising advances towards the acceptance of the often unpredictable freeform geometries in non-standard glass panels.

Conclusion
Viscous Catenary succeeds in questioning the formal and structural potential of matter-driven, multi-curved architectural glass assemblies.

ACKNOWLEDGMENTS
Academic advisors at the Bartlett School of Architecture, UCL: Chris Leung, Victor Huyghe, Tom Svilans.

12 **Conceptual drawing and** digital design in Grasshopper - excerpts

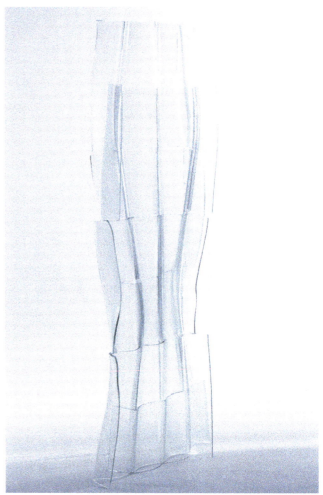

13 Final Prototype (photo by Sarah Lever, 2019 ©).

REFERENCES

Oxman, Neri. 2010. "Per Formative: Towards a Post Materialist Paradigm in Architecture," in *Perspecta #43, Special Issue: TABOO*: 19-30.

Rice, Peter, and Hugh Dutton. 1995. *Structural Glass*. English translation by Martine Erussard. London: Spoon Press.

Ritchie, Ian. 2004. "Aesthetics in Glass Structures." In *Structural Engineering International*, Vol.14 (2): 73-75.

McGee, Wes, Catie Newell, and Aaron Willette. 2012. "Glass Cast: A Reconfigurable Tooling System for Free-form Glass Manufacturing." In *Synthetic Digital Ecologies: Proceedings of the 32nd Annual Conference of the Association for Computer Aided Design in Architecture*, ed. Jason Kelly Johnson, Mark Cabrinha, and Kyle Steinfeld, 47-49. San Francisco: ACADIA.

IMAGE CREDITS

Figures 4, 6, 13-14: © Photographer Sarah Lever, 2019

All other drawings and images by the authors.

Gosia (Malgorzata) Pawlowska has pursued research with a focus on materials in architecture as a student at Cornell University in New York (2011-16) and The Bartlett School of Architecture in London (2018-19). She is currently practicing as an architectural designer while continuing to explore fabrication techniques, working with glass in particular- a material whose applications range from the precisely engineered to the whimsical.

14 Final Prototype (photo by Sarah Lever, 2019 ©).

Ashen Cabin

Leslie Lok
Cornell University/HANNAH

Sasa Zivkovic
Cornell University/HANNAH

1   The robotically sliced wood envelope meets the 3D printed concrete chimney at the northern corner. All bent surfaces made use of irregular timber geometries. (HANNAH, 2019).

Ashen Cabin is a small building 3D-printed from concrete and clothed in a robotically fabricated envelope made of irregular ash wood logs. From the ground up, digital design and fabrication technologies are intrinsic to the making of this architectural prototype, facilitating fundamentally new material methods, tectonic articulations, forms of construction, and architectural design languages.

Ashen Cabin challenges preconceived notions about material standards in wood. The cabin utilizes wood infested by the Emerald Ash Borer (EAB) for its envelope which, unfortunately, is widely considered as 'waste'. At present, the invasive EAB threatens to eradicate most of the 8.7 billion ash trees in North America (USDA 2019). Due to their challenging geometries, most infested ash trees cannot be processed by regular sawmills and are therefore regarded as unsuitable for construction. Infested and dying ash trees form an enormous and untapped material resource for sustainable wood construction. Ashen Cabin presents a pathway to address the massive environmental problem caused by the Emerald Ash Borer in North American forests. By implementing high precision 3D scanning and robotic fabrication, the project upcycles Emerald-Ash-Borer-infested "waste wood" into an available, affordable, and morbidly sustainable building material for the Anthropocene.

The project borrows strategies from traditional wood craft and manufacturing that utilizes irregular timber (Blondeau and Du Clairbois 1783) and aims to increase the yield of tree usage in construction. Currently, only around 35% of the wood of a tree is estimated to be

PRODUCTION NOTES

Designer: HANNAH
Status: Completed
Site Area: 100 sq. ft.
Location: Upstate New York
Date: 2019

2   KUKA KR200/2 with custom built 5hp bandsaw end-effector cutting a curved tree fork. (Andy Chen, 2019)

3   Detail of sliced curved boards. The bandsaw blade is less than 1 mm thick which ensures a tight-fit between the boards. (HANNAH, 2019).

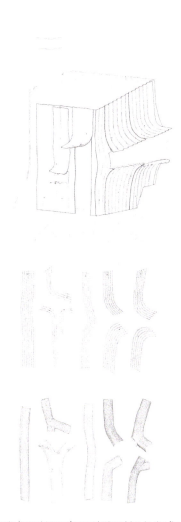

4   Diagram of log to board to surface relationships in the final design of the cabin envelope.

used in construction (Ramage, et al. 2017), mainly straight tree trunks and generally omitting curved timber altogether.

Using a KUKA KR200/2 with a custom 5hp band saw end effector, the team can saw irregular tree logs into naturally curved boards of various and varying thicknesses (down to 2 mm thin). To integrate the non-standardized material, the sliced boards are arrayed into interlocking SIP facade panels. By adjusting the thickness of the bandsaw cut, the robotically carved timber boards can be assembled as complex single curvature surfaces or double-curvature surfaces. The SIPs are insulated using a two component closed-cell foam for which a fully biodegradable option is available. The facade assembly is fully ventilated, detailed to manage shrinkage and transformation of wooden boards to offset the air drying process, and does not require an additional rain screen. The wood is left untreated to naturally grey over time. Geometric form-finding and assembly protocols from form-to-log and log-to-form have been developed for this project while high-precision 3D scanning is utilized for fabrication and timber stock inventory

selection. Ash wood is conducive to this type of fabrication process due to its relatively low moisture content (approximately 20%) compared to other types of green timber.

Architecturally, Ashen Cabin walks the line between familiar and unfamiliar, between technologically advanced and formally elemental. The project expands on research projects such as Wood Chip Barn (Mollica and Self 2016) at Hooke Park (Self 2016), industry applications developed by companies such as WholeTrees Structures (WholeTrees LLC 2019), and establishes a dialogue with projects such as Herb Greene's Prairie Chicken House (Greene 1976). The undulating wooden surfaces accentuate the building's program and yet remain reminiscent of the natural log geometry which they are derived from. The curvature of the wood is strategically deployed to highlight moments of architectural importance such as windows, entrances, roofs, canopies, or provide additional programmatic opportunities such as integrated shelving, desk space, or storage. While transformed, the natural tree remains legible in the design. Ashen Cabin is a fully functional but simple building

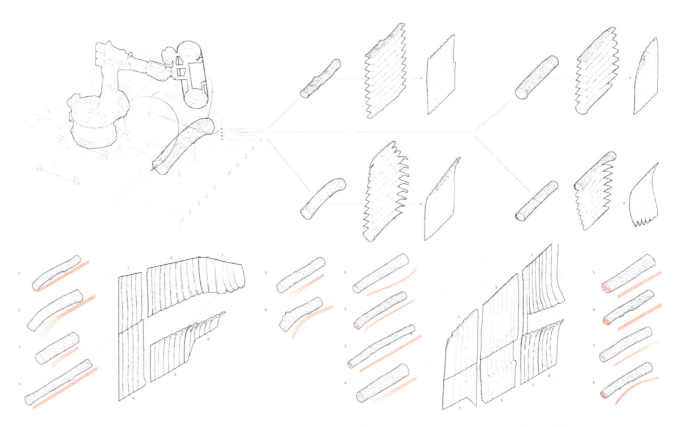

5   The robotically carved timber boards can be assembled into double-curvature surfaces by strategically adjusting the thickness of the bandsaw cut. Log geometries and resulting wall surfaces.

6   Detail of the corner window and undulating ash boards. (Andy Chen, 2019).

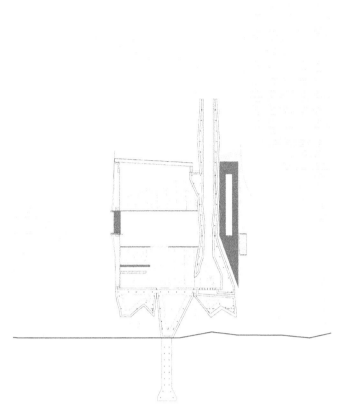

7   Section through 3D printed chimney.

8   Detail of the fully insulated and ventilated SIP envelope including window assembly, connection to concrete structure, and roof structure.

constructed from concrete and wood. Its architectural expression and function are profoundly derived from the digital design and fabrication technologies developed for this project.

ACKNOWLEDGMENTS

HANNAH project leadership: Leslie Lok and Sasa Zivkovic (Principals) / Project team concrete: Christopher Battaglia, Jeremy Bilotti, Elie Boutros, Reuben Chen, Justin Hazelwood, Mitchie Qiao / Assembly and documentation team concrete: Alexandre Mecattaf, Ethan Davis, Russell Southard, Dax Simitch Warke, Ramses Gonzales, Wangda Zhu / Project team wood fabrication and design: Byungchan Ahn, Alexander Terry / Wood studies: Xiaoxue Ma, Alexandre Mecattaf / Assembly and documentation team wood: Freddo Daneshvaran, Ramses Gonzalez, Jiaying Wei, Jiayi Xing, Xiaohang Yan, Jingxin Yang, Sarah Elizabeth Bujnowski, Eleanor Jane Krause, Todd Petrie, Isabel Lucia Branas Jarque, Xiaoxue Ma / Visual Representation: Byungchan Ahn, Kun Bi, Brian Havener, Lingzhe Lu. Project realized with scientific support from the Cornell Robotic Construction Laboratory (RCL) / Sponsors: AAP College of Architecture, Art, and Planning; AAP Department of Architecture; Cornell Atkinson Center for a Sustainable Future, Cornell Arnot Teaching and Research Forest. Special thanks to: Andrea Simitch and Val Warke.

REFERENCES

Blondeau, E-N., and Vial Du Clairbois, H-S. 1783. *Encyclopédie méthodique: Marine*. Paris: Chez Panckoucke.

Greene, Herb, and H. Greene. 1976. *Mind & Image: an Essay on Art & Architecture*. Lexington, KY: University Press of Kentucky.

Mollica, Z., and M. Self. 2016. "Tree Fork Truss'" in *Advances in Architectural Geometry 2016*, ed. S. Adriaenssens, F. Gramazio, M. Kohler, A. Menges, and M. Pauly. 138-153. Zürich: Hochschulverlag,

Ramage, M. H., H. Burridge, M. Busse-Wicher, G. Fereday, T. Reynolds, D.U. Shah, G. Wu, G, L. Yu, P. Fleming, D. Densley-Tingley, J. Allwood, P. Dupree, P.F. Linden, O. and Scherman. 2017. "The Wood From the Trees: The use of Timber in Construction". *Renewable and Sustainable Energy Reviews*, 68 (Part 1): 333-359.

Self, M. 2016. "Hooke Park: application for timber in its Natural Form", in *Advancing Wood Architecture: A Computational Approach* ed A. Menges, T. Schwinn, and O. D. Krieg. London: Routledge.

9   View of southeast corner of the cabin within the site context. Surfaces transform from planar to curved conditions to strategically highlight moments of programmatic importance such as views, entrances, awnings, and roof drainage. (Andy Chen, 2019).

10   View of northeast corner showing the peeling of wood surfaces to reveal an articulated roof scupper and pronounced corner windows.. (Andy Chen, 2019).

          Ashen Cabin Lok, Zivkovic

11 Detail of wooden door surface, window frame, and 3D printed concrete structure. (Andy Chen, 2019).

12 View of northeast corner showing the peeling of wood surfaces to reveal an articulated roof scupper and pronounced corner windows.

USDA Forest Service and Michigan State University, *Emerald Ash Borer Information Network*, http://www.emeraldashborer.info. Accessed 6 October 2019.

WholeTrees. Research and Development, *WholeTrees*, https://wholetrees.com/technology/. Accessed 18 June 2019]

IMAGE CREDITS

Figure 1,3: © HANNAH, 2019

Figures 2, 6, 9-12: © Andy Chen, 2019

All other drawings and images by the authors.

Leslie Lok is a co-principal at HANNAH, an experimental design practice based in Ithaca, NY. HANNAH was recently awarded the 2020 Architectural League Prize and was named Next Progressives by Architect Magazine in 2018. Lok is also an Assistant Professor at Cornell University Department of Architecture. Her teaching and research explore the intersection of housing, urbanization, and mass-customized construction methods. Her work brings together

material specificity, construction protocols, and housing design to address broader sets of architectural, urban, and cultural narratives.

Sasa Zivkovic is a co-principal at HANNAH, an experimental design practice based in Ithaca, New York. HANNAH was recently awarded the 2020 Architectural League Prize and was named Next Progressives by Architect Magazine in 2018. Zivkovic is also an Assistant Professor at Cornell University AAP where he directs the Robotic Construction Laboratory (RCL), an interdisciplinary research group that develops and implements novel robotic construction technology. Interdisciplinary in nature, the work integrates cutting-edge materials, advanced fabrication, mechanical design, architectural computation, structural optimization, and sustainable construction. Zivkovic received his Master of Architecture degree at Massachusetts Institute of Technology.

Realtime Architecture Platform Collab Wood

Alexander Grasser
Institute of Architecture and
Media, TU Graz

Alexandra Parger
Institute of Architecture and
Media, TU Graz

Urs Hirschberg
Institute of Architecture and
Media, TU Graz

1   Realtime Architecture Platform. Personalized clusters of parts to collaborative whole

Realtime Architecture Platform

This project proposes a realtime architecture platform. It's based on previous research on collaborative architecture (Grasser 2019) as well as research on combinatorial design (Sanchez 2016), digital architecture (Carpo 2013), and discrete mereologies (Koehler 2019).

The platform was applied in a design studio at the Institute of Architecture and Media at Graz University of Technology with 20 Masters students. Due to restrictions of the global pandemic, we worked in a distributed mode of telepresent teaching. The implementation of this new working method further accelerated the focus on digital collaboration in architecture. Using the platform to collaborate in real time, the Collab Wood prototype was designed and realized.

The importance of real-time shared events can be seen by the current increase of live social media applications, digital meeting and conferencing tools, and massively multiplayer online games hosting events. Their collective goal is to unite a high number of users that are geographically distributed but temporarily available to create a global common ground. As a consequence of these interactions and accessible digital instruments, the meaning of presence is evolving. At its core, architectural practice and academia rely on interaction and feedback in close proximity. This workflow has to shift towards distributed digital design and realtime collaboration.

2   Realtime Architecture Platform. Multiple screenshots of a collaborative design session in Unity

The "Realtime Architecture Platform," developed by the authors, enables an innovative workflow to collaborate and design in unity. A custom application, developed in the game engine Unity, provides an online persistent environment for shared architectural design (Figures 1, 2). Furthermore, it provides a flexible framework to streamline data via Grasshopper to Rhinoceros.

Collaborative Objects

The work method is based on the concept of collaborative objects and distributed designers. These collaborative objects are the shared content, discrete parts, prefabs, or blocks that enable interaction, communication, and collaboration with and between users and owners. The distributed designers can contribute to a shared architectural project by instantiating these collaborative objects. By placing an object, the users react in real time to the local neighboring conditions and therefore add their embodied design decision to the global architecture. The users experience this common creative flow by communicating through the integrated chat or digital calls, discussing strategies,

debating on design intentions, analyzing the built structure, and scanning for improvements. This pervasive collaboration lays the foundation for a democratization of the design process (Grasser, Parger, Hirschberg 2020).

Collab Wood

As a proof of concept, the platform was applied with 20 students in a telepresence design studio. The participants embraced the real-time workflow and worked with the collaborative tool throughout the semester from different locations and time zones to develop architectural projects in small groups as well as to design and build a collective project: the Collab Wood prototype. In the platform, each student was represented by a color to identify their placed objects as the structure consisted of discrete parts. The students could contribute to this shared architectural project either by placing just one part or by sharing clusters of parts that follow individual design intentions and combinatorial rules (Figure 3). First, in small groups, participants collaboratively experimented and elaborated real-time design strategies, defining global design

3 Personalized clusters of discrete parts

intentions, and playing with local constraints. Then all 20 students met in scheduled real-time design sessions in the platform to design together. These design sessions aimed to create structures such as columns and roofs (Figures 4, 5). Digital design behavior and communication between the participants improved with every session in distributed proximity.

The final design, Collab Wood, was built as a 1:1 prototype using local and accessible material. Respecting social distancing, we scheduled individual time slots to build the wood structure outdoors, student by student (Figures 3, 7, 8). The assembly was supported by Augmented Reality (AR) applications. Here our developed platform enabled real-time AR on mobile devices, using Unity's AR Foundation and Fologram with a HoloLens headset. AR helped to identify the student's clusters and provided a holographic construction manual. To further differentiate the wooden parts, the student's name, as well as an individual polyline pattern, were engraved on the parts.

This added layer of information allowed an ambiguous reading of personalized clusters of parts to the collaborative whole of the Collab Wood prototype (Figure 6).

The global pandemic accelerated the importance of collaboration. Our response, providing an accessible common platform for realtime interaction, design, and collaboration, can be regarded as the first step in how we might work together in the future.

ACKNOWLEDGMENTS

The design studio Collaborative Matter(s) was led by Alexander Grasser, Urs Hischberg, and Alexandra Parger at the Institute of Architecture and Media at TU Graz. With the support of our student tutors: Eszter Katona, Kilian Hoffmann, Nora Hoti. With a great group of students: Alina Boss, Angelika Bernhart, Anton Kussinna, Constanze Feitzlmayr, Daniel Buchacher, Donia Elmenshawi, Felix Zitter, Francesco Doninelli, Franciska Kozul, Janine Witzany, Julie Belpois, Kenan Isakovic, Kerstin Grangl, Kilian Hoffmann, Maria Matthäus, Max Frühwirt, Sebastian Meisinger, Ronald Tang Pak To, Tilen Sagrkovic. March- June 2020.

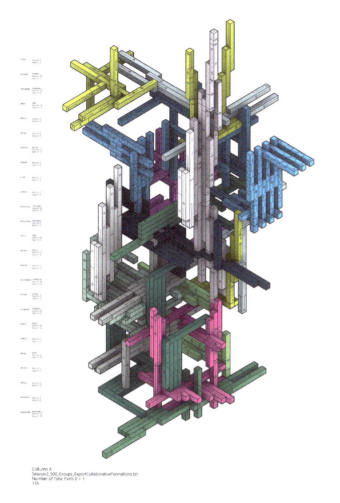

Column A
Session2_500_Groups_ExportCollaborativeFormations.txt
Number of Total Parts 0 + 1:
316

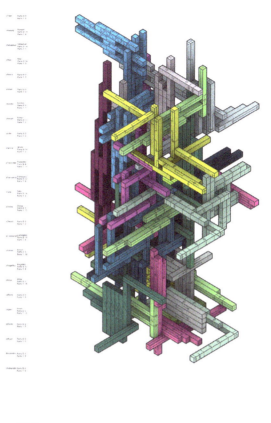

Column B
Session3_400_All_ExportCollaborativeFormations.txt
Number of Total Parts 0 + 1:
296

4   Realtime session 2: collaborative column

5   Realtime session 3: collaborative column

We thank our guest critics for their time and valuable input: Ryan Vincent Manning, Manuel Jiménez Gracia, Daniel Köhler, and Jörg Stanzel. And finally, thanks to our collaborators and partners: Fifteen Seconds, Exit Games, Pro Holz and Felber Holz.

REFERENCES

Carpo, Mario. 2013. *The Digital Turn in Architecture*. Chichester: Wiley

Claypool, Mollie, Gilles Retsin, Manuel Jimenez-Garcia, and Vicente Soler, eds. 2019. Robotic Building: Architecture in the Age of Automation. Munich: Detail Verlag.

Grasser, Alexander. 2019. "Towards an Architecture of Collaborative Objects." In *Architecture in the Age of the 4th Industrial Revolution: Proceedings of the 37th eCAADe and 23rd SIGraDi Conference - Volume 1*, edited by J. Sousa, J. Xavier, and G. Castro Henriques, 325-332.

Grasser, Alexander, Parger, Alexandra and Urs Hirschberg. 2020. "Pervasive Collaboration and Tangible Complexity in Realtime Architecture." In *Anthropologic: Architecture and Fabrication in*

the cognitive age: Proceedings of the 38th eCAADe Conference - Volume 1, edited by L. Werner and D. Koering, 393-400.

Jahn, Gwyllim, Cameron Newnham, Nick Van Den Berg, and Matthew Beanland. 2018. "Making in Mixed Reality." In *ACADIA 2018 Recalibration: On Imprecision and Infidelity: Proceedings of the 38th Annual Conference of the Association for Computer Aided Design in Architecture*, ed. by P. Anzaline, M. del Signore and A.J. W, 88-97. Mexico City: ACADIA.

Koehler, Daniel. 2019. "Mereological Thinking: Figuring Realities within Urban Form." *Architectural Design* 89: 30-37.

Sanchez, Jose. 2018. "Platforms for Architecture: Imperatives and Opportunities of Designing Online Networks for Design" In *ACADIA 2018 Recalibration: On Imprecision and Infidelity: Proceedings of the 38th Annual Conference of the Association for Computer Aided Design in Architecture*, ed. by P. Anzaline, M. del Signore and A.J. W 108-117.

Sanchez, Jose. 2016. "Combinatorial design: Non-parametric Computational Design Strategies." In *ACADIA 2016: Posthuman Frontiers: Data, Designers, and Cognitive Machines; Proceedings of*

6   Collab Wood

7   Collab Wood, column a

8   Collab Wood, column b

the 36th Annual Conference of the Association for Computer Aided Design in Architecture, ed. K. Velikov, S. Ahlquist, M. del Campo, G. Thun, 1-13. Ann Arbor: ACADIA.

IMAGE CREDITS

All drawings and images by the authors.

Alexander Grasser is an architect and researcher based in Graz and Vienna. He is teaching at the Institute of Architecture and Media at TU Graz. His research is focusing on collaborative objects, realtime architecture and platform applications in architecture. Alexander studied architecture at TU Vienna and Innsbruck University and gained professional experience working in offices in Vienna, Berlin and Shanghai, with ongoing collaborations with architectural practices in Texas, Berlin and Vienna. His works were widely published and exhibited internationally.

Alexandra Parger is an architect currently working in Berlin. Born in Vienna, she is fluent in several languages and is increasingly committed to social and ecological issues. During her studies of Architecture at TU Vienna, she founded her jewelry Label NANAdesign. Specializing in 3D printing, she landed collaborations with the fashion industry and other customized merchandising projects. In 2019 she started teaching at TU Graz focusing on tools and design thinking methods applying a wide range of media and technologies, such as AR. Alexandra combines cross-creating design processes in multi-disciplinary settings.

Urs Hirschberg is Professor for the Representation of Architecture and New Media at Graz University of Technology and Head of the Institute of Architecture and Media (IAM). Born and raised in Switzerland, he gained his Architecture Diploma and Doctorate from ETH Zurich. Before TU Graz he served as the Chair of Architecture and CAAD at ETH Zurich and at the Harvard Graduate School of Design. He is a founding editor of GAM, the Graz Architecture Magazine and Director of the TU Graz Field of Expertise Sustainable Systems.

Pulse v2

Nick Puckett
OCAD University
Puckett Research & Design

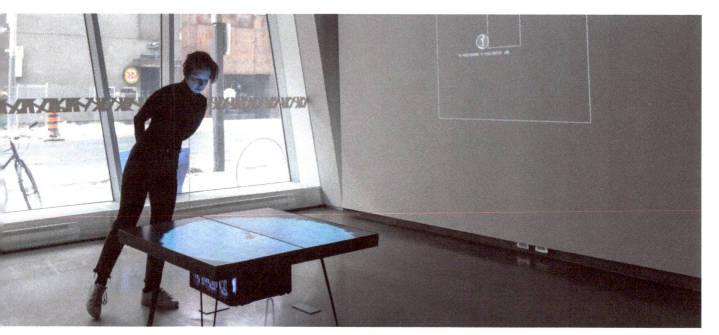

1   Real-time Response based on location of all people visible in the room (Yuula Benivolsk, 2020)

Overview

Pulse v2 is an interactive installation designed to investigate how real-time lidar data can be used to develop new spatial relationships between people and an autonomous digital agent through dynamic visual expressions.

The first iteration of this research, Pulse v1, used a single point lidar with a 160 degree field of view in conjunction with 240 servo-actuated antennas that visualized the position and movement of visitors via their vibrations. This second iteration blends digital and physical materiality to create a synthetic organism that fully integrates sensing, computation, and response into its form. Simultaneously, the raw data feed it "sees" is projected onto the wall in real time, allowing visitors to experience both the response and the logic.

The data feed is supplied by a 360 degree field of view, 2D lidar scanner. This type of scanner is typically used by small autonomous robots to map and navigate their environments. However, in this installation, the relationship is inverted to allow a stationary agent to respond to a dynamically changing environment. The sensor is mounted under the displays and provides a real-time slice of the space at the height of 20cm. An algorithm filters this data stream into trackable blobs by recognizing people via their ankles. The agent analyzes this stream of data and filters it through a series of micro and macro expressions that play out on the screen in the form of a digital microorganism.

PRODUCTION NOTES

Architect: Nick Puckett
Software: Java / GLSL
Sensor: RP Lidar A1M8
Location: Toronto, Canada
Date: 2020

2 Positions of people are determined via lidar mounted under the screen
(Yuula Benivolsk, 2020)

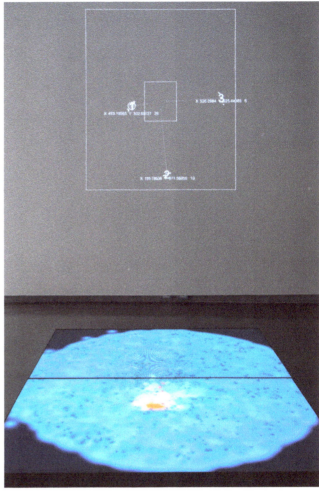

3 The 2D pointcloud generated via Lidar is filtered to trackable blobs.

4 Organism response and raw machine vision are shown simultaneously.
(Yuula Benivolsk, 2020)

System Input

The core input of this system comes via a 2D lidar, which
provides approximately 400 unique points at a rate of 5 Hz.
These points run through a multilayered filtering process
that ultimately converts them into trackable blobs that
represent individual people in the room as 2D coordinates.
When the system initially calibrates, it captures 12,000
points that are tagged as "background."

These points can represent the overall bounds of the room
or other fixed objects within the laser's line of site. With
each revolution of the sensor, a new set of XY coordinates
are sent and are first measured against the existing list
of background points. Only points that are a significant
distance from stored points are filtered into the active
tracking list. Once this list is established, a second filter
iterates over this list, measuring the distance and angle
between sequential points. This algorithm was optimized
based on the height of the lidar from the floor, which is
trained to understand ankles. This ultimately creates the
final list of points by grouping like points together and

calculating their centroid. These XY coordinates provide the
locations of multiple people in real time. These blob positions are projected onto to the wall as they are calculated.

Though conceptually similar to background removal and
tracking in computer vision systems, the spatial data
provided from the lidar can be filtered and grouped using
simple trigonometry. Lidar is a line-of-site technology, so
people obstructed by others may not be accurately tracked.
Current research is working to address this issue by
having multiple lidars in the space that can capture the
point cloud from multiple locations.

System Response

Though the organism appears as a singular object, it is
composed of 10-20,000 individual agents that are driven
by a 2D physics engine and displayed via a GLSL shader.
The overall behavior has multiple, layered methods that
create both instant feedback for people in the room and
longer moves that evolve over time: immediate responses,
creeping, and cyclical. Immediate responses consist of

5   The size of the individual subcells increases based on the current population of the room

visitor investigating behavior and growing or shrinking
based on population changes. Creeping behavior causes
the system to gradually slide towards the average position
of all visitors. Cyclical behavior triggers system regeneration with a different number of particles with different mass
based on amount of previous interaction that day.

ACKNOWLEDGMENTS

This work was exhibited in January 2020 as part of the CodeX exhibition at OnSite Gallery in Toronto.

The software is written in Java using the Processing framework
and utilizes the PixelFlow and oscP5 libraries under public license.

REFERENCES

Diewald, Thomas. PixelFlow. V.1.3.0. 2018

Fry, Ben and Casey Reas. Processing. V. 3.5.2. Processing
Foundation. 2020

Schlegel, Andreas. oscP5. V.09.8. 2011

IMAGE CREDITS

Figures 1, 2, 4 : Courtesy of Onsite Gallery, OCAD University. Yuula
Benivolsk

All other drawings and images by the author.

Nick Puckett is the founding director of Puckett Research & Design,
a design practice that explores near-future speculative design
for the built environment through the creation of new tools and
technologies that radically alter the process and product of design.
This collaborative research spans software, robotics, biological
agents, chemical engineering, and material behaviour to generate
new potentials for the design of intelligent environments. Before
founding Puckett RanD, he worked as an architect and software
developer at Zaha Hadid architects. Nick is currently an Associate
Professor, Co-Director of the ANThill Lab, and Chair of the Digital
Futures undergraduate program at OCAD University.

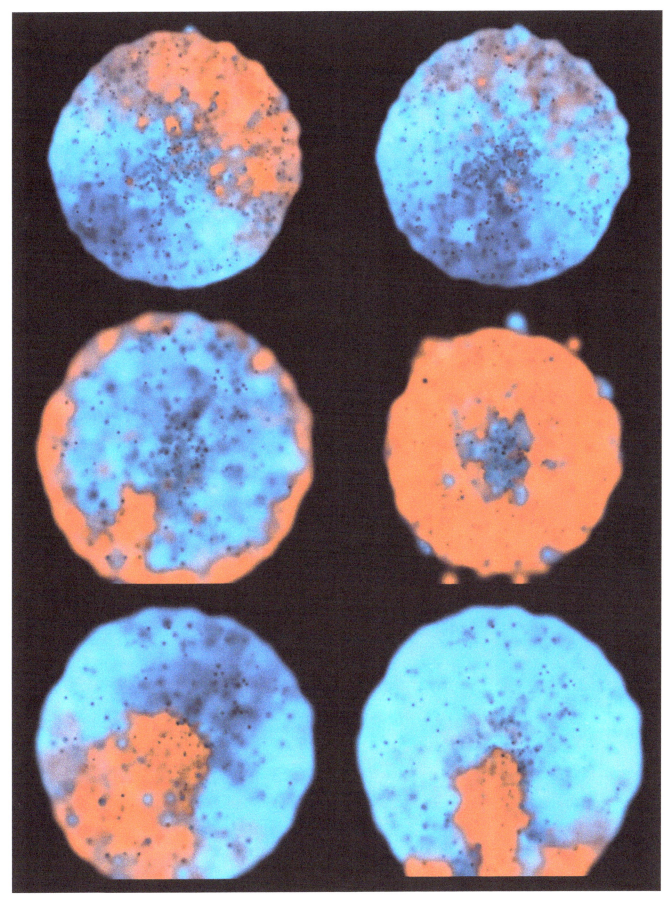

6   The organism is composed of approx. 20,000 subcells whose behaviour are driven via custom software and a GLSL shader

MELTING 2.0

Water Soluble Formwork for Reinforced Concrete

Shelby Elizabeth Doyle
Iowa State University

Erin Linsey Hunt
Harvard Graduate School of
Design

1   Water soluble formwork after four months of weather exposure, October 2020.

This project presents computational design and fabrication methods for locating standard steel reinforcement within 3D printed water-soluble polyvinyl alcohol (PVA) molds to create non-standard concrete columns. Previous methods from "Melting: Augmenting Concrete Columns with Water Soluble 3D Printed Formwork" and "Dissolvable 3D Printed Formwork: Exploring Additive Manufacturing for Reinforced Concrete" (Doyle & Hunt 2019) were adapted for larger scale construction, including the introduction of new hardware, development of custom programming strategies, and updated digital fabrication techniques. Initial research plans included 3D printing continuous molds with a KUKA-1100 industrial robotic arm. However, Covid-19 university campus closures led to fabrication shifting to the author's home and instead relied upon a LulzBot TAZ 6 (build volume of 280 x 280 x 250 mm) with a HS+ tool head (1.2 mm nozzle diameter).

Two methods were developed for this project phase. New 3D printing hardware and custom G-code production were tested on the fabrication of three non-standard columns designed around the location of five standard #3 reinforcement bars (3/8" diameter): Woven, Twisted and Aperture. Each test column is eight inches in diameter (the same size as a standard Sonotube concrete form) and 4 ft tall, approximately half the height of an architecturally scaled 8 ft tall column. Each column's form was generated from combining the constraints of standard reinforcement placement with minimum necessary concrete coverage. The first two molds were printed, assembled, cast, and then submerged in water to dissolve the molds away from the concrete cast. This mold-dissolving process limits

2   Aperture Column immediately after casting, June 2020

3   Aperture Column after four months of weather exposure, October 2020.

the applicable scale for the work as it transitions from the research lab to a construction site. Therefore, the final column cast was placed outside with its formwork intact to explore if weather exposure alone can dissolve the mold, in lieu of submersion (Figures 1-3).

Digital Concrete Construction

Architectural and engineering research goals in digital concrete constructions are varied across scales and design intents. These range from the design of parametric formwork (Howe 2013), to flexible formwork (Peters 2014), to structural optimization (Søndergaard 2012), and full-scale concrete printing (Zeeshan 2016). Recent research in digital construction has focused on eliminating or reducing the use of formwork through fused deposition modeling (FDM) of concrete (Leach et. al. 2012). The incorporation of tensile reinforcement to concrete additive manufacturing continues to present design and construction challenges. Strategies for rebar placement in digital construction are identified in "Incorporating reinforcement into digital concrete construction," and additional background can be

found in that article (Nerella, Ogura, & Mechtcherine 2018).

Woven Column

This column design advances the research presented in "Dissolvable 3D Printed Formwork: Exploring Additive Manufacturing for Reinforced Concrete" (Doyle & Hunt 2019) using a new and larger nozzle for desktop scale fabrication. The HS+ tool head (1.2 mm nozzle diameter) reduced printing times, and this design explored how geometry can be used to mask the location of the standard reinforcement through the appearance of woven "strands" of concrete. Additionally, this design removes any interior concrete that is not necessary to provide minimum rebar coverage, resulting in reduced material use as well as the potential for unique apertures and light qualities (Figure 4).

Twisted Column

This mold was intended to be robotically 3D printed to create a continuous mold. Unfortunately, restrictions resulting from Covid-19 prevented lab access. Prior to the pandemic, a custom method using Grasshopper for

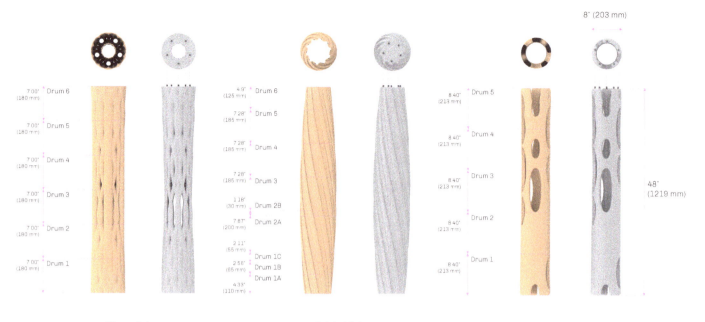

| Woven Column | Twisted Column | Aperture Column |

8" (203 mm)

Woven Column
7.00" (180 mm) Drum 6
7.00" (180 mm) Drum 5
7.00" (180 mm) Drum 4
7.00" (180 mm) Drum 3
7.00" (180 mm) Drum 2
7.00" (180 mm) Drum 1

Twisted Column
4.9" (125 mm) Drum 6
7.28" (185 mm) Drum 5
7.28" (185 mm) Drum 4
7.28" (185 mm) Drum 3
1.18" (30 mm) Drum 2B
7.87" (200 mm) Drum 2A
2.11" (55 mm) Drum 1C
2.56" (65 mm) Drum 1B
Drum 1A
4.33" (110 mm)

Aperture Column
8.40" (213 mm) Drum 5
8.40" (213 mm) Drum 4
8.40" (213 mm) Drum 3
8.40" (213 mm) Drum 2
8.40" (213 mm) Drum 1

48" (1219 mm)

4   The top diagram indicates how the mold was segmented for desktop fabrication on the Lulzbot Taz 6. Each drum indicates a single print. The bottom image shows the three columns after casting: Woven, Twisted, and Aperture. The Aperture column at right is still contained in the PVA formwork, July 2020.

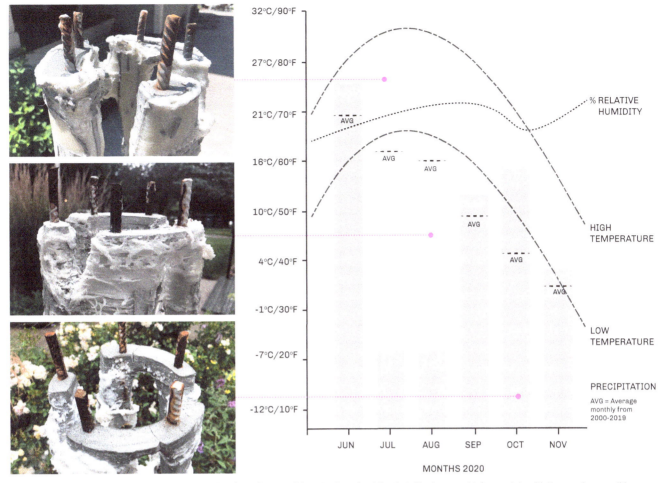

5   The Aperture Column was exposed to six months of weather conditions (at time of publication). The images at left correlate with the weather conditions from June–December 2020: high and low temperature, relative humidity, and precipitation. A drought in July and August was followed by above average precipitation in September–November.

Aperture column

This column design used the Cocoon plug-in for Grasshopper (Stasiuk 2015) to test the placement of apertures in locations where no reinforcement was present. The meshed results were then refined to create an illusion of softness. This design allowed for less concrete use than the Woven Column as well as unique openings which may be useful in future assembly strategies (Figures 2, 4, and 5).

Dissolution

Earlier fabrication studies were submerged in warm water to facilitate dissolution of the PVA. As the column designs increased in size, an inflatable pool was used to dissolve the water-soluble formwork (Figure 9). Due to remote fabrication during Covid-19, it was possible to leave the Aperture Column outdoors for six months to explore whether dissolution was possible through only weather exposure. There was a significant drought in July and August, slowing the formwork's decomposition. Above average precipitation in September and October led to significant dissolution (Figures 5, 8, and 9). PVA is classified as not hazardous

McNeel Rhinoceros was developed to allow for a variable number of shells to be created from a single contoured surface generating a single curve for the tool path. Since this was the first time the authors would be using a robotic workflow for 3D printing, the goal was to avoid retraction. This custom Grasshopper definition allowed both the input robotic tool path and the G-code given to the HS+ tool head to be identical. An author was able to bring a LulzBot TAZ 6 with a HS+ tool head home during quarantine which acted as a stand-in for future robotic fabrication. Each column mold section was printed with two shells which successfully replicated the designed column, while the custom G-code produced a continuous curve suitable for robotic 3D printing. As a result, a third column design was explored at the desktop scale to further the possibility of placing apertures within column designs. Since the quarantine left desktop 3D printing as the only fabrication option, a design which required retraction as a result of its apertures was explored (Figures 4, 6, and 7).

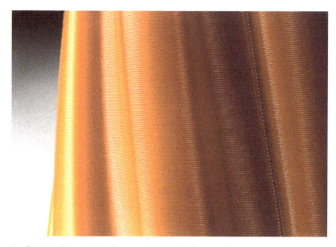

6   Twisted Column PVA formwork detail, before casting.

7   Twisted Column after casting and PVA formwork dissolved. The seam, shown at right, was a design decision to create evidence of the fabrication method from the printer moving up in the Z-axis after each pass.

8   Despite full submersion in warm water, the remnants of the Woven Column formwork remained on the cast as a film, or skin, and continued to dissolve through weather exposure. Future iterations will continue to explore alternative dissolution methods.

by the 2012 OSHA Hazard Communication Standard (PVA MSDS, 2020). However, the environmental impacts of transitioning from lab to site require further evaluation.

Conclusion

The experiments in this project demonstrate the potential of non-standard fabrication of concrete using standard reinforcement. The three augmented concrete casts apply existing concrete fabrication knowledge to develop intelligent computational design strategies and digital fabrication workflows. Once access to the industrial robotic arms is restored, it is planned to design and cast full scale (8 ft columns) which integrate a second body of research from "Melting: Augmenting Concrete Columns with Water Soluble 3D Printed Formwork" and "Dissolvable 3D Printed Formwork: Exploring Additive Manufacturing for Reinforced Concrete" (Doyle & Hunt 2019). The next iteration of this research will explore the potential of robotically printed non-standard molds with robotically placed standard reinforcement.

REFERENCES

Doyle, Shelby, Hunt, Erin. 2019. "Melting: Augmenting Concrete Columns with Water Soluble 3D Printed Formwork." In *ACADIA 2019: Ubiquity and Autonomy: Proceedings of the 39th Annual Conference of the Association for Computer Aided Design in Architecture*, edited by Kory Bieg, Clay Odom, 92-97. Austin, Texas, USA: ACADIA

Doyle, Shelby, Hunt, Erin. 2019. "Dissolvable 3D Printed Formwork: Exploring Additive Manufacturing for Reinforced Concrete." In *ACADIA 2019: Ubiquity and Autonomy: Proceedings of the 39th Annual Conference of the Association for Computer Aided Design in Architecture*, edited by Kory Bieg, Clay Odom, 178-188. Austin, Texas, USA: ACADIA.

Feringa, J., and A. Søndergaard. 2012. "An Integral Approach to Structural Optimization and Fabrication." In *ACADIA 2012: Synthetic Digital Ecologies; Proceedings of the 32nd Annual Conference of the Association for Computer Aided Design in Architecture*, ed J.K. Johnson, M. Cabrinha, K. Steinfeld, 491-497. San Francisco: ACADIA.

Hack, Wangler, Mata-Falcón, Dörfler, Kumar, Walzer, Kohler. 2017. "Mesh Mould: an onsite, robotically fabricated, functional formwork." In *11th High Performance Concrete and Concrete Innovation Conference*, author Hammer Tor Arne, Tromsø, Norway: HPC

Howe, N. 2013. "FluidScape: Research in Parametric Concrete Formwork." In *Proceedings of the 17th Conference of the Iberoamerican Society of Digital Graphics*, 405-409. Chile, Valparaíso: SIGraDi.

Leach, N., A. Carlson, B. Khoshnevis, and M. Thangavelu. 2012. "Robotic Construction by Contour Crafting:The Case of Lunar Construction." *International Journal of Architectural Computing* 10(3), 423-438.

Leschok, Matthia, Dillenburger, Benjamin. 2019. "Dissolvable 3DP Formwork." In *ACADIA 2019: Ubiquity and Autonomy: Proceedings of the 39th Annual Conference of the Association for Computer Aided Design in Architecture*, edited by Kory Bieg, Clay Odom, 188-197. Austin, Texas, USA: ACADIA

MSDS PVA. 2014. "Material Safety Data Sheet - PVA filament."Lulzbot MSDS Sheet, Shenzhen Esun Industrial Co. Polyvinyl Alcohol Filament. Accessed November 27, 2020. https://www.lulzbot. com/sites/default/files/msds_esun_pva.pdf.

Naidu Nerella, Venkatesh, Ogura, Hiroki, Mechtcherine, Viktor. 2018. "Incorporating Reinforcement into Digital Concrete Construction." In *Creativity in Structural Design: Proceedings of the International Association for Shell and Spatial Structures Symposium*, edited by Caitlin Mueller, Sigrid Adriaenssens, Boston, Massachusetts, USA: IASS

Peters, B. 2014. "Additive Formwork: 3D Printed Flexible Formwork." In *ACADIA 2014: Design Agency; Proceedings of the 34th Annual Conference of the Association for Computer Aided Design in Architecture*, ed. D.J Gerber, A. Huang, J. Sanchez., 517-522. Los Angeles: ACADIA.

Stasiuk, David. Cocoon. 2015. https://www.bespokegeometry. com/2015/07/22/cocoon/

Weather Underground. 2020. https://www.wunderground.com/history/monthly/us/ia/des-moines

Zeeshan, Ahmed, Freek, Bos, Wolfs, Rob, Salet, Theo. 2016. "Design Considerations Due to Scale Effects in 3D Concrete Printing." In *Proceedings of 8th International Conference of the Arab Society for Computer Aided Architectural Design*, ed. A. Al-Attili, A. Karandinou, B. Daley, 115-124. London, United Kingdom: ASCAAD.

ACKNOWLEDGMENTS

This work was supported by a 2019 Autodesk ACADIA Emerging Research Award.

IMAGE CREDITS

All drawings and images by the authors.

9   The Twisted Column cast and printed formwork was submerged in an inflatable pool of warm water for 24 hours to allow for dissolution of the PVA formwork.

Shelby Elizabeth Doyle, AIA is an assistant professor of architecture at the Iowa State University College of Design, co-founder of the ISU Computation & Construction Lab (CCL) and director of the ISU Architectural Robotics Lab (ARL). Doyle received a Fulbright Fellowship to Cambodia, a Master of Architecture from the Harvard Graduate School of Design, and a Bachelor of Science in architecture from the University of Virginia.

Erin Linsey Hunt is Master in Design Studies in Technology candidate at the Harvard Graduate School of Design. She is a computational designer whose research interests include applications for additive manufacturing technology. She holds a Bachelor of Architecture degree from Iowa State University.

Live L'oeil – Through the Looking Ceiling

Jonathan A. Scelsa
Pratt Institute

Jennifer Birkeland
Cornell University

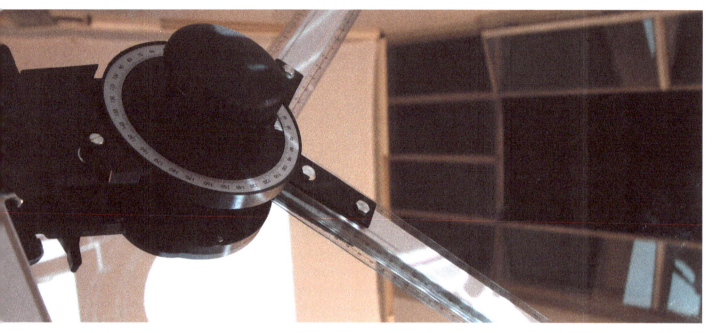

1   The mirror is central to the image spectacle of the architectural illusion of Sant'Ignazio, as in the space of the nave, the mirror is being used by spectators to gaze upwards, herein the projector reverses the process (op.AL, 2018).

Following the proliferation of linear perspective during the Renaissance, the hegemony of the vantage point was often problematically used to signify the patron's dominance. During the mannerist era, we witnessed the creation of elaborate rooms, painted in architectural linear perspective establishing the illusionary space of faraway lands—a measure of optic imperialism wherein the conquests of the west played out in the domestic decoration of the elite later provided to the public as a societal spectacle in the form of the panorama. Within these architectural illusions, or *quadratura* as they were named in Italy, lies the most notable and justifiable critique of design by vantage point, the question "which vantage point is privileged?"

Not surprisingly, history reveals that the typical vantage point was most problematically centered at one and three-quarter meters above the ground—coincident with five centimeters below the average height of a human European male. Design of architectural form through view or spatial image has arguably perpetuated this act of optic bias.

This project addresses this problematic practice of design by vantage point by utilizing motion sensors to liberate the virtual space of a canonic example of *quadratura* from its confines within a singular vantage point.

PRODUCTION NOTES

Architect: op. Architecture Landscape

Client: The American Academy in Rome

Location: Rome, Italy

Date: 2018

2 The image of the linework of the virtual geometry through anamorphic projection distorts to the localized vantage points of the viewer based on their sensed position (op.AL, 2018).

The authors digitally modeled the projective space of Andrea Pozzo's vision for the Church of Sant'Ignazio di Loyola in Rome, scaled and fit to a gallery space outfitted with a canvas to inform a ceiling plane. Anamorphic images of the virtual heavenly space, as seen through the canvas ceiling picture plane, were created from the digital model, and encoded to the individual moments in the room. Individuals who moved through the gallery were followed by the illusion of the heavenly space, creating a live l'oiel distortion.

ACKNOWLEDGMENTS

Many thanks to the American Academy in Rome for their support in the production of this installation. A special thanks to Stefano Silva, Lexi Eberspacher, and Peter Benson Miller.

REFERENCES

Oleksijczuk, Denise Blake. 2011. *The First Panoramas: Visions of British Imperialism*. Minneapolis, MN: Minnesota Press, 4.

3 Diagram of the sensor mapping the room (op.AL, 2018).

4 Image of Pozzo's projection through a window (op.AL, 2018)

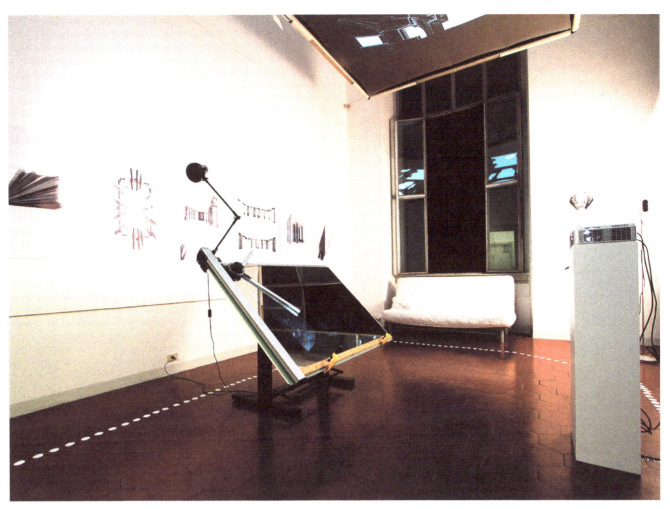

5   The movement of the body in circumambuliation of the room is tracked by a sensor (op.AL, 2018)

IMAGE CREDITS

Figures 1-5: © op.AL, 2018

Jonathan A. Scelsa Jonathan A Scelsa Jonathan is an Architect, Urbanist, and educator. Prior to the founding of op.AL, Jonathan worked in several international offices including Foreign Office Architects, Hashim Sarkis Studios, Smith-Miller + Hawkinson, and Bohlin Cywinski Jackson. As an educator, Jonathan is an Assistant Professor of Architectural Design + Technology at Pratt Institute in Brooklyn, NY. Jonathan is a Licensed Architect in the state of New York and a Fellow of the American Academy in Rome. He received his Master of Architecture in Urban Design with Distinction from Harvard University. He received his Bachelor of Architecture from Carnegie Mellon University.

Jennifer Birkeland is currently an Assistant Professor of Landscape Architecture at Cornell University in the College of Agriculture and Life Sciences. She is a licensed landscape architect in the state of New York, a Fellow at the American Academy in Rome, and a LEED accredited professional. Jennifer received her Master of Landscape Architecture at Harvard University and has a Bachelor of Science in Landscape Architecture from California Polytechnic State University Pomona. Jennifer has worked with internationally renowned offices such as West 8, OLIN, and Ken Smith Workshop.

DE:Stress Pavilion

Print-Cast Concrete for the Fabrication of Thin Shell Architecture

Christopher A. Battaglia
Ball State University

Martin Miller
Cornell University

Kho Verian
Laticrete International, Inc

1   DE:Stress Pavilion: Concrete 3D Printed Panelized Shell (Hadley Fruits, September 2019).

Intro & Context

Print-Cast Concrete investigates architectural-scale concrete 3D printing in robotically tooled recyclable green sand molds for the fabrication of rapidly constructed, structurally optimized, architectural-scale concrete structures. Utilizing a three-dimensional extrusion path for deposition, this process expedites the production of doubly curved concrete geometries by replacing traditional formwork casting or horizontal corbeling with spatial concrete arching. Creating robust non-zero Gaussian curvature in concrete, this method increases speed for mass customized concrete elements, eliminating two-part mold casting by combining robotic 3D printing and extrusion casting. Through the casting component of this method, concrete 3D prints have greater resolution along the edge condition resulting in tighter assembly tolerances between multiple aggregated components.

Methodology

In exploring the intersection of mass customization, rapid manufacturing techniques, concrete 3D printing, and pre-cast construction, this research developed a process of robotic fabrication combining both CNC robotic milling and concrete material deposition. Looking at low-cost reusable aggregate formwork, a green sand mixture was utilized for the creation of bespoke molds. Used in the casting of molten metal and glass sand molds, green sand can resist materials with high temperatures and retain resolution when making molds of intricate geometries. The green sand is utilized for the fabrication of the Print-Cast molds as it is inexpensive to produce in large quantities, can be CNC tooled at high

PRODUCTION NOTES

Architect: Battaglia+Miller
Client: Exhibit Columbus
Status: Temporary Exhibit
Location: Columbus, Indiana
Date: 2019

2   Print Cast Concrete Green Sand Tooling (Hadley Fruits, June 2019).

3   Finished Print Cast Panel (Hadley Fruits, June 2019).

4   Robotic Print Casting in Sand Mold (Hadley Fruits, June 2019).

speeds, and can be recycled, remolded, and reshaped with little effort. Utilizing all six robotic axes, the sand mixture was strong enough to perform undercut milling geometries into the side wall of the sand forms, proving the concept of precise interlocking plug to socket edges could be implemented into the design process.

With the sand mold processed, the material deposition of 3D printable mortar can begin. Switching end effectors from the CNC spindle to the concrete extrusion end effector, 3D printable mortar is weighed and mixed in relation to the toolpath generated for the Print-Cast Panel. Partnering with LATICRETE International, Inc, 3D printing mortar was developed that exhibited an open extrusion time between 45 minutes to one hour, could deposit and stack 9 mm layers consistently, and had a load bearing capacity of 29.2 MPa after a curing period of 28 days. Over-extrusion was utilized along the sand mold edges to press the material against the mold and cast into the undercut edge geometry necessary for the panel-to-panel connections.

The process of Print-Cast Concrete was developed in conjunction with the necessity to produce a full-scale architectural installation commissioned for Exhibit Columbus 2019. The proposal was to design and fabricate a concrete 3D printed compression shell, spanning 12 meters in length, 5 meters in width, and 3 meters in height, with four parabolic arches allowing entry into the proposed project, consisting of 110 bespoke panels ranging in weight of 45 kg to 160 kg per panel. Using this production method, the project had the ability to be assembled and disassembled within the timeframe of the temporary outdoor exhibit, produce <1% of waste mortar material in fabrication, and utilize 60% less material to construct than cast-in-place construction.

Looking at pure compression structures, the application of Print-Cast Concrete centered around shell design and typology. The design of the concrete shell was tasked to respond both to material, form, site, and context within the scope of the overall exhibition. Using evolutionary solvers, one parameter of the shell was to touch down to

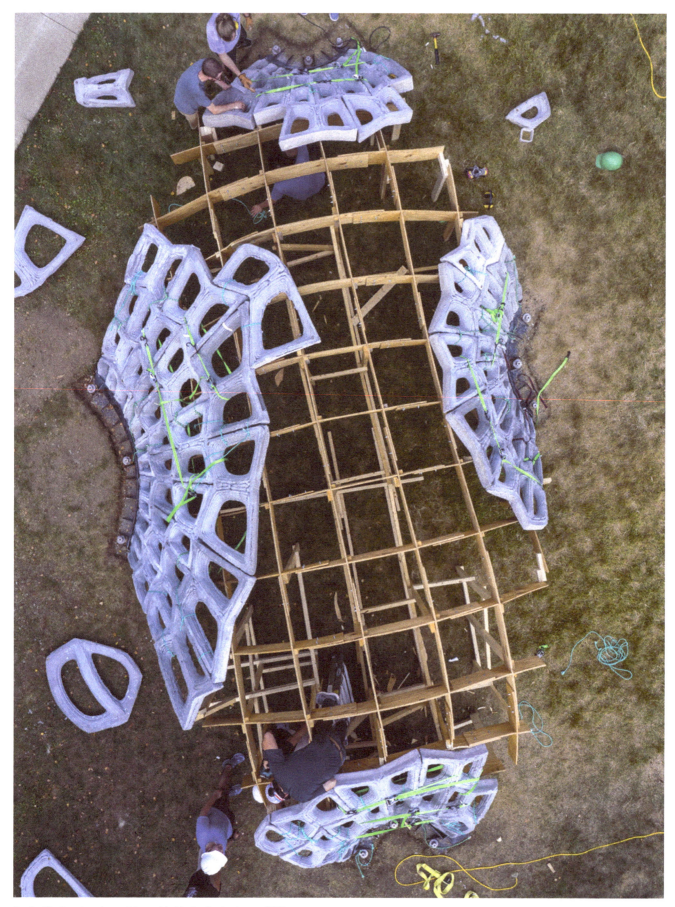

5   On Site Construction and Assembly (Hadley Fruits, August 2019).

6   On Site Construction and Assembly (Hadley Fruits, August 2019).

7   DE:Stress Pavilion: Interior Shell (Hadley Fruits, September 2019).

8   DE:Stress Pavilion: Interior Shell (Hadley Fruits, September 2019.

the ground plane at four locations with curvilinear radii. The resulting parabolic arches of various heights created the openings into the structure that responded to both compression forces and site conditions. Structural analysis integrated into compression form-finding algorithms produced the curvature of the overall geometry placing the project in a state of pure compression. Since the installation was temporary, 6.35 mm steel cabling and tension rods spanned over the exterior of the shell placing additional compression forces on the arches and spans. The addition of this force load was to ensure that an acting force of an unexpected live load would not shift the structural integrity of the structure.

The shell geometry was subdivided into 110 bespoke panels, with constraints determined by the bounding box geometries of the compressed sand mold blanks and reach of the Kuka kr60 robotic platform. Form generation for these panels looked at interlocking geometries that when placed into compression would interlock within one another. Formally resembling a bow tie, the edge seams between

panels would not span across multiple rows of individual geometry. Panel sub-divisions and openings within each of the panel geometries corresponded to the optimized force loads moving through the structure, resulting in the reduction of weight and material usage. Due to the fabrication process, the material texture on the panel's interior inherits the ornamentation of tooling and casting while the exterior layering expresses the extrusion process.

Results

Using the sand mold to contain the edge conditions of each panel geometry, the Print-Cast technique allows for precise geometry along the edges. To increase the pavilion's resistance to shear forces, interlocking nesting geometries are integrated into each edge condition of the panels. Not exceeding 0.785 rad of undercut, the CNC spindle end effector on the robotic platform tooled out the plug and socket sand geometry. Utilizing the precision of casting during the printing process insures accuracy and tight tolerances within concrete 3D printing. When nested together, the edge condition informs the construction

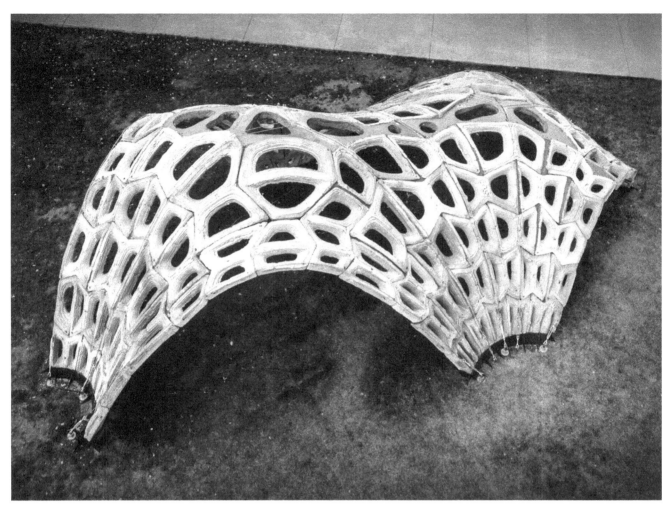

9   DE:Stress Pavilion Completed Shell Structure (Hadley Fruits, 2019).

logic of both the panel's placement and orientation for the temporary concrete panelized shell. This project was fabricated by 2-4 team members over the course of three months utilizing one robotic arm, simulating a larger manufacturing cycle. For on site assembly, a temporary waffle form was utilized for panel placement and then disassembled upon shell completion.

ACKNOWLEDGMENTS

Acknowledged here is the design collaboration of Battaglia+Miller along with Kho Verian designing and testing the 3D Mortar for this project. Special thank you to the design, fabrication, and construction efforts of the students and faculty of Ball State University, Fabrication Associate Ethan Jones, Josh Coggeshall, Janice Shimizu, James Kerestes, Brian Havener, our material sponsor Laticrete International, fabrication sponsor Mid West Metals, Fuller Hard Woods, and the many volunteers of Exhibit Columbus. The work could not have been completed without generous grants from Exhibit Columbus, CAP Design Makes Grant, and Laticrete International.

IMAGE CREDITS

Figures 1-10: © Hadley Fruits, 2019

REFERENCES

Bos,F., Wolfs, R. Ahmed, Z.Salet, T. 2016 "Additive Manufacturing of concrete in construction: potentials and challenges of 3D concrete printing." *Virtual and Physical Prototyping* 11(3): 209-225.

Ballard, G., N. Harper, T. Zabelle. "Learning to see work flow: an application of lean concepts to precast concrete construction." *Engineering, Construction and Architectural Management*, Vol. 10 (1): 6-14.

Battaglia, C., M. Miller, S. Zivkovic. 2019 "Sub-Additive 3D Printing of Optimized Double Curved Concrete Lattice Structures." In. *Robotic Fabrication In Architecture, Art, And Design 2018, Vol. 1*, ed. J. Willmann, P. Block, M. Hutter, K. Byrne, T. Schork, 245-255. Heidelberg: Springer.

Zivkovic, S., C. Battaglia. 2018 "Rough Pass Extrusion Tooling, CNC Post Processing of 3D-Printed Sub-additive Concrete Lattice Structures." In *ACADIA 2018 Recalibration: On Imprecision and Infidelity:*

10 DE:Stress Pavilion Completed Shell Structure (Hadley Fruits, 2019).

Proceedings of the 38th Annual Conference of ACADIA, ed. by P. Anzaline, M. del Signore and A.J. W, 302-311. Mexico City: ACADIA.

Banchhor, R, K. Ganguly. 2014 "Optimization in Green Sand Casting Process For Efficient, Economic, Economical and Quality Casting." *International Journal of Advanced Engineering Technology*. Vol. V (1): 25-29

Verian, K. P., S.R. Kowaleski, M.D. Carli, R.P. Bright, E. Maandi, and G. Still. 2020. "The Properties of 3D Printing Mortar and Development of 3D Construction Printing," *Transportation Research Record*, vol. 2674 (2): 1-9.

Christopher A. Battaglia was formerly the Design and Innovation Fellow and Associate Research Professor at Ball State University College of Architecture and Planning, researching concrete 3D printing robotics, heavy timber construction, and structural optimization techniques. Battaglia's work looks to the intersection of material handcraft through the lens of digital tools and experimental processes. Battaglia teaches studios and seminars focused on architectural design-build projects in collaboration with industrial partners.

Martin Miller is primarily concerned with how the digital onslaught will define our future realities, both physical and virtual. He is the co-founder of the design office AntiStatics Architecture based in Beijing and New York City. Defining a mantra which is ever adaptive to emerging technologies, AntiStatics' work seeks to find a balance between our convergent existences. Miller is currently a Professor of Practice at Cornell University's AAP, where he teaches graduate studios as well as seminars focused on the implementation of computational design techniques including artificial intelligence, simulation, and robotic fabrication.

Dr. Kho Verian is a scientist at LATICRETE International, Inc. He graduated with a bachelor's degree from the Civil Engineering Department of Universitas Katolik Parahyangan, Indonesia in 2008. He earned his MSCE (2012) and PhD (2015) from the Department of Civil Engineering at Purdue University, USA. His current research focuses on the innovation and development of sustainable construction materials. One of his works in innovation is in developing LATICRETE® 3D Printing Mortars, which have been used in several 3D construction printing projects worldwide.

Object-Field

Samuel Bernier-Lavigne
Laval University

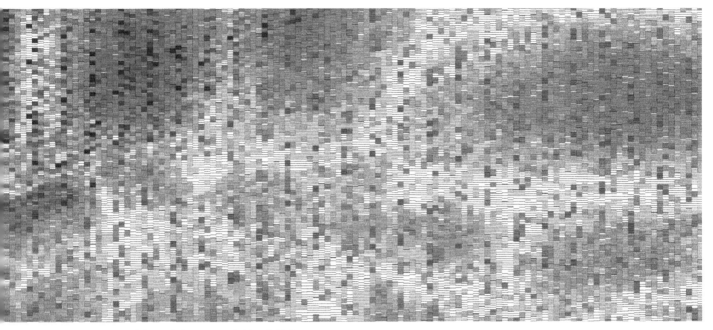

1   Close-up on the high-resolution system of object-field_2.

This project aims to continue the correlative study between two fundamental entities of digital architecture: the *object* and the *field*. Following periods of experimentation on the *field* (materialization of flows of data through animation), the *field of objects* (parametricism), and the *object* (OOO), we investigate the last possible interaction remaining, the *object-field*, by merging the formal characteristics of the object with the structural flow of its own internal field. This will be done by exploring the high-resolution features of 3D printing, in the design of autonomous architectural objects expressing specific materiality, and through the use of topological optimization.

To start, the objects are generated by an iterative process of volumetric reduction, resulting in an ensemble of finely cut monoliths. Four of them are selected and analyzed through topological optimization in order to extract their internal fields, and a series of high-resolution algorithmic systems translate the structural information into 3D printed materiality.

The Object-Field_1 serves as an introduction to the project, materializing a result close to identical to the optimization, giving the keystone to understanding the other object-fields. Moreover, it expresses the spatial qualities of this network that evolves into the body of the object. We discover the high-resolution aspect when manipulating the printed object, where a fine texture, almost invisible to the naked eye but perceptible to the touch, subtly reveals the other theme of the project.

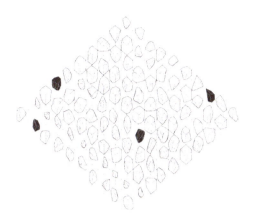

2 Generative process of the monolithic objects.

3 The four selected objects.

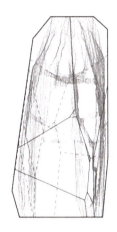
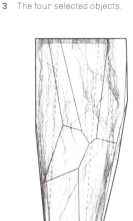

4 Internal field of the objects, emerging from the topological optimization process.

The Object-Field_2 expresses the structural flows as a source of information defining the outer surface of the monolith. This time, the high-resolution system becomes essential in the definition of the project, where an algorithm will first decompose the total volume into a cluster of 1 mm voxels. The voxels are then informed by the optimization, with extrusion following the normals of the initial volume. This has the effect of stiffening the structure where it is needed by generating a new topography on the object. To amplify these fine variations, shades of grey are assigned to the voxels according to their proximity to the underlying field.

The Object-Field_3 aims for complete integration of the structural flows through a transparent monolith, pure from the outside but extremely detailed from the inside. Here, a vertex displacement algorithm is used to thicken parts of the inner walls, giving it a texture that is both crackling and fluid, following the direction of the forces. Fabricated as an ultra-clear resin 3D print exhibiting the accuracy of 15 microns per layer, this object-field could almost be

apprehended as an entity that would have been formed by a growth process rather than manufactured.

The Object-Field_4 decomposes both the formal data of the initial monolith and the structural flows to blur the boundaries between object and field. This is done through the mereological assembly of simple linear elements. The algorithmic procedure divides the initial shape into a series of thin vertical members, extracting the periphery of the object, and an iterative loop run several thousand times gradually organizes the horizontal micro-elements according to the optimization data, slowly solidifying the whole.

Each of these four object-fields rests on a base, a heavy block counterbalancing the light weight of the object placed on it. Although completely white as an abstract volume, its upper surface is milled to express the intensity of the field acting in the object while reinterpreting at another resolution the system of translation. This notion of multi-resolution also has great repercussions

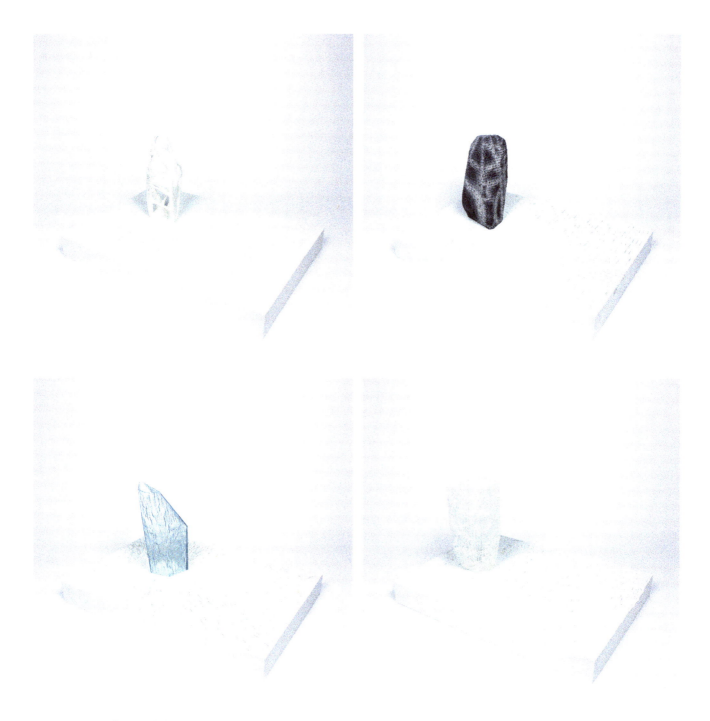

5   The four object-fields on their bases.

on the representation of the project. We have deliberately restricted our investigation to line drawings in order to explore the flexibility of this medium, to see if it could speak this language. For each object-field drawing, a specific algorithmic procedure is developed, deriving from the peculiarities of its complex geometry, aiming to catalyze coherence throughout the project, where similarities, hitherto kept apart by the multiple materialities, begin to dialogue.

ACKNOWLEDGMENTS

I would like to thank all the collaborators involved in the project: Julien Beauchamp, Hugo Thibaudeau, Pascal Labelle, Alexandre Marceau and Romy Brosseau. This project was made possible by the funding of the Conseil des Arts du Québec and the Fonds de Recherche Société et Culture du Québec.

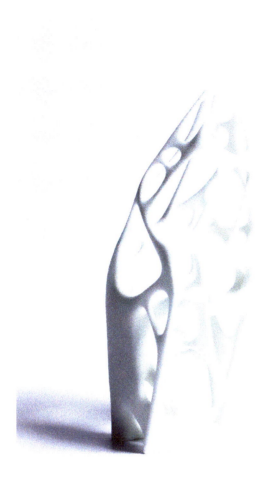

6   Object-field_1.

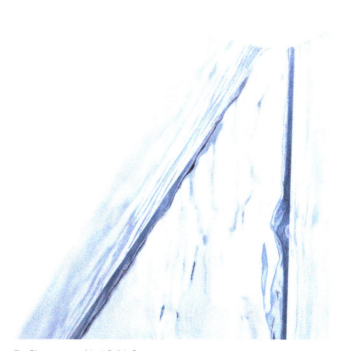

7   Close-up on object-field_3.

8   Close-up on object-field_4.

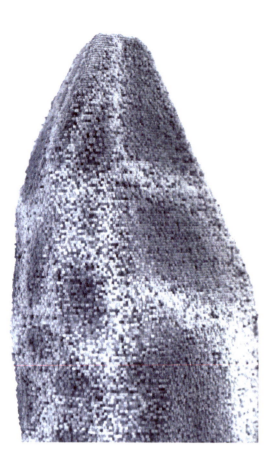

10 Elevation of object-field_2.

9 Close-up on object-field_2.

11 Plan of object-field_4.

REFERENCES

Bendsoe, Martin and Ole Sigmund. 2003. *Topology Optimization: Theory, Methods, and Applications*. Switzerland: Springer Science & Business Media.

Bernier-Lavigne, Samuel. 2019. "Object-field; An adaptive interplay between autonomy and contingency." In *Black Box: Articulating Architecture's Core in the Post-Digital Era*, ACSA 107th Annual Meeting, edited by J. Ficca, A. Kulper and G. La, 640-645. Pittsburgh: ACSA.

Bryant, Levy. 2011. *The Democracy of Objects*. Minneapolis: University of Minnesota Press.

Hui, Yuk. 2016. *On the Existence of Digital Objects*. Minneapolis: University of Minnesota Press.

Nakamura, Hiroshi. 2010. *Microscopic Designing Methodology*. Tokyo: Lixil Publishing.

Young, Michael. 2015. *The Estranged Object*. Chicago: Graham Foundation.

IMAGE CREDITS

Figures 3,5-9, © Photos by Samuel Bernier-Lavigne, Romy Brosseau, Julien Beauchamp.

All other drawings and images by the author.

Samuel Bernier-Lavigne Ph.D., is a tenured professor at Laval University's School of Architecture (Québec, Canada), founder of the FabLab ÉAUL and director of the xFab research group. He holds a doctorate in architecture (theory, design and digital fabrication), in addition to being a recipient of the Henry Adams Medal of Honor (AIA) and the Royal Architectural Institute of Canada (RAIC) Medal. He has notably worked for Studio Cmmnwlth, Gramazio & Kohler (ETHz), and UNStudio. He is co-author of the book *Alfred Neumann - L'architecture de la morphologie*, published in 2020 by Editions B2 in Paris.

12 Plan of object-field_3.

13 Point cloud drawing of object-field_3.

Casa Covida

Mud Frontiers III - Zoquetes Fronterizos III

Ronald Rael
UC Berkeley

Virginia San Fratello
San Jose State University

Alexander Curth
MIT Computation

Logman Arja
Georgia Tech

1   Casa Covida, 3D printed in-situ with a mixture of local earth, straw and water.

Abstract

Casa Covida advances large scale earthen additive manufacturing by establishing new methods for the creation of interconnected, partially enclosed dome structures using a lightweight SCARA robotic arm and custom toolpathing software in combination with traditional earthen construction techniques. In the time of Covid-19, digital fabrication and construction are made difficult by a diminished supply chain and the safety concerns associated with a large team. In this project, local material, dug from the site itself is used for construction coordinated by a team of four people working in a remote location. Three rooms are printed on site 500 mm at a time by moving the 3D printer between stations connected by a low cost 4th axis constructed from plywood. This system allows essentially simultaneous construction between domes, continuously printing without waiting for drying time on one structure so that a continuous cycle of printing can proceed through the three stations 2-4 times in a day, thereby minimizing machine downtime. The machine control software used in this project has been developed from the framework of Potterware, a tool built by our team to allow non-technical users to design and 3D print functional ceramics through an interactive web interface.

All material is excavated from the alluvial soil deposits in a field adjacent to the site (within 500 meters) and processed by hand through a 1/4" (1 cm) screen to remove any large gravel from the mix. Chopped wheat and barley straw from a local supplier (14 miles, 26 km) is combined with water and local soil, which contains an ideal mixture of clay, sand, silt

PRODUCTION NOTES

Designer:	Emerging Objects
Status:	Complete
Location:	San Luis Valley, Colorado
Date:	2020

2   A static 4th axis constucted on site facilitates multiple printing positions.

3   The SCARA arm printing from within the structure.

4   The first doubly-walled prototype frustum space under construction..

and aggregate, in a portable cement mixer before being loaded into the hopper of the mortar pump. The foundation consists of a two foot (0.6 meter) compacted gravel pad collected in the earth sifting process. The system is designed to demonstrate the feasibility of sustainable construction through the use of local earthen material and low-cost robotics. The material used in the project contains no synthetic stabilizers or cement; it is local soil mixed with straw and water, left to dry using only wind and sun (Rael 2010).

Lightweight, low-cost construction robotics
The 3D printing system combines a 3-axis SCARA (Selective Compliance Articulated Robot Arm) purpose-built for on-site additive manufacturing, with a continuous flow, stator-driven mortar pump (Makino 2014). The printing system uses a stator-driven mortar pump to deliver material to the toolhead. For the latest application of this system we have mounted the arm on a 4th axis rail which creates a rigid structure between printing positions, greatly expanding the range of the machine. The total build

area is 8000 x 2667 mm (~26'x8'). This setup was carried to the site by two people, assembled, and calibrated in less than an hour. Relocation between stations on the 4th axis takes around five minutes. The complete robotic system was developed for a fraction of the cost of a gantry printer system of equal build area.

This lightweight, quick to assemble system does not share the fine precision of an industrial milling or inspection robot arm, however, it performs within the tolerances of the material and process for which it is intended.

Flexible toolpathing software
The machine control software used in this project has been developed from the framework of Potterware, a tool built by our team to allow non-technical users to design and 3D print functional ceramics through an interactive web interface. For this application, G-code is organized into 4-8 layers segments which are drip-fed to the SCARA arm via WiFi. Pauses and positional checks are programmed into the toolpath to allow time for operators to load the pump

5　The entry hearth and seating, both functional elements 3D printed into the structure.

Casa Covida Rael, San Fratello, Curth, Arja

6   A space for bathing occupies east room of Casa Covida.

7   The space for sleeping includes a built up adobe bed covered in sheepskins and custom textiles.

hose into the machine nozzle at each station and confirm accurate Z-height relative to the previous layer. By taking this piecewise approach we are able to detect and compensate for inconsistencies in the structure resulting from non-uniform drying due to prevailing wind direction, rain, and sun. Layer height progressively decreases relative to slope angle to ensure better layer adhesion. Feed rate can be adjusted in real time by multiple members of the team via WiFi using a tablet or smartphone.

ACKNOWLEDGMENTS
Project Team: Ronald Rael, Virginia San Fratello, Logman Arja, Alexander Curth, Mattias Rael and Danny Defelici at 3D Potter.

REFERENCES
Makino, Hiroshi. 2014. "Development of the SCARA." Journal of Robotics and Mechatronics 26 (1): 5–8. https://doi.org/10.20965/jrm.2014.p0005.

Ronald Rael. 2010. Earth Architecture. Princeton Architectural Press.

Ronald Rael and Virginia San Fratello. 2018. Printing Architecture. Princeton Architectural Press.

IMAGE CREDITS
Figures 1,5,7,8: © Elliot Ross, 2021.

Figures 2,3,4,6: © Emerging Objects, 2021

—————

Ronald Rael is a Professor and the Chair of the Graduate Committee in the Department of Architecture at UC Berkeley. He directs the printFARM Laboratory (print Facility for Architecture, Research and Materials), He is a partner in Rael-San Fratello and Emerging Objects with Virginia San Fratello. Rael is the author of Borderwall as Architecture: A Manifesto for the U.S.-Mexico Boundary, which advocates for a reconsideration of the barrier dividing the U.S. and Mexico through design proposals that are hyperboles of actual scenarios that have occurred as a consequence of the wall, and Earth Architecture, a history of building with earth in the modern era to exemplify new, creative uses of the oldest building material on the planet.

8   The space for sleeping with a view to the sunset beyond..

Virginia San Fratello is an architect, artist, and educator. She is a Professor in the Department of Design at San Jose State University where she also serves as Chair. San Fratello, along with her partner Rael, is the author of the book Printing Architecture: Innovative Recipes for 3D Printing. Her work with Rael has been published widely, including in the New York Times, Wired, MARK, Domus, Metropolis Magazine, PRAXIS, Interior Design and the Architects Newspaper and is included in the permanent collections of The Museum of Modern Art in New York, The Cooper Hewitt Smithsonian Design Museum, The San Francisco Museum of Modern Art, and the Design Museum in London.

Sandy Curth is a designer and computational researcher at the Massachusetts Insitutue of Technology. His work focuses on the development of tools for democratization and access in the world of architectural additive manufacturing. He was a 2019 Norman Foster Foundation Robotics Scholar and has worked with UC Berkeley's Flexible Hybrid Structures Lab and the XR Lab developing digital fabrication strategies. Previously he worked on the Long Now Foundation's 10,000 Year Clock Project.

Logman Arja is a Ventulett NEXT Generation Fellow and Assistant Professor at the Georgia Institute of Technology where his research focuses on RURALISM and RURAL ARCHITECTURE. Arja is working to advance earth architecture and ceramic production via additive manufacturing technology in rural communities and contexts. Currently, he is leading efforts to adopt the technology of additive manufacturing in Sub-Saharan Africa with a long-term goal of producing sustainable housing solutions and rural micro-infrastructures.

LightWing II

A Cyber-Physical Journey

Uwe Rieger
arc/sec Lab
University of Auckland

Yinan Liu
arc/sec Lab
University of Auckland

1   Kinetic XR installation LightWing II

LightWing II is a kinetic installation at the intersection of architecture, art, and digital spatial technologies. The project follows a hybrid design strategy that allows the augmentation of a physical structure with 3D projected imagery and spatial sound. A key component of this project was the development of a new rendering principle that allows the accurate projection of stereoscopic images on a moving target screen. Thus the interactive installation expands the principles of contemporary Augmented Reality (AR) headsets from isolated viewing towards a communal multiviewer event.

As a "hands-on" experience, LightWing II creates a mysterious sensation of tactile data and allows the user to navigate through holographic narratives assembled in four scenes. These include the interaction with a swarm of three winged creatures, being immersed in a silky bubble, the journey through a velvet wormhole, and the arrival in a forest of dandelions releasing hundreds of creatures when being touched lightly by the wing.

The project was developed at the arc/sec Lab for Cyber-Physical Architecture and Interactive Systems at the University of Auckland. Giving equal attention to both design aspects, the physical and the digital, the Lab explores user-responsive constructions where dynamic properties of the virtual world influence the material world and vice versa. Embedded in the School of Architecture, the Lab's vision is to reconnect the intangible computer world to the multisensory qualities of architecture and urban spaces. With a focus on intuitive forms of user interaction, the arc/sec Lab uses large-scale prototypes

PRODUCTION NOTES

Architect:	Uwe Rieger & Yinan Liu
Client:	Ars Electronica
Status:	Completed
Location:	Lentos Art Museum.
	Linz , Austria
Date:	2019

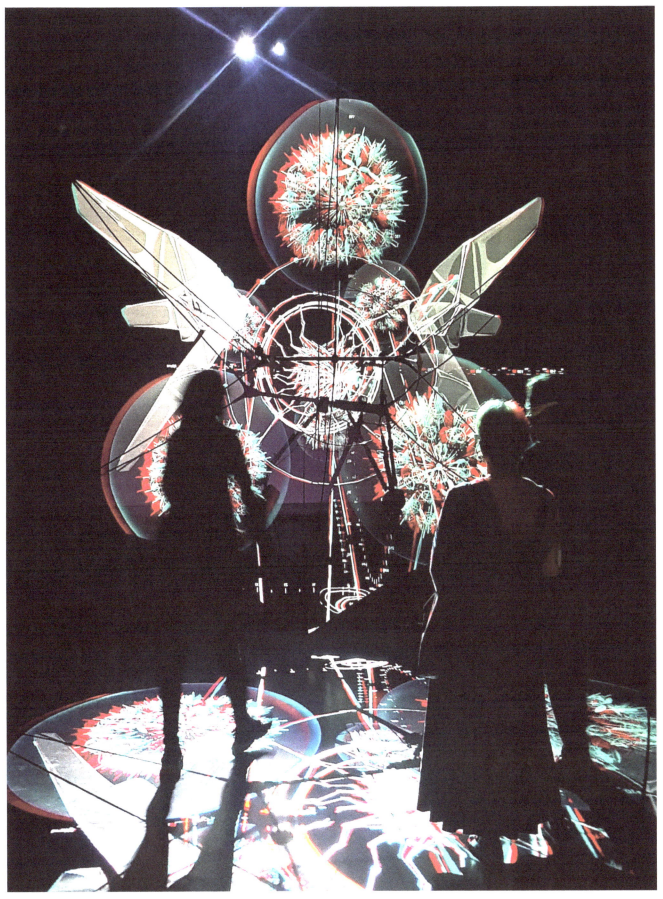

2   LightWing II at the Ars Electronica Festival 2019

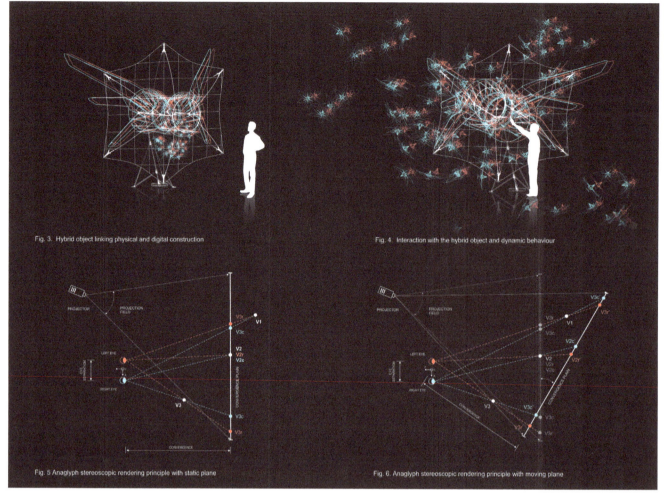

Fig. 3. Hybrid object linking physical and digital construction

Fig. 4. Interaction with the hybrid object and dynamic behaviour

Fig. 5 Anaglyph stereoscopic rendering principle with static plane

Fig. 6. Anaglyph stereoscopic rendering principle with moving plane

3-6 Stereoscopic projections on a moving target screen

and installations as the driving method for both the development and the demonstration of new cyber-physical design principles.

LightWing's main constructive components consist of thin, flexible, carbon fiber tubes holding a fine transparent mesh in tension. This is used as an almost invisible projection screen and refers to a classical theater effect known as "Peppers Ghost" (Nickell 2005). The total size of the tensile structure is 3.7 m x 3.7 m. It rests on a single needle-point support, which is placed off-center and balanced by a counterweight. The joint allows for three degrees of freedom (pitch, roll, and yaw). It enables the visitor to rotate the structure without noticeable friction or resistance. The asymmetric position of the pivot point adds an impression of unpredictability when in motion.

An Inertial Measurement Unit (IMU) is used to identify orientation, speed, and acceleration of the object (Corke et al. 2007). Analyzing the movement also unveils the character of the user interaction, for example, if it is calm or

aggressive. Thus the information from a single sensor is sufficient for the programming of a gaming engine to generate synchronized audio-visual animations that respond directly to user behavior (Figures 3, 4).

With public settings in mind, the installation takes advantage of an anaglyph projection principle (Bourke 2018), which allows effortless stereoscopic viewing by using basic 3D glasses with a red/cyan filter. The use of inexpensive cardboard glasses avoids the need for user instructions, technical servicing, and the handout or collection of viewing devices.

A further innovative element was the programming of a stereoscopic rendering system featuring a non-static convergence plane (display screen). In the case of LightWing II, this plane changes in relationship to three parameters: the orientation in space, the orientation to the viewer, and the orientation in relation to the data projectors (Figures 5, 6). This principle differs significantly from traditional 3D cinema, where all three parameters remain

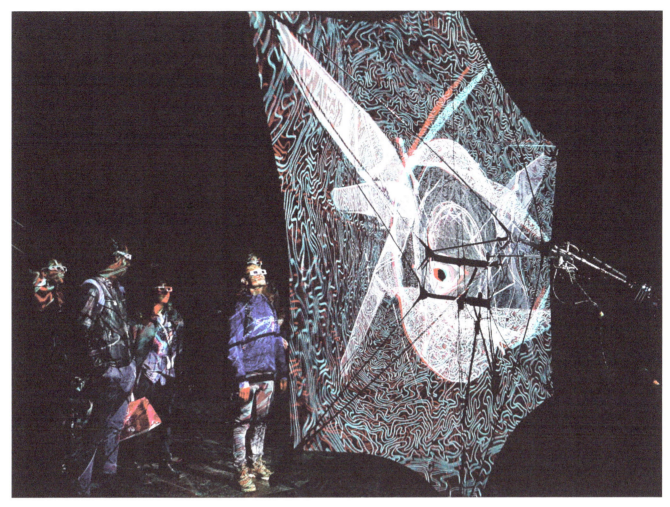

7   LightWing II creates a communal XR experience

fixed (Southard 1992). It is also more complex than stereo rendering with AR/VR headsets where only the location and orientation of the display is changing in relation to the space.

In a final step, the physical and digital settings of the installation are linked through a 1:1 calibration process. This allows one to precisely superimpose the virtual world with both the kinetic carbon fiber structure and the surrounding environment. The aesthetics of the graphics, the responsive animations, and the correlating sound are designed to naturally merge with the object and to expand its behavior.

LightWing II dissolves the user interface through direct linkage between the physical construction and the dynamic digital content. Handling the object means handling the attached digital information. The combination of physical structure, sensors, and real-time information creates a cyber-physical navigation tool which takes its user on a journey that blurs the boundaries between the tactile and the virtual.

ACKNOWLEDGMENTS

Music by: Kyung Ho Min

Graphical, technical and digital contributions: Yan Li, Jacky Zheng, and Zane Egginton

Supported by the University of Auckland

REFERENCES

Nickell, Joe. *Secrets of the Sideshows*. 4th ed. Kentucky: University Press of Kentucky, 2005.291.

Corke, Peter, Jorge Lobo, and Jorge Dias. "An Introduction to Inertial and Visual Sensing." *The International Journal of Robotics Research* 26, (June 2007): 519-535.

Bourke, Paul. "Calculating Stereo Pairs" Accessed May 20, 2018. http://paulbourke.net/stereographics/stereorender/

Southard, David A. "Transformations for stereoscopic visual simulation." *Computers and Graphics 16*, (Winter 1992): 401-410.

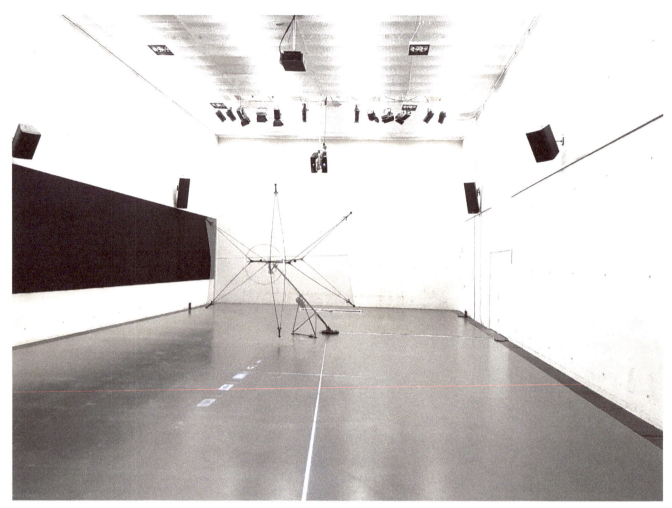

8   Setup at Lentos Art Museum, Linz, Austria

IMAGE CREDITS

All drawings and images by the authors.

Uwe Rieger is a co-founder of the Berlin-based interdisciplinary group [kunst + technik] e.V. and the architecture office XTH-berlin. Since 2006, he is an Associate Professor for Design and Design Technology at the University of Auckland, where he has established the arc/sec Lab for Cyber-Physical Architecture and Interactive Systems. As an architect and researcher, Uwe's work focuses on responsive architectural systems using cross reality concepts. His large-scale installations have been exhibited at renowned institutions such as the Museum of Modern Art Barcelona, the Venice Architecture Biennale, Ars Electronica, the International Building Exhibition IBA, the National Museum of Indonesia, and the National Museum of New Zealand Te Papa Tongarewa. www.arc-sec.com

Yinan Liu received a MArch(Prof)(Hons) degree from the University of Auckland. She is the lead technologist at the arc/sec Lab and Research Associate at the Digital Research Hub at the School of Architecture and Planning, University of Auckland. Yinan is the founding partner of arc/sec Solutions ltd., which develops customised applications for cross-reality environments. www.arc-sec.com

9   LightWing II: the swarm scene

Interlocking Shell

Transforming a block of material into a
self-standing structure with no waste

Alireza Borhani
California College of the Arts
(CCA)

Negar Kalantar, PhD
California College of the Arts
(CCA)

1   Using custom-designed modules (with force-fitting connections) to create self-supporting vaults without the need for mortar or mechanical connectors.

With a specific focus on robotic stereotomy, two full-scale vault structures (Figure 1) were designed to explore the potential of self-standing building structures made from interlocking components; these structures were fabricated with a track-mounted industrial-scale robot (ABB 4600) at the Autodesk Technology Center in Boston. To respond to economic affordances and efficiency of robotic subtractive cutting, all uniquely shaped structural modules came from one block of material (48"x96"x36") (Figure 2). Through the discretization of curvilinear tessellated vault surfaces into a limited number of uniquely shaped modules with embedded, form-fitting connectors (Figure 3), the project exhibited the potential for programming a robot to cut ruled surfaces to produce freeform shells of any kind.

Representing nearly zero-waste construction, the developed technology can potentially be used for self-supporting emergency shelters and field medical clinics, facilitating easy shipping and speedy assembly. Without using any scaffolding or tools, a few people are able to erect and dismantle an entire mortar-free structure. The disassembled structure occupies minimal space in storage (Figure 4), and the structure's pieces can be transported to the site in stacks. This process will reduce both transportation and construction costs (Figure 5).

Robot milling is a common technique for removing material to transform a block into a sculptural shape. Unlike milling techniques that produce significant waste and dust, we

PRODUCTION NOTES

Team:	Negar Kalantar, Alireza Borhani, William Palmer, Amir Behzadan, Zofia Rybkowski, Julian Kang, and Neeraj Yadav
Sponsor:	Texas A&M University
Status:	Completed
Location:	Autodesk Technology Center in Boston
Date:	Summer 2018

2   Using a block of material to crete a vault+ using a custom-built wire cutting end effector of 4' length to complete the cutting sequence of a half-length block through a process of eight cuts.

3   The cutting sequence of a vaulted geometry: 1. Divide the block in half lengthwise. 2. Slice each half into eight modules with varying geometry while making a series of successive cuts. 3. Cut male-and-female joints at both ends of each module.

used a hot wire that sliced through a Geofoam block to create almost no waste pieces. Since the front side of every module was concurrent with the backside of the next one, just one cut per front side of each module was required (Figure 6). In this case, by having three cuts, two neighboring modules were fabricated (Figure 7). Due to the reduction of the cutting sequence that emerged from the constraints of wire cutting, our method contributed to more economical fabrication processes while overcoming high machining time and cost of milling. In this project, the

form of the entire structure and its modules emerged from the constraints of the fabrication technique, which were dictated by using a robot-mounted hot wire end effector. Since the wire remained in a straight line, the design was limited to ruled surfaces. The challenge was matching the pieces together in an arch so that they each came out of a single block of Geofoam without the production of waste material (Figure 8).

In addition to the limited width of the U-shaped metal

4   Since the geometry of the front and back sides of modules were entirely interdependent, the vault modules were rearranged into a block.

5   The interlocking male-and-female joints were allowed the vaults to be constructed without using any scaffolding, formwork, or tools, offering ease of assembly and disassembly.

6   The joint geometry typologies created a condition for having a self-supporting structure and transferred bending loads between the modules

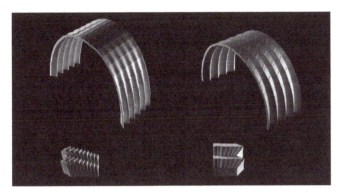

7   By controlling the wire's tilt throughout the cut, the backside of each module and the front side of its adjacent module were congruent.

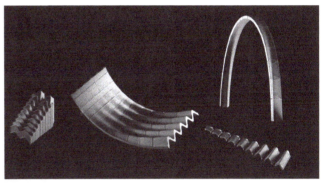

8   While accomplishing the ease of transportation and cost reduction, the final structures were the product of the limits imposed by a wire cutter.

bow end effector, as well as hot wire cutting speed and temperature, the shape of the modules was constrained by the robot's limited workspace and the size of the foam block.

The methodology can be used with wire sawing systems, diamond wires, or a waterjet head mounted on a robotic arm to make these shells out of stone, wood, or concrete (Figure 9). A similar approach could be utilized to make molds for poured concrete. By using the logic of our method to make a series of pieces in stacks, different components of freeform shells can be 3D printed on top of one another. In such cases, the surface of each piece could be used as a printing substrate for the next.

In this project, the goal was to establish a feedback loop between geometry, material, simulation, and tool. By establishing geometric data via Grasshopper, a customized tessellation script was made to breakdown a vault into its modular ruled surface constructs.

This script allowed the process of differentiation and serialization of the modules' geometries and their force-fitting connections. By conducting several Finite Element Analysis through Fusion 360 (Figures 9-11), we studied the connectivity of joints under various load scenarios and shear forces. To generate the required cutting toolpaths, custom speed setting, and RAPID code, we used the TACO plugin within Grasshopper. Then, we used RobotStudio for simulation and collision detection.

ACKNOWLEDGMENTS

As a collaborative effort between the Department of Architecture and Construction Science at Texas A&M University, this project was completed at Autodesk BuildSpace in Boston. The authors appreciate all team members' efforts, including William Palmer, Amir Behzadan, Zofia Rybkowski, Julian Kang, and Neeraj Yadav. The project became possible with the financial support of $50,000 provided by Dr. Patrick Suermann, the Department Head of Construction Science. Special thanks to Rick Rundell, Nathan King, Athena Moore, Adam Allard, and Joseph Aronia from Autodesk.

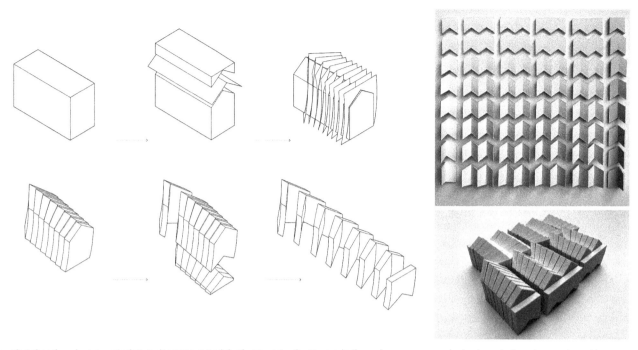

9   By using abrasive wires or waterjets to decrease material volume waste, the same robotic work processes can be implemented on stone and wood to create a self-standing structure.

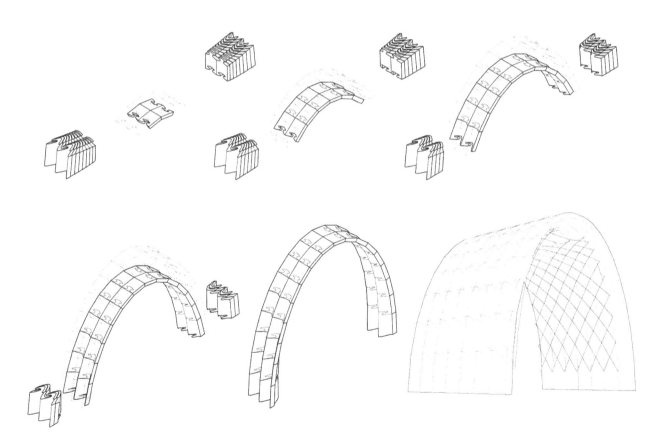

10 The vault can be erected from the middle part and gradually raised up.

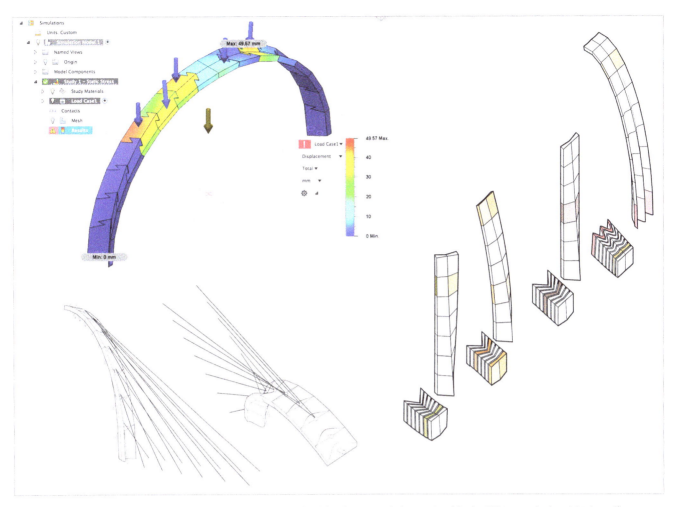

11 Several structural performance studies were conducted through the Finite Element Analysis capacity of Fusion 360 to examine how joints' specific geometry could support structural performance.

IMAGE CREDITS

All drawings and images by the authors.

Alireza Borhani is an innovator, architect, educator, and co-Principal of the transLAB. His interdisciplinary experience has allowed him to expand his career into a broad scale and type of projects at the intersection of design computation, emerging material systems, additive manufacturing workflows, and robotics. At the forefront of kinematic structures, ranging from architectural-scale shelters to small products, Borhani has been immersed in the world of transformable and adaptive design for the past twenty years. At the California College of the Arts, Texas A&M, and Virginia Tech, Alireza has taught architecture studios, concurrent with research and practice, for over a decade.

Dr. Negar Kalantar is an associate professor of Architecture and a Co-Director of the Digital Craft Lab at California College of the Arts (CCA) in San Francisco. Her cross-disciplinary research focuses on materials exploration, robotic and additive manufacturing technologies to engage architecture, science, and engineering as platforms for examining the critical role of design in global issues and built environments. Kalantar is the recipient of several awards and grants, including the Dornfeld Manufacturing Vision Award 2018, the National Science Foundation, Autodesk Technology Center Grant, and X-Grant 2018 from the Texas A&M President's Excellence Fund on developing sustainable material for 3-D printed buildings.

Calligraphies of Disturbances

Erzë Dinarama
The Polytechnic University of Milan
Department of Architecture

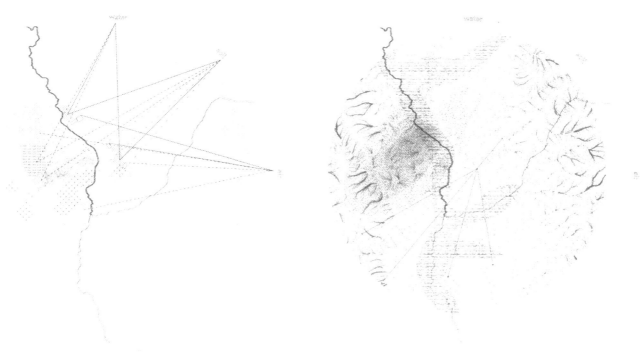

1 Contaminants and their flows.

Introduction

A testing ground for augmented ecologies, this project explores disturbances through the lens of landscape and architecture. Disturbance is a concept used in ecology to describe changes in environmental conditions that cause changes in the ecosystem. The project recognizes disturbances as a constant state of landscape and architecture and investigates how this concept can generate an architectural and landscape idea through ecological thinking and computational tools.

The toxic landscape in the vicinity of Prishtina—a coal mining site and its surroundings—is transformed into an open seed bank and a site of ecological research. The constructed ecology studies mutations in ecological patterns on a constantly disturbed site. The design proposal builds on the ecological pattern that exists on site and considers geology, hydro-geology, hydrography, topography, climate conditions, and vegetation as interconnected and inseparable layers of the site, using the instability of ecology as a foundation for the project.

Method

The flows of toxins produced by the coal mining industry are traced by an agent based system as they travel through soil, water, and air. By building new microecologies, a remediation process is proposed in the designated paths that extend beyond the mining activities following the traced flows.

PRODUCTION NOTES

Architect: Erzë Dinarama
Date: 2020

2 Ecological pattern datascape: geology, hydrogeology, hydrography, topography, and climate.

The open seed bank or "data landscape" is conceived as a public work and knowledge accumulation site for scientists. It provides an understanding of the interaction between heavy metals and the natural systems on site, which serves the scientific community globally and likewise collects knowledge and data on how to combat climate change locally. Acting as a large public work, it aims to include the public in the process of remediation through learning about endemic and invasive species, the end or transition of coal mining activities, recording of the toxins on the ground through indicatory gardens, etc. As such, it renders our interrelationship with non-human agents visible.

As the industry continues to operate, overburden machines that normally place the waste material would also engage in creating landwork on the riverbed of the river that passes through the mining site, which, since it is an active flood area, is particularly polluted. Following the curvature of the river, the mining overburden machines are used to create a performative landwork that serve as wetlands that sustain the cycles of the flood and remediate the soil and water. The signs of the industry are transformed into landwork that acts as a monument to the finale of the industry. Once the overburden machines stop being used and the industry ends, the landwork pattern will change its shape, following other constructed wetland patterns.

Following the constructed wetlands, an architectural instrument is placed on the lowest point of the new topography where the water passes before being filtered to aquifers. It serves as a research center, facilitating the functioning of the overall ecological system, as well as an exhibition and data center for plants. The constructed artificial porosity layer on the underground creates a mycorrhizae effect that benefits the remediation process, this way designing symbiotic relationships that are characteristic of ecological objects. Architecture is used to create environments as well as ideas about the environment.

At the territorial scale, computational design is used as a tool that enables access to knowledge from other disciplines through the use of GIS and visual programming.

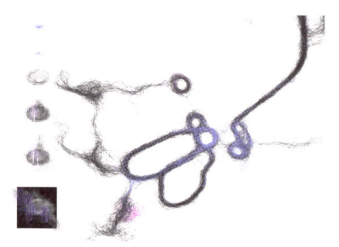

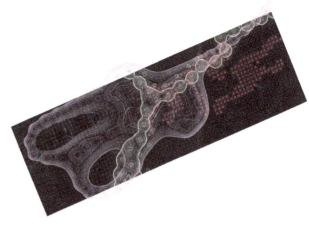

6 Generated path for the placement of microecologies. The intervention tests different species of vegetation on site and their interaction with heavy metals, following the idea of hyperobjects and the appearance and disappearance of toxins as an essential characteristic of the site. This is done by placing landscape instruments on the micro basins of the landscape, augmenting these points and generating an ecology and space.

7 Flows and influences of placed microecologies. The microecologies constructed on site have different fields of influence and effects on the territory.

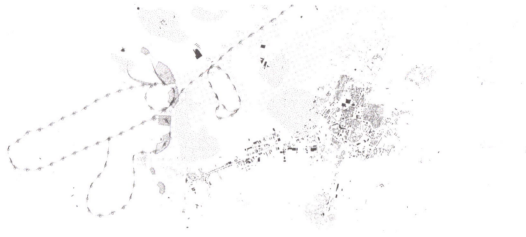

8 Performative landwork and microecologies generate the remediation site and the open seedbank.

rendering the project and process of design transdisciplinary, crucial to ecological thinking. At the tectonic scale, visual programming is used to generate the landscape and architecture modules that are used as performative instruments in the project. The module becomes the most important feature of architecture, generated by discretizing the space into voxels. This approach extracts the connection of each voxel, allowing the voxels to mutate into a range of different connections between them.

Conclusion

The project explores new methodologies and representation for territorial design in the contemporary environment. In particular, disturbances are related to the new calligraphy of the world, a new drawing, and a new geography.

ACKNOWLEDGMENTS

The author would like to thank mentor and friend Prof. Elisa Cattaneo for the continuous exciting insights and support. Also, thanks to Iacopo Neri for the valuable computational support.

REFERENCES

Picon, Antoine. 2013. "Substance and Structure II: The Digital Culture of Landscape Architecture." *Harvard Design Magazine, Landscape Architecture's Core?*, no. 36 (S/S 2013).

Cattaneo, Elisa. 2014, *Weakcity: Notes on Landscape Urbanism.* Barcelona: List Publisher.

Morton, Timothy. 2013. *Hyperobjects: Philosophy and Ecology after the End of the World.* Minneapolis: The University of Minnesota Press.

Forman, Richard and Michel Godron. 1986. *Landscape Ecology.* Canada: John Wiley & Sons.

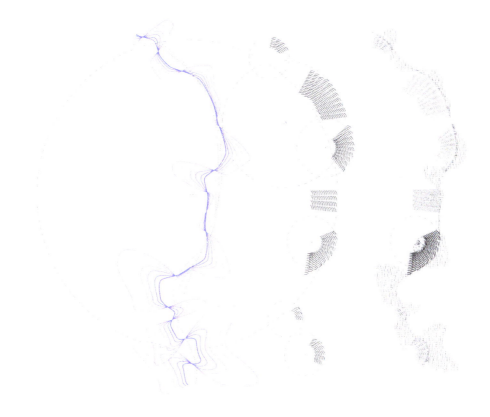

10 Performative landwork - Constructed wetlands. The dynamics of the river and its shape - positive and negative curvature of the riverbed are used for the designing of the performative landwork.

Kepes, Gyorgy.1963. *The New Landscape in Art and Science.* Chicago: Paul Theobald and Co.

Gissen, David. 2009. *Subnatures: Architecture's Other Environments.* New York: Princeton Architectural Press.

Ghosn, Rania and El Hadi Jazairy. 2018. *Another Architecture for the Environment.* Barcelona: Actar Publishers.

Ma, Yidong and Weiguo Xu. 2017. "Physarealm: A Bio-inspired Stigmergic Algorithm Tool for Form-Finding". In *Proceedings of the 22nd International Conference of the Association for Computer-Aided Architectural Design Research in Asia (CAADRIA) 2017, Suzhou, China, April 5-18 2017,* edited by P. Janssen, P. Loh, A. Raonic, M. A. Schnabel, 499-509. Hong Kong: The Association for Computer-Aided Architectural Design Research in Asia (CAADRIA).

Graham, James, Caitlin Blanchfield, and Jacob Moore. 2016. *Climates: Architecture and the Planetary Imaginary.* New York: Columbia Books on Architecture and the City.

IMAGE CREDITS

All drawings and images by the author.

Erzë Dinarama is an interdisciplinary designer and researcher working at the intersection of architecture, landscape architecture, and ecological design.

Erzë holds a Bachelor's Degree in Architecture at The University of Prishtina, a Masters Degree in Architecture with Distinction at The Polytechnic University of Milan. Additionally, she holds a Professional Certificate Degree in Advanced Architecture at The University of Berkeley, California, with a Distinction in Design, and has done exchange programs at the University of Bologna and Czech Technical University.

Erzë has practiced in Italy, Kosovo, Germany, and Austria, and has also been involved in teaching activities at the Polytechnic University of Milan.

Fast Complexity

Additive Manufacturing for Bespoke
Concrete Slabs

Ana Anton
D-ARCH/ETH Zurich

Andrei Jipa
D-ARCH/ETH Zurich

Lex Reiter
D-BAUG/ETH Zurich

Benjamin Dillenburger
D-ARCH/ETH Zurich

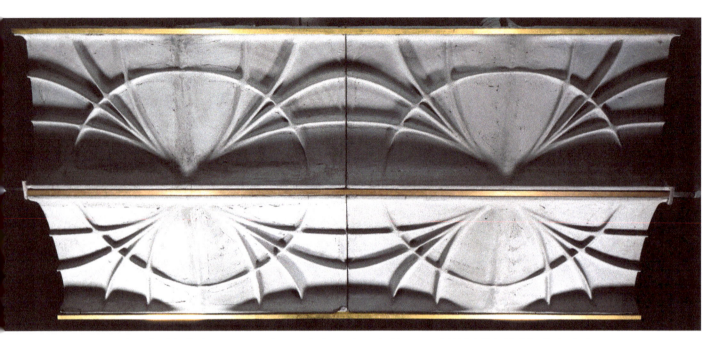

1   View towards the soffit of the final prototype covering a 1 m by 2 m surface. (Axel Crettenand, 2020, © Digital Building Technologies).

Context

Worldwide, the concrete industry produces 2.8 Mt of greenhouse gases per year, roughly 8% of the global emissions (Scrivener 2018). Hence, using concrete more efficiently can have a significant benefit to the environment. However, material efficiency often translates into complex, optimized shapes.

Such shapes present a fabrication challenge for commercial formwork systems with limited customizability. Digital fabrication with concrete aims to overcome the geometric limitations of standardized formworks and implicitly reduce the ecological footprint of the building industry. Recent research has demonstrated that complex geometries can reduce concrete use in building elements by up to 70%.

Fast Complexity

One of the most significant material economy potentials is in structural slabs because they represent 85% of the weight of multi-story concrete structures. Despite this significant proportion, slabs are almost exclusively over-dimensioned monolithic boxes with flat surfaces. To address this opportunity, Fast Complexity proposes an automated fabrication process for highly optimized slabs with ornamented soffits (Figure 1). The process combines reusable 3D-printed formwork (3DPF) and 3D concrete printing (3DCP).

2 Calibration of the binder-jetted substrate for the 3DCP phase.

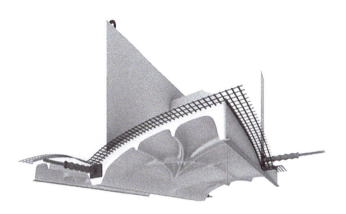

3 Fabrication setup for one module.

4 Fabrication sequence: the production of one module.

3DPF uses binder-jetting, a process with submillimeter resolution that can produce complex shapes of up to 8 m³. A polyester coating is applied to ensure reusability and smooth concrete surfaces that are otherwise not achievable with 3DCP alone. 3DPF is selectively used only where high-quality concrete surfaces are necessary, while all other surfaces are fabricated formwork-free with 3DCP.

The 3DCP process was developed interdisciplinarily at ETH Zurich and employs a two-component material system consisting of Portland cement mortar and calcium aluminate cement accelerator paste (Anton 2020). The two materials are mixed just before they are extruded on the 3DPF. The concrete viscosity varies dynamically through the amount of dosed accelerator. The variable viscosity enables the use of a fluid concrete that perfectly emulates the surface of the formwork and a fast hardening concrete for the upper structure. This fabrication process provides a seamless transition from digital casting to 3DCP in a continuous automated process.

Prototype

Fast Complexity was demonstrated with the design and fabrication of a 2 m² structural slab prototype composed of two 1 m² modules. The prototype is an excerpt of a prefabricated post-tensioned structural slab system that consists of a bi-directional grid of structural upstand ribs and a 20 mm thin articulated soffit (Figure 4).

A single 3DPF is reused for both modules of the entire slab, while the grid of upstand ribs is fabricated using 3DCP. The upstand structure requires no formwork, is customized with variable heights according to the structural requirements, and integrates custom voids for building services.

The prototype incorporates post-tensioning tendons in the ribs and a continuous carbon fiber mesh for controlling shrinkage cracks in the soffit surface (Figure 8). Due to the layered nature of 3DCP, the post-tensioning ducts and reinforcement mesh can be precisely positioned during concreting without temporary spacers.

5 Details like brass profiles can be integrated into the formwork and later on applied to the concrete slab, as decoration or as functional enhancement (Axel Crettenand, 2020, © Digital Building Technologies).

Fast Complexity Anton, Jipa, Reiter, Dillenburger

6 Fabrication sequence: filling the main geometric features of the substrate.

7 Fabrication sequence: inserting the post-tensioning tube for the main beam.

8 Fabrication sequence: adding the carbon fiber mesh after the first layer.

9 Fabrication sequence: printing the main ribs.

Conclusion

Fast Complexity selectively uses two complementary additive manufacturing methods, optimizing the fabrication speed while delivering high-quality complex surfaces. In this regard, the prototype exhibits two different surface qualities, reflecting the specific resolutions of the two digital processes.

3DCP inherits the fine resolution of the 3DPF strictly for the smooth, visible surfaces of the soffit, for which aesthetics are essential. In contrast, the hidden parts of the slab use the coarse resolution specific to the 3DCP process, not requiring any formwork and implicitly achieving better fabrication speeds.

In the context of an increased interest in construction additive manufacturing, Fast Complexity explicitly addresses the low resolution, lack of geometric freedom, and limited reinforcement options typical to layered extrusion 3DCP, as well as the limited automation and the problematic resource efficiency of single-use 3DPF. Based on these considerations, Fast Complexity challenges current practices and promotes contextualized design to fabrication solutions.

ACKNOWLEDGMENTS

This research was supported by the NCCR Digital Fabrication, funded by the Swiss National Science Foundation (NCCR Digital Fabrication Agreement #51NF40-141853). We acknowledge the contribution of Philippe Fleischman to the development of the ABB robot user interface for the 3DCP process in the Robotic Fabrication Lab, ETH Zürich. We also thank our colleagues and partners for their support: Eleni Skevaki, Yoana Taseva, Tobias Hartmann, Mathias Bernhard, Pietro Odaglia, Axel Crettenand from Digital Building Technologies, Andreas Reusser and Achilleas Xydis from ETH Zürich and Stefan Miesel from BASF Master Builders Solutions.

REFERENCES

Anton, A, A. Jipa, L. Reiter, B. Dillenburger. 2020. "Fast complexity: Additive manufacturing for prefabricated concrete slabs". In *Second RILEM International Conference on Concrete and Digital Fabrication*, ed. F. Bos, S. Lucas, R. Wolfs, T. Salet, 1067–1077. doi:10.1007/978-3-030-49916-7_102.

K. L. Scrivener, V. M. John, and E. M. Gartner. 2018. "Eco-efficient cements: Potential economically viable solutions for a low-CO2 cement-based materials industry," *Cement and Concrete Research* 114: 2-26.

10 Detail of the concrete soffit: the two post-tensioned components precisely fit given the high resolution of the binder-jetted formwork (Axel Crettenand,2020, © Digital Building Technologies).

IMAGE CREDITS

Figure 1, 5, 10: Axel Crettenand © Digital Building Technologies 2020

Figure 11: Andrei Jipa © Digital Building Technologies 2020

All other drawings and images by the authors.

Ana Anton is a PhD Candidate at the chair for Digital Building Technologies, ETH Zurich and associated to the National Center for Competence in Research – Digital Fabrication. She received her architectural degree, cum laude, from TU Delft in 2014. Her current research, Tectonics of Concrete Printed Architecture, focuses on robotic concrete extrusion processes for large scale building components.

Andrei Jipa is a doctoral student with Digital Building Technologies. He studied architecture at the Ion Mincu University in Bucharest, the University of Sheffield and the University of Westminster in London. After his diploma, he founded jamD, a digital fabrication and parametric design studio based in London and taught Computational Design to MArch and MSc students at the University of Westminster. His current research focuses on 3D-printed formwork for functional concrete building components.

Lex Reiter, PhD is post-doc researcher at ETH Zürich working on early age strength build-up and its control for digital fabrication processes with concrete among which layered extrusion. His research interest is in the physical and chemical processes that allow building without formwork and at high vertical rates as well as associated processing challenges.

Benjamin Dillenburger, PhD is Assistant Professor at the Institute of Technology in Architecture at the Department of Architecture, ETH Zurich. He is leading the research group Digital Building Technologies, which investigates computational design and digital fabrication with a focus on large scale additive manufacturing in architecture.

11 Detail of the concrete soffit (Andrei Jipa,2020, © Digital Building Technologies).

DISTRIBUTED PROXIMITIES
FIELD NOTES

Field Notes are a new submission type introduced for the 2020 ACADIA Conference. The intent was to provide an alternative to the typical peer-reviewed technical paper, and to encourage shorter pieces that are more critical, reflective, and contemplative—particularly in the context of the global Covid-19 pandemic. The call invited authors to submit shorter pieces that may include provocative artifacts regarding the culture and practice of computational design: experimental ideas, behind-the-scenes observations, brief narratives, provocations, and manifestos. Authors submitted a short text, annotated images, or an image-based essay, with the emphasis on content rather than format. The six Field Notes selected for presentation and publication reflect a diverse range of research interests yet share a reflective perspective on computation's limits and possibilities in this moment.

Waiting to Get Cut Out

Zach Cohen
The Ohio State University

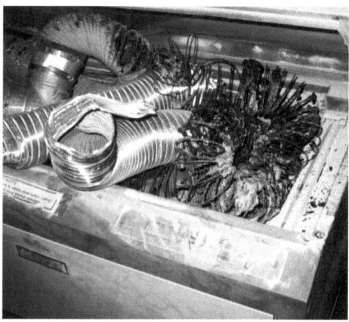

1   "What can happen when you leave a laser cutter unsupervised" (from the website of the MIT Center for Bits and Atoms).

Anyone can find the "laser cutter room" in a school of architecture: you simply follow the smell of burning cardboard. At any given time, if a passerby were to peer into one of these rooms' required "observation windows," they might observe a common sight: a sleepless student, head on hand, elbow on machine, dozing, while they wait for their pieces to get cut out. If they aren't already asleep, this student might instead be pacing nervously, getting angry at the machine's bugs, or robotically browsing social media on their smartphone, thus, if only for the brief moment that it takes for a post to load, compounding their wait. For the duration of their "cut time," this student is confined to an invisible cell next to the machine; it is a compulsory perch from which they must stand guard, just in case the laser sets their model (or the building) ablaze.

Another academic discipline might reason that having sleepy, stressed-out students next to fire-breathing machines isn't a good idea. And yet, in the discipline of architecture, our current, often impatient, relationship with fabrication is such that we not only grant students round-the-clock access to these incendiary automata, but we also continually ask ourselves: what other making (and thinking) can digital fabrication machines do for us? Our seemingly insatiable desire for automation has most recently prompted investigations into the ways in which machine learning can be used to further remove slow and unpredictable human interactions from digital fabrication processes.

The irony of the automation appetite that we are cultivating in aspiring architects is that it will actually result in future architectural practices composed of even more waiting; put simply, the more that we fill our schools and offices with automated fabrication technologies, the more time we will have to spend waiting for them to make our things. And so, we need to, for our own safety, both teach and learn how to wait better.

In other words, how can we productively use our waiting time? The answer that we find most often in both education and practice is multitasking. For instance, an industrious architecture student might (to the chagrin of fabrication shop staff) turn the plexiglass lid of a laser cutter into an ad hoc model-making station; in doing so, this student satisfies the requirement of staying beside the machine while it completes their job. However, in placing their model-making materials on top of the machine's transparent lid, the student has also literally blinded themselves to what is going on inside. Multitasking, or the skill of doing as many things as possible at one time, often has the result of doing none of those things very well: if we multitask, our ability to wait suffers.

Instead of waiting for the machine (and dozing off), not waiting by the machine at all (and risking a fire), or almost waiting for the machine (but really multitasking), I propose that we attempt to wait-*with* digital fabrication machines. The difference is more than mere semantics: waiting-for encourages antagonism, whereas waiting-with encourages companionship—companionship opens the possibility of mutualistic interactions.

For example, in waiting-with, the interaction between architect and fabrication machine can be recast as a kind of performance: we give the machine a digital file to make; it performs the making of that file for us, not just as a proxy, but as an actor. Every once in a while, the digital fabrication machine even breaks the fourth wall—it glitches—and, in doing so, provides us with a glimpse into its innerworkings. If we embrace the role of audience, and pay attention, we can unlock instrumental knowledge that can inform the ways in which we use digital fabrication machines to design and make. Further, we can use such knowledge to fix glitches and keep the performance going.

If digital fabrication machines are worked for long enough, they eventually do become exhausted; their exhaustion typically manifests in something getting fried or incinerated—these machines are most dangerous when they are fatigued. Waiting is also a necessarily exhausting task. Therefore, waiting-with machines can be a means to empathize with their exhaustion. In this act of solidarity, we might come to see the machines' mechanics as foils for our own. We can then study how machines physically work in order to become more aware of the bodies we are waiting in.

Despite recent efforts to make digital fabrication machines more automated and "intelligent," empirical knowledge and self-awareness are still part of what distinguishes us from them and, thus, part of our enduring relevance in design and fabrication processes. Waiting-with digital fabrication machines can provide designers with opportunities to cultivate such virtues. And so, if we wait-with digital fabrication machines, we can avoid, or at least delay, getting cut out.

IMAGE CREDITS

Figure 1: © Massachusetts Institute of Technology, Center for Bits and Atoms

---

Zach Cohen is an architectural designer, educator, and researcher. He is currently the Christos Yessios Visiting Assistant Professor at the Knowlton School of Architecture at The Ohio State University and co-principal of the Brooklyn-based architecture studio commoncraft.

Reconfigurable Space: Transformable Prototypes Produced during the Outbreak

Rachel Dickey
University of North Carolina, Charlotte

Noushin Radnia
University of North Carolina, Charlotte

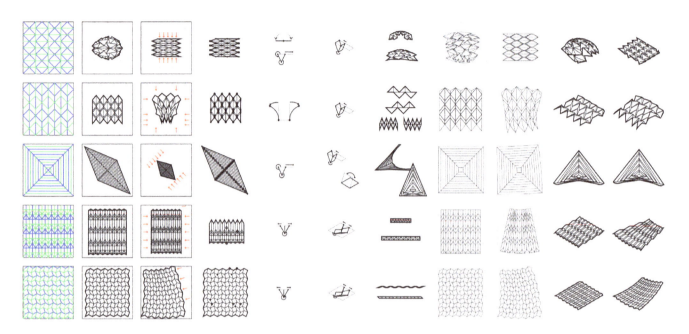

1   Excerpt from folding strategy notes cataloging the range of transformation.

As a result of the global pandemic, advanced fabrication researchers have experienced interruption in workflows and processes, shifting from material-based study and prototyping produced with access to tools and facilities to remote, work-from-home practices. This field note outlines the development of a collection of scalable prototypes for the transformable design of reconfigurable spaces, produced during COVID-19 stay-at-home orders. The research finds opportunity within the constraints of limited tools and materials and re-embraces analog computation and DIY informed rapid prototyping.

While traditional definitions of space in architecture fall under the domain of floor area measured by the square foot, this research focuses on the definition of space as a volumetric condition, measured by the cubic foot. It suggests the delineation of space is not solely based on a 2D plane articulated by a floor plan, but is instead a 3D condition observed from multiple orthographic and 3D views. Importantly, this notion of transformation uses the evaluation of change in volume as a criterion for evaluation rather than a transformation of floor area. The notion of reconfigurable space, defined for the sake of this research, is the arrangement and rearrangement of a collection of parts to influence change in volume and form (Figure 1).

Methodology

The research explores ways to create mechanisms that convert a simple push or pull over a collection of parts to cause change in size and shape. More specifically, the research focuses on spatially reconfigurable systems produced by combining folding strategies and reconfigurable polyhedra as a means for exploring transformable geometries. The following research objectives guide the development of the work:

1. To create a family of forms that convert a simple push or pull into an overall change in size and shape.

2. To program an object's behavior and motion by designing its form.

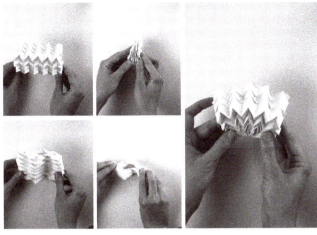

2   Stages of transformation for laminated v-form surface.

3   Stages of transformation for angled accordion pleated surface.

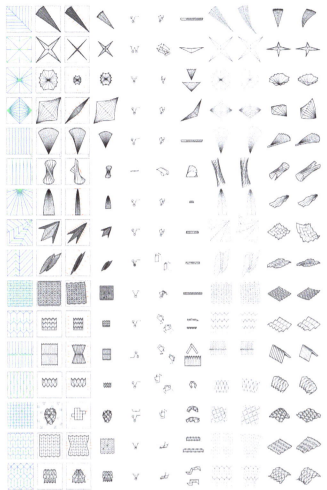

4   Excerpt from folding strategy taxonomy and catalog.

3. To explore fabrication techniques and their relationship to kinetic principles and formal transformation.

4. To explore integrated actuation strategies which use minimal amounts of energy to produce maximum change in shape.

This field note includes a collection of experiments in response to the first two of the research objectives. The figures provided in addition to this summary illustrate some of the investigations of kinematics based on folding strategies and transformational polyhedra.

Transformable Folds
The first set of investigations sought to study change in shape by folding and collapsing and then unfolding and expanding. In these explorations, the team observed the behavior and transformation of folding operations. The variables included different folding patterns and the location and amount of applied force applied to each form. To establish a mutual understanding throughout the project

between the relationship of folding and motion, the team recorded and cataloged our findings based on the different folding patterns. The team studied each pattern in a relaxed state (the neutral position after application of directional force) and compressed state (where deformation occurs during the application of directional force), and then documented each type in various views within the original 6x6 boundary to evaluate the change in size as well as range of motion of the form (Figure 4). These variables provide a set of metrics for evaluating the folding patterns for future increased-scale prototypes.

Transformable Polyhedra
The second collection of prototypes include the study of reconfigurable polyhedra with rotational hinge joints. These polyhedra are of interest because of their potential for pairing with the earlier outlined folding strategies. The geometric relationship between the polyhedra and folded figures is inherent due to triangulation and their rotational and translational attributes. In addition to the digital models, the research team developed a set of small-scale

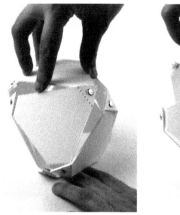

5   Stages of transformation from octahedron to cuboctahedron.

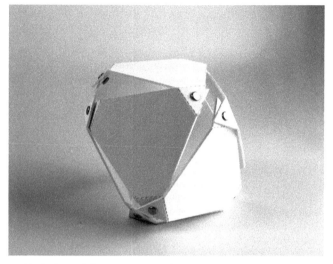

6   Physical model of octahedron transforming into cuboctahedron.

physical prototypes using a rotational hinge with rivets and perforated edges, produced with a hand held rotary cuter with a perforation blade, to accommodate the transformational node. Figures 5-8 outline the geometry of each of the polyhedra and the change in volume as a result of the transformation. As seen in Figure 6, the reshaping of the octahedron to the cuboctahedron yields the largest volumetric change, with the resulting polyhedron being five times larger. With these small prototypes, it was important for the rivet to provide enough rigidity and tightness between panels for the form to hold its shape in addition to limiting resistance and friction in order to allow for rotation between the panels.

Next Steps

Future stages of research involve the production prototypes, which gradually increase in scale and explore various ways of integrating actuators. The research team will test actuation in relationship to material logic (incorporating hard and soft materials) and fabrication procedures involving laminated assemblies with integrated flexure along fold creases. Based on these tests and integration of actuators the studies will provide determining factors for narrowing development to a specific architectural element for a full-scale prototype which changes the degree of enclosure and subdivision of space through programmed actuation.

ACKNOWLEDGMENTS

This research was funded by the Architectural Research Center Consortium (ARCC) Research Incentive Award. Special thanks to our research team: Alex Cabral, Arghavan Ebrahimi, Will Hutchins, Robby Sachs, and Elvie Sumner.

REFERENCES

Jackson, Paul. 2011. Folding Techniques for Designers: From Sheet to Form. London: Laurence King Publishing.

Schumacher, Schaeffer, and Vogt. 2010. MOVE: Architecture in Motion - Dynamic Components and Elements. Birkhäu-ser Basel.

Sweeney, Richard. 2016. Paper Sculpture: Fluid Forms. Gringko Press.

7   Physical model of cuboctahedron transforming into rhombicuboctahedron.

8   Physical model of icosidodecahedron transforming into rhombicosidodecahedron.

IMAGE CREDITS

All images and drawings by the authors.

Rachel Dickey is an Assistant Professor at the University of North Carolina at Charlotte and is founder of Studio Dickey, an experimental design practice based in Charlotte. She holds a Master of Design Studies with a concentration in technology from the Graduate School of Design at Harvard University and a Bachelor of Science in Architecture and a Master of Architecture from Georgia Tech. Dickey has held appointments as a visiting critic at Cornell University and Design Innovation Fellow at Ball State University. Her research and work has been published in *Architectural Review; Arteca; Robotic Fabrication in Architecture, Art, and Design;* and *Paradigms in Computing.* Additionally, she has exhibited at the Office for the Arts at Harvard, Des Cours in New Orleans, and the Museum of Design in Atlanta. Dickey's particular area of interest examines ways of engaging the body and technology to uncover design approaches which demonstrate the influential capacity of architecture to impact and enhance the lives of those who encounter it.

Noushin Radnia is a Post-Graduate Teaching Fellow in the School of Architecture at the University of North Carolina at Charlotte. She has worked as a designer, researcher, and educator in Iran and the United States. She holds a Master of Architecture and Master of Science in Information Technology from UNCC and a Bachelor of Architecture from Azad University of Tabriz, Iran. Radnia has pursued her research in the Digital Arts Lab at UNCC at the intersection of architecture and technology, centered around the dialogue between physical and digital space and how they impact human experience.

Pandemic Pause

Jacob Gasper
Iowa State University

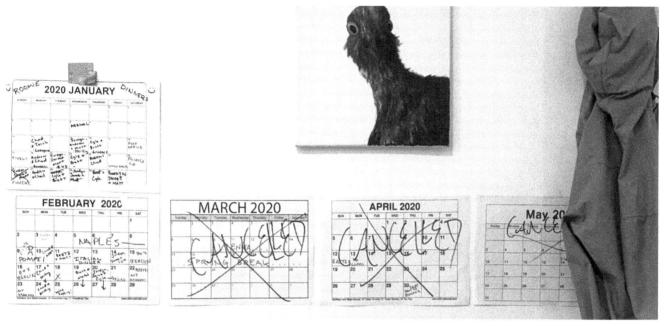

1   Cancelled.

My name is Jacob Gasper, a 5th BArch student from Manchester, Iowa. When I began this set of drawings, it was day 128 of COVID-19 turning my world upside-down and day 39 of my socially distant summer in Ames at Iowa State University. In the past five months, I have been recalled from studying abroad in Italy, lost my summer internship in Rome, and moved four times (Figure 1). Now the rapidly spreading virus and our country's refusal to muster a coordinated response makes the future uncertain. In the following pages, I catalog this current moment at the ISU Computation and Construction Lab (CCL) located in Ames, Iowa, where I worked socially distanced and alone for summer 2020 (Figure 2). Documented as field notes, these drawings capture a space simultaneously frozen in time and transitioning to a new future.

These orthographic drawings capture a reality, for me and this lab, that was not planned. Through the months of March and April 2020, the CCL produced 2,000-3D printed face shields for area hospitals. The seminar space became a factory and assembly line for life-saving personal protective equipment (PPE). This rapid response involved commandeering 30 3D printers scattered around the College of Design to print around the clock. Six other undergraduates and I, continuously rotated our times to change over the prints, sew elastic, and place plastic—all while socially distanced. We partnered with Alliant Energy to fund our efforts and disperse batches of face shields to hospitals and nursing homes across the state of Iowa. The last group of face shields went out in early May, at the beginning of a upward-trending summer.

As the recent grads found jobs—or didn't—I was left to work solo. I dedicated the majority of my summer to developing FDM printing workflows for both concrete and clay using the KUKA robots, which I had zero experience with up to this point (Figure 3). I walked in every morning and sat in the same spot, facing the wall. I usually listened to *The Daily*, a *New York Times* podcast, which slowly detailed the fractures in the nation's COVID response, democracy, and racial relations.

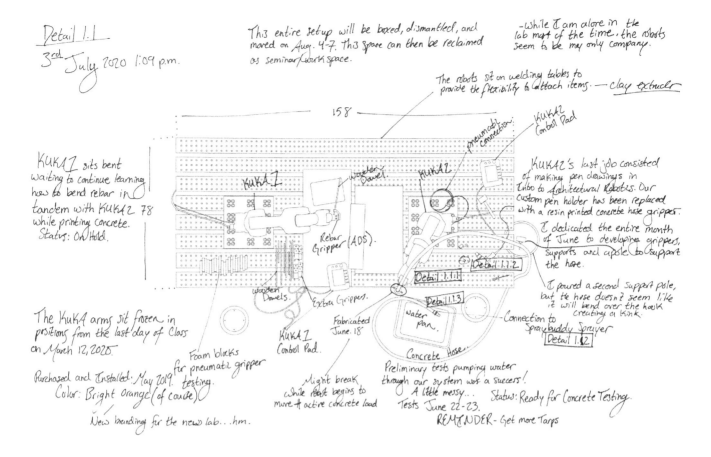

2 KUKA industrial robotic arms; in progress, moving.

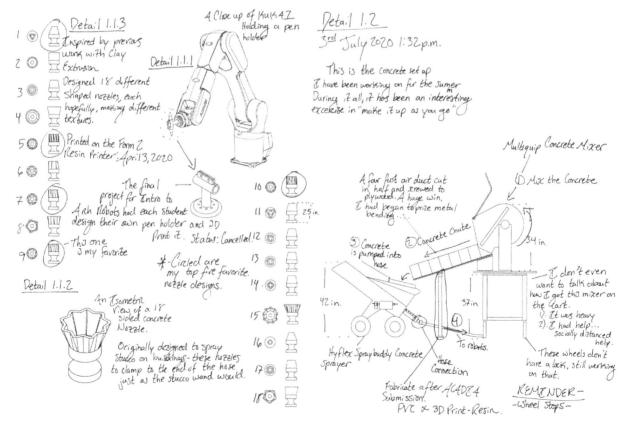

3 Concrete 3D-printing workflow preliminary notes.

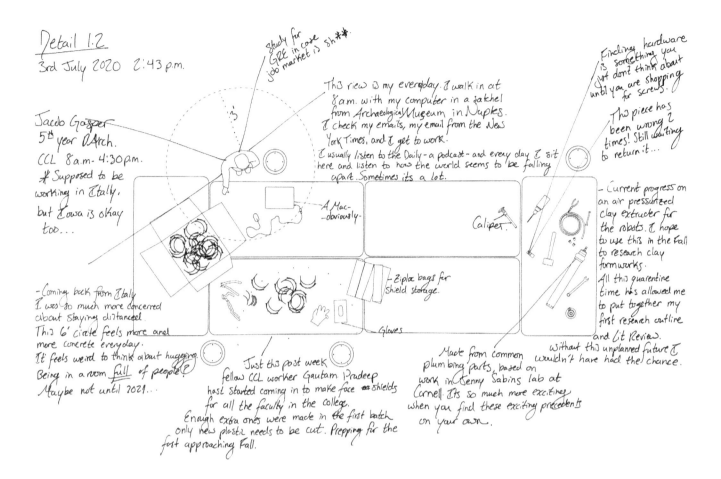

Detail 1.2
3rd July 2020 2:43 p.m.

Jacob Gasper
5th year D.Arch.
CCL 8 a.m.- 4:30 p.m.
* Supposed to be working in Italy, but Iowa is okay too...

study for GRE in case job market is sh**

This view is my everyday. I walk in at 8 a.m. with my computer in a satchel from Archaeological Museum in Naples. I check my emails, my email from the New York Times, and I get to work. I usually listen to the Daily - a podcast - and every day I sit here and listen to how the world seems to be falling apart. Sometimes its a lot.

Finding hardware is something you just don't think about until you are shopping for screws.

This piece has been wrong 2 times! Still waiting to return it...

- Current progress on an air pressurized clay extruder for the robots. I hope to use this in the Fall to research clay formworks.
All this quarentine time has allowed me to put together my first research outline and Lit Review.
Without this unplanned future I wouldn't have had the chance.

- A Mac -obviously-

Caliper.

- Ziploc bags for shield storage.

Gloves

- Coming back from Italy I was so much more concerned about staying distanced. This 6' circle feels more and more concrete everyday. It feels weird to think about hugging. Being in a room full of people? Maybe not until 2021...

Just this past week fellow CCL worker Gautam Pradeep has started coming in to make face shields for all the faculty in the college. Enough extra ones were made in the first batch only new plastic needs to be cut. Prepping for the fast approaching Fall.

Made from common plumbing parts, based on work in Jenny Sabins lab at Cornell. Its so much more exciting when you find these exciting precedents on your own.

4   PPE production.

On my first day at the CCL in April 2019, I was given an N95 mask if I needed to assist in making clay for the Potterbots. It lived in a plastic bag with my name on it, pinned to the wall. I didn't end up using this mask until almost a year later, in circumstances I could have never guessed: making face shields for a pandemic.

Initially scheduled to move into the new Architectural Robotics Lab on March 23, 2020 KUKA pneumatics, grippers, and packing material lay boxed and unboxed waiting to be transported. The KUKA arms themselves sat frozen in positions from the last day of class on March 12, 2020 (Figure 2). I spent the final two weeks of my solo work experience inventorying, boxing, and bubble-wrapping countless robot parts and research materials (Figure 5). The move finally happened—4 months and 11 Days after the initially scheduled date—on August 3. Unpacking and organizing an entire lab during a pandemic promises to be an interesting ongoing challenge for the rest of 2020.

The Computer Numerical Controlled (CNC) router is chiefly used for site models and experimental molds in Intro to Fabrication. Throughout the pandemic it became a very large and sturdy storage surface for my lunch, packing supplies, and miscellaneous tools and materials. An expensive table...

For the fall semester, the CCL decided to cancel Intro to Fabrication. The constant threat of transitioning to online classes made our ability to support the class uncertain. Can a student learn to fabricate distanced? Is that even the point? These questions address the importance of design labor and understanding how much time and effort it actually takes to not only design but also fabricate the object and clean and maintain the machine used. Socially distanced production misses this. The time searching for extra screws, loading a tube with clay, spilling grease on your pants, turning things on and off five times, labeling print files "PLSSS WORK," sweeping shavings ... all these things matter greatly to the process of the making in this space.

These field notes capture something rare in architectural design and education: a pause. I am surrounded by

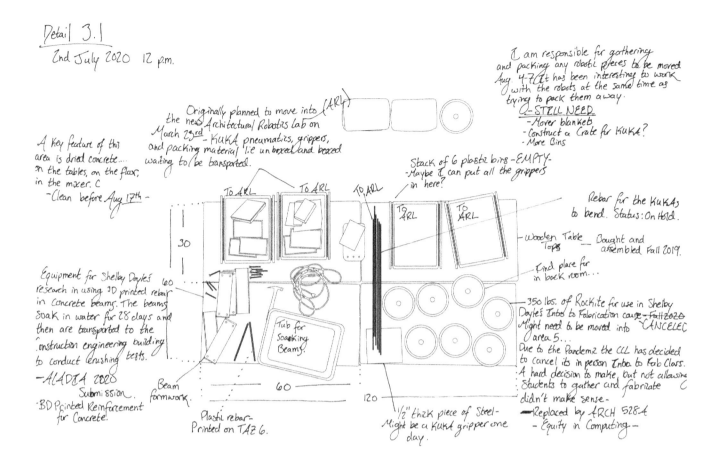

Detail 3.1
2nd July 2020 12 p.m.

I am responsible for gathering and packing any robotic pieces to be moved Aug 4-7. It has been interesting to work with the robots at the same time as trying to pack them away.
- STILL NEED
  - Mover blankets
  - Construct a Crate for KUKA?
  - More Bins

Originally planned to move into (ARL) the new Architectural Robotics Lab on March 23rd - KUKA pneumatics, grippers, and packing material lie unboxed and boxed waiting to be transported.

A key feature of this area is dried concrete... on the tables, on the floor, in the mixer. C
- Clean before Aug 17th -

Stack of 6 plastic bins - EMPTY - Maybe I can put all the grippers in here?

Rebar for the KUKAs to bend. Status: On Hold.

TO ARL   TO ARL   TO ARL   TO ARL   TO ARL

Wooden Table Tops - Bought and assembled Fall 2019.

Find place for in back room...

Equipment for Shelby Doyle's research in using 3D printed rebar in concrete beams. The beams soak in water for 28 days and then are transported to the construction engineering building to conduct crushing tests.
- ACADIA 2020
  Submission.
- 3D Printed Reinforcement for Concrete.

350 lbs. of Rockite for use in Shelby Doyle's Intro to Fabrication course - Fall 2020 Might need to be moved into CANCELED area 5...

Due to the Pandemic the CCL has decided to cancel its in person Intro to Fab Class. A hard decision to make, but not allowing students to gather and fabricate didn't make sense.
- Replaced by ARCH 528A
- Equity in Computing -

Tub for Soaking Beams.

Beam formwork

Plastic rebar - Printed on TAZ 6.

1/2" thick piece of Steel - Might be a KUKA gripper one day.

30

60

60

120

5 Packing research materials.

machines and tools that usually support digital fabrication classes, design studios, Intro to Architectural Robotics, and five undergraduate research assistants. A group of 40 or more people making use of the space, now down to one. Usually bustling with activity and constantly changing, the CCL currently exists frozen in time. In our world of fast turnarounds and deadlines, this pause allows one to focus on the space and its artifacts—traces of people now distanced. Emphasis is usually placed on the outputs of our creative spaces and not the space itself. Now I sit in silence, alone in 3,000 square feet, made aware that the Lab isn't about the equipment, or even the space; it's about people and the vibrant, challenging, animated conversations at the heart of design work.

ACKNOWLEDGMENTS

The ISU CCL PPE design and production team: Tyler Beers, Anna Lukens, Michael Oddo, Gautam Pradeep, Michael Stanley, and Hannah Underwood. The development of this field note was supported by Shelby Doyle, Assistant Professor of Architecture at Iowa State University, Co-founder of the ISU Computation & Construction Lab, and Director of the Architectural Robotics Lab.

IMAGE CREDITS

All drawings and images by the author.

Jacob Gasper is a 5th-year Bachelor of Architecture Student at Iowa State University College of Design where he is an undergraduate research assistant at the ISU Computation & Construction Lab. Gasper is conducting ongoing research titled "Robotic Architectural Clay Formwork" in collaboration with Cyle King in the Architectural Robotics Lab at the new Student Innovation Center at Iowa State University.

Unknowing

Catie Newell
University of Michigan

Zackery Belanger
Arcgeometer

Wes McGee
University of Michigan

Misri Patel
University of Michigan

1   Variations in openings and curvature of a glass pane created through the application of heat and a range of auxetic behaviors.

As digital fabrication and computation move deeper into the building sector, impressive contributions have relied on precision in complexity: heroic feats of geometry, innumerable custom parts, or the success of a prefabricated fit. Working over a design and its production in practice, even through the advancements made in physical iterations and informed simulations, often still depends on knowing precisely what you will get.

This determinacy can necessitate a reliance on *knowns*: rules, established conventions, and proofs. So much of how we operate is built on these elements. Questioning them—recognizing their limitations, identifying gaps in their reach, realizing they might be false or imperfect—can be a successful project unto itself. For almost 50 years, acoustic researchers accepted the known speed of sound as a truth. Then, in 1986, acoustician George S. K. Wong, while calibrating microphones, revealed that the "known" speed was slower by 0.16 meters per second than the value that had been accepted for decades (Wong 1986). In the science of acoustics, the speed of sound is an important constant. In architecture, it is fundamental to how sound reverberates in a space. In the interminable precision of science, the error discovered by Wong was tremendously large. For architecture, we must discern whether such an error is consequential in the determination of the shape or material of a space or, as often occurs with continuous variables, whether a threshold will be crossed between success and failure. If inconsequential now, will it remain so as fabrication technology and design evolve? Will it propagate or even compound with the uncertainties of other quantities? How precisely must it be known?

Material behaviors can be uncertain in ways that only experienced fabricators can understand. Even homogeneous materials can show unpredictable behavior triggered by thickness, shape, center of gravity, or temperature, to name a few traits. Acoustic architecture, an important physical and experiential condition of a space, adds more dimensions to this uncertainty, as temporally varying sound energy interacts with surfaces and fills spaces. Acoustics can invite a false sense of precision: if the target

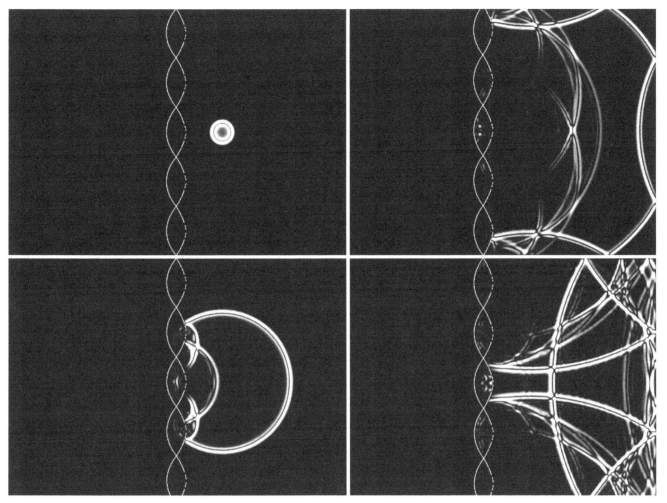

2   Stills from a simulation sequence demonstrating acoustic reflection, diffusion, and access to cavities through openings of limited dimension.

reverberation time for a room is less than 1.00 second, then is a time of 1.01 seconds a failure while a time of 0.99 seconds a success? The difference would not be distinguishable even to the most sensitive ear, and reverberation time itself is a gross oversimplification of the behavior of sound with its own uncertainties and their propagation. Even with unlimited precision, the idea of knowing what you will get can be called into question.

Adjacent to creating (or predicting) with precision is approaching the performance and experiential aspects of a material system via exploration of the troubling indeterminate area. Acoustics has a confusing relationship with the term "material." Fiberglass batt is labeled an acoustic material for its sound-absorbing properties, but a flat sheet, also made of glass and reflective to sound, is usually not. This distinction is fine for selling acoustic products driven by efficiency and influence. But since form is all that separates glass fibers from panes, what does the immense geometric area between the two have to offer? Does such a range apply to other materials as well? (It does.) An intriguing

realm of exploration for digital fabrication and computation is understanding and mastering variation within the gray areas, in this case between absorption and reflection. Seemingly opposite behaviors can arise from material configuration; everything between them also exists and can be accessed (Belanger 2021).

Panes of glass are cut and placed into a custom kiln, where they are heated to slump into the third spatial dimension. They move from acoustically reflective into the gray area. Shaped panels will diffuse sound, but this is not just about creating diffusers. This is about continuous change of form and acoustic properties. If the glass is assembled into cavities with the right balance of openings, they can exhibit Helmholtz resonance and absorb, touching on the realm dominated by fiberglass batt. And if assembled into arrays, the panels become an aggregate surface that approaches enclosure. The geometric result of slumping can be tuned by a number of variables: temperature ramp-up, maximum, and ramp-down; shape of the perimeter frame; thickness and color of the glass, and cuts made through the

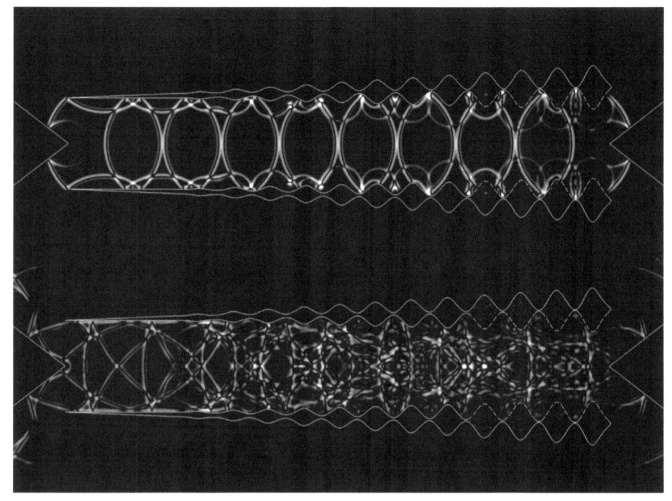

3   Simulation stills of sound in a 2D corridor made of rigid boundaries. From left to right the energy is coherent, then dispersed, then reduced. This demonstrates continuity between acoustic reflection, diffusion, and absorption.

glass surface. If the cuts are auxetic, then another layer of control is added or, better yet, is productively lost: the material itself can unwind at different rates and produce shapes not accessible with more static patterns. Each method of transformation has productive consequences that shift the acoustic behavior of the pane of glass, not necessarily in a linear fashion. This compounding indeterminacy clarifies the deception that occurs in giving precise definitions to moments along a spectrum and reveals unexpected behaviors, leading to new knowledge.

Continuous acoustic behavior and an unwinding material system sum together to give access to indeterminate regions of possibility, including transitions, boundaries, limits, and points of dramatic shift like a phase change or the crossing of a threshold. With the scale of operation, this shift cannot be precisely pinpointed within the known definitions. And maybe the known definitions are not necessary. It is challenging to diagram the acoustics of a variable system using the accepted categories of behavior—transmissive, reflective, diffusive, absorptive—and if shape is a

primary determining factor of performance, then the visual appearance of the surface becomes its own best acoustic diagram. This combination has removed the ability to find the exact knowns, and that might be how the most gains will be made in mastering variation, and therefore glimpsing what is possible.

In this time of a world of unknowns; in this moment of a strange pause, a time to rethink how we make, the why and what are thrown into question as well. It was within this pause that uncertainty within this material system went from a hindrance to the greatest value. Our understanding of the connections between form and aural performance has strengthened. There is productive value in abandoning precise definitions.

ACKNOWLEDGMENTS

Project Team: Misri Patel, Oliver Popadich, Elizabeth Teret, Dan Tish, Maryam Alhajri, Ryan Craney, Hannah Kirkpatrick, Amin Aghagholizadeh.

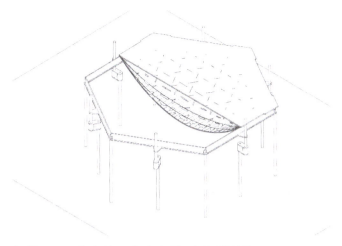

4   Glass pane altering formally during the slump process.

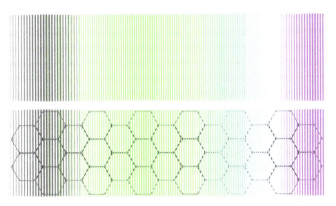

5   Diagram indicating a range of acoustic behaviors along the length of a wall for a given frequency.

6   A volume created between two slumped panes.

Funding support: Guardian Industries, Taubman College of Architecture and Urban Planning, University of Michigan, Arcgeometer LC.

REFERENCES

Belanger, Zackery. 2021. *Acoustic Ornament*. Detroit: Arcgeometer.

Wong, George S. K. 1986. "Speed of Sound in Standard Air." *The Journal of the Acoustical Society of America* 79: 1359.

IMAGE CREDITS

All drawings and images by the authors.

Catie Newell is the Director of the Master of Science in Digital and Material Technologies and Associate Professor of Architecture at the University of Michigan's Taubman College of Architecture and Urban Planning. Newell is also a founding principal of the architecture and research practice Alibi Studio.

Zackery Belanger is the founder and director of Arcgeometer, a Detroit-based studio dedicated to design, research, and implementation of the intrinsic acoustic properties of architecture.

Wes McGee is an Associate Professor in Architecture and the Director of the Fabrication and Robotics Lab at the University of Michigan's Taubman College of Architecture and Urban Planning, as well as a principal at Matter Design.

Misri Patel is an Indian architect and researcher. She earned her MS DMT from the University of Michigan, during which she assisted Sean Ahlquist. Patel gained professional experience at sP+ a, Mumbai, and LOT-EK, New York. Currently, she is a Research Associate at Taubman College and most recently served as the 2019-2020 Ballard Fellow at the CoAD, Lawrence Technological University.

Remote Impressions: Roboformed Prototypes for a Nomadic Studio

Thomas Pearce
The Bartlett School of Architecture

Gary Edwards
The Bartlett School of Architecture

1   SPIF toolpath overlay of both skins of the prototype wall, showing the transformation between interior and exterior ladder.

Someone walking past the robotics lab, seeing the steel panel with the shape of a chair pressed into it, asks us how we have managed to vacuum-form steel. The chair belongs to James, we explain, the sculptor with whom we are designing and building a mobile artist studio. James has become famous for making fantastically absurd sculptures—he is just finishing a boat that will pull itself up the bank of the Thames, inspired by the comical amphibian mudskipper after which it is named. Like all of James Capper's sculptures, it actually works.

Now we are collaborating on the next amphibious sculpture inspired by lizard locomotion. The chair is one of many objects that will come on its expeditions and will be stowed away into the wall of the extremely compact studio. We picked the old-fashioned piece, with its leather upholstering, turned legs, and backrest stiles, because it conjures up images of Admiral Nelson's chair on the HMS *Victory*—except that now, in an odd hybridization of preindustrial and postindustrial manufacturing processes, it is 3D-scanned and robotically formed.

All of the 50+ panels of the 1:1 prototype wall that we are currently building are fabricated using robotic Single Point Incremental Forming (SPIF). But it is while prototyping this chair panel, with its awkward geometry and challenging depth, that we tear the most sheets, blunt the most end effectors—and consequently learn the most. We learn that the flexible timber framework backing the panels, which we developed because it was quick, cheap, and variable, had the added advantage of yielding to forces, which compensates for the more unforgiving material constraints of the sheet steel we are forming. We learn that, as the robot gradually presses the panel into shape, the timber substructure tends to creak like an old sailing boat. We learn that our end effector should equally be softer than the material it is forming and finally settle on a brass stylus, which we have to sharpen like a pencil between forming.

Because the chair is difficult (and perhaps slightly silly), because it tells the fabrication process what to do rather than just listening to what it has on offer, we learn how to analyze and optimize formable geometries: filtering the

2   The thick wall of the artist studio (photograph by Greg Storrar).

3   Overlay of studio locomotion (photograph by Greg Storrar).

4   A difficult chair (photograph by Thomas Pearce).

scan according to draft angles, smoothing and relaxing the mesh, modeling the surface between the scan and the edge of the formable surface according to allowable geometrical constraints (many quantifiable, many intuited) for robotic forming. We learn to generate toolpaths that minimize the common SPIF "pillow effect" and continue to battle what we call the "pinching effect", an extreme case of pillowing that appears specifically at the point where the long valleys around the chair's legs close in on themselves and accumulate (or "pinch") excess material.

Our dialogue with the chair, or rather the dialogue between the chair and the sheet, with us as mediators, becomes more interesting when more voices join in. A conversation between the studio's two skins unfolds. The exterior 0.9mm steel skin is riveted onto a structural frame (the very same frame we use for forming, with a set of standardized clamping plates, to secure the blank panels in the first place), whereas the interior 0.9mm aluminum skin is hung, thermally separated, from the load-bearing exterior frame. The conversation between the two skins is marked

by transformations and productive mistranslations: an axe head inside offers a boot scraper outside; the swing of James's knee, sitting at his desk on the inside, presses into the aluminum skin, the knee cap traced by a secondary toolpath expressing the patella structure, and translates as a bulge on the outside, where it is used as a leg-up to climb an exterior ladder and access the studio's roof. A secondary dotted pattern, added to the upper leg, provides extra grip to this step. The inner sitter helps the outer climber.

Without touching, through the mediation of the thick in-between of the physical wall, of the digital modeling process and the material and robotic fabrication constraints, the two skins modulate each other, resulting in strange hybrids. The exterior ladder, for example, echoes a moveable ladder on the inside, transforming the intersection of its treads and stringers to form three pairs of circular protrusions, "nipples" that accept the bent rungs for the exterior ladder. Below these nipples, another knee emerges, which, rather than an echo of an internal knee, follows the need for an

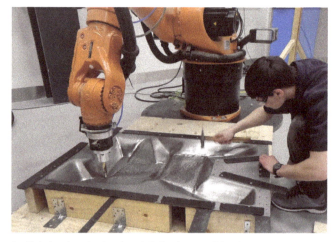

5　Digital and analog forming of chair (photograph by Thomas Pearce).

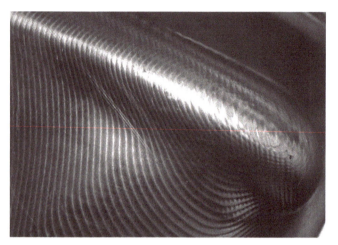

6　Interior knee with patella toolpath (photograph by Thomas Pearce).

7　Capper with prototype wall and interior ladder (photograph by Theo Tan).

additional step between the first knee and the first rung. The ladder's knee is the deepest and steepest piece of forming we do.

We have nearly forgotten the person who had prompted our train of thought with the initial question about the chair panel—and who is still listening, though seeming slightly puzzled about how the conversation has moved from a timber chair to walls growing nipples and ladders begetting knees. Perhaps the project's conceptual framework has escalated? But then again, perhaps by doing so, it has continued to challenge us as digital makers? And perhaps, within the cross-contamination between bodies, objects, skins, and code, another type of knowledge has emerged—a hybrid knowledge? In the background, the creaking boat sound grows louder and louder, it is time we sharpen our brass pencil.

ACKNOWLEDGMENTS

Monitor, the mobile studio discussed in this piece, is a project by James Capper, Thomas Pearce, and Greg Storrar.

The team at The Bartlett School of Architecture (University College London): Thomas Pearce, project lead, design; Greg Storrar (ARB), design; Gary Edwards (ARB), robotics; Theo Tan and Cristina Garza Lasierra, research assistants.

This project is made possible thanks to generous support from the Higher Education Innovation Fund (UCL Knowledge Exchange grant), the Bartlett's Architectural Project Fund, Hannah Barry Gallery (London), Izolyatsia (Kyiv), and Tata Steel. Many thanks to the staff at B-Made for enabling and supporting our research. The robotic incremental sheet-forming in this project was initially based on a research project developed by Cristina Garza Lasierra (DfM) in collaboration with Vincent Huyghe of B-Made

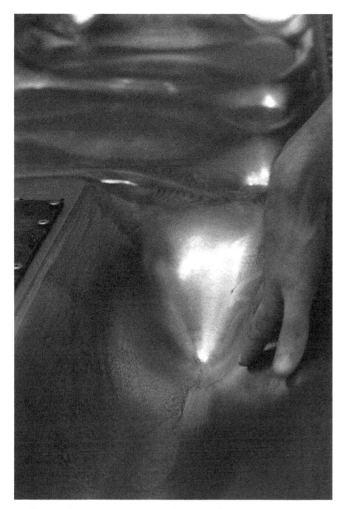

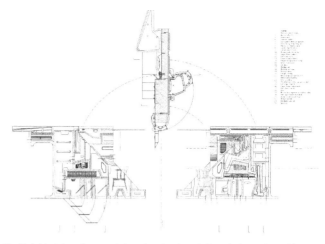

9   Unfolded elevations and plan, showing translations between two skins.

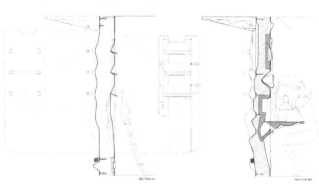

10   Cross-sections illustrating bodies transforming through the two skins.

8   The exterior ladder's leg-up knee (photograph by Thomas Pearce).

IMAGE CREDITS

Figure 1-3: © Greg Storrar

Figure 7: © Theo Tan

All other drawings and images by the authors.

Thomas Pearce is a Lecturer at the Bartlett School of Architecture, where he currently teaches in the MArch Design for Manufacture program. His collaborative design research practice straddles the boundaries between architectural design and fabrication, historical reconstruction and speculation, performance and technological subversion. He has worked extensively in practice as a specialist for digital capture, design, and fabrication. Pearce holds a BA and MA (KULeuven, Belgium) in Cultural History and a BSc (TUBerlin) and MArch (Bartlett) in Architecture, and is currently finishing his PhD thesis in Architectural Design at the Bartlett.

Gary Edwards is a Chartered Architect, researcher, and computational designer. Having studied at the Bartlett (Unit 23), he is no stranger to analog and robotic methods of fabrication. He works closely with free and open source communities developing bespoke design tools that bridge digital and physical realms. He worked a number of years at the global engineering firm Arup, where he was Software and Tools Leader for Architecture. He has taught at the Bartlett and AA Schools of Architecture as well as in industrial settings. He currently runs his own consultancy and design practice.

There Has Never Been a Patient Zero

Tiziano Derme*
MAEID / University of
Innsbruck

Daniela Mitterberger*
MAEID / ETH Zürich

Gonzalo Vaillo*
MORPHtopia / University of
Innsbruck

Jordi Vivaldi*
IAAC Barcelona

*Authors contributed equally to the work

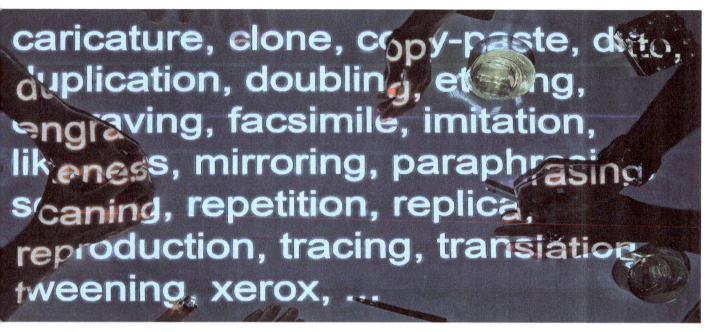

1 "We argue that to reveal the opportunities embedded within this techno-perceptive condition demands that we delve into the concepts orbiting around the notion of copy".

Transparency Society and Sliding Perception

The arrival of the notion of "Hyper-Communication" and its associated "Transparency Society"[1] (Han 2015) reveals a new media condition: an informational framework characterized by being carnal, recursive, omnipresent, immediate, intimate, and exact. This optimized and embodied gaze constructs a pervasive communicative scenario that differs from the predigital era by a paradoxical fact: while the amount of information exposed has been massively expanded, the exposure time of each informational phenomena, particularly visual representations, has been considerably reduced. This results in a drastic decrease of the amount of time available for its cognition and the exhaustion of its Value-Information (Baudrillard 1981). This cognitive framework responds to a 21st-century technological condition in which iterative algorithmic repetition (Sadin 2013) has become the mode of production par excellence. The massive, immediate, embodied, and ubiquitous proliferation of information characteristic of our age, widely celebrated—by themselves and in themselves—through our social networks, constructs a regime of sameness inaugurating a new form of sensibility: a perceptual condition defined here with the expression "sliding perception." Rather than intermittent attention operating through discrete jumps and accumulations of ratios, sliding perception is, above all, a scrolled perception based on perpetual replacement and iterative substitution.

It is constituted as a sensibility characterized by a frictionless and wandering attention: an elongated scrolling and an insistent deferral, an oscillating—almost ludic—dérive, always incomplete, always voracious, but, paradoxically, at the same time, always saturated, always flooded. Always doubting between the "enough" and the "more," always alternating between the "tedious" and the "colorful," sliding perception does not imply a mere de-sensibilization, but a re-sensibilization orchestrating a twofold action: the eye is being hypo-sensitized as a tool for sensing differentiation, while it is being hypersensitized as a tool for sensing repetition.

2 "Hyper-communication as a media condition is associated with the 'Transparency Society'."

4 "Sliding perception: It is always incomplete, always voracious, but, paradoxically, at the same time, always saturated, always flooded. It is always oscillating between the 'enough' and the 'more.'"

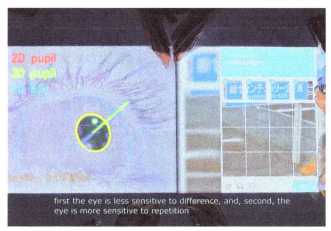

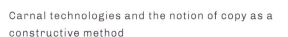

3 "Sliding perception is not just a passive act receiving information, but simultaneously it is an active act producing information. It links our body with the devices...."

5 "The landmark exhibition *Les Immateriaux* by Lyotard foreshadowed the turning point of a technology that partially might lead to disembodiment, globalization, and an accelerated rate of information exchange."

Carnal technologies and the notion of copy as a constructive method

In this scenario, this text argues that to reveal the opportunities embedded within this techno-perceptive condition demands that we delve into the concepts orbiting around the notion of copy, an approach already taken by Hannah Arendt (1972) and Jacques Derrida (2005) with the notion of the lie. Today, the old dichotomy "repetition/differentiation" dissolves into a myriad of derivatives associated with the former: replica, paraphrase, duplication, transcript, reproduction, mimesis, copy-paste, tweening, scanning, doubling, cloning, repetition, ditto, engraving, or facsimile emerge as the modes of production par excellence of the 21st century. Those mechanistic tendencies fall today into a new literacy and creative abilities based primarily on short attention span: recursive algorithms, databasing, data trailing, recycling, remixing, appropriation, intentional plagiarism, identity ciphering, and intensive reprogramming (Goldsmith 2011). These actions are used as daily intensifiers shaking the notions of identity, media, and culture as

they have been established by the industrial paradigm of the 20th century. Thus, the notion of "copy," traditionally marginalized by the Western glorification of the idea of creation and its secularization through the modern myth of the tabula rasa, is redeemed: in the 21st century, copying, in its plethora of modulations, has the potential to fuel new modes of contribution. However, a question arises: How to produce difference in a regime of transparency? How to produce distinction in a regime of sameness? How to produce originality when there is no Patient Zero? Under the regime of the algorithmic copy, the notion of originality demands reconsideration: rather than approaching what is original as what is distinct, the former must be read as what is originative. The original is no longer only what is necessarily different, disparate, or divergent, but what originates: while what is distinct necessarily refers to the past in order to differ from it, what is fertile cannot but refer to the future in order to inseminate it.

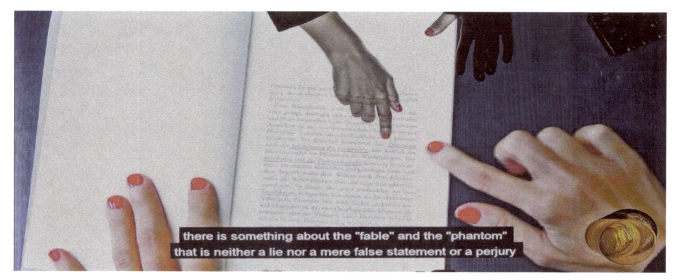

there is something about the "fable" and the "phantom" that is neither a lie nor a mere false statement or a perjury

6   "We argue that to reveal the opportunities embedded within this techno-perceptive condition demands that we delve into the concepts orbiting around the notion of copy."

Thus, the notion of copy exposed here opposes both its modern and postmodern equivalents: while modernism relies on the spatial copy of an optimized standard, post-modernism relies on the historical copy of a calligraphic gesture. However, in what specific way does the notion of algorithmic copy instrumentalized here differ from the one done by these two precedents? Is it in its computational nature? Is it in its autonomous vocation? Is it in its ubiquitous condition? Is it in the iinformation's increment, or in the reduction characteristic of algorithmic copying processes? And, above all, how is this specificity associated with our technological scenario?

In this sense, Lyotard's landmark exhibition *Les Immateriaux* foreshadowed a turning point: it prophesied a technological insurrection advocating for radical disembodiment, globalization, and an accelerated rate of information exchange. However, the fact that our body is still—maybe more than ever—intimately associated with immaterial technologies radically transforms the way we perceive and produce information: it opens the door to interactive processes whose immediacy and ubiquity might partially circumvent the moral, political, and aesthetic filters associated with our consciousness. Thus, the Hyper-Communication society is, above all, an embodied society disrupting any unitarian conception of the notion of subject: it impacts our bodies, emphasizing its relational, affective, and transversal dimension; it constructs desynchronized, kaleidoscopic, and diffracted corporalities collaboratively linked to a material network of organic and nonorganic beings. In light of this embedded scenario, a hybrid techno-natural regime emerges: defined here with the expression "carnal technologies", it capitalizes on one fact of crucial relevance in our cultural landscape: the

recursive and intimate association between (in)organic bodies and digital agents.

The projection on this technological scenario of the algorithmic register of the notion of copy, together with all of its associated terminological universe, aim at unveiling, understanding, and contextualizing new logics of production: a set of modes of action linked to recursive protocols that are intimately interlaced to a massive and carnal management of data.

However, the centralization of the notion of copy in light of this technological context raises a number of questions: For example, does our celebration of "copy" cancel the value of creativity? Or, should we still produce originality? Can we produce originality? Is the notion of newness intrinsically implying a modern attitude towards design? And, above all, can a copy, in the foliated structure characteristic of its algorithmic register, be a critical contribution?

FOOTNOTES

[1] The thinker Byung-Chul Han posits that the notion of transparency is a false ideal in contemporary society. According to Han, things presented without singularity or depth are "transparent" and are only governed by the "exhibition value," posing no meaning at all. See Byung-Chul Han, *The Transparency Society* (2012; repr., Stanford, CA: Stanford University Press, 2015). Our approach takes Han's concept neither as an endemic condition of the current technological age that denigrates the old romantic and contemplative social dynamics nor as technological positivism, but as an opportunity to reconsider the value systems, categorizations, and beliefs within the already-established regime of hyper-communication.

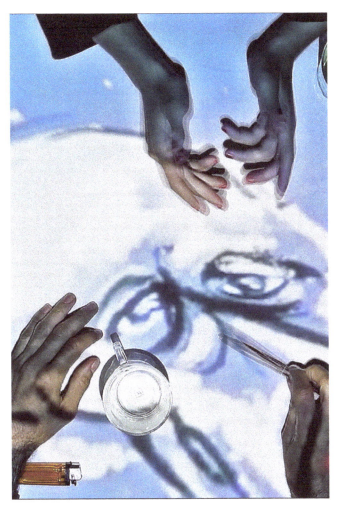

7 "In this biopolitical regime of sameness where there is no Patient Zero, the notion of "copy," traditionally marginalized by the Western canonization of the idea of creation is redeemed."

REFERENCES

Arendt, Hannah. 1972. *Crises of the Republic: Lying in Politics*. Boston: Houghton Mifflin Harcourt.

Baudrillard, Jean. 1981. *Simulacra and Simulation- The implosion of Meaning in the Media*. Paris: Éditions Galilée & Semiotext(e).

Derrida, Jacques. 2005. *Without Alibi*. Stanford: Stanford University Press.

Goldsmith, Kenneth. 2011. *Uncreative Writing: Managing Language in the Digital Age*. New York: Columbia University Press.

Han, Byung-Chul. 2015. *The Transparency Society*. Stanford, CA: Stanford University Press. First published 2012.

Sadin, Eric. 2013. *L' humanité augmentée*. Paris: Editions L' échappée.

IMAGE CREDITS

Figure 1-7: © by the authors.

Tiziano Derme is an architect, researcher, and media artist, co-founder and director of MAEID-FutureRetrospectiveNarrative, an interdisciplinary design practice based in Vienna. His work ranges between biomaterials, robotics, and design performativity. Derme's work has been widely recognized with several grants and has been exhibited at various events, institutions, and galleries. Derme is currently a researcher at the University of Applied Arts Angewandte, and Assistant Professor and PhD fellow at the University of Innsbruck with the chair of Marjan Colletti at the Institute for Experimental Architecture, where he researches robotic fabrication and applied bio-fabrication.

Daniela Mitterberger is an architect and researcher with a strong interest in new media, human/body relationship, digital fabrication, and emerging technologies. Mitterberger is cofounder and director of MAEID-FutureRetrospectiveNarrative, a multidisciplinary architecture practice based in Vienna. Currently, she is a PhD researcher at Gramazio-Kohler Research at the ETH Zurich, focusing on intuition in digital design and robotic fabrication. Previously, Mitterberger was a lecturer at several international graduate and postgraduate programs. Her award-winning work has been widely exhibited at various galleries, institutions, and events such as La Biennale di Venezia, Ars Electronica Linz, Melbourne Triennial, Academy of Fine Arts Vienna, and HdA Graz.

Gonzalo Vaillo is a registered architect and designer based in Vienna. He is the founder and director of MORPHtopia, a studio committed to the reciprocal relationship between speculation and tangible, efficient formalizations in architecture, product design, and art installations. His theoretical work focuses on aesthetics, technology, and philosophy for the development of a design theory of the unknown as a design material. Vaillo has taught at the University of Applied Arts Vienna, Texas A&M University, and is a University Assistant at the Institute for Experimental Architecture. Hochbau at the University of Innsbruck.

Jordi Vivaldi is a writer, philosopher, and architectural theorist based in Vienna, and is a PhD Architect and PhD Philosopher (cand.). Vivaldi works as a theory faculty in the Institute for Advanced Architecture in Barcelona, UCL Bartlett in London, and the Institute of Urban Design in Austria. His research capitalizes on the notion of "limit," both as an ontological device of com-pression/ex-pression and as an architectural form of space. Besides several essays and lectures, his work has crystallized in two forthcoming books, with Actar Publishers): *The Threefold Logic of Advanced Architecture* and *In-Limit: Space and Agency in a Subjectless World*.

VIDEOS

Videos are a new submission type introduced for the 2020 ACADIA Conference. The intent was to showcase innovative work that lends itself to a video format viewed online. The video submissions were reviewed and selected by an external jury consisting of Kristy Balliet of SCI-Arc, Hina Jamelle of the University of Pennsylvania Weitzman School, Mara Marcu of the University of Cincinnati, and Tsz Yan Ng of University of Michigan Taubman College.

TERRAMIA
Housing Prototypes

Stephanie Chaltiel
MuDD Architects

Maite Bravo
British Columbia Institute
of Technology (BCIT), MuDD
Architects

The three housing prototypes were commissioned by Regione Lombardia, Isola Design District 2019, and built during the Milan Design Week on Regione Lomardia head-quarters. The exhibit highlighted how new technologies applied to housing could tackle certain aspects of a global housing crisis.

Terramia is an emergency mud-shell housing prototype aimed at highlighting the potential of using drone spraying of locally sourced raw mortars on light formworks.

To deploy the prototypes, thin bamboo arches were arranged in bundles to provide a suitable geometry for the light formwork and were transported and secured into position on site. A tailor-made jute fabric was designed to fit into each dome and was set on site with the help of a drone to lift up the large fabrics over the arches, and tensioned by hand to provide a suitable surface for the spraying stage. Once the light formwork was set in place, the drone spraying sessions started by depositing a succession of carefully formulated mortars. In addition to spraying a series of viscous earthen mortars, the drone was also

blowing a byproduct of the local agriculture, rice husks, to increase the insulation of the resulting vaults. The three mud shells were completed in only five days.

Besides exhibiting the technique to a large audience, this project helped the teams involved to map the drone trajectories, to set up suitable distances to the surface, to establish drone spraying pressures for each stage, and to formulate construction protocols for future permanent projects that could be built using this technique.

The highly multidisciplinary team involved in the project includes bamboo experts (Canya Viva) and two engineering firms focused on innovation and sustainability (Summum Engineering and AKT II).

ACKNOWLEDGMENTS

Regione Lombardia

Isola Design District

Design and Modeling Team

Stephanie Chaltiel, Fabio Gatti | MuDD Architects

Jonathan Cory-Wright | CanyaViva

Structural Engineering

Diederik Veenendaal, Francesco Verzura | Summum Engineering

Gavin Sayers, Edoardo Tibuzzi | AKT II

Construction

Jonathan Cory-Wright | CanyaViva

Michan Daris | RC Take off

Sébastien Goessens | Université catholique de Louvain, Belgium

Euromair

Francesco Verzura | Summum Engineering

Construction Volunteers

Nadia Avezzano, Alessandra Benigno, Miriam Ceravolo, Michele Francia, Giulia Rosa, Mark Witte.

IMAGE CREDITS

Studio Naaro

Diego Delgado

Stephanie Chaltiel is a French architect and interior designer working with innovative techniques and natural materials, offering unique designs for each project. She began her career in Mexico and French Guyana building houses by hand with local dwellers. After working for Bernard Tschumi in New York, OMA, and Zaha Hadid, she started her own practice. Her award-winning projects marrying cutting-edge technology and raw materials (ACADIA, MIT 2017, part of the ICON Design 100 Talents 2019 and Dezeen Awards Winners Highly Commended mention, Fast Company World Changing Ideas Awards 2020) have been presented and exhibited worldwide. She taught at SUTD Singapore, Westminster London, AA London, Ravensbourne London, at the architectural school at the University of Brighton, and more recently at Elisava Barcelona. She was also an EU Marie Curie scholarship recipient for four years, during which she developed the drone spray technology for sustainable architecture and refurbishments.

Maite Bravo is an architect, educator, and researcher studying concepts and design methodologies emerging from the use of digital design and its immersion into the architectural praxis, with emphasis in architectural theory, built shell structures, robotic fabrication techniques, and bio-climatic design. She holds degrees of Architecture (U. of Chile), a Master of Advanced Architecture (IAAC), a Master of Architectural Design (ETSAB-UPC), and a PhD

International Mention "Cum Laude" distinction (ETSAB-UPC). She is currently senior faculty at the British Columbia Institute of Technology (BCIT), leading the Architectural Building Technology-Architectural Elective, and senior faculty at IAAC Master in Advanced Computation for Architecture and Design, MaCAD . Her working experience includes several architectural firms in Chile, GBL architects as associate (Canada), collaborations with the Barcelona Municipality and the Barcelona Regional Agency, research with MuDD architects (Spain), and partner at B3 Arquitectes (Chile). Her ground-breaking work has been featured in several international publications and exhibitions, including the ACADIA 2017 research award on Robotic Fabrication for Monolithic Earthen Shells for her ongoing collaborations with Stephanie Chaltiel.

Patty & Jan

Brandon Clifford
MIT / Matter Design

Tyler Swingle
Matter Design

Davide Zampini
CEMEX Global R&D

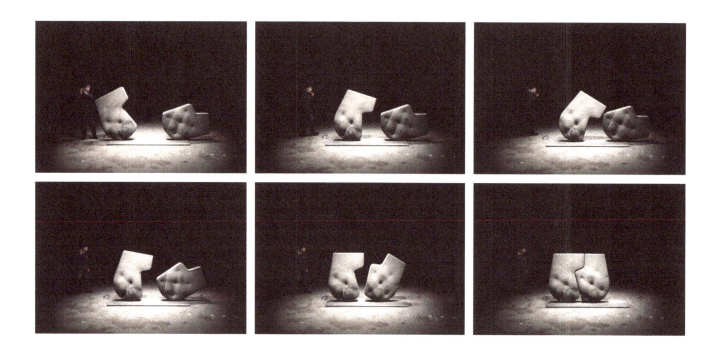

Patty & Jan is a massive concrete assembly that explores the curious and playful possibilities of architecture by focusing on the process of construction rather than the end product. By extending and magnifying the process, even impractically, with movement, momentum, and impact, *Patty & Jan* incorporate colossal collisions as performative moments that encourage human engagement. Like other civilizations past and present such as the Amish's use of community for barn raisings, the Inka's use of ritual to engender eternal construction, or the Rapanui's use of ceremony to transport massive stones, human engagement during construction is a social generator and impacts the units of construction and the construction technique (Swingle et al. 2019). As a medium, audiovisuals, although unintentionally chronological, capture and communicate the visual and audible energy of *Patty & Jan*'s timing, kinetics and physics associated with both their human engagement and construction process.

As a reciprocal partnership between a pair of massive concrete masonry units (MCMU), *Patty & Jan* ensures one cannot assemble without the other. Starting in static positions at a predetermined distance apart from one another, a weighted tool is effortlessly removed from *Patty* by a human to alter the center of mass (CoM) and create a righting moment. As *Patty* is released from both the human and tool, the audiovisual depicts both the change of state from static to dynamic, as well as an acceleration during the dynamic state, relaying a moment of tension and suspense as *Patty* quietly rolls towards *Jan* with increasing speed. After rotating, the nose of *Patty*, embedded with a high-strength concrete, collides with *Jan* and strikes a resounding echo that fills the air and awakens *Jan*. The controlled impact triggers *Jan* to first rotate backwards, rebound off its braking surface, and then counter-rotate towards *Patty*. The different speeds of *Patty & Jan* seen in the audiovisual represent the difference in both the calculated weight and rotational energy of each MCMU. As the two roll towards each other and meet along their assembly surfaces in the middle, a slight grinding sound can be heard as the two slip into their assembled position. Confirmed by the lack of motion and noise, *Patty & Jan* are together.

In addition to the performance at the "From Lab to Site: Innovation in Concrete" symposium (Matter Design and CEMEX Global R&D, 2019), recordings of calculating and testing *Patty & Jan* were shown because the different speeds, accelerations, and collisions provide a more holistic understanding of *Patty & Jan's* characteristics. Compared side by side at the same time, the dynamic differences are more accentuated and depict the variability of the movement *Patty & Jan* had throughout the prototype phases. In the audiovisual, the energy of *Patty & Jan's* timing, kinetics, and physics are represented as both a construction process and a social generator such as a spectacle or performance. This harmony is the foundation for thinking about larger and more complex construction choreographies that engage material as well as human bodies in the building of architecture.

ACKNOWLEDGMENTS

This research is produced in collaboration between Matter Design and CEMEX Global R&D. The recursion solver is generated through a custom definition that employs Anemone (theobject.co/anemone). The former, a plugin developed by Object to resolve recursion in Grasshopper (grasshopper3d.com), yet another plugin developed by David Rutten for the Robert McNeel developed program, Rhinoceros (rhino3d.com).

REFERENCES

Matter Design and CEMEX Global R&D. "Patty & Jan." Performance at the "From Lab to Site: Innovation in Concrete" conference hosted by the University of Michigan Taubman College of Architecture and Urban Planning and the University of Michigan College of Civil and Environmental Engineering. Ann Arbor, MI, November 1, 2019.

Swingle, Tyler, Davide Zampini, and Brandon Clifford. 2019. "Walking Assembly: A Method for Craneless Tilt-Up Construction." In *Design Modelling Symposium Berlin*, 237–249. Cham: Springer.

IMAGE CREDITS

All images by the authors.

Brandon Clifford mines knowledge from the past to design new futures. He is best known for bringing megalithic sculptures to life to perform tasks. Clifford is the director of Matter Design and Associate Professor at the Massachusetts Institute of Technology. As a designer and researcher, Clifford has received recognition with prizes such as the American Academy in Rome Prize, a TED Fellowship, the SOM Prize, and the Architectural League Prize for Young Architects & Designers. Clifford is dedicated to reimagining the role of the architect. His speculative work continues to provoke new directions for the digital era.

Tyler Swingle is Research Lead and Project Manager at Matter Design and holds a lecturer position at McGill University. In his work, he is committed to exploring the reciprocity between materials and computational methods. His role as part of Matter Design includes both ancient building techniques and new material technologies.

Davide Zampini has over 30 years of experience in the construction materials industry and is best known for pushing the limits of innovation in cement-based products and building solutions. Adopting a design- and industrially driven innovation approach, Zampini leads a multidisciplinary and culturally diverse team at CEMEX's Center for Innovation and Technology. Through adaptive research and development conceived with versatility in mind, Zampini's team at CEMEX in Switzerland develops novel functionalities in cement-based materials that incorporate customer-centered strategies and are designed to create solid emotional ties to a material that for ages has been considered "gray."

Terrestrial Reef: Robotic Gardens from the Series Artificial Ecologies

Tiziano Derme
University of Innsbruck/
MAEID

Daniela Mitterberger
MAEID/ETH Zurich

Marjan Colletti
University of Innsbruck/UCL

Terrestrial Reef is a 21st-century techno-organic garden consisting of both natural and synthetic elements. The project reflects on the often troubled, incompatible, and even oppressive binary relationship between the built environment and the natural environment as defined by western modernity, while proposing an alternative to the current cultural associations to nature as "green" or "sustainable"(Karafyllis 2003). The project offers an alternative material-driven design approach where processes of robotic fabrication are coupled with natural systems and environmental agents (Mitterberger and Derme, 2020).

Within this framework, *Terrestrial Reef* tries to reorient us away from the word "Nature" and towards the word "Terrestrial." The term Terrestrial" refers to the idea that animate and inanimate beings are not limited by frontiers and dichotomies but embedded into and within one another. The vital character of this approach and its coordination within the biotechnological continuum demonstrate the potential novel transformations of borders of life and the classification of the terms "natural," "living," "artificial," or

"synthetic" (Šlesingerová 2017). Within this context, humans, species, and technologies are not specified but considered as "Earthbound" (Latour 2018). We may start to look at the word "Terrestrial" as a point of departure to encompass and promote other agencies, deoptimizing the way we look at the world, deconstructing the false belief of precision and control over new forms of intelligence and autonomy. The *Artificial Ecologies* series describes the ubiquitous reality of computing not just by introducting information media into surfaces, but also by how it nurtures what is already there. It extends its ubiquity into a new material substrate of things through biochemical heterogeneity, nested diversity, transversal contamination, and symbiotic transmission. *Terrestrial Reef* is constituted simultaneously by in situ and in vitro technologies, the first applied to the production of computed substrates, while the second is applied through micropropagation techniques that cultivate in a controlled environment the *Ganoderma lucidum* fungal species. The blending of biology and technology—or, more precisely, biological life and fabricated environments—constitutes a novel diagram of the built environment governed by renewal evolution and degradation. The project considers the discipline of design within quite different regulatory boundaries, dissolving existing differences through processes of integration and translation. This condition refers to a context where design is understood as a vehicle to create dissensus—not as a medium of harmonizing parts to the whole, but rather as a condition of coexistence between different agents and velocities. It redirects design towards a new ethics of ecological information: modes of action capable of augmenting the capacities of exposed surfaces and entire organisms, while expanding their interaction beyond a command-and-control state.

ACKNOWLEDGMENTS

This video is an excerpt from the silver-medal-winning project at the Gardening Will Save the World – IKEA & Tom Dixon pavilion at the 2019 RHS Royal Chelsea Flower Show. The project follows the project *Pahoehoe Beauty* (presented at the Ars Electronica Festival in 2018) and is situated within a series of techno-organic gardens titled *Artificial Ecologies* developed by MAEID (Tiziano Derme and Daniela Mitterberger). This research would not have been possible without the support of the University of Innsbruck, Marjan Colletti (Faculty of Architecture, Institut fur experimentelle Architektur, REX|LAB), and UCL (The Bartlett School of Architecture). We would like to thank especially Tyroler Glückspilze GmbH (fungi research), BMade at The Bartlett School of Architecture University College London (robotic arm), REX|LAB at Innsbruck University (facilities), and the entire team involved in the construction of the garden (Moritz Riedl and Lukas Vorreiter).

REFERENCES

Mitterberger, Daniela, and Tiziano Derme. 2020. "Digital Soil: Robotically 3D-Printed Granular Bio-Composites." *International Journal of Architectural Computing* 18 (2): 194–211. https://doi.org/10.1177/1478077120924996.

Karafyllis, Nicole C. 2003. "Renewable Resources and the Idea of Nature – What Has Biotechnology Got to Do With It?" *Journal of Agricultural and Environmental Ethics* 16 (1): 3–28. https://doi.org/10.1023/a:1021747521534.

Latour, Bruno. 2018. *Down to Earth: Politics in the New Climatic Regime*. Cambridge: Polity Press.

Šlesingerová, Eva. 2017. "Biopower Imagined: Biotechnological Art and Life Engineering." *Social Science Information* 57 (1): 59–76. https://doi.org/10.1177/0539018417745164.

IMAGE CREDITS

All video stills by the authors.

Tiziano Derme is an architect and researcher interested in the application of biotechnologies in the context of architectural design. He is the co-founder and director of MAEID - FutureRetrospectiveNarrative, an interdisciplinary design practice based in Vienna. His work ranges between biomaterials, robotics, and design performativity. Derme's work has been widely recognized with several grants and has been exhibited at various events, institutions, and galleries. Derme is currently a researcher at the University of Applied Arts Angewandte, Assistant Professor and PhD fellow at the University of Innsbruck with the chair of Marjan Colletti at the Institute for Experimental Architecture, where he researches robotic fabrication and applied bio-fabrication.

Daniela Mitterberger is an architect and researcher with a strong interest in new media, human/body relationship, digital fabrication, and emerging technologies. Mitterberger is co-founder and director of MAEID - FutureRetrospectiveNarrative, a multidisciplinary architecture practice based in Vienna. Currently, she is a PhD researcher at Gramazio-Kohler Research at the ETH Zurich, focusing on intuition in digital design and robotic fabrication. Previously, Mitterberger was a lecturer at several international graduate and postgraduate programs. Her award-winning work has been widely exhibited at various galleries, institutions, and events such as La Biennale di Venezia, Ars Electronica Linz, Melbourne Triennial, Academy of Fine Arts Vienna, and HdA Graz.

Marjan Colletti is an architect, designer, educator, researcher, and author. He is a professor and part-time Chair Building Design and Construction and head of the Institute of Experimental Architecture as well as the founder of REX|LAB, the robotic experimentation laboratory at the University of Innsbruck. He is also a part-time full Professor of Architecture and Postdigital Practice (first worldwide) and co-director of the MArch Architecture (ARB/RIBA Part 2) at The Bartlett School of Architecture UCL London. Colletti has exhibited over 90 times in international venues. He publishes and lectures regularly on design research and research-led education, and acts as scientific reviewer for several major funding bodies in the UK, Switzerland, Canada, Russia, and Australia.

Bioplastic Robotic Materialization

Sina Mostafavi
TU Delft and Dessau Institute
of Architecture, DARS.hub

Manuel Kretzer
HS Anhalt, Dessau Department
of Design, Materiability Group

Bioplastics or biopolymers are substances that are composed of renewable organic biomass sources, such as starch, cellulose, or sugar. Because of their biological origin, they are inherently biodegradable, which means that they can easily be broken down into carbon dioxide, water, energy, and cell mass with the aid of microbes, rendering them largely carbon-neutral. On top of their ecological advantages to standard plastics, which are largely derived from petrochemicals and can take hundreds of years to degrade, they help to conserve fossilized raw materials and the dependency on mineral oil. Within this collaborative course between the Dessau Department of Design and the Dessau Institute of Architecture, we set out to explore the potentials of such bioplastic materials in combination with cutting-edge robotic fabrication in order to produce compostable products. The learning objectives of this course were twofold. On the one hand, the participants became acquainted with the fundamentals of parametric design for robotic production. On the other hand, they performed systematic scientific experiments with bioplastic in order to develop the perfect material for robotic production. Following a phase of experimental research, the overall goal was to design and robotically produce lampshades made from self-made bioplastic material. According to the outcomes of the experiments and design explorations, relevant techniques of robotic fabrication such as subtractive or additive manufacturing as well as cutting were used.

ACKNOWLEDGMENTS

As the coordinators of the Bioplastic Robotic Materialization collaborative project between Dessau Department of Design and Dessau Institute of Architecture, the authors acknowledge and admire the efforts of tutor assistants, students, and colleagues involved in this course.

Coordinating Tutors: Manuel Kretzer (DDD), Sina Mostafavi (DIA)
Students:

Changing customs — Vegan Bioplastic Chandelier: Tania Sabrina Ortiz Ramírez, Delta Carolina Gómez Linares, Valmir Kastrati, Louise Meyer, Marie Philine, Frances Rockmann, Tang Yuanfeng
Second Skin: Johanna Muller, Dominique Lohaus, Amro Hamead, Neady Oduor, Quenna Leer
Fruit Lamp: Hossameldin Badr, Kyanoush Bitafaran, Juan Antonio Herrera Gonzalez, Ludwig Epple, Erik Scherenberg

Lifelight: Luise Eva Maria Oppelt, Martin Naumann, Julia Ziener, Adib Khaeez, Kamal Amgad, Jason Hage
Araneo: Toni Pasternak, Anian Till Stoib, Iwan Mazlan, Mohamed Mansour, Jakob Emmerling, Gulfia Kutlahmetova
Tutor Assistants: Mohammed Saad Moharram, Arise Wan
Robotic Workshop Support: Carl Buchmann
Video: Esteban Amon, Dokuteam HS Anhalt
Materiability Research Group, DARS.hub [Design, Architectural Robotics & Systems]

IMAGE CREDITS
All video stills by the authors and project team members.

Sina Mostafavi is a practicing architect, researcher, and educator with expertise in computational design and architectural robotics. He is the founder of the award-winning studio SETUParchitecture. At TU Delft, he is a senior researcher, and has completed his PhD in the Hyperbody group. In Dessau Institute of Architecture, he has initiated and led DARS.hub, a unit that focuses on design systems, architectural robotics, and interdisciplinarity in design research. He has lectured and published internationally, and the results of his work have been exhibited in numerous venues such as V2 gallery, NAi in Rotterdam, and Centre Pompidou Paris. An overview of his work can be found at www.setuparchitecture.com and www.sinamostafavi.com.

Manuel Kretzer is Professor for Material and Technology at the Dessau Department of Design, Anhalt University of Applied Sciences. His research aims at the creation of dynamic and adaptive objects with a specific focus on new smart and biological material performance and their combination with advanced digital design and fabrication tools. In 2012 he initiated Materiability, a free educational platform that attempts to connect architects, designers, and artists and provides access to novel material developments and technologies. Dr. Sc. Kretzer is also a founding partner of Responsive Design studio, based in Cologne. An overview of his work can be found at www.responsivedesign.de and www.materiability.com.

Adaptive City Car

Sina Mostafavi
TU Delft and Dessau Institute
of Architecture, DARS.hub

Manuel Kretzer
HS Anhalt, Dessau Department
of Design, Materiability Group

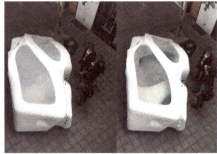
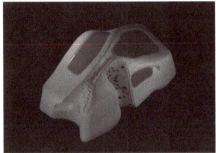

Sponsored by AUDI, Adaptive City Car is the result of a collaborative studio between the Dessau Department of Design and the Dessau Institute of Architecture. Focusing on the future of urban mobility, which is facing tremendous challenges such as increased traffic, air pollution, and a lack of car-free zones, the goal of the three-month course was to build a one-to-one model of an autonomous shared car, since most of today's options are missing a number of important factors in comparison to owning a private vehicle. The Adaptive City Car project aims at radically breaking with current industry standards by offering a visionary solution for a more sustainable urban vehicle. The Adaptive City Car provides better air quality, room for various activities during driving, and, most of all, the feeling of occupying a personal space. The organic design of the car is based on generative principles that try to offer an alternative to the artificial and standardized appearance of ordinary vehicles. In addition to a structure that seems naturally evolved, certain areas of the shell are designed to encourage the growth of moss and lichen to filter air pollutants entering the car's interior. The asymmetric shape of the vehicle allows for more internal space but also the integration of large skylights, made from opacity-changing smart glass, that direct the visual focus of passengers from unpleasant traffic situations to the environment. Sensors that respond to the presence of individuals control integrated light and audio feedback in order to increase the passengers' identification with the self-driving vehicle. The 1:1 model was robotically produced from 92 bespoke components that are coated with up to three layers of polystyrene adhesive, sanded, and then assembled together. Once all units were in place, the completed vehicle was painted, and the adaptive technologies and organic materials installed. Groups of architects and designers in this interdisciplinary studio conducted research in four clusters: computational design, smart materials, robotic fabrication, and communication design.

ACKNOWLEDGMENTS

As the supervisors of the Adaptive City Car Collaborative Studio between Dessau Department of Design and Dessau Institute of Architecture, the authors acknowledge and admire the tremendous efforts by tutors, students, colleagues, and the main sponsor of this project, AUDI.

Students: Saeed Abdwin, Niloufar Rahimi, Aleksander Mastalski, Neady Oduor, Marina Osmolovska, Ashish Varshith, Jan Boetker, Otto Glöckner, Nate Herndon, Dominique Lohaus, Marie Isabell Pietsch, Katja Rasbasch, Fu Yi Ser, Lam Sa Kiu, Anian Till Stoib, Laura Woodrow

Tutors: Adib Khaeez, Valmir Kastrati, Shazwan Mazlan, Manuel Lukas

Supervision: Sina Mostafavi, Manuel Kretzer

Audi Support: Mike Herbig

CG Artist: Mohammed Mansour

Robotic Support: Carl Buchmann

Video: Yoshua Wilm, Esteban Amon

Additional Support: Vanessa Rüpprich, Anton Roppeld, Mo Sayed Ahmad, Yulia Surova, Melissa-Kim Petrasch, Ludwig Epple, Jessica Bösherz, Vanessa Busch, Niklas Menzel

IMAGE CREDITS

All video stills by the authors and project team members.

Sina Mostafavi is a practicing architect, researcher, and educator with expertise in computational design and architectural robotics. He is the founder of the award-winning studio SETUParchitecture. At TU Delft, he is a senior researcher, and has completed his PhD in the Hyperbody group. In Dessau Institute of Architecture, he has initiated and led DARS.hub, a unit that focuses on design systems, architectural robotics, and interdisciplinarity in design research. He has lectured and published internationally, and the results of his work have been exhibited in numerous venues such as V2 gallery, NAi in Rotterdam, and Centre Pompidou Paris. An overview of his work can be found at www.setuparchitecture.com and www.sinamostafavi.com.

Manuel Kretzer is professor for Material and Technology at the Dessau Department of Design, Anhalt University of Applied Sciences. His research aims at the creation of dynamic and adaptive objects with a specific focus on new smart and biological material performance and their combination with advanced digital design and fabrication tools. In 2012 he initiated Materiability, a free educational platform that attempts to connect architects, designers, and artists and provides access to novel material developments and technologies. Dr. Sc. Kretzer is also a founding partner of Responsive Design studio, based in Cologne. An overview of his work can be found at www.responsivedesign.de and www.materiability.com.

Parti!Wall: Autonomous Wall Partition Navigating Office Space

Marta Nowak
UCLA

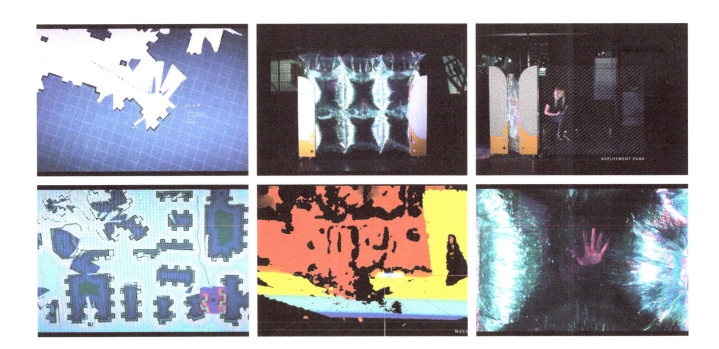

The wide implementation of open office layouts, in response to ossified cubicles of the sixties, has improved collaboration, enhanced social interactions, and resulted in many economic benefits. However, the open office has also contributed to workspace distraction and loss of privacy for both individuals and teams. Meanwhile, while 78% of unplanned meetings in an open office occur on the office floor rather than in meeting rooms, the open office is not usually equipped to support such spontaneous events. For instance, when two or three individuals in a team decide to work out a problem with a whiteboard, they risk distracting their neighboring colleagues, both visually and acoustically, and they lack privacy themselves. In other words, there is no possibility to create micro spaces within the macro space of the office floor. Parti!Wall attempts to resolve this through a robotic mobile solution that is summoned to create a small space around a team. Space is created on demand and it encloses six to eight people. Using Simultaneous Localization and Mapping (SLAM) and robotic toolkit TurtleBot, the mobile wall can map the environment and navigate to its destination autonomously while avoiding collision with people or objects. Once it arrives, the partition wall creates an inflatable enclosure around a working team to provide visual and acoustic privacy.

IMAGE CREDITS

Videography: Nathan Su

Marta Nowak is a founding principal of AN.ONYMOUS. She is a licensed architect and is currently a Senior Innovation Manager at Google R+D for Built Environment. Prior to establishing AN.ONYMOUS, she had taught in various universities, including the University of California, Los Angeles (UCLA), ArtCenter College of Design, and Northeastern University. Marta holds degrees in studio arts from St. Catherine University in Minnesota, and in architecture from Harvard University.

Ferro Field: Emergent Forms and Ornamentation

Emmanuel Osorno
Princeton University

Yinong Tao
Princeton University

Zaid Kashef Alghata
Princeton University

Experiment B - Manual Horizontal Pour Test   Experiment L - Robot-Assisted Pour Result   Experiment D - Result

Catalyzed by an interest in the relationship between technique and ornamentation, *Ferro Field* explores how to record invisible magnetic fields acting upon a reactive ferrous mass to generate emergent forms with unique textural qualities. To achieve this, the project employs ferro resin, a composite material that consists of a mix of fast-curing epoxy resin and iron oxide powder. The project moved rapidly and sequentially through a series of manual tests that shed light on the behavior and cure speed of the material, providing valuable insights that informed the robotic-assisted process that followed. In order to exploit the temporal workability of the material, two neodymium magnets were mounted to the end effectors of two UR3e cobots, whose movements were synchronized to manipulate and control the ferro resin mass. This final process, which required the design and fabrication of a custom tool that could be reused, incorporated two key movements: first, a constant rotation along the center axis to minimize the effects of gravity such that only the magnetic field is materialized; and second, a translation that increased the distance between the magnets and, in doing so, redistributed the ferro resin mass towards the ends of the objects.

Even though the objects produced resemble columns, *Ferro Field* does not aim to create a structure per se, but rather to isolate and study the effects a shifting magnetic field has on the formation of textures on the surface of the ferro resin mass. The resulting objects do, however, inspire conversations about ornamentation and, perhaps, the proposal of a new column order, in which robotic agents supplant human labor.

IMAGE CREDITS

Emmanuel Osorno is an architect and designer based in Trenton, NJ, and the founder of Eostudio. Prior to that, he worked for five years at Eric Owen Moss Architects in Culver City, CA, where he was involved in the design and construction of several renowned projects. Currently, he is a research assistant at the c.r.e.A.t.e lab, led by Stefana Parascho, and has been a teaching assistant for multiple design studios while completing his Post-Professional MArch II at the Princeton School of Architecture. He holds a BArch from California Polytechnic State University, San Luis Obispo, and is a registered architect in the state of California.

Yinong Tao is currently completing his Post-Professional MArch II at the Princeton School of Architecture. He holds a BArch and BFA from Rhode Island School of Design (RISD).

Zaid Kashef Alghata is the founder of House of ZKA, before which he worked at Gensler (Los Angeles) and UN Studio (Hong Kong). He co-taught studio at the graduate level with Jesse Reiser and the undergraduate thesis level with Marcelo Spina. He was a research assistant to Sylvia Lavin for a media archive project and to Todd Gannon for a publication on Craig Hodgetts. He continues to conduct his one-on-one interview series with architects and theorists under the moniker "Clashes and Intersections." Alghata is currently completing his Post-Professional MArch II at the Princeton School of Architecture and holds a BArch from SCI-Arc.

Extending the Robotic Workspace by Motion Tracking

Victor Sardenberg
Leibniz Universität Hannover

Marco Schacht
Leibniz Universität Hannover

Mirco Becker
Leibniz Universität Hannover

Stationary robotic arms always have a defined working range.

With real-time tracking, we compute the correct TCP.

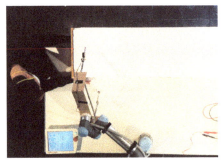

Problem Definition

Stationary robots have a defined workspace, which limits the size of workpieces. Industrial robots usually expand these limits by adding an additional axis, thus relying on expensive, low-tolerance hardware and custom integration to the system. Contemporary collaborative robots have allowed novel ways of human-robot collaboration by providing a safe robotic work environment. While far more agile than industrial robots, these collaborative robots still have the same size-to-workspace ratio and thus the same limitations in handling larger workpieces.

Solution

We suggest a solution where a low-cost motion tracking system, HTC Vive, is attached to the workpiece, which then updates the robotic toolpath in real time. This allows an operator to manually move large pieces of material through the stationary robotic workspace. The robot then performs local manipulations in the area of the workpiece, which is at that point in time in reach of the robot's end-effector. Such a scenario would widen the application of robots in the realm of fabricating architectural components as well as bringing traditional craftsmanship and robots closer together.

Proof of Concept

To test this concept, we defined a task of fabricating a series of 2 meters tall architectural columns employing robotic hot-wire cutting large Styrofoam workpieces using a UR5 robot. Each column was cut out of a single block of 2000 mm x 400 mm x 400 mm material. The workpiece was equipped with two Vive trackers. The material was manually pushed along a linear guide. The technical set-up for this proof-of-concept is built around Rhino, Grasshopper, and the Robots plug-in for generating UR-Script code and sending it to the controller via a socket connection. The Vive position was acquired via the Steam VR API and streamed into Grasshopper.

IMAGE CREDITS
All video stills by the authors.

Victor Sardenberg is an architect and researcher. He is Associate Researcher in Digital Methods in Architecture at Leibniz Universität Hannover, where he develops a computational framework for quantification of the architectural aesthetics experience. He holds a postgraduate MA with a specialization in Architecture and Urban Design from the Städelschule Architecture Class, Frankfurt am Main, and a bachelor's degree in Architecture and Urbanism from Mackenzie University, São Paulo.

Marco Schacht is a master's student of Architecture and Urban Planning at Leibniz Universität Hannover. He started working as a student assistant in Digital Methods in Architecture during his bachelor's degree and continued his work during his master's studies, where he was also able to take part in research and teaching. During his studies, he mainly focuses on digital fabrication, especially robotics.

Mirco Becker has been a Professor of Digital Methods in Architecture at the Leibniz Universität Hannover faculty of Architecture and Landscape since August 2016. From 2012 to 2016 he was Stiftungsprofessor of Architecture and Performative Design at the Städelschule Architecture Class, Frankfurt. He holds an MArch degree from the Architectural Association, London, where he graduated from the AA Design Research Lab in 2003. In 2012 he founded informance, a Berlin-based design-integration consultancy for the building industry. Earlier, he pursued his particular interest in computational design in architecture with Zaha Hadid Architects, Foster & Partners Specialist Modeling Group, and Kohn Pedersen Fox Computational Geometry Group, which he led for five years as a Senior Associate Principal.

Machine Vision for Reassembly

Bastian Wibranek
TU Darmstadt

Anna Braumann
TU Darmstadt

Lucia Martinovic
TU Darmstadt

Nastassia Sysoyeva
TU Darmstadt

Oliver Tessmann
TU Darmstadt

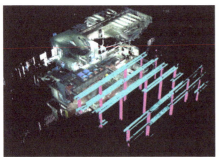
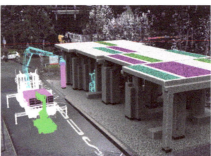
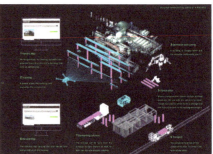

The construction industry makes a significant contribution to global resource consumption. A major reason is that many of its material flows are still linear and not traceable. In the case of mineral materials and components, in particular, a large proportion of them could be valuable for a second use (Durmisevic 2006).

While at least there are guidelines for using recycled concrete on the material level, there is no approach for reuse on the component level. This means that the primary energy bound in buildings by the production process is largely lost, although existing buildings already consist of finished components. An essential reason for not reusing those components from existing buildings is the lack of information on the material and structural composition of existing buildings (Koźmińska and Rynska 2018). Although current digital planning tools enable model-based planning (BIM) and digital documentation, they do not offer an approach for the digital acquisition and dismantling of existing buildings on the component level.

The project presents a strategy to reuse concrete elements from an obsolete building, the Faculty of Architecture at the TU Darmstadt. The building was first digitally recorded with the aid of 3D-scanning technologies into a 3d point cloud (Bastian Wibranek et al. 2020).

Based on this point cloud, the building was reconstructed, and the concrete elements were extracted. These parts could be stored in a temporary building—in our case, a bus stop—for tomorrow's buildings and could form the basis for reusing existing buildings at the component level in an end-to-end digital workflow.

With the help of these novel digital processes, reinforced concrete components from existing buildings destined for demolition could be recovered as reusable components for future buildings (Salama 2017). Ultimately, this might move the construction industry from current protocols of demolition to protocols of intelligent disassembly, treating our built environment not as a burden but instead as a modality for the future.

ACKNOWLEDGMENTS

3D scanning was supported by Christian Hickel and the FG Geodätische Messysteme und Sensorik from Prof. Andreas Eichhorn at TU Darmstadt.

REFERENCES

Durmisevic, Elma. 2006. *Transformable Building Structures*. Delft: Cedris M&CC.

Koźmińska, Urszula, and Elżbieta Dagny Rynska. 2018. "Harvest Map – Alternative Sources of Building Materials." In *1st Sustainable Solutions for Growth: SSG 2018 Conference Harvest Map–Alternative Sources of Building Materials*: 61. Wojciech Budzianowski Consulting Services

Salama, Wasim. 2017. "Design of Concrete Buildings for Disassembly: An Explorative Review." *International Journal of Sustainable Built Environment* 6 (2): 617–635. https://doi.org/10.1016/j.ijsbe.2017.03.005.

Wibranek, Bastian, Anna Braumann, Lucia Martinovic, Nastassia Sysoyeva, and Oliver Tessmann. 2020. "Machine Vision for Reassembly." February 28, 2020. https://www.youtube.com/watch?v=6-bdJM5PEFo&t.

IMAGE CREDITS

All video stills by the authors.

Bastian Wibranek joined the Digital Design Unit at the Faculty of Architecture at TU Darmstadt in 2015. He is currently a PhD candidate and a research assistant, teaching in the area of computational design and robotic fabrication. Wibranek's research focuses on how we will share our future buildings with intelligent machines. He proposes that the practice of architecture must define modes of co-existence and man-machine collaborations for design and production. He holds a Diploma in Architecture from the University of Applied Sciences and Arts Dortmund and a Master in Advanced Architectural Design from the Städelschule, Frankfurt am Main.

Anna Braumann, Lucia Martinovic, and Nastassia Sysoyeva were students at the Faculty of Architecture at TU Darmstadt. They participated in the design studio Design for Reassembly at the Digital Design Unit in the Winter Semester 2019-20, supervised by Prof. Oliver Tessmann and Bastian Wibranek. During the studio course, they were introduced to different 3D-scanning and animation techniques. The video was a preliminary study for a bus stop design for a student competition at IBA Basel 2020. Their proposal for the Future Stops competition was awarded a prize.

Oliver Tessman is a Professor for Digital Design at the Technical University Darmstadt School of Architecture. His teaching and research revolve around computational design and digital manufacturing in architecture. In 2008 Tessmann received a doctoral degree from the University of Kassel. From 2008 to 2011, he headed the performativeBuildingGroup in the renowned engineering office Bollinger + Grohmann and worked at the Staedelschule Architecture Class as a guest professor. From 2012 to 2015, he was an Assistant Professor at the Royal Institute of Technology Stockholm.

Urbach Tower: Self-Shaping Wood for a Curved CLT Structure

Dylan Wood
ICD - University of Stuttgart

Achim Menges
ICD - University of Stuttgart

Simon Bechert
ITKE - University of Stuttgart

Lotte Aldinger
ITKE - University of Stuttgart

Jan Knippers
ITKE - University of Stuttgart

Philippe Grönquist
ICD - University of Stuttgart

Simon Bechert
Empa / ETH Zurich

Markus Rüggeberg
Empa / ETH Zurich

The Urbach Tower is a unique wood structure. The design of the tower emerges from a new self-shaping process of curved wood components. This pioneering development constitutes a paradigm shift in timber manufacturing from elaborate and energy-intensive mechanical forming processes that require heavy machinery to a process where the material shapes entirely by itself. This shape change is driven only by the wood's characteristic shrinking during a decrease of moisture content. Components for the 14m tall tower are designed and manufactured in a flat state and transform autonomously into the final, programmed curved shapes during industry-standard technical drying. This opens up new and unexpected architectural possibilities for high-performance and elegant structures, using a sustainable, renewable, and locally sourced building material. The Urbach Tower constitutes the very first structure worldwide made from self-shaped, building-scale components. It not only showcases this innovative manufacturing approach and resultant novel timber structure; it also intensifies the visitors' spatial involvement and landscape experience by providing a striking landmark building for the Remstal Gartenschau 2019.

ACKNOWLEDGMENTS

The authors would like to especially thank Robert Faulkner, the boys and girls of Blumer Lehmann AG, Empa, and ETH Zurich for their extended efforts to produce this project video.

REFERENCES

Wood, D., P. Grönquist, S. Bechert, L. Aldinger, D. Riggenbach, K. Lehmann, M. Rüggeberg, I. Burgert, J. Knippers, and A. Menges. 2020. "From Machine Control to Material Programming: Self-Shaping Wood Manufacturing of a High Performance Curved CLT Structure — Urbach Tower." In *Fabricate 2020: Making Resilient Architecture* edited by J. Burry, J. Sabin, B. Sheil, and M. Skavara. London: UCL Press.

Grönquist, P., D. Wood, M. Hassani, F. Wittel, A. Menges, and M. Rüggeberg. 2019. "Analysis of Hygroscopic Self-Shaping Wood at Large Scale for Curved Mass Timber Structures." *Science Advances* 5 (9): eaax1311. doi:10.1126/sciadv.aax1311.

Aldinger, L., S. Bechert, D. Wood, J. Knippers, and A. Menges. 2020. "Design and Structural Modelling of Surface-Active Timber Structures Made from Curved CLT – Urbach Tower,

Remstal Gartenschau 2019." In *Impact: Design With All Senses*
[Proceedings of the Design Modelling Symposium 2019], edited by
C. Gengnagel, O. Baverel, J, Burry, M. Ramsgaard Thomsen, and S.
Weinzierl. Cham: Springer International Publishing, 419-432. doi:
10.1007/978-3-030-29829-6 33.

J. Brütting, A. Menges. 2018. "Self-Forming Curved Timber Plates:
Initial Design Modeling for Shape-Changing Material Buildups." In
IASS – Creativity in Structural Design [Proceedings of the IASS
Symposium 2018].

Wood, D., D. Correa, O. Krieg,, A. Menges: 2016. "Material
Computation— 4D Timber Construction: Towards Building-Scale
Hygroscopic Actuated, Self-Constructing Timber Surfaces."
International Journal of Architectural Computing (IJAC), Vol. 14 (1):
49–62. doi: 10.1177/1478077115625522.

IMAGE CREDITS

Video: Robert Faulkner for the Institute for Computational Design
and Construction, University of Stuttgart

Dylan Wood is a Senior Research Associate and group leader
at the Institute for Computation Design and Construction at the
University of Stuttgart. At ICD, Dylan leads the Institute's research
on Material Programming and supervises graduate students in the
associated topics. His research focuses on developing intelligent
design principles for smart shape-changing materials as a form of
material robotics that can be applied in building systems, construction, and manufacturing. In practice, he has a range of experience
developing, adapting, and deploying experimental methods for
high-performance building construction, with a special focus on
timber construction.

Achim Menges is an architect in Frankfurt and full Professor at
the University of Stuttgart, where he is the founding director of
the Institute for Computational Design and Construction (ICD) and
the director of the Cluster of Excellence Integrative Computational
Design and Construction for Architecture (IntCDC). In addition, he
has been Visiting Professor in Architecture at Harvard University's
Graduate School of Design and held multiple other visiting professorships in Europe and the United States. His work focuses on
integrative design at the intersection of computational design
methods, robotic manufacturing, and construction, as well as
advanced material and building systems.

Simon Bechert is a structural engineer and research associate
at the Institute of Building Structures and Structural Design
(IKTE) at the University of Stuttgart. His research focuses on
the development of building systems, connection strategies, and
integral structural design processes for segmented timber-shell
structures.

Lotte Aldinger is a structural engineer and holds a Master of
Science with distinction from the ITECH master's program at the
University of Stuttgart. Aldinger's primary interest lies in an integrative process for the structural design of shell structures with
informed fiber layouts by applying computational design.

Jan Knippers is a practicing consulting engineer and, since 2000,
head of the Institute for Building Structures and Structural Design
(ITKE) at the University of Stuttgart. His interest is in innovative
and resource-efficient structures created at the intersection
of research and development, and practice. From 2014 to 2019
Knippers was the coordinator of the DFG collaborative research
center Biological Design and Integrative Structures. Since
2019, he has been Deputy Executive Director of the Cluster of
Excellence Integrative Computational Design and Construction
for Architecture and Vice-Rector for Research of the University of
Stuttgart. He is the author of several books, numerous scientific
publications, and a member of various advisory boards.

Philippe Grönquist is a research assistant in the Wood Materials
Science lab at the Institute of Building Materials, ETH Zurich. His
research about wood includes both a fundamental aspect where
scale-dependent structure property relations are explored and an
applied aspect for employing such knowledge in timber engineering
and architecture. He specializes in mechanical behavior and
theoretical and applied computational mechanics for materials
simulations. Grönquist has worked with research partners from
ICD, University of Stuttgart on the development and application of
self-shaping wood for timber structures. He holds a BSc and MSc
in civil engineering from ETH Zurich.

Markus Rüggeberg is Senior Scientist at the Institute for Building
Materials at ETH Zurich, and at Empa, Dübendorf, Switzerland.
He received his PhD in Biology from the University of Freiburg,
Germany, and worked at the Max-Planck-Institute of Colloids and
Interfaces, Potsdam, Germany. He has positioned his research
on wood at the interface of engineering, material science, and
molecular biology, covering fundamental and applied research on
structure-mechanics relationships and wood-water interaction. A
focus of Rüggeberg's work is rethinking the materiality of wood by
turning its drawbacks into new capacities, for example, utilizing
dimensional instabilities and its affinity to water for developing self-
forming manufacturing.

Tailored to Time

Maria Wyller
ICD, University of Stuttgart

Maria Yablonina
ICD, University of Stuttgart
John H. Daniels Faculty, University of Toronto

Martin Alvarez
ICD, University of Stuttgart

Achim Menges
ICD, University of Stuttgart

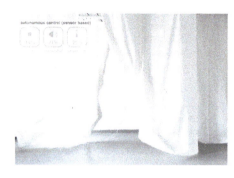

A common motivation for designing adaptive structures is to save resources. However, many systems fall into the paradox of using a lot of resources, both through production and maintenance. Adaptive architecture often relies on numerous actuators, expensive computing, and a continuous power supply to operate, usually due to the structural load applied to the mechanical elements.

In *Tailored to Time*, the aim is to form a textile into adaptive, kinematic spaces and able to respond to its environment using distributed, on-site, on-material, mobile robotic connectors. Together, the material and the connectors compose a lightweight, energy-efficient system capable of producing a significant architectural change with minimal mechanical actuation. This project hopes to contribute to the search for adaptive systems that consume less while providing a great spatial impact.

A common objective of adaptive systems is to alter spatial parameters such as light, acoustics, temperature, and space division (Schnädelbach 2010). Textiles' inherent material qualities allow them to influence all of these

factors just by being present (Bendixen 2010; Quinn 2006). They are well-suited for adaptation because they can have a significant reversible impact on space through quick manipulation. By augmenting a textile element with a mobile robot, one can further leverage the results that these materials can offer towards scenarios where they can alter geometric and ambient characteristics of architectural space through continuous kinematic behaviors.

To keep the technology-to-material ratio at a minimum, the material relocation is conducted by a lightweight, two-part mobile robotic textile joint—the connector. It is considered an extension of the textile itself, there to augment already innate material qualities. The control code produces and evaluates real-time environmental sensor data against preset, user-defined goals, and from this produces motor values that trigger the connector to move until the textile has taken on a configuration where the target is reached. The combination of the precise, computerized control of the connectors and the unpredictability of the textile's folding allows the system to respond to user-defined goals with unique configurations.

Whereas adaptive architecture often is approached through the development of project and location-specific adaptive building components, this project proposes an inherently flexible system, ready to be attached or detached, and thus can make any static space, new or old, small or large, adaptive.

REFERENCES

Bendixen, Cecilie. 2010. "The Textile Form of Sound ." *Duck: Journal for Research in Textiles and Textile Design* 1 (1).

Quinn, Bradley. 2006. "Textiles in Architecture." Architectural Design: 22–26. https://doi.org/10.1002/ad.348.

Schnädelbach, Holger. 2010. "Adaptive Architecture—A Conceptual Framework." In proceedings of *MediaCity: Interaction of Architecture, Media and Social Phenomena*, edited by J. Geelhaar, F. Eckardt, B. Rudolf, S. Zierold, and M. Markert, 523–555. Weimar, Germany.

IMAGE CREDITS

All video stills by the authors.

Maria Wyller is an architect and designer working at David Chipperfield Architects in Berlin. With a background in computational design and digital fabrication, she is currently exploring the relationship between tradition, technology and sustainability. She completed the MSc ITECH Program at the University of Stuttgart in 2019.

Maria Yablonina is an architect, researcher, and artist working in the field of computational design and digital fabrication. She is currently Assistant Professor at the John H. Daniels Faculty of Architecture, Landscape, and Design at the University of Toronto. Her work lies at the intersection of architecture and robotics, producing spaces and robotic systems that can construct themselves and change in real time. Such architectural productions include the development of hardware and software solutions, as well as complementing architectural and material systems in order to offer new design spaces.

Martin Alvarez is a former Research Associate at the Institute for Computational Design and Construction. He studied Architecture at the University of Buenos Aires (UBA) where he received his architectural degree in 2008 and continued teaching as a tutor in the chairs of Prof. Lombardi and Prof. Solsona. After graduating, he employed computational methods in many international projects at Ciro Najle General Design Bureau and completed various constructions at Estudio Ruiz Orrico in Argentina. Before joining the Institute for Computational Design and Construction in 2017, he collaborated with arch22 (Stuttgart) and completed the ITECH program (Dist). His current research focuses on the design of robotically sewn lightweight timber structures.

Achim Menges is a practicing architect in Frankfurt and full Professor at Stuttgart University, where he is the founding director of the Institute for Computational Design and Construction (ICD) and the director of the Cluster of Excellence Integrative Computational Design and Construction for Architecture (IntCDC). In addition, he has been Visiting Professor in Architecture at Harvard University's Graduate School of Design and held multiple other visiting professorships in Europe and the United States. He graduated with honors from the Architectural Association, where he subsequently taught as Graduate Studio Master and Diploma Unit Master.

The focus of Menges's practice and research is on the development of integrative design at the intersection of computational design methods, robotic manufacturing and construction, as well as advanced material and building systems. His work is based on an interdisciplinary approach in collaboration with structural engineers, system engineers, production engineers, computer scientists, material scientists, and biologists.

ARCHITECTS & PPE PRODUCTION

The early days of the COVID-19 pandemic shifted the digital fabrication community from research into the urgent production of Personal Protective Equipment (PPE) for healthcare workers. The six projects selected for this panel reflect a diverse range of approaches yet share a considered perspective on the limits and possibilities of computational design's engagement with ongoing crises. The following text summarizes and reflects on the results of several PPE initiatives: an entanglement of aspirations, technical knowledge, politics, and logistics.

Special Session:
Architects and PPE Production

Ersela Kripa
Texas Tech College of
Architecture

Shelby Doyle
Iowa State University

Alvin Huang
University of Southern
California

Manuel Jimenez Garcia
UCL Bartlett

Heath May
HKS LINE

Jenny Sabin
Cornell University

INTRODUCTION
ERSELA KRIPA, SESSION CHAIR

The pandemic has deepened the already existing asymmetries of power, inequity, and systemic racism. This result is supported by data that tracks the geographies of death and the direct relationship between race, socioeconomic strife, and lack of access to healthcare. The deep inequities of the US healthcare system are currently mitigated in crisis mode by healthcare workers—the frontliners. However, there are other fronts that are emerging more clearly: one such front is biometric surveillance in the name of crisis management, otherwise known as contact-tracing. These surveillance mechanisms have arisen as a way to manage the failure of policy to provide safety standards for such contact. They seem to apply only to areas of high density, or service, or blue-collar work, not to the already self-isolated wealthy. Fortunately, there are yet other fronts where designers can act: education, civic engagement, and protest. Our discipline has a complicated history of supporting dictatorships, as well as imagining socially equitable systems. While some architects support infrastructures of exclusion and death, others model behaviors of inclusivity and altruism. To this end, and after we've made the thousands of PPE, I invite designers to think about where our mobilization would more precisely affect positive change. We cannot continue to use our design knowledge to subsidize a failed system.

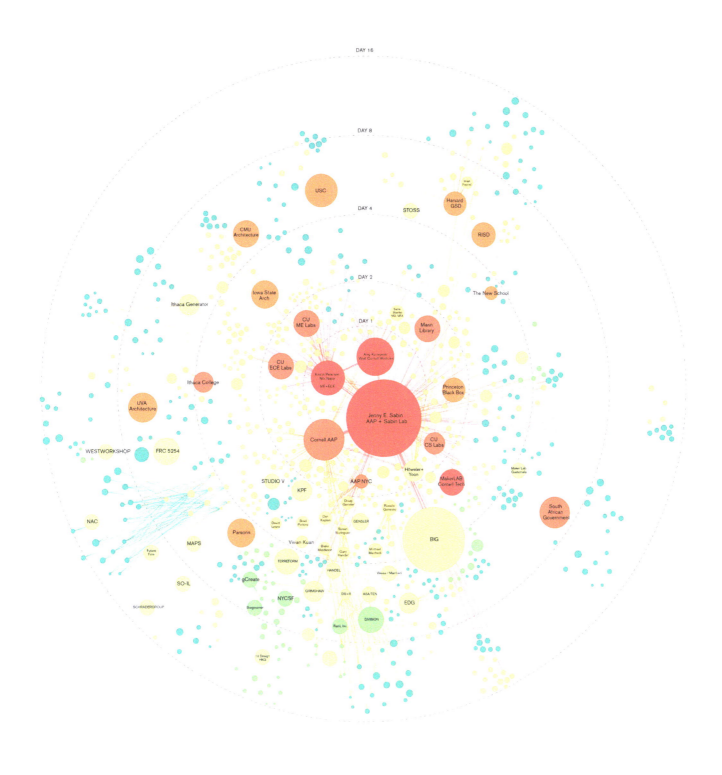

DAY 16

DAY 8

DAY 4

DAY 2

DAY 1

USC

Harvard GSD

STOSS

RISD

CMU Architecture

Iowa State Arch

Ithaca Generator

The New School

CU ME Labs

Mann Library

CU ECE Labs

Amy Kortepeter Weil Cornell Medicine

Ithaca College

Krison Petreser Nik Najdo
ME+ECE

UVA Architecture

Jenny E. Sabin AAP + Sabin Lab

Princeton Black Box

WESTWORKSHOP   FRC 5254

Cornell AAP

CU CS Labs

STUDIO V

KPF

AAP NYC

Höweler + Yoon

MakerLAB Cornell Tech

Maker Lab Guatemala

NAC

Doug Gensler

Rosala Gonesto

South African Government

David Lewis

Dan Kaplan

GENSLER

Parsons

Susan Rodriguez

BIG

MAPS

Vivian Kuan

Blake Middleton

Gary Handel

Michael Manfredi

Future Firm

TERREFORM

Weiss / Manfredi

SO-IL

gCreate

HANDEL

SCHRADERGROUP

NYCSF

GRIMSHAW

DS+R

AISA-TEN

EDG

Boogsanter

Ratti, Inc.

DIVISION

19 Design +BIG

1   Diagram of Operation PPE launched by engineers and architects at Cornell University, demonstrating the rapid distribution of digital models and files through a network of architects and designers who retooled academic and professional labs to produce Personal Protective Equipment in the early days of the COVID-19 pandemic. Image courtesy of Sabin Lab.

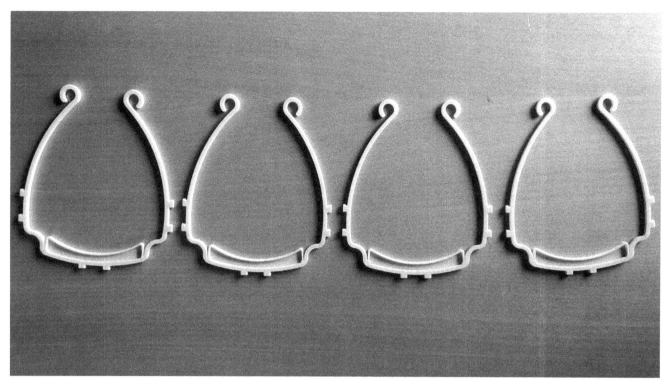

2   3D printed headbands for face shields.. Image courtesy of Sabin Lab.

OPERATION PPE @CORNELL AAP
JENNY E. SABIN

The Sabin Lab at Cornell Architecture, Art, and Planning (AAP) is a transdisciplinary design research lab with specialization in computational design, data visualization, and digital fabrication. We investigate the intersections of architecture and science, and apply insights and theories from biology, robotics, computer science, mathematics, materials science, physics, fiber science, and engineering to the design, fabrication, and production of responsive material structures and constructed assemblies. Our research, including bio-inspired adaptive materials, DNA 3D printed bricks, robotic fabrication, and 3D Kirigami assemblies, has been funded substantially by the National Science Foundation, Autodesk, the Grainger Foundation, and the National Academy of Engineering. We engage in transdisciplinary design research where problem and knowledge generation is done through collaborative design research processes that are emergent, transforming, and evolving for innovative applications across disciplines and disciplinary frameworks. Operation PPE is one such initiative.

Operation PPE + Informal Fabrication leverages the participatory and networked space of design and making across disciplines to innovate design solutions that can rapidly respond to gaps in supply chains at times of extreme crisis. The Sabin Lab and the Material Practice Facilities at Cornell AAP launched Operation PPE with collaborators in the Engineering school at Cornell University on March 24, 2020, to respond to an urgent request from Weill Cornell Medicine in New York City for PPE face shields. The initiative has since inspired clusters of makers and designers across the country and internationally. Our New York regional network of Cornell faculty, students, staff, alumni, industry partners, and home 3D printing enthusiasts has since delivered over 25,000 face shields to regional and NYC-based hospitals. This effort is a collective effort across the Cornell community. The design and print file for the visor component of the shield comes from 3D Verkstan and was tested and verified by Weill Cornell Medicine. The polyethylene transparent sheet (the shield) is laser cut to fabricate hundreds of shield components at a time. The sheet can either be sanitized for reuse or be tossed and a new one clipped on to the visor.

Early in the initiative, it became clear that it was important to distribute and scale the effort quickly. We consolidated the print files and instructions on the Sabin Lab website (https://www.sabinlab.com/operation-ppe) and launched

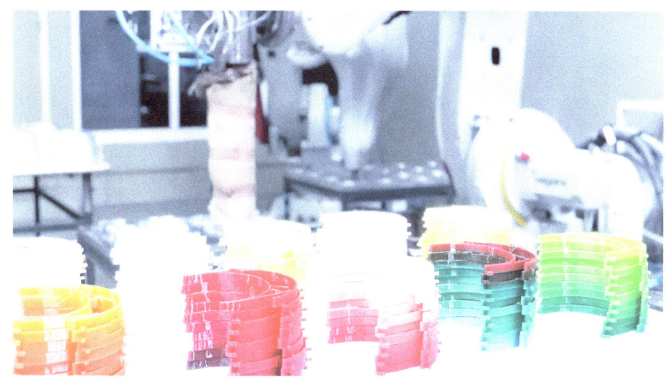

3   Robotic 3D printed face shields at Nagami. Image courtesy of Nagami.

a Slack Channel to communicate efficiently. With the support of AAP's Dean Meejin Yoon, we reached out to our incredible AAP alumni network, and within 24 to 48 hours, our alumni not only joined the 3D printing efforts but also leveraged their own networks. Within hours, NYC-based architecture firms, including Handel Associates, KPF, BIG, Grimshaw, and Terreform ONE started 3D printing the PPE face-shield visors and laser cutting the protective shield. AAP alumni practice leaders Vivian Kuan, Blake Middleton, Michael Manfredi, Dan Kaplan, Brad Perkins, Doug Gensler, Susan Rodriguez, David Lewis, and Rosalie Genevro also leveraged their networks. Through those networks, industry partners such as g-Create, a 3D printer manufacturer, and organizations such as NYSCF (New York Stem Cell Foundation Research Institute) and faculty at Parsons also joined the effort. Together, we worked around the clock, sharing materials, dropping off materials and parts at garages and doorsteps, and in the end, we made a very big and real impact in a short amount of time through the informal, democratic, and collective DIY network that digital fabrication and design afford across disciplines and practice.

The Sabin Lab continues to innovate design solutions for PPE during the pandemic, including award-winning mask designs that incorporate off-the-shelf materials and custom tools and algorithms such as the "living hinge" to address fit, comfort, and ease of fabrication through DIY 3D printing networks.

DISTRIBUTED INMEDIATE MANUFACTURING
MANUEL JIMENEZ GARCIA

The pandemic hit Spain particularly hard, as it was one of the most infected countries in the early stages of the outbreak in Europe. The country saw its hospitals surpass their maximum capacity in just a matter of weeks, leading to the hiring of medical students and retired doctors to help combat the virus. To accelerate the supply of equipment to guarantee their safety, makers from all over the world have organized platforms to distribute manufacturing, using 3D printers as a global network where on-demand production could occur locally. Manuel Jimenez Garcia and his robotic manufacturing company Nagami developed a new face shield that can be printed with a robot in just seven minutes. The company put their furniture production on hold to dedicate themselves fully to a much more urgent matter: producing as many face shields as they could to help fight the spread of COVID-19. For more than four months, Nagami printed 500 PPEs per day, and the entire

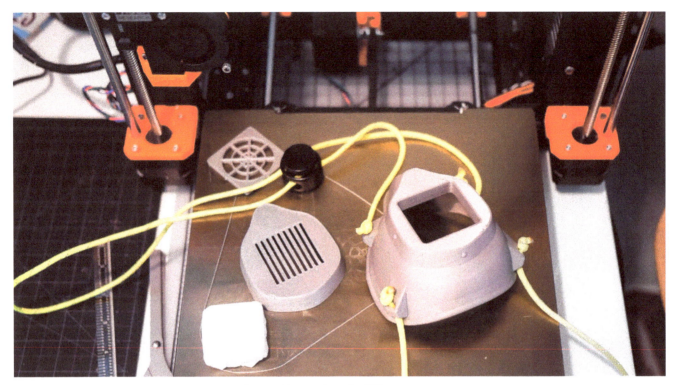

4   One example of a 3D-printed mask. Image courtesy of USC Architecture Operation PPE.

city of Avila, where the company is based, collaborated in this initiative, sponsoring material and offering support of multiple kinds. Furthermore, Jimenez Garcia's UK-based design and tech consultancy AUAR (Automated Architecture Ltd) developed a mobile app to streamline communication between material suppliers, manufacturers, and hospital staff in the UK, to ease the supply of PPE in the country and take real advantage of distributed manufacturing and local delivery. COVID-19 has uncovered how distributed digital manufacturing technologies give greater flexibility, allowing companies to immediately jump into the production of a completely new and urgently needed product, and to do so at a short distance from the consumer, drastically reducing the CO_2 emissions inherent to long-range shipping. Together with their partners Parley for the Oceans, Nagami is planning to develop a compact recycling/3D printing unit which can upscale distributed manufacturing, favoring the production of not only medical equipment but also shelters and housing created from local waste and local delivery. COVID-19 has uncovered how distributed digital manufacturing technologies give greater flexibility, allowing not only to immediately jump into the production of a completely new and urgently needed product, but also doing so in a short distance from the consumer, drastically reducing the CO_2 emissions inherited to long-range shipping. Together with

their partners Parley for the Oceans, Nagami is planning to develop a compact recycling/3dprinting unit which can upscale distributing manufacturing, favoring the production of not only medical equipment but also shelters and housing created from local waste.

TEMPORAL PROXIMITY
HEATH MAY

The COVID-19 pandemic revealed information about us that was there all along. It was subliminal, and likely masked by the ubiquitous stimulation of progress around us. While some of what we observed and experienced indicates gaps in our systems and infrastructure—a sobering and even painful indicator of our susceptibility to novel stressors such as the virus—intrinsic strengths of our personal and professional relationships were also revealed. Mobilization of discrete fabrication efforts across geographic distance is possible through technology, yet dependent on human relationships. The diversity of our network improves our ability to react and should remain a focal point as we move forward, with the lessons of partnering, scalability, supply-chain logistics, and resource sharing offering particularly poignant relevance in assessing our ability to respond

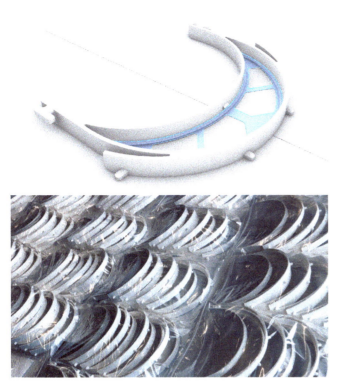

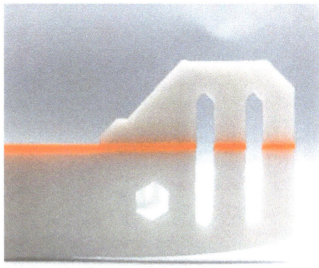

5   Screenshot of 3D model for customized snap-in closure piece model for face shield headbands and the resulting 3D prints packaged for distribution. Images courtesy of HKS LINE.

6   Layering together ends of filament rolls to use of even small amounts of available material. Image courtesy of Computation & Construction Lab.

to such a crisis again. As our shared challenges and our technologies evolve, so will our need to grow and foster our personal and professional relationships. This session offers an introductory critical dialogue around these issues, and we can benefit from advancing and expanding the conversation toward a wider network.

OPERATION PPE @USC
ALVIN HUANG

"Technology is the answer ... but what was the question??" asked Cedric Price in his seminal lecture at the AA in London in 1966. Flash forward to March of 2020, and the question was staring the global digital fabrication community in the face. In the midst of a global pandemic with a massive shortage of personal protective equipment (PPE), the question was how could we, as designers invested in the application of design and fabrication technologies, leverage our skills, abilities, and capabilities to assist in the production of PPE?

The answer was that we could leverage the ethos of open-source digital fabrication (which was championed by the early protagonists of our movement such as Bernard

Cache) alongside our existing resources of 3D printers and the emerging suite of remote collaboration platforms at our disposal, such as Zoom, Slack, and Google Drive, to mobilize, organize, and enable a global network of designers, students, and enthusiasts to 3D print PPE in response. At USC and in Los Angeles, our network grew to include 334 volunteers with 278 3D printers distributed throughout Southern California, resulting in the production of over 6,500+ pseudo N95 face masks and 11,000+ face shields that were distributed to USC Keck Medicine, USC LA County Hospital, Children's Hospital Los Angeles, MLK Hospital in Watts, Chinle Chapter Government in Chinle, Arizona , and the Bureau of Education for the Colorado River Indian Tribes.

In hindsight, perhaps 2020 gave the global design community an immense opportunity to rethink, reassess, and reconsider our navel-gazing ways. For myself, I would like to think that Operation PPE was just the beginning of the opportunity. While my design work and design research have previously been guilty of being invested in technological answers to technological questions, Operation PPE gave me an opportunity to reflect on how design innovation might better focus on questions that involve society as a whole. The COVID-19 pandemic has not only been a global health crisis, it has exposed and magnified a series of social and cultural inequities in our society including, but not limited to, systemic racism, housing shortages, economic disparity, and environmental crisis. I, for one, am taking the opportunity to reflect on how design, computation, and technology might be leveraged to engage a different set of questions.

FABRICATING A RESPONSE
SHELBY DOYLE

On Thursday March 12, 2020—due to the COVID-19 pandemic—Iowa State University (ISU) moved all of its courses online, effectively closing the fabrication spaces of the Computation and Construction Lab (CCL). As Jacob Gasper documents in the ACADIA 2020 Field Note "Pandemic Pause," this meant that the CCL, like many labs, had to figure out how to function in a pandemic. The idea of fabricating face shields came to us through a network of colleagues and fabrication labs. We began with files from Prusa Labs in the Czech Republic that were edited by Storrs Lab at UNC-Charlotte and then continued integrating feedback from local healthcare workers in Iowa. We arrived at a final prototype which was posted to social media and led to a local donor, Alliant Energy, offering to support scaling-up the project. To increase production, we brought all 30 of the Department of Architecture's 3D printers into the CCL and began printing 24 hours a day. What followed was an exercise in supply chain and material procurement: we stood in socially distanced lines outside of JoAnn Fabric to purchase rolls of elastic and drove to Kansas City to buy rolls of clear plastic from a sign-making company for face shields. This is a summary of the process we developed: Print, Remove, Sew, Add Top Piece, Add Bottom Piece, Clean, Bag, Box, Distribute. A 60-word disclaimer from ISU Counsel was attached to the outside of each box, and this short text allowed the very existence of the project.

We fabricated these face shields to aid in bridging the gap in Iowa between the need for PPE, industrial production capacity, and government policy. Since the beginning of the pandemic, one in nine residents have been infected in Story County, where ISU is located (Iowa Department of Health, April 2021). In the early days of the pandemic, this work seemed urgent: Iowa never imposed a full stay-at-home order and issued a temporary, partial, mask-mandate. This project asks several questions: How can designers and the digital fabrication community prepare to engage in ongoing and future crises? And should we? Particularly when there are clear frictions of liability and misalignments with existing institutional and political structures?

Shelby Elizabeth Doyle, AIA, is a registered architect, co-founder of the ISU Computation and Construction Lab (CCL), director of the ISU Architectural Robotics Lab (ARL), and an Assistant Professor of Architecture at Iowa State University, where she teaches design studios and seminars in digital technology. Doyle's education includes a Bachelor of Science in architecture from the University of Virginia, a Master of Architecture from the Harvard Graduate School of Design, and a Fulbright Fellowship to Cambodia. The central hypothesis of her research, and of the CCL, is that computation in architecture is a material, pedagogical, and social project. Computation is both informed by and productive of architectural cultures, and her research entails not only the "how" (skills and techniques) of computational design but also the "why" (processes and impacts). This hypothesis is explored through the fabrication of built projects, writing, exhibition, and material experiments.

Alvin Huang, AIA, NOMA, is a Los Angeles-based architect with a global profile. He is an award-winning architect, designer, and educator specializing in the integrated application of material performance, emergent design technologies, and digital fabrication in contemporary architectural practice. His work spans all scales, ranging from high-rise towers and mixed-use developments to temporary pavilions and bespoke furnishings. He is the founder and principal of Synthesis Design + Architecture and an Associate Professor at the University of Southern California, where he is also the Director of Graduate and Post-professional Architecture. Prior to establishing SDA, he gained significant experience working in the offices of Zaha Hadid Architects, Future Systems, AL_A, and AECOM. He received an MArch from the Graduate Design Research Laboratory at the Architectural Association in London and a BArch from the USC School of Architecture in Los Angeles.

Manuel Jimenez García is founding partner and CEO of Nagami, a robotic manufacturing / design brand, based in Avila, Spain; co-founder and principal of madMdesign, a computational design practice based in London; and co-founder of AUAR (Automated Architecture Ltd), a design-tech consultancy based in London. His work has been exhibited worldwide in venues such as Centre Pompidou (Paris), Victoria & Albert Museum (London), Canada's Design Museum (Toronto), Royal Academy of Arts (London), and Zaha Hadid Design Gallery (London). Alongside his practice, Manuel is a lecturer at The Bartlett School of Architecture UCL (London). He is program director of MSc/MRes Architectural Computation (AC), and unit master of RC4 at the MArch Architectural Design (AD), both part of The Bartlett B-Pro. In addition, he is also co-founder of UCL Design Computation Lab, recently rebranded as AUARLabs, and the curator of Plexus, a lecture series based on computational design.

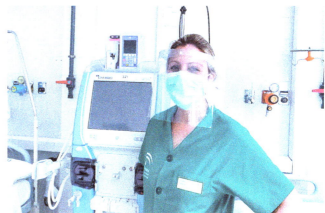

7   Spanish medical workers with PPE fabricated by Nagami. Images courtesy of Nagami.

Ersela Kripa is an Assistant Professor and Acting Director at Texas Tech College of Architecture (CoA)–El Paso, and Director of Projects at POST (Project for Operative Spatial Technologies), a CoA research center. Her awards include the Rome Prize in Architecture and the Emerging Voices award from The Architectural League of New York, among others. Ersela holds a Master of Science in Advanced Architectural Design from Columbia University GSAPP and a BArch from NJIT. Ersela is an architect and founding partner of AGENCY, a design and research practice which leverages spatial design and information to counteract nascent forms of global and urban insecurity. Located on the US–Mexico border, AGENCY works in protracted conflictual contexts to consistently shift the narrative, developing targeted methods to identify, appropriate, and subvert subperceptual urban and atmospheric events that violate human rights. Her recent book, co-authored with Stephen Mueller, *FRONTS: Military Urbanisms and the Developing World* (AR+D, 2020), compiles original urban research and analysis, revealing a growing geography of codependence between the global security complex and the urban morphologies of the developing world which it increasingly incriminates.

Heath May, AIA, is Principal and Director of HKS Laboratory for INtensive Exploration (LINE). He leads a studio responsible for projects that have been recognized for their progressive design with numerous awards. His work and research include data-driven design optimization, simulation, and digital design, fabrication, and delivery. Heath has taught advanced graduate design studio as an Adjunct Assistant Professor at the University of Texas Arlington, CAPPA, School of Architecture. Practicing across multiple sectors, his recent projects featuring the design and/or collaboration of LINE include SoFi Stadium, Pacific Plaza Pavilion, and Alcon-Novartis Café. He practices in San Francisco, with a current focus on collaborative digital platforms.

Jenny E. Sabin is an architectural designer whose work is at the forefront of a new direction for 21st-century architectural practice—one that investigates the intersections of architecture and science and applies insights and theories from biology and mathematics to the design of responsive material structures and adaptive architecture. Sabin is the Arthur L. and Isabel B. Wiesenberger Professor in Architecture and Associate Dean for Design at the College of Architecture, Art, and Planning at Cornell University, where she established a new advanced research degree in Matter Design Computation. She is principal of Jenny Sabin Studio, an experimental architectural design studio based in Ithaca and Director of the Sabin Lab at Cornell AAP. Her book, *LabStudio: Design Research Between Architecture and Biology*, co-authored with Peter Lloyd Jones, was published in 2017. Sabin won MoMA & MoMA PS1's Young Architects Program with her submission of Lumen, 2017.

DISTRIBUTED PROXIMITIES
WORKSHOPS

As part of the *Distributed Proximities* conference, ACADIA offered a lineup of fourteen two-day workshops led by expert instructors from around the globe. The online format allowed ACADIA to offer more workshops to a greater number of attendees than typically participate in the annual workshop program: over 260 participants from 22 countries. The conference chairs curated a selection of workshops that uniquely addressed the conference's theme of distributed modes of working and collaboration, including topics such as remote robotics, long-distance collaborative design, machine learning, 3D scanning, and generative writing. Funding from Autodesk provided sixty scholarships and grants to students and professionals in partnership with NOMA, NOMAS, and schools of architecture in Mexico.

KUKA|crc: Cloud Remote Control

Ethan Kerber
RWTH Aachen University

Sven Stumm
Robots in Architecture

As architects, engineers, educators, and builders, we rely on working closely together to create innovative structures. Inspired by new need for social distancing, Robots in Architecture Research has developed a cloud-based approach to working remotely with robotics: KUKA|crc. Cloud Robot Control enables industrial access through online collaboration. In this workshop, participants learned to remotely simulate robotic movements, program robots over the cloud, monitor fabrication progress, and adapt in real time to inaccuracies in material, all while controlling the process from their own international location. The goal of this workshop is to advance the capability of remote robotic fabrication while prototyping new methods of adaptivity based on available process data. Construction relies on large international teams collaborating in close quarters to create ambitious structures. Inspired by this challenge, the aim of Cloud Robot Control is to extend remote robotic capabilities to the building site, enabling automated, adaptive, and collaborative processes to bring a new level of digitization and innovation to the construction industry. Through the ACADIA 2020 Cloud Robot Control Workshop, an international group of artists, architects, and engineers had a chance to experience automated construction in a new digital way.

Images courtesy of the workshop leaders.

Dual-Additive Manufacturing Combining Timber and In-Process Bio-Based 3D-Printing

Hans Jakob Wagner
Dylan Marx Wood
Tiffany Cheng
Luis Orozco
Yasaman Tahouni
ICD University of Stuttgart

Chai Hua
ICD University of Stuttgart /
Tongji University

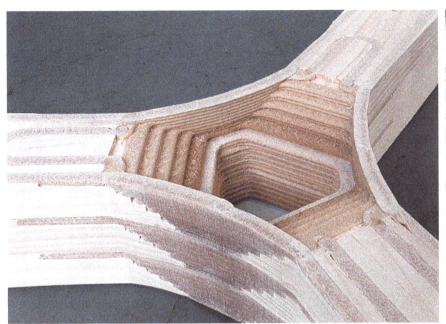

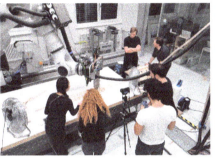

This workshop explored the novel potentials for timber construction and computational design that arise at the intersection of rapid additive robotic assembly of timber elements and in-process bio-based 3D-printed connections. Participants entered a virtual control room that was ready-equipped with finely crafted digital tools that allowed them to collaboratively control and directly initiate a robotic construction process in the Computational Construction Laboratory of the Institute of Computational Design and Construction at the University of Stuttgart, Germany. A heavy-duty industrial robot arm on a 12m linear axis was equipped with a vacuum-gripper and a 3D printing effector that achieves bead-widths of up to 5mm thickness. The focus was on developing novel additive assembly sequences and interfaces leveraging the unique fabrication setup. The intent was to then automate the production of a series of small-scale prototype components, each with a different internal material arrangement. In parallel, the production sequence for a larger slab component was explored and analyzed digitally, and the internal arrangements documented through a series of layered line drawings. In a fast-paced cyber-physical robotic fabrication charrette, this 4 x 2m large structural timber slab was produced by taking turns in collaboratively controlling the time-agnostic robotic setup according to each participant's global time zone.

Images courtesy of the workshop leaders.

ART: Augmented Robotic Telepresence

Ebrahim Poustinchi
Mona Hashemi
Kent State University /
Robotically Augmented Design
Lab

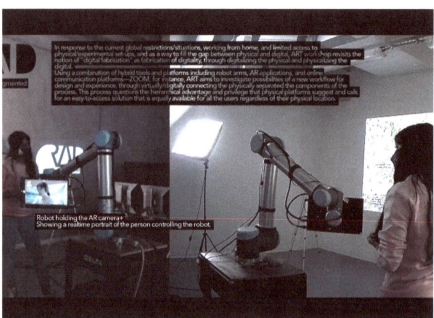

Robot holding the AR camera+
Showing a realtime portrait of the person controlling the robot.

Augmented Robotic Telepresence (ART) revisits the concept of "digital fabrication" as fabrication of digitality, through digitalizing the physical and physicalizing the digital. Employing native digital/physical interpreters—robot arms and augmented reality platforms—ART investigates possible mediums to hybridize realities of actual and virtual, to establish a workflow between a custom-made AR camera mounted on a robot arm and a curated robotic motion, remotely programmed/controlled, as means of telepresence.

Looking at telepresence from a conceptual perspective, the ART workshop considers motion and modification as two means of "presence." Through the use of robotic movement, ART aims to mimic "motion" in the space, and by employing AR platforms, it makes it possible for participants to "modify" the physical space through the projection of virtual content.

Using the virtual workshop platform as an opportunity, the ART workshop allowed participants to remotely utilize the Robotically Augmented Design (RAD) Lab resources at Kent State University, move in the space, and "modify" it. The workshop instructors enabled the safe use of the robots, videography/AR tools mounted on the robots, projection mapping, and custom robot end-effectors, for participants. Workshop participants engaged in a hybrid digital/physical workflow: developing a robotic walkthrough path for the UR10 robot arm to capture a curated "presence" at RAD Lab, through hybridized real-time videography of the AR "scene," developed using Maya and Unity3D.

Images courtesy of the workshop leaders.

Sequin Sequencing

Amina Blacksher
Atelier Office / Columbia GSAPP

Mitch McEwen
Atelier Office / Princeton

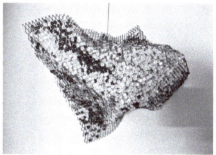

se·quin /sēkwin/ (noun): a small, shiny disk sewn as one of many onto clothing for decoration.

This workshop focused on part-to-part relationships that can define surface behaviors and visual effects. The tectonic logic tasks the decorative parcel to perform collectively as structure. In this workshop, the part of interest was the sequin. Because the spatially as a node with a defined center and materially as a module, techniques of assembly were explored to articulate a link logic to arrive at a self-supporting construction. Working with industry partner Zahner, participants gained an introduction to robotic prototyping for full-scale distributed construction from file preparation and machine tacit knowledge. The workshop guided participants through a sheet-metal detailing tutorial, illustrating how to represent metal panels in paper and connection types. Paper was used as a stand-in for sheet metal components, allowing for simplified fabrication methods while still surfacing the challenges inherent in a full digital fabrication workflow for part-to-part assembly. Participants gained an introduction to materials and finishes through a discussion of base materials, finishes, polishing, alloys, coatings, patina, aging, etc. The guidance focused on qualities of the sequins both as individuals and aggregates to calibrate the simulation of an assembly.

This workshop was sponsored by and led in collaboration with A. Zahner Company.

Images courtesy of the workshop leaders.

Generative Physics: Dynamic Systems within Immersive Projection-Mapped Environments

Alida Sun
Artist

Jeffrey Halstead
Architect

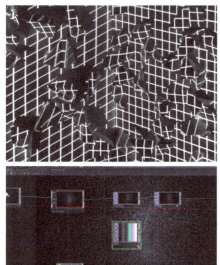

This workshop introduced participants to new methods of collaboration and communication across the disciplines of art and architecture, as well as to tools and workflows that respond to our current condition of being online, but without sacrificing the value or caliber of the work. Workshop participants were guided through projection mapping techniques and their real-time integration with physics simulation and live-action modeling/sculpting, producing a singular work that is simultaneously developed and experienced in different parts of the world. Participants were introduced to a series of generative art techniques using algorithmic systems and physics simulators. In addition, workshop participants were introduced to a variety of tookits to convey ideas of form that register different actions and events that have taken place over a period of time or are occurring in real time. Participants also received an overview of TouchDesigner to develop and augment workflows that can alter form or perception of form with a visual thesis in mind. Finally, students designed environments to be re-rendered in real time and projected onto an assemblage of materials arranged in a physical space designed by workshop leaders. TouchDesigner was employed to integrate and transform multiple action-based visuals into immersive projections.

Images courtesy of the workshop leaders.

Thanks to TouchDesigner for providing software licenses for this workshop.

Digital Borgo: From 3D Scanning and Digital Surveys to Collective Spaces of Design

Maya Alam
AP Practice / University of Pennsylvania

Daniele Profeta
AP Practice / Syracuse University

This workshop focused on contemporary surveying and imaging technologies in an effort to challenge the semantic tropes that are produced when dealing with historical artifacts in a monolithic way. How can design practices leverage these modes of vision to develop a multifaceted understanding of the built environment? Can these digital traces of the city stimulate participatory design protocols to construct a collective space of design? The workshop introduced photogrammetry, mesh editing workflows, and animation strategies to construct immersive digital surveys of existing building environments. Participants were introduced to a variety of methodologies to obtain digital survey data, ranging from individual photogrammetry models to GIS data clouds and Google Earth, as well as animation and compositing techniques in Autodesk Maya and Adobe After Effects. The final output was a short video where multiple animated point-cloud environments began to speculate on the role of representation in practices of adaptive reuse. The workshop participants collaboratively constructed what we call a "Digital Borgo." *Borgo* is an Italian word referring to small villages that historically emerged outside the defensive infrastructure of larger political centers to survey, manage, and control peripheral territories of the region. In the space of this workshop, each participant contributed a digital trace from their physical territory—a collective act of sharing to lay a common ground for speculation.

Images courtesy of the workshop leaders.

Collaborative Computation with Hypar

Andrew Heumann
Hypar / Columbia GSAPP

Eric Wassail
Hypar

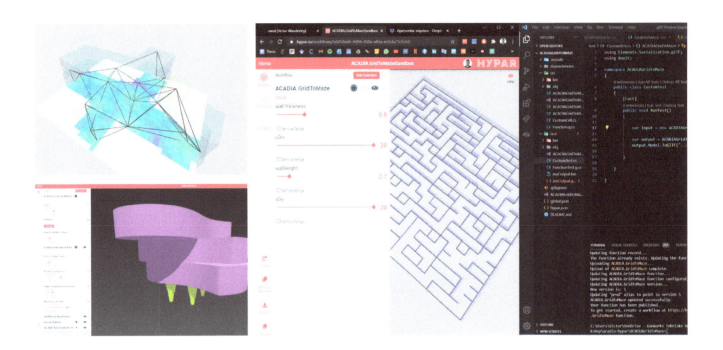

In this workshop, participants explored the potentials of Hypar, a new cloud-based computational and generative design platform, to collaborate and co-design through the sharing and encapsulation of design knowledge as algorithmic functions. Participants learned to use Grasshopper and/or C# to author Functions on Hypar, which encapsulate a single step in a design process, and can be combined into more complex workflows. We leveraged Hypar's fully web- and cloud-based computational design platform to explore new possibilities for remote collaboration and creative production. As a group, we built up a library of reusable functions which can be shared and composed into workflows and projects. Together we designed a range of sculptural architectural "follies" utilizing each other's Functions. Over the course of the workshop, participants explored many conceptual issues above and beyond the technical specifics of Hypar's platform, including algorithmic knowledge capture, architectural problem decomposition, and schematized object ontologies.

Images courtesy of the workshop leaders.

Thanks to Hypar for providing software licenses for this workshop.

Architectural Geometry and Morphing Patterns

Angelica Videla
Universidad de Chile /
Arquitectura Grupal

Gonzalo Muñoz
Universidad de Chile /
Arquitectura Grupal

Alberto Fernández
Universidad de Chile + UCL
Bartlett

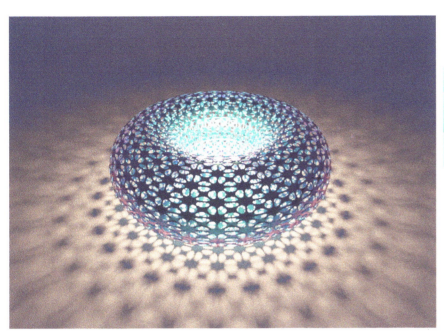

In this workshop, the participants explored procedural polygon modeling methodology in Maya and Blender by a process that breaks down a complicated task into discrete modeling operations. In addition to procedural polygon modeling, the participants also learned how to integrate topological patterns into the low-poly modeling workflow through morphing patterns. A series of procedural polygon modeling techniques was demonstrated and provided to the participants as a set of strategies for undertaking the design work. The ambition of the workshop was to develop formal and aesthetic qualities; furthermore, the goal was to achieve qualities that are not indifferent to their processes.

The workshop used building skins as the playground for this design investigation. The skills that were explored in the workshop include low-poly geometry components and organizational logic, sculptural mesh modeling, and discrete modeling operations. The workshop was taught using Maya and Blender. Workshop participants designed highly expressive building facades that integrate surface, structure, and ornament into an irreducible assemblage of compressed tectonics.

Images courtesy of the workshop leaders.

In Silico, In Vitro, In Vivo: Programming in Processing and in Life

Martyn Dade-Robertson
Hub for Biotechnology in the
Built Environment, Newcastle
University

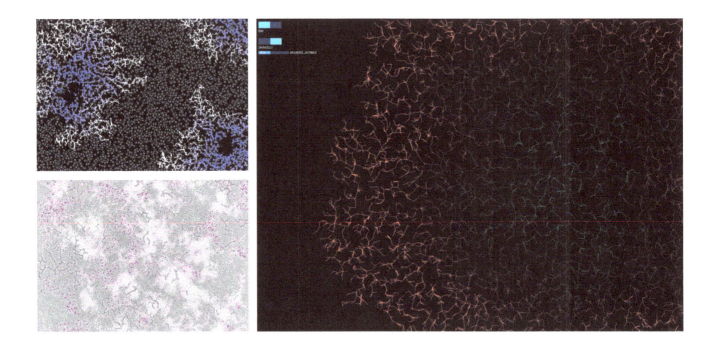

This workshop introduced biological modeling using the Processing programming language. The backbone of the workshop was a series of two five-hour crash courses in the Processing language for complete beginners. This acted as an introduction to the core concepts of programming and Object-Oriented Programming, including writing functions and objects. The workshop was organized around the building of a simple Diffusion Limited Aggregation (DLA) system that simulates agents (cells) which aggregate in response to a simulated chemical signal. The resulting aggregations lead to branching patterns in 2D and possibly 3D. Developing this simple biological model, we also explored ideas of self-organizing systems and emergence in biological pattern-forming and show the universality of certain types of models. The DLA model we developed, for example, can be effective at modeling viral transmission (which is itself a type of biological patterning). The workshop gave the participants some of the fundamentals they need to begin to code for biological simulations. We also introduced fundamentals of biological pattern making and the field of synthetic biology - looking to the future of biology as a programmable medium for design.

This workshop included contributions from Carolina Ramirez Figueroa (Royal College of Art) and various members from the Hub for Biotechnology in the Built Environment.

Images courtesy of the workshop leader.

Writing with the Machine

Mitchell Akiyama
University of Toronto

I close the zoom session and place the computer away. Oh my, is trying to be living between black screens every day.

I do my hair, put on my clothes, a yellow sweater, and pattern jeans. And, then socks and a pair of black boots.

I am ready.

Don't forget the mask! Yes, don't forget the face mask.

And as I put on my colorful mask, my heart starts racing. Will people keep their distance? Will they have a face mask? And will they even wearer, right?

You are fine, it is nothing.

And then again, the heart goes wild.

It is okay, and you are going to be fine, lets go,today is nice outside.

This workshop led participants through a series of guided writing exercises that are intended to nudge writers away from the inherited, freighted language of conventional academic writing. Over several years of teaching creative writing to architects and artists, the workshop leader has observed that many people, if not most, really don't like to write, and very few write with a natural ease or personal flair. The workshop began on day one with a discussion about literary voice and form, after which participants engaged in a series of exercises designed to defamiliarize conventional modes of writing. During the second session, participants workshopped these texts, focusing on voice and style. The workshop then turned to an exploration of the influence of artificial intelligence (AI) and machine learning (ML) on creative production (in general) and on creative writing (in particular). The goal for this work was to start a loop in which humans and machines write together, hopefully leading to a more nuanced understanding of how AI Natural Language algorithms work, but more importantly, we will ask, what do we want from AIs?

Images courtesy of the workshop leader.

DeepDesign: Architecture and 2D-to-3D Style Transfers with Neural Networks

Alexandra Carlson
University of Michigan

Sandra Manninger, PhD
University of Michigan

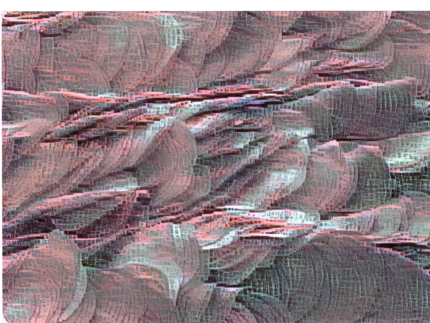

The rise of artificial intelligence (AI) and machine learning (ML) in recent years has posed a challenge to the architecture community. How will this novel technology impact our profession? This workshop interrogated the rise of ML from two distinct directions: the implication for the discourse of the discipline and the technical know-how to make an impact as an architect in the emerging ecology of ML applications. The goal of the DeepDesign workshop was to introduce participants, uninitiated in the use of ML in architecture, to a specific method of design with neural networks, 2D-to-3D neural style transfer. This method allows for back-propagating the stylistic qualities of images onto a 3D model. AI design technologies might be the first genuinely 21st-century design techniques, as they question the role of the sole genius, perpetuated by the postmodern era, and propose a conversation between the creativity and ingenuity of both mind and machine. In close collaboration with Michigan Robotics, participants learned how to employ neural networks in a design protocol. This training was designed to introduce participants to the workings of ML applications.

Images courtesy of the workshop leaders.

Thanks to PaperSpace for sponsoring this workshop.

Space Frames for a Space Fleet

Mathias Bernhard
Digital Building Technologies
ETH Zurich

Masoud Akbarzadeh
Polyhedral Structures
Laboratory / University of
Pennsylvania

This workshop explored the design of space frame structures and network trusses, focusing specifically on how specialized design tools can produce customized one-of-a-kind components that are geometrically unconstrained, have a high level of detail, and have a constant cost regardless of complexity. Participants were introduced to PolyFrame by PSL, a Rhino plugin that allows the construction and manipulation of reciprocal polyhedrons for structural form-finding, and Axolotl by DBT, a Grasshopper plugin that allows the creation, combination, and modification of shapes in constructive solid geometry trees using volumetric modeling (VM). The goal of the workshop was to establish a workflow from the abstract, purely topological layout of a space frame structure all the way to the generation of different formats of print data. Instructors demonstrated a sequence of both standard and highly specialized custom design instruments, provided help for their successful, and highlighted opportunities for possible interventions. The design task for the workshop participants was to imagine, invent, and plan a hypothetical vehicle: a Mars rover. In addition to introducing workshop participants to a new palette of design instruments for their daily architectural practice, the workshop resulted in a virtual fleet of imaginary vehicles in the form of renderings, 3D models, and the data ready for their digital fabrication.

Images courtesy of the workshop leaders.

Constructing Cognition

Alessio Erioli
University of Bologna /
Co-de-iT

Alessandro Mintrone
University of Bologna

This workshop explored iterative assemblages of discrete parts driven by an implementation of the Wave Function Collapse algorithm, combined with machine learning techniques operating at the decisional level, focusing on the generation of complex and heterogeneous spatial conditions. Participants worked with a discretized representation of space (a 3D voxel matrix) and explored how the inception of an AI system can lead to a cognitive understanding and deployment of emergent qualities in the assemblage. The workshop explored ways to short-circuit the analysis and the design phases, developing an agency to learn from experience and then produce an inherent sensibility. Working in Tensorflow and Unity 3D, participants developed procedural aggregations by arranging a collection of geometric tiles according to adjacency and frequency. Utilizing machine learning techniques, participants then trained a neural network to explore how different spatial conditions can emerge in the aggregation. Participants also learned bespoke visualization techniques in order to produce video and still images that showcase the spatial qualities of the outcomes while keeping track of the training process with Tensorboard.

Images courtesy of the workshop leaders.

Generative Design In and Beyond Revit

Lilli Smith
Autodesk

Zach Kron
Autodesk

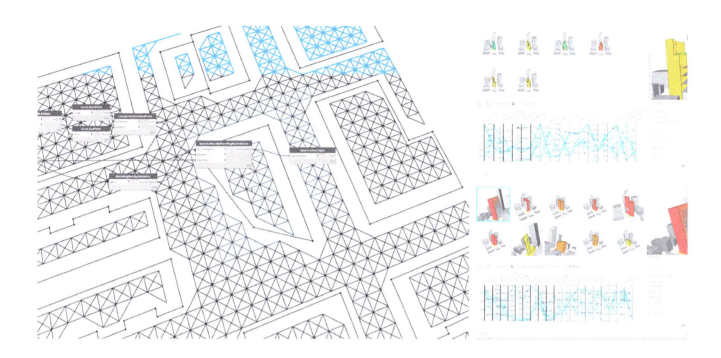

A parametric model contains many possible design states and configurations. How can we navigate this vast landscape of possibilities to find high-performing designs? This workshop introduced workflows that help answer such a question using Dynamo and the new Generative Design in Revit functionality, an Autodesk tool for design option generation, search, optimization, and sharing. During this workshop, participants learned how to build geometry generators and evaluators using visual programming in Dynamo, how to use these generators and evaluators to drive multi-objective optimization towards specified goals, and how to evaluate optimal solutions and integrate these designs back to Revit. Each section included discussion of generative design thinking and then hands-on creation of these ideas using Dynamo and Revit. Session 1 focused on Dynamo basics: how to create a model for generative design studies. Participants began by developing a common

understanding of the mechanics of Dynamo, and then built a set of graphs together that included some basic geometric applications and Revit integration. Session 2 focused on adding evaluation methods and generating design options. Participants reviewed the fundamentals of optimization and how to frame a design problem in terms of goals and constraints in order to drive multi-objective optimization and evaluation. Participants explored the various ways our problem definition can affect the result of the optimization. Session 3 demonstrated methods to explore and filter the design options that were generated and to tell a story about a design direction.

Images courtesy of the workshop leaders.

Thanks to Autodesk for sponsoring this workshop.

Design to Experience: Leveraging Speckle as a Conduit for Unreal Engine in AEC

Mark Cichy
Mateusz Gawad
Rotimi Seriki
Christopher Zoog
HOK Architects

Jakir Hussain
AKT II

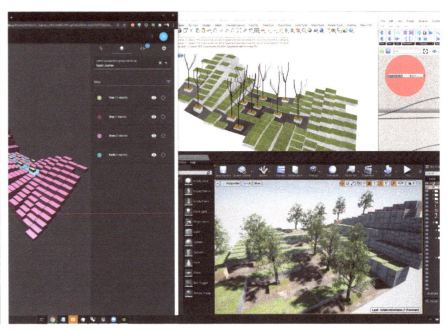

The workshop focused on real-time streaming design content from Rhino and Grasshopper to Unreal Engine via Speckle, an open data platform for AEC. Process workflows were presented and investigated through a series of applied exercises where attendees were encouraged to bring their own design content. Workshop leaders and participants leveraged open-source plugins developed under the Epic Mega Grants program to bridge the gap between design-stage authoring and game engine visualization. The first part of the session focused on procedural mapping and content preparation, and primarily emphasized the capabilities available in experimental packages and workflows. The latter half of the workshop immersed attendees in their independent projects as they produced tangible geometric and visual outcomes. Leaders presented various methods of automating operations on streamed content and used their applied experience to support the individual effort of the attendees. The goal of the workshop was to provide attendees with the knowledge required to effectively generate and transfer AEC collateral for coordination and collaboration via game engine technologies in real time. The outcomes were threefold: (1) optimized AEC models and design content, (2) robust procedural streaming workflows, and (3) experiential real-time visualization content.

Images courtesy of the workshop leaders.

Thanks to Epic Games for sponsoring this workshop.

Workshop Participants

KUKA|crc: Cloud Remote Control
Max Zorn
Lior Skoury
Ziyu Huang
Carl Eppinger
Felicia Wagiri
Jorge Tubella
Luca Lu
Kyu Hwan Lee
Pablo C Herrera
Ludovic Mallegol
Petr Krejcirik
Valmir Kastrati
Mahdi Jandaghimeibodi
Pengfei Zhang
Namjoo Kim
Miguel Zúñiga Ramírez
Lisha Shankar
Ricardo Agustin Leon Rojas
Anirudh Rathi
Farzaneh Eskandari

Dual-Additive Manufacturing Combining Timber and In-Process Bio-Based 3D-Printing
Eric Peterson
Fatima Javeed
Mahdieh Hadian Rasanani
George Guida
Melis Çetin
Kshitij Nashine
Yelda Gin
Ana Gatóo
Slate Werner
Kyle Vansice
Darcy Zelenko
Mitchell Ransome
Severi Virolainen
Hex Ceballos

Varalikaraj Singh
Emilio Robles
Erick Vernon-Galindo
Lourdes Robles
Camila Martinez Alarcon
Elif Akbaş
Isla Xi Han

ART: Augmented Robotic Telepresence
Biayna Bogosian
Yu-Ting Chang
Jingyuan Hu
Jackie Doyle
Yu-Hung Chiu
Wenyi Zheng
Maryam Liaghatjoo
Nicole Zsoter
Paola Sanguinetti
Katerina Vejrostova
Sean Mckeever
Melissa Goldman
Marcos Rojas
Marc Northstar
Ruxin Xie

Sequin Sequencing
Sheung Yuk Liu
Baris Doga Cam
Zheng Li
Mingjia Chen
Habeeb Muhammad
Fabian Hubner
Moti Tavassoli
Doga Tuven
J. Alejandro Forni
Hanieh Kouchaki
Sanaz Zarghami
Mahshid Tabatabaei
Amirhossein Sattari

Generative Physics: Dynamic Systems Within Immersive Projection-Mapped Environments
Tatiana Estrina
Ben Lawson
Scott Sandifer
Xinjie Zhou
Sarah Nail
Lucas Warfield
Jill Shah
Campbell Argenzio
Natalie Allison
Vasundhra Aggarwal
Albert Maksoudian
Nathan Braithwaite
Jimmy Simmons
Vernelle Noel
Johnathan Greenage
Katia Sondang Sitompul
Adriana Martínez Toxqui
Shayna Karuman
Dimah Ghazal
Luca Meza Sorrentino

Digital Borgo: From 3d Scanning and Digital Surveys to Collective Spaces of Design
Shengnan Gao
Alya Rapoport
Yingzi Hu
Ezgi Nalci
Alec Rovensky
Anastasia Tsamitrou
Mariam Adamjee
R Weissenböck
Niko Mcglashan
Larissa Korol
Feras Nour

Roberto Antinogene
Sophia Cabral
Gizem Ulusoy
Anastasia Malafey
Yongsan Huang
Andrew Bako
Christine Yogiaman
Sachin Gupta
Erik Molina

Collaborative Computation with Hypar
Lucas Denit
Victor Wanderley Barbosa
John Chun
Erika Stadnik
Luke Gehron
Xavier Garnavault
Marco Juliani
Kristen Forward
Ph Chen
Rui Liu
Sierra Jensen
James Mcintyre
Marios Tsiliakos
Efthymia Douroudi
Kate Mcphee

Architectural Geometry & Morphing Patterns
Jo Mccallum
Qianhua Fu
Meysam Ehsanian Mofrad
Julie Kress
Cristina Soto
Monik Jayantilal Gada
Ana Hernandez
Elizabeth Frias
Michael Levison
Grisel Gastélum

Vijender Singh
Kamile Öztürk Kösenciğ
Simin Nasiri
Angela Rodriguez
Ayaan Abbas Ansari
Ahmed Hassan
Matías Sánchez
Kennedy Geraldo
Samaneh Karimelahi

In Silico, In Vitro, In Vivo: Programming in Processing and in Life
Hao Wu
Jorge Soto
Dona Al-Alula
Nijat Mahamaliyev
Martin Krčma
Eduardo Nunez Luce
Natalie Alima
Canhui Chen
Daniel Tran
Natalia Piorecka
Stefana Zapuc
John Cirka
Kory Bieg
Ting Song
Curime Batliner
Dongyeop Lee
Israa El-Maghraby
Trevor Kemp
Santiago Brown
Daniel Panameño Corvera
Juan Ontiveros
Noé Guzmán
Hanieh Sotudeh
Gharebaagh
Mayur Mistry

Writing With The Machine
Aidan Crossey
Mario Ezekiel Hernandez
Ana Goidea
Sidney Brown
Alicia Delgado
Marina Rodríguez Das
Neves

Deepdesign: Architecture & 2D to 3D Style Transfers with Neural Networks
William Garner
Kyuseung Kyoung
Virginia Melnyk
Jingyu Xu
Dongyun Kim
Yael Braha
Jeremy Bowen
Michael Pryor
Mason Mo
Timothy Hanson
Karen Mercedes
David Rico-Gomez
Ahmed Meeran
Alvaro Salinas
Joy Mondal

Space Frames for a Space Fleet
Will Reynolds
Manish Bilore
Jiries Alali
Mackenzie Bruce
Ayush Kamalia
Andrea Menardo
Arnost Vespalec
Fatemeh Amiri
Ali Ghazvinian
Zhenxiang Huang

Diana Yan
Shahe Gregorian
Jack Hatcher
Felipe Villanueva
Gabriel Lopez Romero
Isaac Medina Zarco
Selda Pourali Behzad
Mehdi Shirvani
Andrea De La Piedra
June Grant
Ian Ting

Constructing Cognition
Nic Onions
Melinda Bognár
Satoshi Hoshino
Roxana Milliani
Frank Quek
Louis Daumard
Daniel Vianna
Lorenzo Villaggi
Christina Doumpioti
Shermeen Yousif
David Maples
Parvin Farahzadeh
Emmanouil Vermisso
Sumer Singh
Yağmur Bulut
Deepika Raghu

Generative Design In and Beyond Revit
Kai Ching Yip
Anna Mytcul
Yen-Chieh Chung
Daniel Anderi
Harry Moller
José Luis Rodríguez
Hernández
Randa Omar

Maryam Al-Irhayim
David Diez
Iulia Tenea
Adriana Davis
Mitra Maghsoudloo
Arantxa Nava
Thesla Collier
Jessica Elizalde
Michael Hiebert
David Skaroupka
Ahmed Halim
Robert Woodbury
Marlene Astrid Membrillo
Solis
Archi Martinez
Florencia Ramírez
Keshava Narayan
Maryam Nafez
Rodrigo Cabrera

Design to Experience: Leveraging Speckle As A Conduit for Unreal Engine in AEC
Pawel Sapiecha
Roberto Antinogene
Luis López
Byunghun Lee
Zheng Li
Katie Macdonald
Alyssa Haas
Andrew Kudless
Andrew Swartzell
Ronan Bolaños
Trevor Patt

DISTRIBUTED PROXIMITIES
ACADIA 2020 CREDITS

CONFERENCE CHAIRS

Viola Ago is an architectural designer, educator, and practitioner. She directs MIRACLES Architecture and is the current Wortham Fellow at the Rice University School of Architecture. Previously, Viola held the Christos Yessios Visiting Professorship at the Knowlton School of Architecture at OSU and the William Muschenheim Design Fellowship position at the Taubman College of Architecture, University of Michigan. Viola has also previously taught at Harvard's GSD, RISD School of Architecture, and SCI-Arc. She earned her M.Arch degree from SCI-Arc and a B.ArchSci from Ryerson University in Toronto. Prior to teaching, Viola worked as a lead designer in the Advanced Technology Team at Morphosis Architects in Los Angeles.

Viola's work has been exhibited in Los Angeles, Boston, Houston, Ghent NY, San Francisco, Miami, Columbus, Ann Arbor, and Cincinnati. Her written work has been published in *Log*, *AD Architectural Design Magazine* (Wiley), *Instabilities and Potentialities* (Routledge), Sci-Arc's *Offramp*, ACADIA Conference Proceedings, *TxA Emerging Design and Technology*, *Journal of Architectural Education*, *Architect's Newspaper*, and Archinect. Viola held a digital fabrication residency at the Autodesk Build Space in Boston, a University Design and Research Fellowship with Exhibit Columbus, and an artist residency at the MacDowell Colony.

Dr. Matias del Campo, a registered architect and designer, is an Associate Professor of Architecture at the University of Michigan's Taubman College of Architecture and Urban Planning. He is best known for the application of contemporary technologies in architectural production. His award-winning architectural designs are informed by computational methodologies (Artificial Intelligence, Algorithmic Modeling), contemporary theory, and philosophical inquiry. In 2003, he co-founded (with Sandra Manninger) the architectural practice SPAN in Vienna. SPAN gained wide recognition for its winning competition entry for the Austrian Pavilion at the 2010 Shanghai World Expo, as well as the new Brancusi Museum in Paris.

SPAN's work was featured at Venice Biennale in 2012; at ArchiLab 2013 in Orléans, France; at Architecture Biennale in Beijing in 2008 and 2010; and in the solo show, "Formations" at the Museum of Applied Arts (MAK) in Vienna in 2011. In 2017, SPAN's work was shown in a solo exhibition at the Fab Union Gallery in Shanghai. Most recently, del Campo was awarded the Accelerate@CERN Fellowship, served as technical chair of the ACADIA 2016 Conference, and guest-edited an issue of *Architectural Design*.

He earned his Master of Architecture from the University of Applied Arts Vienna and his PhD from the Royal Melbourne Institute of Technology.

Shelby Elizabeth Doyle, AIA is a registered architect, co-founder of the ISU Computation & Construction Lab (CCL), and an Assistant Professor of Architecture at Iowa State University, where she teaches design studios and seminars in digital technology. Her education includes a Fulbright Fellowship to Cambodia, a Master of Architecture from the Harvard Graduate School of Design, and a Bachelor of Science in Architecture from the University of Virginia.

The central hypothesis of her research, and of the CCL, is that computation in architecture is a material, pedagogical, and social project; computation is both informed by and productive of architectural cultures. This hypothesis is explored through the fabrication of built projects, writing, exhibition, and material explorations. The CCL is invested in questioning the role of education and pedagogy in replicating existing technological inequities, and in pursuing the potential for technology in architecture as a space of and for gender equity.

Adam Marcus is a licensed and registered architect and educator. He directs Variable Projects, an independent architecture practice in Oakland, and he is a partner in Futures North, a Minneapolis-based public art collaborative dedicated to exploring the aesthetics of data. Adam is an Associate Professor of Architecture at California College of the Arts in San Francisco, where he teaches design studios in computational design and digital fabrication, co-directs the Architectural Ecologies Lab, and collaborates with CCA's Digital Craft Lab. From 2011 to 2013, Adam was Cass Gilbert Assistant Professor at University of Minnesota School of Architecture, where he chaired the symposium "Digital Provocations: Emerging Computational Approaches to Pedagogy & Practice." He has also taught at Columbia University and the Architectural Association's Visiting School Los Angeles. Adam is a graduate of Brown University and Columbia University's Graduate School of Architecture, Planning and Preservation.

Brian Slocum holds a Master of Architecture from the Graduate School of Architecture, Planning and Preservation of Columbia University and a Bachelor of Science in Architecture from Georgia Tech. He is currently an Adjunct Professor in the Department of Architecture, Urbanism, and Civil Engineering at the Universidad Iberoamericana in Mexico City, where he teaches a design studio entitled Exogenous Protocols//Endogenous Properties (#prexpren), which focuses on analog material research employing computational and performative design strategies. Brian is the founder of tresRobots, an independent studio for design and architectural technologies research and co-founder of the architecture firm Diverse Projects, with offices in the United States and Mexico; he is licensed in the State of New York. In 2008, Brian was the recipient of an Individual Research Grant for ad hoc infrastructures from the New York State Council on the Arts. He was also a participant in the group exhibition *Landscapes of Quarantine* at Storefront for Art and Architecture in 2009-2010, where he presented *Context/Shift*, a prosthetic piece installed on a door panel in the gallery designed by the architect Steven Holl and the artist Vito Acconci. Brian has also contributed essays to the journal *CLOG* and *Pamphlet Architecture #23: MOVE Sites of Trauma*, by Johanna Saleh Dickson. Brian currently serves as the Secretary for the Association for Computer Aided Design in Architecture (ACADIA), and was Conference Co-chair for ACADIA 2018 Mexico City, *Recalibration: On Imprecision and Infidelity*.

Maria Yablonina is an architect, researcher, and artist working in the field of computational design and digital fabrication. Her work lies at the intersection of architecture and robotics, producing spaces and robotic systems that can construct themselves and change in real-time. Such architectural productions include the development of hardware and software solutions, as well as complementing architectural and material systems in order to offer new design spaces.

Maria's practice focuses on designing machines that make architecture: a practice that she broadly describes as Designing [with] Machines (D[w]M). D[w]M aims to investigate and establish design method-ologies that consider robotic hardware development as part of the overall design process and its output. Through this work, Maria argues for a design practice that moves beyond the design of objects towards the design of technologies and processes that enable new ways of both creating and interacting with archi-tectural spaces.

Maria has been commissioned and exhibited by institutions including Milan Design Week, Ars Electronica (Linz), Kapelica Gallery (Ljubljana), The Cooper Union, and the Moscow Institute of Architecture. She has also collaborated internationally on research with both universities and companies, including Autodesk Pier 9 (San Francisco), ETH Zurich, WeWork (New York), and the Bartlett School of Architecture (London).

SESSION CHAIRS

Viola Ago is an architectural designer, educator, and practitioner. She directs MIRACLES Architecture and is the current Wortham Fellow at the Rice University School of Architecture. Previously, Viola held the Christos Yessios Visiting Professorship at the Knowlton School of Architecture at OSU and the William Muschenheim Design Fellowship position at the Taubman College of Architecture, University of Michigan. Viola has also previously taught at Harvard's GSD, RISD School of Architecture, and SCI-Arc. She earned her M.Arch degree from SCI-Arc and a B.ArchSci from Ryerson University in Toronto. Prior to teaching, Viola worked as a lead designer in the Advanced Technology Team at Morphosis Architects in Los Angeles.

Viola's work has been exhibited in Los Angeles, Boston, Houston, Ghent NY, San Francisco, Miami, Columbus, Ann Arbor, and Cincinnati. Her written work has been published in *Log*, *AD Architectural Design Magazine* (Wiley), *Instabilities and Potentialities* (Routledge), Sci-Arc's *Offramp*, ACADIA Conference Proceedings, *TxA Emerging Design and Technology*, *Journal of Architectural Education*, *Architect's Newspaper*, and Archinect. Viola held a digital fabrication residency at the Autodesk Build Space in Boston, a University Design and Research Fellowship with Exhibit Columbus, and an artist residency at the MacDowell Colony.

Masoud Akbarzadeh is a designer with a wide academic background and experience in architectural design, computation, and structural engineering. He is an Assistant Professor of Architecture in Structures and Advanced Technologies and the Director of the Polyhedral Structures Laboratory (PSL). He holds a D.Sc. from the Institute of Technology in Architecture, ETH Zurich, a Master of Science in Architecture Studies (Computation), and a M.Arch from MIT. He also has a degree in Earthquake Engineering and Dynamics of Structures from the Iran University of Science and Technology and a BS in Civil and Environmental Engineering. His main research topic is Three-Dimensional Graphical Statics, a novel geometric method of structural design in three dimensions. He has published widely in various peer-reviewed journals and received multiple awards, including the renowned SOM award for his architecture thesis in 2011 and the National Science Foundation CAREER Award in 2020 to extend 3D/Polyhedral Graphic Statics for Education, Design, and Optimization of High-Performance Structures.

Marcella Del Signore is an architect, urbanist, educator, scholar, and the principal of X-Topia, a design-research practice that explores the intersection of architecture and urbanism with technology and the public, social and cultural realm. She is an Associate Professor and Director of the Master of Science in Architecture, Urban and Regional Design at the New York Institute of Technology, School of Architecture and Design. Her research focuses on interscalar design approaches that engage socio-technical systems through computation, prototyping, material and fabricated assemblies, data-driven protocols, and adaptive environments. She is the author of Urban Machines: Public Space in a Digital Culture (LISTLab, 2018; OROEditions, 2020; with G. Riether) and the editor of *Data, Matter, Design: Strategies in Computational Design* (2020, Routledge; with F. Melendez, N. Diniz). In 2018, she co-edited *Recalibration: On Imprecision and Infidelity* paper and project proceedings (with P. Anzalone and A. J. Wit) published during the 2018 ACADIA Conference where she served as technical co-chair. In 2018, she co-curated the 'Data & Matter' exhibition at the ECC during the 2018 Architecture Venice Biennale, and she is currently invited to exhibit at the 17th Architecture Venice Biennale in 2021.

Maya Alam is a German/Indian architect and designer. She holds a degree of Dipl. Ing. of Interior Architecture from the Behrens School of Arts in Düsseldorf and a Master of Architecture with Distinction from the Southern California Institute of Architecture in Los Angeles. Maya was the inaugural recipient of the 2016/17 Harry der Boghosian Fellowship. She was awarded the AIA Henry Adams Certificate and a Selected Best Thesis Award at SCI-Arc. She has worked in Germany, India, Switzerland, China, Italy, and the United States with P-A-T-T-E-R-N-S, NMDA, UNStudio, and Studio Fuksas, among others. She has taught at Southern California Institute of Architecture, Syracuse University, and Yale University and is currently part of the faculty at the University of Pennsylvania, Weitzman School of Design.

Maya is one of the founding partners of Alam/Profeta, a collaborative partnership with Daniele Profeta. Their projects combine everyday digital habits, contemporary imaging technologies, and traditional craftsmanship to surpass an introverted conversation and open up novel forms of practice. Past work ranges from small scale public installations to sites of speculative re-use. Weaving existing conditions with contemporary manufacturing technologies and aesthetics, engaging with the heterogeneous, often contradictory set of evidences of a given context, their practice focuses on constructing inclusive interventions that embrace and critically address the multi-faceted nature of our reality.

The work of A/P Practice has received support from the Smithsonian National Museum of American History in Washington DC, the Anchorage Museum in Alaska, the A+D Museum of Architecture and Design in Los Angeles, Syracuse University, Kent State University and the Festival des Architectures Vives in Montpellier, France.

Biayna Bogosian's academic and professional background extends in the fields of architecture, environmental design, computational design, data science, and immersive media design. Biayna's interdisciplinary research has allowed her to understand innovation in design and technology within a broader environmental context and explore data-driven and participatory methods for improving the built environment. Biayna is a PhD candidate in the Media Arts and Practice (iMAP) program at the USC School Cinematic Arts. Her dissertation focuses on the application of participatory immersive media for environmental monitoring, literacy, and policymaking. She is currently an Assistant Professor of Architectural Technology at Florida International University (FIU), where her research is supported by several National Science Foundation (NSF) grants. She has also taught at Columbia University GSAPP, Cornell University AAP, University of Southern California SoA, and Tongji University CAUP, and the American University of Armenia among other universities. She has been one of the co-organizers of the DigitalFUTURES World 2020 events and CAAD Futures 2021 conference.

June Grant, RA, NOMA, is Founder and Design Principal at blink!LAB architecture; a boutique research-based architecture and urban design practice. Launched in 2014, blink!LAB is based on Ms. Grant's 20 years of experience in architecture, design and the urban regeneration of cities and communities. Her design approach rests on an avid belief in cultural empathy, data research and new technologies as integral to design futures and design solutions. blink!LAB has three mandates: A commitment to Design Exploration, Advocacy for Holistic Solutions, and the Integration of Technology as a central component for a regenerative society.

Ms. Grant is also the current President of the San Francisco Chapter of the National Organization of Minority Architects (SFNOMA).

Kevin Hirth is an Assistant Professor at the University of Colorado Denver College of Architecture and Planning, and the founder of Kevin Hirth Co, which he began in 2013. He holds a Master's of Architecture with distinction from the Harvard Graduate School of Design and a Bachelor's of Science in Architecture from the University of Virginia.

The work of his firm focuses on the rural and urban condition of the American West. Projects in exploration include single family homes down unnamed roads in the mountain wilds and mixed-use towers pushing up against the edge of the Midwestern plains.

In 2017, he was awarded the Architectural League of New York's League Prize. In 2020 he was awarded an Architects Newspaper Best of Design Award.

Dr. Negar Kalantar is an Associate Professor of Architecture and a Co-Director of Digital Craft Lab at California College of the Arts (CCA) in San Francisco. Her cross-disciplinary research focuses on materials exploration, robotic and additive manufacturing technologies and engaging architecture, science, and engineering as platforms for examining the critical role of design in global issues and built environments.

Kalantar is the recipient of several awards and grants, including the Dornfeld Manufacturing Vision Award 2018, the National Science Foundation, Autodesk Technology Center Grant, and X-Grant 2018 from the Texas A&M President's Excellence Fund on developing sustainable material for 3-D printed buildings.

Some of the outcomes of her work have been featured in *The Guardian*, on the BBC, in science-focused magazines, and by the National Science Foundation. Her research has been presented at the Technical University of Vienna and Berlin, ETH Zurich, University of Maryland, Tehran University, Virginia Tech, Texas A&M University, and New York 3D Print Show. She has organized national and international workshops on additive manufacturing, robotics, and materials advancement in digital fabrication and architecture.

Christoph Klemmt received his diploma from the Architectural Association in London in 2004. He is Assistant Professor at the Department of Design, Art, Architecture and Planning at the University of Cincinnati, where he received a grant to set up the Architectural Robotics Lab. He taught and gave work-shops at the AA Visiting Schools, Tsinghua University, Tongji University, and he directed the AA Visiting School at the Angewandte in Vienna.

He worked amongst others for Zaha Hadid Architects and Tezuka Architects. In 2008 he co-founded Orproject, an architect's office specialising in advanced geometries with an ecologic agenda. Orproject exhibited at the Palais De Tokyo in Paris, the China National Museum in Beijing and the Biennale in Venice. The work of Orproject was featured world-wide in magazines and books such as *Domus*, *Frame*, and *AD*, and the practice won several international Awards.

Mara Marcu is an Assistant Professor at the University of Cincinnati, School of Architecture and Interior Design. She is the founder of MMXIII (Merely Maybe x Idyllic Imagination Inflicted—or simply—MM Thirteen). She structures her work around various collections, focused on the peculiar and the outcast over the ever-changing architectural style.

Leslie Lok is an Assistant Professor at Cornell University Department of Architecture and a co-founder at HANNAH, an experimental design practice for built and speculative projects across scales. HANNAH's work utilizes novel material applications and innovative forms of construction to address subjects of architecture and urbanism. The work aims to mine the tension between machine means and architectural ends. Her teaching and research explore the intersection of housing, urbanization, and mass-customized construction methods. She has previously taught at McGill University and received her Master of Architecture from MIT.

HANNAH is the recipient of the 2020 Architectural League Prize and was named Next Progressives by Architect Magazine in 2018. Her contributions were exhibited at the 2019 Bi-City Biennale of Urbanism/ Architecture in Shenzhen, Art OMI, the Pinkcomma Gallery, the Momentary, and the Canadian Centre for Architecture. Her work has been published at FABRICATE, Rob|Arch, and ACADIA, as well as featured in *Architectural Record*, the *New York Times*, *Dwell*, and *Digital Trends*, among others.

Sandra Manninger is a registered architect and educator.

"In her office, SPAN Architecture, that she founded together with Matias del Campo in 2003, she is constructing an epistemological framework from practice and procedures that are based on the newly acquired knowledge that we increasingly employ through science and technology. The result does not come from a formal effort, but rather as a consequence of a union of evolutionary attempts based on very rigid design procedures. These involve design protocols that go beyond the tools itself, leaving space for a true ecology of digital thinking. The research highlights how to go beyond beautiful data to discover something that could be defined voluptuous data. This coagulation of numbers, algorithms, procedures and programs uses the forces of thriving nature and, passing through the calculation of multi-core processors, knits them with human desire."

— Excerpts from Sabina Barcucci, *digimag* 64

Tsz Yan Ng's material-based research and design primarily focus on experimental concrete forming (hard) and textile manipulation (soft), often times in direct exchange and incorporating contemporary technologies to develop novel designs for building and manufacturing. A common thread to her work investigates questions of labor in various facets and forms – underscoring broader issues of industrial manufacturing innovation, of human labor, crafting, and aesthetics. She's the principal of an independent architecture and art practice and works collaboratively across disciplines and scales. She joined Taubman College, University of Michigan as the Walter B. Sanders Fellow (2007-2008) and is currently an Assistant Professor. She was also the Reyner Banham Fellow at the University of Buffalo from 2001-2002. Her co-edited book *Twisted* was released in 2018 and was co-editor for the *JAE* theme issue *Work* (2019).

Alida Sun is an artist, futurist, and activist based in Berlin and New York. Her practice comprises building extended realities both virtual and augmented, machine learning paradigms, and interactive installations. Her current projects include developing decolonial protocols in AI and blockchain techology, exploring anti-fascist traditions in performing arts and digital culture with Düsseldorf Schauspielhaus, and generating immersive cyberfeminist narratives for Transmediale. She graduated from RISD with a BFA in Industrial Design. Her works have been presented in new media exhibitions and audiovisual festivals around the world.

DISTRIBUTED PROXIMITIES
ACADIA ORGANIZATION

The Association for Computer Aided Design in Architecture (ACADIA) is an international network of digital design researchers and professionals that facilitates critical investigations into the role of computation in architecture, planning, and building science, encouraging innovation in design creativity, sustainability and education.

ACADIA was founded in 1981 by some of the pioneers in the field of design computation including Bill Mitchell, Chuck Eastman, and Chris Yessios. Since then, ACADIA has hosted 40 conferences across North America and has grown into a strong network of academics and professionals in the design computation field.

Incorporated in the state of Delaware as a not-for-profit corporation, ACADIA is an all-volunteer organization governed by elected officers, an elected Board of Directors, and appointed ex-officio officers.

PRESIDENT
Kathy Velikov, University of Michigan
president@acadia.org

VICE-PRESIDENT
Jason Kelly Johnson, California College of the Arts
vp@acadia.org

SECRETARY
Brian Slocum, Universidad Iberoamericana
secretary@acadia.org

VICE-SECRETARY
Mara Marcu, University of Cincinnati

TREASURER
Phillip Anzalone, New York City College of Technology
treasurer@acadia.org

VICE-TREASURER
Jason Kelly Johnson, California College of the Arts

MEMBERSHIP OFFICER
Jane Scott, Newcastle University
membership@acadia.org

TECHNOLOGY OFFICER
Andrew Kudless, University of Houston
webmaster@acadia.org

DEVELOPMENT OFFICER
Matias del Campo, University of Michigan
development@acadia.org

COMMUNICATIONS OFFICER
Adam Marcus, California College of the Arts
communications@acadia.org

BOARD OF DIRECTORS, 2020
Brandon Clifford
Shelby Doyle
Behnaz Farahi
Mara Marcu
Adam Marcus
Tsz Yan Ng
Jane Scott
Lauren Vasey
Andrew John Wit
Maria Yablonina
Viola Ago (alternate)
Phillip Anzalone (alternate)
Kory Bieg (alternate)
Matias del Campo (alternate)
Melissa Goldman (alternate)
Christoph Klemmt (alternate)

DISTRIBUTED PROXIMITIES
CONFERENCE MANAGEMENT

CONFERENCE CHAIRS

Viola Ago, Wortham Fellow, Rice University

Matias del Campo, Associate Professor, University of Michigan Taubman College of Architecture and Urban Planning

Shelby Doyle, Assistant Professor, Iowa State University

Adam Marcus, Associate Professor, California College of the Arts

Brian Slocum, Adjunct Professor, Universidad Iberoamericana

Maria Yablonina, Assistant Professor, John H. Daniels Faculty, University of Toronto

SPECIAL ADVISOR

Kathy Velikov, Associate Professor, University of Michigan Taubman College of Architecture and Urban Planning

CONFERENCE PLATFORM DESIGN & FULLSTACK ENGINEERING

Oliver Popadich, AltF4 Design

MMMURMUR CHAT PLATFORM

Ultan Byrne, PhD student in architecture, GSAPP, Columbia University

TECHNICAL ASSISTANTS

Jiries Alali, California College of the Arts

Pablo Espinal Henao, John H. Daniels Faculty, University of Toronto

David Kalman, John H. Daniels Faculty, University of Toronto

CONFERENCE WEBSITE

Adam Marcus

COPY EDITING

Rachel Fudge, Paula Woolley, Mary O'Malley

GRAPHIC IDENTITY

Adam Marcus, Viola Ago, Alejandro Sánchez Velasco

GRAPHIC DESIGN

Alejandro Sánchez Velasco

LAYOUT

Carolyn Francis, Sebastian Lopez, Shelby Doyle, Adam Marcus

PEER REVIEW COMMITTEE

Henri Achten _ *Czech Technical University*

Arash Adel _ *University of Michigan*

Mania Aghaei Meibodi _ *University of Michigan*

Viola Ago _ *Rice University*

Chandler Ahrens _ *Washington University St. Louis*

Masoud Akbarzadeh _ *University of Pennsylvania*

Ayşegül Akçay Kavakoğlu _ *Altınbaş University*

Phillip Anzalone _ *New York Institute of Technology*

German Aparicio _ *Trimble Consulting*

Imdat As _ *Arcbazar / Scientific and Technological Research Council of Turkey*

Dorit Aviv _ *University of Pennsylvania*

Phil Ayres _ *The Royal Danish Academy of Fine Arts*

Pedro Azambuja Varela _ *University of Porto*

Ehsan Baharlou _ *University of Virginia*

Amber Bartosh _ *Syracuse University*

Efilena Baseta _ *IAAC / NOUMENA*

Leighton Beaman _ *University of Virginia*

Steven Beites _ *Laurentian University*

Brad Bell _ *University of Texas Arlington*

Chris Beorkrem _ *University of North Carolina Charlotte*

Bastian Beyer _ *Royal College of Art*

Vishu Bhooshan _ *ZHA Code / ETH Zurich*

Kory Bieg _ *University of Texas Austin*

Biayna Bogosian _ *Florida International University / University of Southern California*

Ronan Bolaños _ *Universidad Nacional Autónoma de México*

Johannes Braumann _ *Robots in Architecture / University of Arts and Industrial Design Linz*

Nicholas Bruscia _ *University at Buffalo*

Jane Burry _ *Swinburne University*

Mark Cabrinha _ *California State Polytechnic University, San Luis Obispo*

Galo Cañizares _ *The Ohio State University*

Bradley Cantrell _ *University of Virginia*

Mario Carpo _ *The Bartlett, University College London*

Juan José Castellón _ *Rice University*

Gonçalo Castro Henriques _ *Florida Atlantic University*

Yichao Chen _ *The Bartlett, University College London*

Angelos Chronis _ *Austrian Institute of Technology / IAAC*

Mollie Claypool _ *The Bartlett, University College London*

Brandon Clifford _ *Massachusetts Institute of Technology*

Andrew Colopy _ *Rice University*

David Costanza _ *Cornell University*

Kristof Crolla _ *Chinese University of Hong Kong*

Dana Cupkova _ *Carnegie Mellon University*

Pierre Cutellic _ *ETH Zurich*

Daniel Davis _ *Hassell / WeWork*

Matias del Campo _ *University of Michigan*

Marcela Delgado _ *Universidad Nacional Autónoma de México*

Marcella Del Signore _ *New York Institute of Technology*

Ilaria Di Carlo _ *The Bartlett, University College London*

Nancy Diniz _ *University of the Arts London*

Antonino Di Raimo _ *University of Portsmouth*

Mark Donohue _ *California College of the Arts*

Shelby Doyle _ *Iowa State University*

Rebeca Duque Estrada _ *University of Stuttgart, PhD Candidate*

Emre Erkal _ *NOMAD / Erkal Architects*

Gabriel Esquivel _ *Texas A&M University*

Alberto Estévez _ *International University of Catalunya*

Behnaz Farahi _ *California State University, Long Beach / University of Southern California*

Iman Fayyad _ *Harvard University*

Yara Feghali _ *University of California, Los Angeles*

Jelle Feringa _ *Aectual*

Antonio Fioravanti _ *Sapienza University Rome*

Wendy Fok _ *Parsons School of Design*

Michael Fox _ *California State Polytechnic University, Pomona*

Pia Fricker _ *Aalto University*

Madeline Gannon _ *Carnegie Mellon University*

Mark Foster Gage _ *Yale University*

Richard Garber _ *University of Pennsylvania*

Jose Luis García del Castillo y López _ *Harvard University*

Guy Erik Gardner _ *University of Calgary*

Jordan Geiger _ *Gekh*

David Gerber _ *University of Southern California*

Andrei Gheorghe _ *University of Applied Arts Vienna*

Daniel Gillen _ *SOM*

Melissa Goldman _ *University of Virginia*

Kyriaki Goti _ *Pratt Institute*

Marcelyn Gow _ *SCI-Arc*

Onur Yüce Gün _ *New Balance / Massachusetts Institute of Technology*

Jeffrey Halstead _ *University of Michigan*

Erik Herrmann _ *The Ohio State University*

Andrew Heumann _ *Hypar / Columbia University GSAPP*

Kevin Hirth _ *University of Colorado Denver*

Zaneta Hong _ *University of Virginia*

Tyson Hosmer _ *The Bartlett, University College London / ZHA Code*

Kayleigh Houde _ *Buro Happold*

Yasushi Ikeda _ *Keio University*

Ryan Johns _ *ETH Zurich*

Jason Kelly Johnson _ *California College of the Arts*

Nathaniel Jones _ *Massachusetts Institute of Technology*

Damjan Jovanovic _ *SCI-Arc*

Negar Kalantar _ *California College of the Arts*

Ed Keller _ *Parsons School of Design*

James Kerestes _ *Ball State University*

Sumbul Khan _ *Singapore University of Technology*

Joachim Kieferle _ *RheinMain University of Applied Sciences*
Axel Kilian _ *Massachusetts Institute of Technology*
Marirena Kladeftira _ *ETH Zurich*
Christoph Klemmt _ *University of Cincinnati*
Chris Knapp _ *Bond University*
Reinhard Koenig _ *Bauhaus University Weimar*
Daniel Köhler _ *University of Texas Austin*
Axel Körner _ *University of Stuttgart*
Sarah Aipra Kott _ *NBBJ Design*
Oliver David Krieg _ *Intelligent City / University of Stuttgart*
Ersela Kripa _ *Texas Tech University*
Kihong Ku _ *Thomas Jefferson University*
Andrew Kudless _ *University of Houston*
Hyojin Kwon _ *Harvard University*
Riccardo La Magna _ *University of Stuttgart*
Rodrigo Langarica _ *Universidad Anáhuac*
Christian Lange _ *University of Hong Kong*
Brian Lonsway _ *Syracuse University*
Gregory Luhan _ *Texas A&M University*
Katie MacDonald _ *University of Virginia*
Mathias Maierhofer _ *University of Stuttgart*
Elena Manferdini _ *SCI-Arc*
Ryan Vincent Manning _ *quirkd33*
Sandra Manninger _ *University of Michigan*
Mara Marcu _ *University of Cincinnati*
Adam Marcus _ *California College of the Arts*
Mathilde Marengo _ *IAAC*
Bob Martens _ *TU Wien*
Matan Mayer _ *IE University*
Malcolm McCullough _ *University of Michigan*
Duane McLemore _ *Mississippi State University*
AnnaLisa Meyboom _ *University of British Columbia*
Philippe Morel _ *ENSAPM / The Bartlett, University College London*
Sina Mostafavi _ *TU Delft*
Stephen Mueller _ *Texas Tech University*
Alicia Nahmad Vazquez _ *Cardiff University / University of Calgary*
Burçin Nalinci _ *AUX Architecture, Los Angeles*
Rasa Navasaityte _ *University of Texas Austin*
Andrei Nejur _ *University of Montreal*
Catie Newell _ *University of Michigan*
Tsz Yan Ng _ *University of Michigan*
Ted Ngai _ *Pratt Institute*
Sarah Nichols _ *Rice University*
Betül Orbey _ *Doğuş Üniversitesi*
Mine Özkar _ *İstanbul Technical University*
Derya Güleç Özer _ *İstanbul Technical University*
Dimitrios Papanikolaou _ *University of North Carolina Charlotte*
Murali Paranandi _ *Miami University*

Stefana Parascho _ *Princeton University*
Ju Hong Park _ *Massachusetts Institute of Technology*
Kat Park _ *Massachusetts Institute of Technology*
Vera Parlac _ *New Jersey Institute of Technology*
Maria Perbellini _ *New York Institute of Technology*
Chris Perry _ *Rensselaer Polytechnic Institute*
Brady Peters _ *University of Toronto*
Ebrahim Poustinchi _ *Kent State University*
Marshall Prado _ *University of Tennessee Knoxville*
Nick Puckett _ *OCAD University*
Jorge Ramirez _ *Anemonal*
Carolina Ramirez-Figueroa _ *Royal College of Art*
Alexander Robinson _ *University of Southern California*
Christopher Romano _ *University at Buffalo*
Rhett Russo _ *Rensselaer Polytechnic Institute*
Jenny Sabin _ *Cornell University*
Jose Sanchez _ *University of Michigan*
Andrew Saunders _ *University of Pennsylvania*
Simon Schleicher _ *University of California Berkeley*
Axel Schmitzberger _ *California State Polytechnic University, Pomona*
Marc Aurel Schnabel _ *Victoria University of Wellington*
Kyle Schumann _ *University of Virginia*
Mathew Schwartz _ *New Jersey Institute of Technology*
Jane Scott _ *Newcastle University*
Jason Scroggin _ *University of Kentucky*
Nick Senske _ *Iowa State University*
Brian Slocum _ *Universidad Iberoamericana*
Valentina Soana _ *The Bartlett, University College London*
Catherine Soderberg _ *Texas Tech University*
Rajat Sodhi _ *Orproject*
Robert Stuart-Smith _ *University of Pennsylvania*
Daniel Suarez _ *Berlin University of the Arts*
Satoru Sugihara _ *SCI-Arc*
Martin Summers _ *University of Kentucky*
Kyle Talbott _ *University of Wisconsin Madison*
Martin Tamke _ *The Royal Danish Academy of Fine Arts*
Josh Taron _ *University of Calgary*
Peter Testa _ *SCI-Arc*
Geoffrey Thün _ *University of Michigan*
T.F. Tierney _ *University of Illinois Urbana Champaign*
Robert Brandt Trempe _ *Aarhus School of Architecture*
Peter Trummer _ *University of Innsbruck*
Daniel Tish _ *Harvard University*
Zenovia Toloudi _ *Dartmouth College*
Carmen Trudell _ *California State Polytechnic University, San Luis Obispo*
Hans Tursack _ *Massachusetts Institute of Technology*
Manja van de Worp _ *Royal College of Art School of Architecture*

Pavlina Vardoulaki _ *Nike /DesignMorphine*
Theodora Vardouli _ *McGill University*
Lauren Vasey _ *ETH Zurich*
Shota Vashakmadze _ *University of California, Los Angeles*
Kathy Velikov _ *University of Michigan*
Tom Verebes _ *New York Institute of Technology*
Joshua Vermillion _ *University of Nevada Las Vegas*
Gabriel Wainer _ *Carleton University*
Dustin White _ *New York Institute of Technology*
Emily White _ *California State Polytechnic University, San Luis Obispo*
Aaron Willette _ *WeWork*
Shane Williamson _ *University of Toronto*
Andrew John Wit _ *Temple University*
Maria Yablonina _ *University of Toronto*
Shai Yeshayahu _ *Ryerson University*
Christine Yogiaman _ *Singapore University of Technology*
Lei Yu _ *Tsinghua University*
Maroula Zacharias _ *Massachusetts Institute of Technology*
Machi Zawidzki _ *Massachusetts Institute of Technology*
Catty Dan Zhang _ *University of North Carolina Charlotte*
Hao Zheng _ *University of Pennsylvania*
Sasa Zivkovic _ *Cornell University*

DISTRIBUTED PROXIMITIES
SPONSORS

PLATINUM SPONSORS

  Zaha Hadid Architects

SILVER SPONSOR

GRIMSHAW

BRONZE SPONSOR

SPONSORS

TECHNOLOGY SPONSORS

Paperspace

MEDIA PARTNER

The
Architect's
Newspaper

www.ingramcontent.com/pod-product-compliance
Lightning Source LLC
Chambersburg PA
CBHW042320070326
40689CB00059B/4992